business solutions

Charts and Graphs for Microsoft® Office Excel® 2007

Bill Jelen

Contents at a Glance

D1406159

que®

800 E. 96th Street
Indianapolis, Indiana 46240

Charts and Graphs for Microsoft® Office Excel® 2007

International Standard Book Number: 0-7897-3610-1

Library of Congress Cataloging-in-Publication Data

Jelen, Bill.
  Charts and graphs for Microsoft Office Excel 2007 / Bill Jelen.
    p. cm.
  ISBN 0-7897-3610-1
  1. Microsoft Excel (Computer file) 2. Business—Computer programs. 3. Electronic spreadsheets. 4. Charts, diagrams, etc.—Computer programs. I. Title.
  HF5548.4.M523J447 2007
  005.54—dc22

                                   2007004763

Printed in the United States of America

First Printing: April 2007

10   09   08   07   4   3   2   1

Trademarks

All terms mentioned in this book that are known to be trademarks or service marks have been appropriately capitalized. Que Publish-ing cannot attest to the accuracy of this information. Use of a term in this book should not be regarded as affecting the validity of any trademark or service mark.

Warning and Disclaimer

Every effort has been made to make this book as complete and as accurate as possible, but no warranty or fitness is implied. The information provided is on an "as is" basis. The author and the publisher shall have neither liability nor responsibility to any person or entity with respect to any loss or damages arising from the information contained in this book or from the use of the CD or programs accompanying it.

Bulk Sales

Que Publishing offers excellent discounts on this book when ordered in quantity for bulk purchases or special sales. For more information, please contact

U.S. Corporate and Government Sales
1-800-382-3419
corpsales@pearsontechgroup.com

For sales outside of the U.S., please contact

International Sales
international@pearsoned.com

 This Book Is Safari Enabled

The Safari® Enabled icon on the cover of your favorite technology book means the book is available through Safari Bookshelf. When you buy this book, you get free access to the online edition for 45 days. Safari Bookshelf is an electronic reference library that lets you easily search thousands of technical books, find code samples, download chapters, and access technical information whenever and wherever you need it. To gain 45-day Safari Enabled access to this book:

- Go to http://www.quepublishing.com/safarienabled
- Complete the brief registration form
- Enter the coupon code

If you have difficulty registering on Safari Bookshelf or accessing the online edition, please e-mail customerservice@safaribooksonline.com.

Associate Publisher
Greg Wiegand

Acquisitions Editor
Loretta Yates

Development Editor
Laura Norman

Managing Editor
Gina Kanouse

Project Editor
Michael Thurston

Copy Editor
Kitty Jarrett

Indexer
Cheryl Lenser

Proofreader
Water Crest Publishing

Technical Editors
Juan Pablo Gonzalez
Bob Umlas

Publishing Coordinator
Cindy Teeters

Book Designer
Anne Jones

Composition
Gloria Schurick

Contents

About the Author

Bill Jelen, Excel MVP and MrExcel, has been using spreadsheets since 1985, and he launched the MrExcel.com website in 1998. His team provides custom Excel applications to clients around the world. You can see Bill as a regular guest on *The Lab* with Leo Laporte in Australia, in Canada, and on Google Video. Bill produces a daily video podcast about Excel. He also enjoys taking his show on the road, doing a one- to four-hour power Excel seminar anywhere that a room full of accountants or Excellers will show up.

Dedication

To Josh Jelen

Acknowledgments

I wish to thank Gene Zelazny of McKinsey & Company. Gene was generous with his time and feedback. He indirectly taught me a lot about charting over a decade ago, when I did a six-month stint on a McKinsey project team. Kathy Villella and Tom Bunzel also provided advice on presentations. Mala Singh of XLSoft Consulting vetted the chapter on using VBA to create charts.

Mike Alexander, my coauthor on the *Pivot Table Data Crunching* books, helped outline the table of contents for this book and provided many ideas for Chapter 7, "Using Advanced Chart Techniques." You can catch Mike and me on a cool DVD training series by Total Training.

I enjoy the visual delight of every Edward Tufte book. I apologize in advance to E.T. for documenting all the chartjunk that Microsoft lets us add to Excel charts.

Dick DeBartolo is the Daily GizWiz and has been writing for *MAD Magazine* for more than 40 years, since he was 15. The pages of *MAD* were not where I expected to find inspiration for a charting book, but why not? Thanks to John Marcinko, my son's friend who pointed me, in a random conversation, to the *MAD* charts. Thanks to Bob D'Amico for illustrating the charts a la *MAD*. The pie chart in Chapter 4 is a Dick DeBartolo original, created especially for this book. Many thanks to Dick for being a contributor.

I was visiting Keith Bradbury's office in Toronto. Keith makes the completely awesome PDF-to-Excel utility at InvestInTech.com. Between parking the car and Keith's office, I saw the most amazing store, managed by David Michaelides. SWIPE is a bookstore dedicated to art and design. This is a beautiful store to browse, and if you go in and reveal that you work in Excel all day, they will sympathetically be very nice to you. In a clash of worlds, David has the original 1984 Mac way up above his cash register because it was the start of desktop publishing. I pointed out that the Mac was where Excel 1.0 got its start in 1985, so we had a common thread in our respective backgrounds. Stop by 477 Richmond Street West (two blocks west of Spadina) to take a look the next time you are in Toronto.

Thanks to Leo Laporte and everyone else at TechTV in Toronto. By the time this book is out, production will have moved to Vancouver, so I offer my thanks to Matt Harris and everyone else at the Vancouver studio, even though I don't know who you are yet.

Thanks to Dan Bricklin and Bob Frankston for inventing the computer spreadsheet. Thanks to Mitch Kapor for Lotus 1-2-3. Like everyone else who uses computers to make a living, I owe a debt of gratitude to these three pioneers.

Thanks to Lora White, Tracy Syrstad, and Barb Jelen for keeping MrExcel running while I wrote. As always, thanks to the hundreds of people answering 30,000 Excel questions a year at the MrExcel message board. Thanks to Duane Aubin, Wei Jiang, Suat Ozgur, Nate Oliver, and Jake Hildebrand for their programming expertise.

The Microsoft MVPs for Excel are always generous with their time and ideas. Over the years, I've learned many cool charting tricks from websites maintained by John Peltier, Andy Pope, and Charley Kyd. Turn to the appendix for links to their respective websites. MVPs Juan Pablo Gonzalez and Bob Umlas served as great technical editors. I still smile when I recall Bob pointing out that "9. Repeat step 9 for High, Low, and Close lines." was, in itself, a circular reference.

At Pearson, Loretta Yates is an awesome acquisitions editor. Thanks to Judi Taylor, Greg Wiegand, Michael Thurston, Laura Norman, and Lisa Jacobson-Brown at Que. Jean Esposito was a great high school English teacher who used up many red pens marking my papers. Had Kitty Jarrett been around to be my copy editor back then, there would have been no need for red ink at all. Thanks to my agent, William Brown.

Finally, thanks to Josh Jelen, Zeke Jelen, and Mary Ellen Jelen. I wrote 2,500 pages in 2006—way too many to actually pay attention to anything important in my life. 2007 will be better.

We Want to Hear from You!

As the reader of this book, *you* are our most important critic and commentator. We value your opinion and want to know what we're doing right, what we could do better, what areas you'd like to see us publish in, and any other words of wisdom you're willing to pass our way.

As an associate publisher for Que Publishing, I welcome your comments. You can email or write me directly to let me know what you did or didn't like about this book—as well as what we can do to make our books better.

Please note that I cannot help you with technical problems related to the topic of this book. We do have a User Services group, however, where I will forward specific technical questions related to the book.

When you write, please be sure to include this book's title and author as well as your name, email address, and phone number. I will carefully review your comments and share them with the author and editors who worked on the book.

Email: feedback@quepublishing.com

Mail: Greg Wiegand
          Associate Publisher
          Que Publishing
          800 East 96th Street
          Indianapolis, IN 46240 USA

Reader Services

Visit our website and register this book at www.quepublishing.com/register for convenient access to any updates, downloads, or errata that might be available for this book.

INTRODUCTION

A good chart should both explain and arouse curiosity. A chart can summarize thousands of data points into a single picture. The arrangement of a chart should explain the underlying data but also enable the reader to isolate trouble spots worthy of further analysis.

Excel makes it easy to create charts. But although the improvements in Excel 2007 allow you to create a chart with only a few mouse clicks, it still takes thought to find the best way to present your data.

CASE STUDY

Choosing the Right Chart Type

Say that you are an analyst for a chain of restaurants, and you are studying the lunch hour sales for a restaurant in a location at a distant mall. The mall is surrounded by corporations that provide a steady lunchtime clientele during the week. On the weekends, the mall does well in the holiday shopping months but lacks weekend crowds during the rest of the year.

From the data contained in the chart in Figure I.1, you can spot a periodicity in sales throughout the year. An estimated 50 spikes indicate that the periodicity might be based on the day of the week. You can also spot that there is a general improvement in sales at the end of the year, which you attribute to the holiday shopping season. However, there is an anomaly in the pattern during the summer months.

Figure I.1
This chart shows the sales trend for 365 data points.

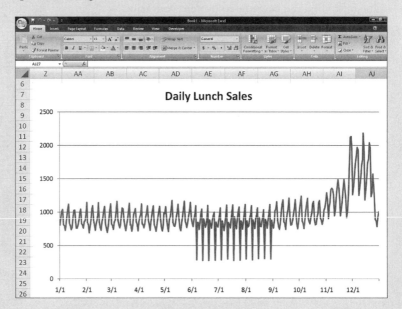

After studying the data in Figure I.1, you might decide to plot the sales by weekday in order to better understand the sales. Figure I.2 shows the same data presented as seven line charts. Each line represents the sales for a particular day of the week. Friday is the dashed line. At the beginning of the year, Friday was the best sales day for this particular restaurant. For some reason, around week 23, Friday sales plummeted.

Figure I.2
When you isolate sales by weekday, you can see a definite problem with Fridays in the summer.

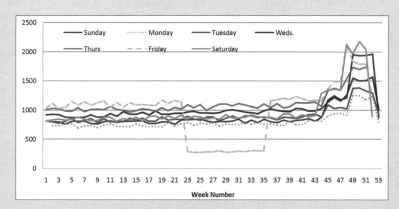

The chart in Figure I.2 prompts you to make some calls to see what was happening on Fridays at this location. You might discover that the city was throwing free Friday lunchtime concerts from June through August and that the manager of the restaurant was offered a concession at the concert location but thought that it would be too much trouble. Using this pair of charts enabled you to isolate a problem and equipped you to make better decisions in the future.

Using Excel as Your Charting Canvas

Excel 2007 offers a complete rewrite of the 15-year-old charting engine from previous versions of Excel. Although the software offers no new charting types, Excel 2007 provides plenty of tools that allow you to make eye-catching charts. In Excel 2007, you have the ability to create better versions of the 11 existing chart types. Maybe in Excel 14, Microsoft will add support for new chart types.

Creating charts in Excel 2007 basically requires these steps:

1. Set up and select your data in an Excel worksheet.
2. Choose the appropriate chart type from the Insert ribbon.
3. Change the chart layout or color scheme by using the Design ribbon.
4. Customize chart elements by using the Layout ribbon.
5. Micromanage formatting for individual data points by using the Format ribbon.

Most charts require steps 1 and 2. The remaining steps are optional and are used with decreasing frequency. It should be rare that you will need to venture to step 5. However, you are likely to change at least a couple items in step 4.

This book covers the improved charting engine in Excel 2007 as well as the new SmartArt graphics that you can use to create business diagrams. You will also learn to use spreadsheet cells to present graphical information.

Besides charts, Excel 2007 offers many other ways to visually display quantitative data. The new conditional formatting features, such as data bars, color scales, and icon sets allow you to add visual elements to regular tables of numbers. In Figure I.3, you can easily see that Ontario has the largest population and that Nunavut has the largest land area. You can add in-cell data bars such as these with a couple mouse clicks, as described in Chapter 9, "Presenting Data Graphically Without Charts."

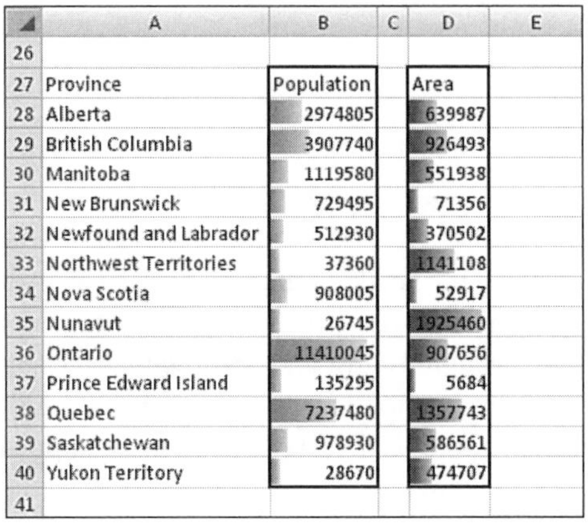

Figure I.3
In-cell data bars draw the eye to the largest values in each column.

	A	B	C	D	E
26					
27	Province	Population		Area	
28	Alberta	2974805		639987	
29	British Columbia	3907740		926493	
30	Manitoba	1119580		551938	
31	New Brunswick	729495		71356	
32	Newfound and Labrador	512930		370502	
33	Northwest Territories	37360		1141108	
34	Nova Scotia	908005		52917	
35	Nunavut	26745		1925460	
36	Ontario	11410045		907656	
37	Prince Edward Island	135295		5684	
38	Quebec	7237480		1357743	
39	Saskatchewan	978930		586561	
40	Yukon Territory	28670		474707	
41					

This book also takes a look at tools that you can purchase to add functionality to Excel. Many vendors offer tools to create sparklines, speedometer charts, and specialized stock analysis tools. Perhaps one of the best tools is a Microsoft product called MapPoint. Using MapPoint, you can easily plot your Excel data in a geographic orientation on a map. See Chapter 10, "Presenting Your Excel Data on a Map Using Microsoft MapPoint," for more information about the cool tricks available with MapPoint.

This Book's Objectives

The goal of this book is to make you more efficient and effective in creating visual displays of information using Excel.

In the early chapters of this book, you will learn how to use the new Excel 2007 charting interface. Chapters 3 through 6 walk you through all the built-in chart types and talk about when you can use each chart type. Chapter 7 discusses about creating unusual charts. Chapter 8 covers pivot charts, and Chapter 9 covers creating visual displays of information right in the worksheet. Chapter 10 covers mapping, and Chapter 11 covers the new SmartArt business graphics, as well as Excel 2007's shape tools. The penultimate chapter presents macro tools you can use to automate the production of charts using Excel VBA. In Chapter 14, you will see several techniques that people may use to stretch the truth with charts. Finally, in Appendix A, I provide you with a list of resources to give you additional help with creating charts and graphs.

A Note About Bugs

Microsoft's complete rewrite of the charting engine for Office 2007 was ambitious. As this book goes to press in March 2007, about a half-dozen charting bugs have surfaced in the initial release of Excel 2007. While I will call these bugs out in the relevant sections of the book, note that most of the bugs should be patched with Service Release 1 in early 2008. If you are using the service release of the software, you may not be able to reproduce the bugs.

Special Elements in This Book

This book contains the following special elements:

> **NOTE**
> Notes provide additional information outside the main thread of the chapter discussion that might be useful for you to know.

> **TIP**
> Tips provide you with quick workarounds and time-saving techniques to help you do your work more efficiently.

> **CAUTION**
> Cautions warn you about potential pitfalls you might encounter. It's important to pay attention to these because they alert you to problems that could cause you hours of frustration.

CASE STUDY

Case studies provide a real-world look at topics previously introduced in the chapter.

DESIGNING CHARTS LIKE THE PROS

Throughout the book, I've asked several non-Excellers to contribute charts unlike those found in Excel. After showing the designer's chart, you can walk through how to adjust the Excel settings to create a chart that approximates the designer's chart.

Next Steps

Chapter 1, "Introducing Charts in Excel 2007," introduces the new Excel 2007 interface for creating charts. You will learn how to create your first chart and understand the various elements available in a chart.

Introducing Charts in Excel 2007

1

What's New in Excel 2007 Charts

The charting engine has been completely rewritten in Excel 2007. After 15 years of the same tired-looking charts, you can now create stunning charts with just a few mouse clicks.

The following list summarizes the new charting features in Excel 2007:

- To create a chart, you usually start with one of the seven new galleries on the ribbon's Insert tab. The first six galleries offer column, line, pie, bar, area, and scatter charts. The remaining chart types—stock, surface, doughnut, bubble, and radar—are grouped in the Other Charts gallery.

- You can display the All Charts gallery, which shows all 73 chart subtypes.

- After you have created a chart, you can customize individual elements of the chart by using the Layout ribbon. The Layout ribbon offers settings for the chart title, axis titles, legend, data labels, data table, axes, gridlines, plot area, chart wall, chart floor, 3-D rotation, trendline, lines, up/down bars, and error bars. In each case, a drop-down menu offers the popular choices, and a More Options choice leads to a formatting dialog that presents all the choices.

- If you are in a hurry, you can head to the Chart Layouts drop-down on the Design ribbon. This drop-down offers a number of preset combinations of the elements from the Layout ribbon. The presets vary from chart type to chart type. For example, while there are 10 presets for column charts, there are 12 presets for line charts, and there are fewer for area charts.

- There is now a gallery of 48 combinations of color and effects. You can choose from the Chart Styles gallery on the Design ribbon to quickly apply a color scheme to a chart. If you don't like the built-in colors, you can choose a new theme from the Page Layout ribbon, or you can head to the Format ribbon to change the colors for each data series.

- If you want micro-control over the shape, fill, outline, or effects of any chart element, you can use the Format ribbon.

- It has always been possible to create a chart with a single keystroke—using the F11 key to build a default chart on a new worksheet. Excel 2007 continues to support this feature, and it also adds Alt+F1 for building a default chart embedded on the current worksheet.

- In Excel 2003, you could define custom formatting for charts by using Chart Type, Custom Types, User Defined, Add. Excel 2007 replaces this functionality with Chart Type, Manage Templates. The main advantage of this change is that it is now easier to move templates from one computer to another computer.

- In many galleries and formatting menus, Excel offers a Live Preview feature. You can see the effect of a change by simply hovering your mouse over the menu selection. You will find yourself hovering over several choices until you find one that looks good, and then clicking that option.

New Charting Tools and Menus

The entry point for Excel 2007 charting is the Insert ribbon. After you have created a chart, three new ribbon tabs appear under the Chart Tools heading. The Design ribbon allows you to choose a different chart type, layout, or style. The Layout tab allows you to add various elements to a chart or remove them from a chart. The Format tab allows you to micromanage individual elements, such as the bevel effect for an individual data series. In general, the tabs progress from more general to more specific as you move from the Design tab on the left to the Format tab on the right. Figure 1.1 shows the icons on the Design, Layout, and Format tabs.

Figure 1.1
Global changes occur on the Design tab, formatting of individual elements on the Layout tab, and micro changes on the Format tab.

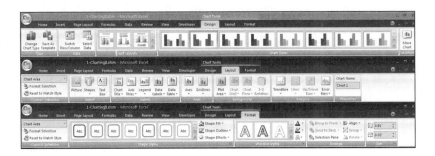

A few other ribbon tabs come into play when you're creating charts. If you don't like the colors used in the Chart Styles gallery on the Design tab, you can visit the Theme drop-down on the Page Layout tab to choose a new theme color for the document.

> **CAUTION**
>
> Note that changing the theme color affects all charts, shapes, and SmartArt diagrams in the workbook.

Also, you can use many of the formatting icons on the Home tab to format titles and labels on a chart. These same icons appear on the mini toolbar when you select text within a title on a chart.

Using the Insert Tab to Select a Chart Type

As shown in Figure 1.2, the Insert tab offers seven drop-down menus in the Charts group. Each drop-down leads to a variety of chart types.

Figure 1.2
Five less-popular chart types are tucked under the Other Charts menu.

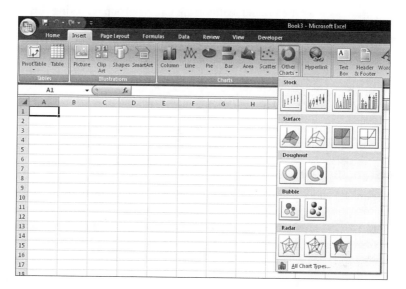

Table 1.1 describes the contents of each drop-down in the Charts group.

Table 1.1   Contents of Each Charts Group Drop-Down

Ribbon Icon	Contents
Column	19 types of column, cylinder, cone, and pyramid charts
Line	7 types of line charts
Pie	6 types of pie charts
Bar	15 types of bar charts
Area	6 types of area charts

continues

1

Table 1.1 Continued	
Ribbon Icon	**Contents**
Scatter	5 types of scatter charts
Other Charts	4 stock charts, 4 surface charts, 2 doughnut charts, 2 bubble charts, and 3 radar charts

Using the Expand Icon to Access a Gallery of All Chart Types

A dialog launcher icon appears in the lower-right corner of some ribbon groups. This icon usually allows you to bypass the ribbon and head straight to a legacy-style dialog box.

Figure 1.3 shows the expand icon for the Charts group. Clicking this icon leads to a dialog box that shows all 73 charting types in one place.

Figure 1.3
You can click the dialog launcher icon to bypass the ribbon and open a charting dialog box.

Dialog Launcher Icon

Understanding the Chart Thumbnail Icons

Figure 1.4 shows the Insert Chart dialog with all 73 built-in chart types.

Figure 1.4
There are 73 chart types available in Excel 2007.

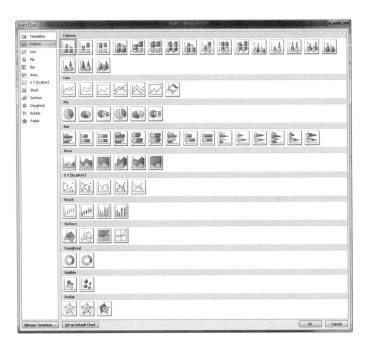

1

The gallery of 73 chart types might seem like a dizzying array of charts. However, in many cases, there are four variations of a given type. When you understand how Excel uses the light and dark blue icons to show you these four charting types, you can quickly choose from the various thumbnails.

For example, consider the fourth through seventh icons in the Column section of Figure 1.4.

The fourth icon in the Column group of Figure 1.4 is for a 3-D clustered column chart. In this type, series 1 and series 2 are plotted next to each other. When they are plotted with different colors, it is easy to compare the height of the similar-colored bars in order to see how a particular value is trending. For example, the top-left chart in Figure 1.5 shows a 3-D clustered column chart. The thumbnail icon shows a light blue element and a dark blue element next to each other. Icons for clustered charts are shown in Figure 1.6.

Figure 1.5

Many chart subtypes offer these four variations on how the data is plotted.

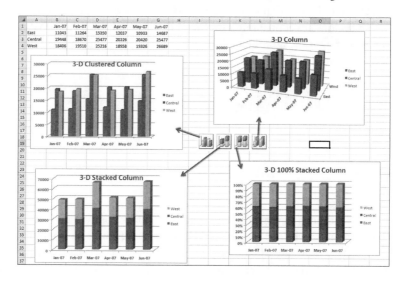

Figure 1.6

Icons for clustered charts show a dark blue and a light blue element at differing heights.

The fifth icon in the Column group of Figure 1.4 is for a 3-D stacked column chart. In this type of chart, the values from series 2 are added to the values for series 1. This type of chart makes it easy to compare totals of all series. The lower-left chart in Figure 1.5 shows this type of chart. Although it is easy to understand how the first series is trending, it is much harder to understand how the third series is trending. Are the West sales for April larger or smaller than those for March? It is hard to tell in a stacked chart. The icons for stacked charts always show the dark blue series on top of the light blue series, and the heights of the blue series vary from point to point. Icons for stacked charts are shown in Figure 1.7.

Figure 1.7
Icons for stacked charts show a dark blue element on top of a light blue element. The total height of the elements differ from category to category.

The sixth icon in the Column group of Figure 1.4 is for a 3-D 100% stacked column chart. These charts are similar to the stacked charts in that they plot series 2 on top of series 1. However, the total height of all series is scaled so that each data point shows 100%. The lower-right chart in Figure 1.5 shows a 100% stacked chart. This type of chart illustrates which regions are contributing to the total. The icons for 100% charts show the dark blue series on top of the light blue series, and the heights of all bars or points are the same. Icons for 100% charts are shown in Figure 1.8.

Figure 1.8
Icons for 100% stacked charts show a dark blue element on top of a light blue element. The total height is the same for each point.

The seventh icon in the Column group of Figure 1.4 is available only for 3-D charts. In 3-D column charts, the data for series 2 is plotted behind the data for series 1. A 3-D column chart works best when there are only a few data series. A basic problem occurs when the values in series 1 are larger than all the values in a later series. The taller bars in the front of the chart obscure the later values. Because none of the 2-D chart types offer this subtype of chart, there are fewer examples of icons that plot one series in front of the other. The six icons are shown in Figure 1.9.

Figure 1.9
Icons for 3-D charts show a dark blue element behind the light blue element.

Because there are four ways to plot multiple series, you can group 46 of the 73 chart types into 14 groups of types, as shown in Figure 1.10.

Figure 1.10
The column, line, bar, and area chart subtypes are really variations of basic types.

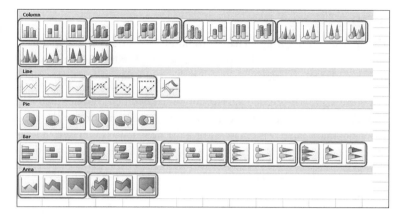

Using Gallery Controls

The charting tools ribbons contain many instances of a new Office interface element known as a gallery. A gallery control allows you to scroll through options one row at a time or click the open gallery button to see all the choices at one time.

For example, the Chart Layouts gallery starts by showing three of the available icons: There are three control icons on the right side of the gallery. The up and down arrow icons allow you to move through the gallery one row at a time (see Figure 1.11).

Figure 1.11
To effectively use the Gallery control, you use the three controls along the right side of the gallery.

A quick trick is to use the bottom control icon, the More icon. You can click the More icon to cause the gallery to open the entire control, as shown in Figure 1.12.

Figure 1.12
When you click the More icon, you can quickly see all choices in the gallery at one time.

Creating a Chart

The first step in creating a chart is to build a worksheet that contains data to chart. Many business charts are created from summary data. If your dataset contains transactional data, you should also consider summarizing the data using either a pivot table or formulas.

In Figure 1.13, the original dataset contained detailed transactional data. In order to create summary data to be used in a chart, new rows were inserted at the top of the worksheet, and a summary table was created using the new SUMIFS function. The formulas in C2:E4 create conditional sums to find the total revenue for each combination of product and year.

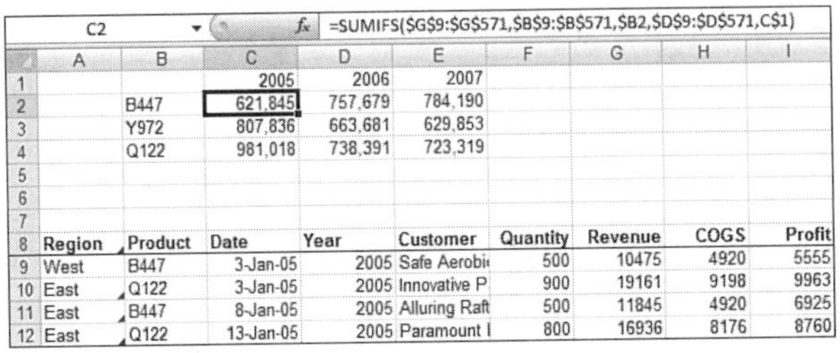

Figure 1.13

The new SUMIFS function makes it easy to create the summary that can be used for charting.

	C2			f_x	=SUMIFS($G$9:$G$571,$B$9:$B$571,$B2,$D$9:$D$571,C$1)			
	A	B	C	D	E	F	G	H	I
1			2005	2006	2007				
2		B447	621,845	757,679	784,190				
3		Y972	807,836	663,681	629,853				
4		Q122	981,018	738,391	723,319				
5									
6									
7									
8	Region	Product	Date	Year	Customer	Quantity	Revenue	COGS	Profit
9	West	B447	3-Jan-05	2005	Safe Aerobi	500	10475	4920	5555
10	East	Q122	3-Jan-05	2005	Innovative P	900	19161	9198	9963
11	East	B447	8-Jan-05	2005	Alluring Raft	500	11845	4920	6925
12	East	Q122	13-Jan-05	2005	Paramount I	800	16936	8176	8760

NOTE

SUMIFS is a new function in Excel 2007. It allows you to perform a SUMIF with multiple conditions. In previous versions of Excel, you had to resort to using a SUMPRODUCT function or an array formula to perform the calculation now offered by SUMIFS.

The formula in cell C2 in Figure 1.13 is =SUMIFS($G$9:$G$571,$B$9:$B$571,$B2,$D$9:$D$571,C$1). To use SUMIFS, you specify a range to be summed (in this case, the revenue in G9:G571). You then specify pairs of arguments representing a criteria range and a criteria value. The second and third arguments of the function specify that the products in B9:B571 should be compared to the product in B2. Excel sums the values in the sum range where all the criteria for that row are true.

For example, the $621,845 is the sum of all revenue in the dataset where both the product is B447 and the year is 2005. Similar logic is used to calculate all of the cells in C2:E4.

Selecting Contiguous Data to Chart

It is easiest to create charts when your data is in a contiguous rectangular block of cells. The left column of the dataset should contain the label for each series to be plotted. The first row of the dataset should contain values to be plotted along the category axis. The top-left cell should be blank. The rest of the cells in the dataset should contain values to be plotted.

In Figure 1.13, the products in B2:B4 will be plotted as individual series on the chart. The years in C1:E1 will be points along the category axis.

Selecting Noncontiguous Data to Chart

It is helpful, but not necessary, for your data to be in a contiguous range. In Figure 1.14, for example, you might want to create a pie chart that includes the category labels in column B and the totals in column F. To select data for creating a chart, you follow these steps:

1. Click in cell B1 and drag to cell B4 in order to select the range of category labels.
2. While holding down the Ctrl key, click in cell F1 and drag down to cell F4 in order to add F1:F4 to the selection.
3. If you have additional series to plot, repeat step 2 for each additional series.

Figure 1.14
Selecting noncontiguous data requires a bit of dexterity, as you attempt to drag while holding down the Ctrl key.

	B	C	D	E	F
1		2005	2006	2007	Sales
2	B447	621,845	757,679	784,190	2,163,714
3	Y972	807,836	663,681	629,853	2,101,370
4	Q122	981,018	738,391	723,319	2,442,728

> **CAUTION**
>
> Excel remembers the order in which you selected the data. Although choosing cell B1 and then individually Ctrl+clicking cells F4, F3, F2, F1, B4, B3, and B2 would lead to a selection that looks the same as Figure 1.14, it would not create an acceptable chart. You must select the category labels first and then Ctrl+click and drag to select the first series.

Creating a Chart by Using the Insert Ribbon Icons

After you have selected the data to be included in a chart, you click the Insert tab of the ribbon. Seven drop-down menus in the Charts group offer a total of 73 different chart subtypes. You can select one of the drop-down menus or click the dialog launcher icon in the lower-right corner of the group (refer back to Figure 1.3).

> **TIP**
>
> The ToolTips in the seven drop-downs are more descriptive than the ToolTips in the Insert Chart dialog. If you are not sure of which chart subtype to use, you can hover your mouse over an icon in a charting drop-down to see a description of that chart subtype (see Figure 1.15).

Figure 1.15
You can hover over any subtype in the ribbon drop-down menus to see a description of the subtype.

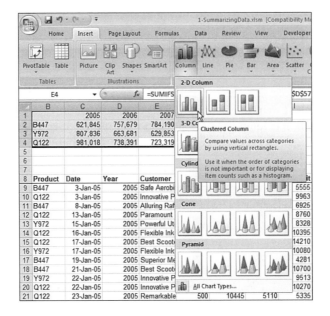

NOTE Live Preview does not work when you're selecting a chart type from either the Ribbon or the Charts dialog. You have to choose one type and click in order to create a chart.

Excel charts are now automatically created as embedded charts. A chart appears somewhere in the range currently visible in the window. You will likely have to move most charts after creating them. In Figure 1.16, for example, the chart has been created in an annoying location. You can also resize a chart to best fit the space by clicking to select it and then dragging a corner handle in or out.

Figure 1.16
Excel randomly inserts a chart somewhere in the visible range of cells. You can move and resize a chart.

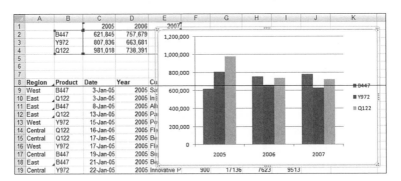

Creating a Chart with One Keystroke

Previous versions of Excel allowed you to create a chart by selecting the data and pressing the F11 key. In response, Excel created a default chart on a new sheet.

Excel 2007 still recognizes that F11 shortcut, and it adds an Alt+F1 shortcut, which creates a default chart as a chart object embedded in the current worksheet. The Alt+F1 keystroke is a time saver when you need to create charts that match the Excel default. When Excel is installed, the default chart is a 2-D column chart. You can easily change the default chart type to best fit the type of charts you create the most. Here's how:

1. Select an existing chart. In the Design ribbon, click the Change Chart Type icon. If you do not have an existing chart in your workbook, click the dialog launcher icon in the Charts group of the Insert ribbon.

2. Click the chart subtype that is closest to the chart type you want to create.

3. In the lower-left of the dialog, click Set as Default Chart. Then click Cancel to leave the dialog box.

After you go through this procedure, you can press F11 or Alt+F1 to create the selected chart type instead of the column chart.

> You can define a custom template as the default chart. This enables you to define custom colors, effects, and settings as the default. See "Creating Your Own Theme" later in this chapter for more information.

Working with Charts

After creating a chart, you may need to rearrange the data or move the chart to a new location. The following topics will assist with these tasks.

Moving a Chart Within the Current Worksheet

As you will see in the following case study, Excel had an annoying habit of locating new charts near the bottom of your dataset. With a large dataset, you may need to move the chart to the proper location thousands of rows away. Some methods are faster than others.

There are several ways to move a chart within the current worksheet. When a chart is selected, a border appears around the chart. Eight resizing handles appear in the border. To move a chart, you click the border but avoid the resizing handles. You can then drag the chart to a new location.

Because it is somewhat difficult to click on a thin chart border, you might try clicking inside the chart in order to drag the chart to a new location. This approach works as long as you can click on some whitespace between the plot area and the chart border. The arrows in Figure 1.17 show areas where you can click and drag in order to move the entire chart. There are many areas inside the chart where clicking and dragging will have a different outcome. For example, if you click on the legend and drag, you move the legend within the chart area. In addition, if you click anywhere inside the plot area and drag, you can nudge the plot area within the constraints of the chart area.

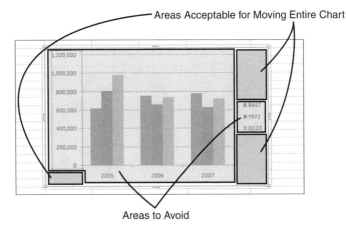

Areas Acceptable for Moving Entire Chart

Figure 1.17
If you can find some whitespace outside the plot area, you can click and drag the whitespace in order to move the entire chart to a new location on the worksheet.

Areas to Avoid

You can easily drag a chart anywhere in the visible window. If you accidentally drop the chart just a pixel outside of the visible window, the chart boomerangs back to its original position.

If you need to move a chart outside of the visible window, drag so that your cell pointer is within one-half row of the edge of the window. Excel will slowly start to scroll in the appropriate direction. As with other Windows programs, you can speed up the scroll by rapidly moving your mouse left and right. However, it is difficult to keep the mouse within the one-half row tolerance while moving left and right.

One option is to use the Zoom slider to show the worksheet at a 10% zoom. You can then move the chart about 375 rows at a time.

Instead of dragging and dropping, the fastest way to relocate a chart might be to cut and paste it. You follow these steps to quickly move a chart within the current worksheet:

1. Select a chart.
2. Press Ctrl+X to cut the chart from the worksheet.
3. Press F5 to display the Go To dialog.
4. Type the address of the cell that you want to contain the top-left corner of the chart and click OK.
5. Press Ctrl+V to paste the chart in the new location.

Of course, instead of taking steps 4 and 5, you could use your favorite navigation method to move to the cell that should contain the upper-left corner of the chart.

Locating a Chart at the Top of Your Dataset

It is easy to build a dataset so you can work along with this case study. Follow these steps to build the dataset.

1. Start a blank worksheet.
2. Type 1 in cell A2.
3. With cell A2 selected, choose Home, Fill, Series....
4. Choose Series in Columns. Enter a Stop Value of 3000. Choose OK to fill in the numbers from 1 to 3000 in column A.
5. Enter the label Result in B1. Enter the number 10 in B2. In B3, enter the formula

   `=B2+RANDBETWEEN(-2,2)`.
6. Select cell B3. Double-click the fill handle to copy the formula down to B3001.

The goal of this case study is to create a chart of the results in A1:B3001. Follow these steps:

1. Start with the cellpointer in A1. While holding down the Shift key, press right arrow, down arrow, End, down arrow. You will have selected A1:B3001. Depending on your screen resolution, you might see rows 2965 through 3001.
2. Choose Insert, Line, 2-D Line, Line. Excel creates a chart in the center of the visible window, with the upper-left corner roughly around G2976. You now have quite a dilemma. The chart is located 2900 rows away from the proper location.

There are several approaches for moving the chart.

- If you grab the border of the chart, drag it to within one-half row of the top of the window, and hold it there, Excel scrolls to the proper location in 8 minutes and 47 seconds. This clearly is not the best solution.
- Another option is to change the Zoom to 10%. You can now drag the tiny chart to within one-half row of the top window and Excel will scroll faster, covering 2900 rows in 1 minute and 40 seconds. Adding in the time to adjust the zoom to 10% and then back to 100%, this method is 75% faster than scrolling at 100%.
- Cutting and pasting is much faster. With the original chart selected, type Ctrl+X to cut, Ctrl+Home to move to cell A1, click in cell D4, and type Ctrl+V to paste the chart at the top of the worksheet. This method takes about 7 seconds, depending on your manual dexterity with the keystroke combinations.

A completely different approach is selecting the original dataset while keeping cell A1 in view. Then, the created chart will be located at the top of your worksheet. Either of these methods will work:

- Start in cell A1. Hold down the Shift key while pressing down, End, down, right. Release the Shift key and type Ctrl+. to move to an opposite corner of the selection.
- Click in cell A2. Type Ctrl+* to select the current region. This will keep the visible window at the top of your dataset.

This case study is an example of how Excel offers many solutions to a problem, but a few of the solutions are dramatically faster than the obvious solution.

Reversing the Series and Categories of a Chart

Excel follows strict rules in deciding whether rows should be series or categories. Luckily, you can reverse this decision with a single button click.

If Excel chooses the wrong orientation for the data in a chart, you can click the Switch Row/Column icon in the Design ribbon. Compare the before and after charts in Figure 1.18. You will see that the years have changed from being category labels to being series labels. The products have changed from being series labels to being category labels.

Figure 1.18
To reverse the orientation of data in a chart, you click Switch Row/Column.

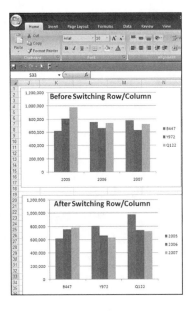

If your data has more columns of data than rows, the headings in the first row become category labels. In Figure 1.19, the eight columns of monthly data become category labels, and the three rows become series.

If your data has more rows than columns, the headings in the first column become category labels. In Figure 1.20, the 11 rows of city data become category labels, and the 4 columns become series.

If your data has exactly the same number of rows and columns, the rows become series.

Figure 1.19

If your data has more columns than rows, the rows become series in the chart.

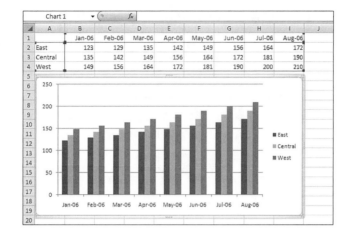

Figure 1.20

If your data has more rows than columns, the columns become series in the chart.

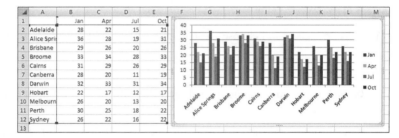

Changing the Data Sequence by Using Select Data

The Select Data icon on the Design ribbon allows you to change the rows and columns of your dataset, and it also allows you to re-sequence the order of the series. When you click this icon, the Select Data Source dialog appears.

As shown in Figure 1.21, buttons in the Legend Entries side of the Select Data Source dialog allow you to add new series, edit a series, remove a series, or change the sequence of a series. A single Edit button on the right side of the dialog allows you to edit the range used for category labels.

Compare Figure 1.20 to Figure 1.22. The series and categories have been reversed. The order of the cities has been re-sequenced from alphabetical to descending order by summer temperature. The month names have been changed to season names.

Figure 1.21
You can use the Select Data Source dialog box for more control over data series.

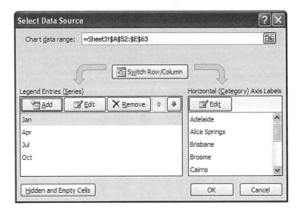

To convert the chart shown in Figure 1.20 to the chart shown in Figure 1.22, you use the Select Data Source dialog, as follows:

1. Select the chart and choose Design, Select Data. The Select Data Source dialog displays.

2. Click Switch Rows/Columns to move the city names to the left side of the dialog.

3. Click Alice Springs on the left side and then the up arrow button until Alice Springs is the first series.

4. Click Broome and then the up arrow button until Broome is the second series.

5. Continue re-sequencing the cities until they are in the desired order.

6. On the Horizontal (Category) Axis Labels side of the dialog, click the Edit button. The data initially points to B1:E1. Change the address in the Axis Labels dialog box to an array by entering the four new labels inside curly braces:
   ={"Summer","Fall","Winter","Spring"}. Click OK to close the Axis Labels dialog box and return to the Select Data Source dialog box.

The modified chart in Figure 1.22 shows the cities based on the warmest summer temperatures.

Figure 1.22
You can control the series
order by using the Select
Data icon.

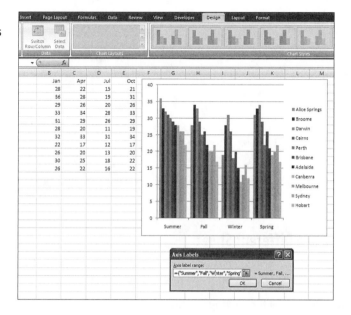

Leaving the Top-Left Cell Blank

In the past, Excel tipsters would tell you to always leave the top-left cell of your dataset blank before creating a chart. This requirement has eased up a bit with Excel 2007.

The old guideline was that if your series or category labels contained either dates or numeric labels, you should leave the top-left cell blank. Excel 2007 has been tweaked a bit. Now, if your labels contain values formatted as dates, there is no need to leave the top-left cell blank. In addition, if your data has been converted to a table, using the Format as Table icon on the Home ribbon, it is impossible to leave the top-left cell blank.

In a few instances, your results improve if the top-left cell is blank. Consider the data in A1:D4 of Figure 1.23. The years in B1:D1 are numeric. If you look at A1:D1, you have text in column A, followed by three numbers in B:D. This is remarkably similar to the data in A2:D4. You have text in column A, followed by numbers in B:D. If you create a chart from this dataset, Excel assumes that you do not have series labels and assumes that A1:A4 represent four category labels. This erroneously produces the top chart in the figure.

Cells A11:D14 in the figure contain exactly the same data as A1:D4, except the Region label was cleared from A11. In this case, Excel correctly sees three series and three categories.

Figure 1.23
The top data is charted incorrectly because of the Region label in cell A1. The bottom data is charted correctly because cell A11 is blank.

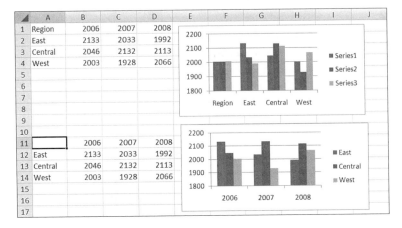

Moving a Chart to a Different Sheet

In Excel 2007, charts always start out as objects embedded in a worksheet. However, you might want to display a chart on its own full-page chart sheet.

There are two options for moving a chart:

- Choose the Move Chart icon at the right edge of the Design ribbon.
- Right-click any whitespace near the border of the chart and choose Move Chart.

Either way, the Move Chart dialog appears, offering the options New Sheet and Object In. The Object In drop-down lists all the worksheets in the current workbook. The New Sheet option allows you to specify a name for a new sheet. (See Figure 1.24.)

Figure 1.24
Move a chart to a different worksheet using the Move Chart dialog.

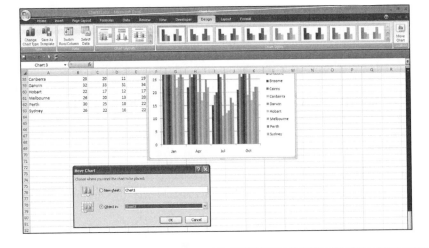

NOTE

When you choose to move a chart to a new sheet, the chart is located on a special sheet called a chart sheet. This sheet holds one chart that can be printed to fill a sheet of paper. You cannot have additional cells or formulas on a chart sheet. Figure 1.25 shows a chart that has been moved to a chart sheet.

Figure 1.25
A chart sheet holds one chart at full screen. There are no cells on the sheet.

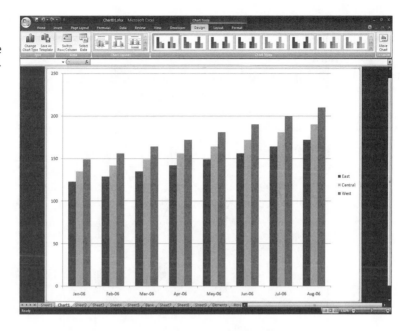

Customizing a Chart by Using the Design Ribbon

The Design ribbon allows you to quickly customize a chart with just a couple clicks. For example, the Chart Styles gallery allows you to change the color scheme and effects for the entire chart. The Chart Layouts gallery offers professionally designed combinations of chart elements.

Choosing a Chart Layout

Depending on the chart type you have chosen, the Chart Layouts gallery offers 4 to 12 built-in combinations of chart elements. When you choose a new chart layout from the gallery, you get a predefined combination of title, layout, gridlines, and so on.

> **NOTE**
>
> Frankly, the combinations offered in the Chart Layouts gallery seem a bit arbitrary. When I look at the options in the gallery, I am not sure why these 12 were chosen out of the 780 quadrillion possible combinations. Assuming that each chart layout controls four different settings, the odds of any given chart layout being the style that you would have selected yourself are ($1/2 \wedge 4$) or less. I do know that at one point in time, one of the Excel developers showed me some chart samples, and I was asked to choose my favorites from the various galleries. Perhaps my opinions and the opinions of thousands of others were combined to choose the styles in the gallery.

Figure 1.26 shows 11 charts created by choosing each of the different column chart layouts from the gallery.

Figure 1.26

The Chart Layouts gallery offers up to a dozen predefined layouts for the current chart type.

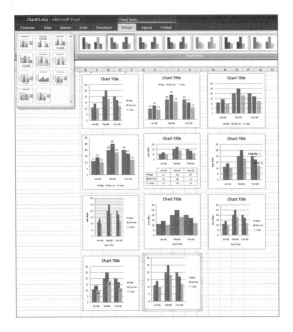

Choosing a Color Scheme

The Design ribbon is also home to the Chart Styles gallery, which offers 48 variations of color and effects. The gallery has columns for each of the six accent colors, monochrome, and mixed colors.

As you proceed down the first four rows of the gallery, each style has a bit more extreme effect applied to the bars. The styles in row 2 have a white border around the bars. The styles in row 3 have a dark gradient. The styles in row 4 have a glass-like surface on the bars. The styles in row 5 have a dark border around the bars, combined with a light tint in the plot area. The final row has a dark background that is suitable, for example, if you are using the chart in a dark-themed PowerPoint presentation.

Figure 1.27 shows the 48 thumbnails in the gallery and a sample of the effects available for accent color 2 in the Office theme.

Figure 1.27
You can choose from eight color schemes when you use the Chart Styles gallery.

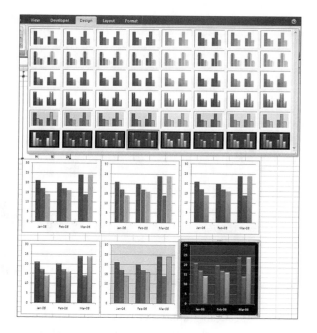

Modifying a Color Scheme by Changing the Theme

The six accent colors and the built-in effects are different in each of the 20 themes that ship with Office 2007. You can change to any of the 20 themes or create your own theme in order to easily access new colors and effects.

On the Page Layout ribbon, you can click the Themes drop-down to choose from the 20 built-in themes. If you choose a new theme from the Themes drop-down, Excel applies a new color and set of effects to all of the charts in the current workbook. If you want to change only the colors or effects, you can use the Colors or Effects drop-down in the Themes group.

In Figure 1.28, you can see that the Opulent theme applies a jeweled effect to the columns.

You should keep the following in mind when changing a chart's theme:

■ Excel, Word, and PowerPoint offer the same 20 built-in themes. If you are building a document that contains elements from more than one Office 2007 product, you should apply the same theme in all the documents.

Figure 1.28
Applying a new theme changes the color and built-in effects.

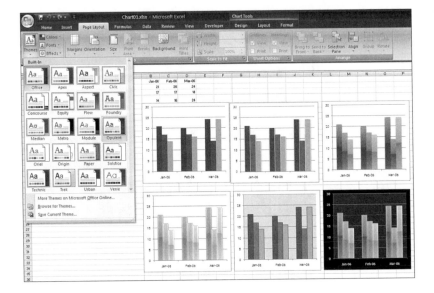

- Changing the theme affects all graphic elements in the workbook. While your Excel workbook might contain mostly numbers and one or two charts, it could make sense to change the theme to easily apply new colors to the chart. In Excel 2007, changing the theme affects any SmartArt graphics in the workbook as well.

> **CAUTION**
>
> In PowerPoint, and to a lesser extent Word, changing the theme affects far more than the occasional chart. The chosen theme also changes the fonts used in the presentation, the slide background, and so on.

- If you want the theme to have an impact on the fonts in your workbook, you should use the Cell Styles drop-down in the Home ribbon to format your cells.
- The Effects drop-down on the Page Layout ribbon contains a lot of subtle information encoded in the thumbnails. See "Choosing Effects for a Custom Theme from an Existing Theme" for details.

Creating Your Own Theme

You might want to develop a special theme. This is fairly easy to do: you basically need to select two fonts and six accent colors. For example, let's say you want to create a theme to match your company's color scheme. The hardest part is probably finding six colors to represent your company because most company logos have two or three colors. The following sections describe how to create a new theme and suggest resources for choosing complementary colors for your company colors.

Choosing Effects for a Custom Theme from an Existing Theme

Unless you plan on editing XML files, you will have to re-use built-in effects from an existing theme for your theme. The thumbnails in the Effects drop-down offer very subtle clues to the types of effects used in each theme.

The formatting galleries generally range from simple effects in the top row, moderate effects in the middle rows, and extreme effects in the bottom row. If you open the Shape Styles gallery on the Format ribbon, the first row is simple, the fourth row is moderate, and the sixth row is extreme.

Open the Effects drop-down on the Page Layout ribbon. You will see three shapes for each theme: a circle, an arrow, and a rectangle. The appearance of the circle provides an indication of the effects used in simple formats (such as from row 1 of the Shape Styles Gallery). The appearance of the arrow provides an indication of the effects used in moderate formats (row 4 of the Shape Styles Gallery). The appearance of the rectangle provides an indication of the effects used in extreme formats (row 6 of the gallery).

Figure 1.29 shows the Effects drop-down in grayscale. Please open this in your computer so you can actually see the effects in color.

Figure 1.29
The circle, arrow, and rectangle apply to simple, moderate, and intense layouts, respectively.

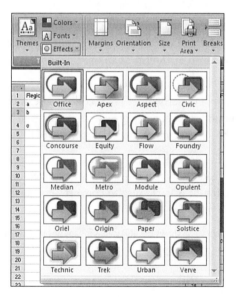

For example:

- The circle in the Civic and Equity themes show a faint line. This indicates that shapes with a simple format applied will have fainter lines when using this theme. The circles in the Module and Concourse theme have an interior reflection or glow.

■ The arrow in the Trek theme has a gradient that starts out light at the top of the arrow and becomes darker at the bottom of the arrow. If you apply a moderate effect to a chart and use the Trek theme, the shapes in the chart will have a similar gradient.

■ The rectangle in the Paper theme has a dark texture applied. The rectangle in the Metro theme has a glass or jeweled affect applied. The rectangle in the Equity theme has a thin white outline around a dark rectangle. If you format your chart with extreme effects, the shapes will have an appearance similar to the rectangle in each thumbnail.

While you can access dialog boxes to control the font and colors in your theme, you simply have to choose one of the 20 built-in effects as a starting point for your new custom theme.

Choose any theme from the Effects drop-down to start building your custom theme.

Understanding RGB Color Codes

Colors on computer monitors are described as a mix of red (R), green (G), and blue (B). Each color channel is assigned a value from 0 to 255. For example, a color of R=255, G=0, B=0 is a bright red. As you add more blue, the red shifts toward a pink or violet color. A color of R=255, G=0, B=128 is a pinkish violet color.

A color of R=0, G=0, B=0 is black. A color of R=255, G=255, B=255 is white. You can create 16.7 million different colors by using combinations of red, green, and blue.

To see a pertinent example of how this works, open your company's home page in a browser. Then, from the View menu in Internet Explorer, choose Source, or, in Firefox, choose View, Page Source.

You should now see the webpage's underlying HTML code. You can find the colors used in the page by searching for a pound sign. A webpage specifies colors in hexadecimal format, using a pound sign followed by six characters (for example, #4F81BD).

Although every webpage uses the hexadecimal notation for describing colors, Microsoft Excel's theme specification instead needs the RGB values for the color. Luckily, as described in the following section, it is fairly easy to convert between the two.

> **TIP**
> The color chooser in Photoshop shows the RGB values for any hexadecimal notation.

Converting from Hexadecimal to RGB

Hexadecimal is a numbering system that has digits 0 through 9 and A through F. Including 0, there are 16 digits in the hexadecimal numbering system. In the decimal system, a 2-digit number can represent 10×10 different combinations. There are 100 numbers, from 00 to 99. In a hex system, a 2-digit number can represent 16×16 different numbers—that is, 256 numbers, from 0 to 255.

In the #123456 nomenclature, the # sign indicates that the number is in hexadecimal. The first two digits are the hex representation of the red value. The next two digits are the hex representation of the green value. The next two digits are the hex representation of the blue value.

If you don't have Photoshop or another tool that converts from a hex color to an RGB value for you automatically, you can use functions in Excel to do the conversion. For example, the worksheet in Figure 1.30 converts from a hex color in Cell B1 to the RGB values in B7:B9:

- The formulas in B2:B4 use the MID function to extract each pair of numbers from the color code. The formula for Cell B2 is shown in Cell C2.

- The formulas in B7:B9 use the HEX2DEC function to convert the two-digit hex number to decimal.

Figure 1.30
This quick Excel worksheet converts from a six-digit hex color code to decimal RGB values.

	A	B	C	D
	B1	▾	f_x	#FF9108
1		#FF9108		
2		FF	=MID(B1,2,2)	
3		91	=MID(B1,4,2)	
4		08	=MID(B1,6,2)	
5				
6				
7	R:	255	=HEX2DEC(B2)	
8	G:	145	=HEX2DEC(B3)	
9	B:	8	=HEX2DEC(B4)	

To represent the color #FF9108 in Excel, for example, you would use R=255, G=145, B=8.

Finding Complementary Colors

If you look at your company's logo and website, you can probably identify two or three colors to use in the theme. You need to come up with a total of six accent colors for a theme.

> **NOTE**   You can use the free web-based tool at http://wellstyled.com/tools/colorscheme2/index-en.html# to find colors that look good together.

To find complementary colors, you follow these steps:

1. Start with a hex representation of one of your logo colors.

2. Open http://wellstyled.com/tools/colorscheme2/index-en.html# in a browser.

3. In the lower-left corner, click the link for Enter RGB (rough conversion).

4. In the window that pops up, enter the portion of the color code after the pound sign (for example, FF9108).

5. Click each of the five icons under the color wheel on the left (for contrast, triad, tetrad, and analogic). In the Triad view, the website shows your original color, three others, and three variations of each, as shown in Figure 1.31. The right side of the website specifies the hex color codes for all the colors shown.

Figure 1.31
This webpage suggests colors that complement your logo colors.

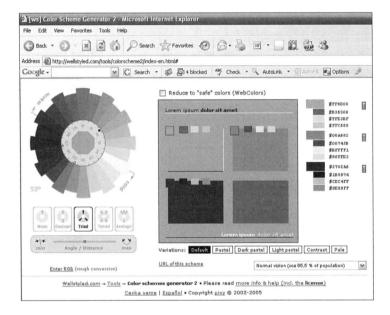

Specifying a Theme's Colors

To specify new theme colors, you follow these steps:

1. Select Page Layout, Themes, Colors, Create New Theme Colors. The Create New Theme Colors dialog appears. Remember that a theme is composed of 2 text colors, 2 background colors, 6 accent colors, and 2 hyperlink colors. These 12 colors are shown in the Create New Theme Colors dialog, as shown in Figure 1.32.

2. To change the first accent color, choose the drop-down next to Accent 1. The color chooser appears.

3. From the bottom of the color chooser drop-down, choose More Colors. The Colors dialog appears.

4. On the Custom tab of the Colors dialog, enter values for red, green, and blue, as shown in Figure 1.33. The New color block shows the color for the values you entered. Click OK to accept the new color.

5. Repeat steps 2–4 for each of the accent colors.

6. If you want to change the colors for Hyperlink, Followed Hyperlink, and Text, repeats steps 2–4 for any of those.

7. In the Name box, give the theme a name, such as your company name.

8. Click Preview to see the theme applied to your workbook.

9. Click Save to accept the theme.

Figure 1.32
The 12 colors in the current theme are shown here.

Figure 1.33
Specify the RGB values for the first color.

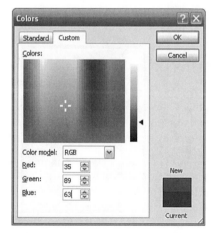

Specifying a Theme's Fonts

To specify new theme fonts, you follow these steps:

1. Select Page Layout, Themes, Fonts, Create New Theme Fonts. The Create New Theme Fonts dialog appears, as shown in Figure 1.34. Remember that a font theme contains a heading font and a body font.

Figure 1.34
A theme is composed of two fonts.

2. Select a font from the Heading Font drop-down. If a custom font is used in your company's logo, using it might be appropriate.

3. Select a font from the Body Font drop-down. This should be a font that is easy to read. Avoid stylized fonts for body copy.

4. Give the theme a name. It is okay to reuse the same name from the color theme.

5. Click Save to accept the theme changes.

Saving a Custom Theme

In order to reuse a theme in other workbooks, you must save it. From the Page Layout ribbon, you select Themes, Themes, Save Current Theme, as shown in Figure 1.35.

Figure 1.35
The option to save a theme is at the bottom of the Themes drop-down.

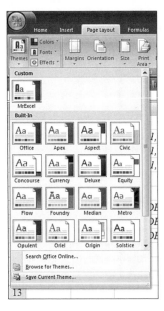

By default, themes are stored in the `Document Themes` folder. This folder is in `%appdata%\Microsoft\Templates\Document Themes\`.

You need to give your theme a useful name and click Save.

Using a Custom Theme on a New Document

After saving a custom theme with your company colors, fonts, and effects, the theme will be available to all workbooks, documents, and slide shows on your computer. The next time that you access the Themes drop-down, your custom themes will appear first in the menu, under a heading of Custom.

Excel automatically generates a thumbnail showing the letter A in your headline font, the letter a in the body text font, and the six accent colors used in the theme.

After saving a theme and opening PowerPoint 2007 or Word 2007, the new custom themes will be available in those applications as well.

Sharing a Theme with Others

If you want to share a theme with others, you need to send them the `.thmx` file from `%AppData%\Microsoft\Templates\Document Themes\`.

> **TIP**
>
> Using `%AppData%` in Windows Explorer is a shortcut to the application data folder in your operating system. On a Windows XP machine, this might be `C:\Documents and Settings\your name\Application Data\`. On a Windows Vista machine, this might be `C:\Users\Your Name\App Data\Roaming`. By typing `$AppData%`, Windows Explorer will navigate to the proper folder.

The people you share the theme with can either copy the `.thmx` file to their equivalent folder or save the `.thmx` file to their desktop and use the Browse for Themes option by choosing Page Layout, Themes, Themes, Browse for Themes.

Next Steps

Chapter 2 describes how to use the Layout tab of the ribbon in order to toggle on or off individual elements of the chart. It also describes how you can micromanage individual elements by using the Format ribbon.

Customizing Charts

2

Accessing Element Formatting Tools

In Chapter 1, "Introducing Charts in Excel 2007," you learned how to create a chart using the Insert ribbon and then how to choose from built-in layouts and styles on the Design ribbon. In real life, you usually want to have some control over the various elements in a chart. Excel provides three additional levels of control:

- The Layout ribbon contains a few popular choices for formatting 15 chart elements. In 80% of cases, you can choose from the drop-down menus on the Layout ribbon in order to create the perfect chart.

- The Format ribbon contains icons that enable you to micromanage the color, fill, outline, and effects for any individual chart element. If you want to apply a soft glow, a metallic finish, and a reflection to the January data point, for example, you can do so using the Format ribbon.

- Powerful format dialog boxes exist for every element in the chart. These dialog boxes provide the ultimate control over individual elements. You can access these dialog boxes in several different ways: You can select an element and press Ctrl+1. Or, simply right-click a chart element and choose Format or use the new Format Selection icons on the Layout and Format tabs. Most of the drop-downs on the Layout tab also lead to a More option.

This chapter walks you through the various chart components that you can customize and offers tips and tricks for creating eye-catching but meaningful results.

Identifying Chart Elements

Many elements of a chart can be customized. You rarely want to include all the available elements in a single chart because having too many elements takes away from the meaning of the data in the chart. You should judiciously use titles, axes, and gridlines to help the reader understand the data presented in a chart.

Chart Labels and Axis

To help you identify the various elements in a chart, Figure 2.1 shows a chart that has too many elements.

Figure 2.1
This chart shows the various components available in a 2-D chart.

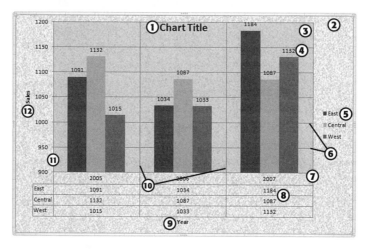

1. Chart Title	7. Horizontal Axis
2. Chart Area	8. Data Table
3. Plot Area	9. Horizontal Axis Title
4. Data Label	10. Vertical Gridlines
5. Legend	11. Vertical Axis
6. Horizontal Gridlines	12. Vertical Axis Title

Figure 2.1 contains the following elements:

- **Chart area**—The chart area is the entire range shown in Figure 2.1. This includes all the area outside the plot area. It is where labels and legends often appear.

- **Plot area**—The plot area is the rectangular area that includes the data series and data markers.

- **Chart title**—The chart title typically appears in a larger font and near the top of the chart. Whereas Excel 2003 always included the chart title outside the plot area, choices in Excel 2007 encourage you to have the title overlaying the plot area.

- **Horizontal axis title**—The horizontal axis title identifies the type of data along the horizontal axis. In case it is not clear that "2005 2006 2007" represents years, you can add a horizontal axis title such as the one shown near number 9 in Figure 2.1.

- **Vertical axis title**—It is common to use the vertical axis title along the left side of a chart to identify the units along the axis. In Figure 2.1, the word "Sales" near number 12 is the vertical axis title.

- **Legend**—The legend initially appears to the right of the plot area. It helps identify which color in the chart represents which series. You can drag the legend anywhere in the chart area or plot area, freeing up space for the plot area to extend further to the right.

- **Data label**—If you want the actual value for each bar or point to appear on the chart, you turn on the Data Labels option. Data labels frequently get overwritten by gridlines and other charting elements. Far too often, I find myself nudging individual data labels so that they can be read.

- **Data table**—Instead of using data labels, you can ask Excel to add a spreadsheet-like data table beneath the plot area. The data table frequently takes up too much space in the chart area and reduces the size available for the plot area.

- **Horizontal axis**—The horizontal or category axis is along the bottom of the chart for column and line charts and along the left side for bar charts. Your main choice is whether the axis contains a time series. If it does, Excel varies the spacing between the points to represent actual dates.

- **Vertical axis**—This is the axis along the left side of the chart in a column or line chart. In some advanced charts, as discussed in Chapter 7, "Advanced Chart Techniques," you might have a second vertical axis on the right side of the chart. This axis typically contains values, and your main choice is whether you want the axis scaled in thousands, millions, and so on.

- **Horizontal gridlines**—Horizontal gridlines run horizontally across the plot area and line up with each number along the vertical axis. If you do not have data labels on a chart, the horizontal gridlines are particularly useful for telling whether a particular point is just above or below a certain level. It is best to keep gridlines unobtrusive. Some of the best charts include gridlines in a faint color so that they do not obscure the main message of the chart.

- **Vertical gridlines**—Vertical gridlines are used less often than horizontal gridlines. If you are considering using them in a line chart or a surface chart, you should consider using drop lines instead.

Special Elements in a 3-D Chart

Some chart elements are editable only in 3-D charting styles. Figure 2.2 shows a 3-D column chart.

Figure 2.2
This chart shows the various components available in a 3-D chart.

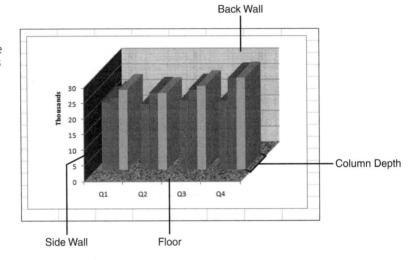

The following are the 3-D chart elements:

- **Back wall**—The back wall in Figure 2.2 is formatted with a texture. In previous versions of Excel, any formatting applied to the back wall also applied to the side wall. In Excel 2007, these are now two separate elements.

- **Side wall**—The side wall in Figure 2.2 is formatted with a dark fill.

- **Floor**—The floor is the surface below the 3-D columns.

- **Column depth**—Column depth is one of the many 3-D rotation settings you can change. In Figure 2.2, each column appears to be a deep rectangular slab. You create this effect by increasing the column depth. The chart has also been tipped forward a bit, so that it appears that the viewer is at a slightly higher viewing angle.

Analysis Elements

The Analysis group on the Layout ribbon includes elements that are of particular importance to scientists. However, some of the elements, such as the trendline, can also be useful in business charting. Figure 2.3 illustrates some of the analysis elements.

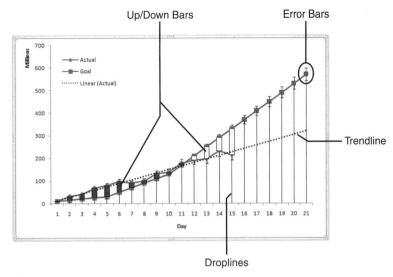

Figure 2.3
This chart shows the various analysis elements.

The following are the analysis elements:

- **Trendline**—If you ask for a trendline, Excel uses regression analysis to fit your existing data points to a statistical line. You can have Excel extend this line into future time periods. In Figure 2.3, the dotted trendline shows that unless you alter the system-generating actuals, you will likely miss the goal.

- **Drop lines**—Drop lines are vertical lines that extend from the data point to the horizontal axis in either line or area charts. These lines are helpful because they enable the reader to locate the exact point where the line intersects the axis.

- **Up/down bars**—When you are plotting two series on a line chart, Excel can draw rectangles between the two lines. In Figure 2.3, the actual exceeds the goal in Days 2 through 11, and the up/down bars are shown in a dark color. The goal exceeds the actual in Days 11 through 15, and the up/down error bars are shown in a contrasting color. If the up/down error bars seem too wide, you can try using high/low lines.

- **Error bars**—The error bar feature is popular in scientific analysis to show the error of an estimate. You might see these used in business charts to indicate the acceptable tolerance from a quality goal. For example, a quality goal might be to achieve 99.5% quality, with anything between 99% and 100% being acceptable. The error bars could be added to the 99.5% goal series in order to show whether the actual quality falls within the acceptable tolerance.

Formatting Chart Elements

When formatting chart elements, you generally start with some of the built-in choices available on the Layout ribbon. This section describes how to do this, as well as how to use the mini toolbar, Home ribbon, Format ribbon, or Format dialog to further customize certain elements.

Formatting a Chart Title

By default, a chart with more than one series is created without any title, as shown in the upper-right chart in Figure 2.4.

To add a title, you use the Chart Title drop-down on the Layout tab. Your choices are a centered overlay title or a title above the chart. When you add the title above the chart, Excel has to shrink the plot area to make room for the title (see the lower-right chart in Figure 2.4). If your title fits, using a centered overlay title leaves more space for the title, but there is the chance that the words in your title and the points plotted in the series will collide, as they do in the chart shown on the left in Figure 2.4.

Figure 2.4
Excel offers two built-in locations for chart titles.

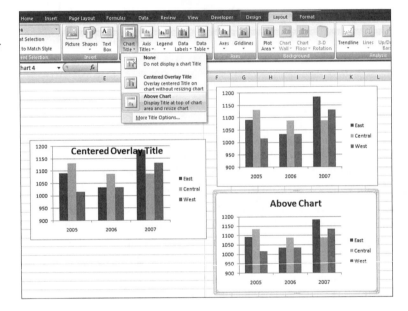

Typing a Title

After you select a title location from the drop-down, Excel adds the generic "Chart Title" placeholder text to the top of your chart. The title is selected by default, so you can immediately start typing the actual title. You see the typed characters appear in the formula bar. When you press the Enter key, Excel replaces "Chart Title" with the words you typed.

Moving a Title

You single-click a title to select it. Then you move the mouse pointer so that it is above the outline of the title. When the mouse pointer changes to a four-headed arrow, you click and drag the title to a new location.

Note that the outline contains only four handles instead of the usual eight. This means you cannot use the handles to resize the title bounding box. However, you do have some control over the size of the title bounding box. If you press the Enter key in the middle of the title, you will force the title bounding box to become vertically larger.

Formatting a Title with the Mini Toolbar

You triple-click a title in order to select all the words in the title. When you move your mouse pointer slightly up and to the right, the mini toolbar appears, allowing you to select the font and other formatting to use in the title (see Figure 2.5).

Figure 2.5
You select text in a title and then move the mouse up and to the right, toward the nearly invisible mini toolbar, to make the toolbar appear.

Formatting a Title with the Home Ribbon Tab

If getting the mini toolbar to display is too frustrating for you, you can use the Home ribbon instead. To do so, you select characters in the title and then display the Home tab of the ribbon. You can use the icons in the Font and Alignment groups to format the title.

TIP If you use the Orientation drop-down to angle your title, there is no setting on the Home ribbon to return to horizontal text. To turn off a selection such as vertical text, you have to re-select that item from the Orientation drop-down.

Formatting a Title with the Format Ribbon

Many options on the Format ribbon allow you to change the fill, font, and line style used in the title. The settings in the Shape Styles group affect the currently invisible rectangle that surrounds the title. You cannot add a reflection, but all the other settings are available.

To add effects to the actual words in a title, you use the drop-downs in the WordArt Styles group of the Format ribbon (see Figure 2.6). You can control the font color, the outline color of the font, shadow, reflection, and glow. Other WordArt features, such as Bevel and Transforms, are not available in charting titles.

Figure 2.6
You select a title and then use the three drop-downs in the WordArt Styles group to format the title.

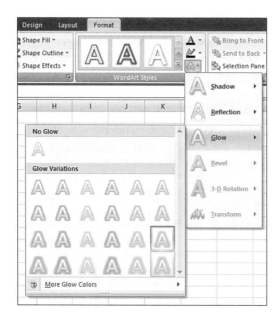

More Title Options

You can right-click a title and then choose Format Chart Title to access the Format dialog. This dialog offers Fill, Border Color, Border Styles, Shadow, 3-D Format, and Alignment sections. The Shadow section gives you micro-control over the shadow transparency, size, blur, angle, and distance.

The Alignment tab allows you to rotate the text in 1 degree increments.

Formatting an Axis Title

Excel has three built-in options for the vertical axis. Figure 2.7 shows these options: Rotated Title (top left), Vertical Title (bottom left), and Horizontal Title (bottom right). In many cases, the Rotated Title option looks the best.

For a horizontal axis title, the only built-in option is to turn the title on or off.

All the formatting options available for the chart title also apply to the axis titles. You can use the mini toolbar, the Home ribbon, or the Format ribbon to change the font, color, fill, and effects for the axis title.

> **TIP**
> You may see charts with "Thousands," "Millions," "Billions," and so on near the top of the vertical axis title area. You should know that this is not part of the vertical axis title. You control this setting by selecting Layout, Axes, Primary Vertical Axis, Show Axis in Thousands.

Figure 2.7
The vertical axis title can be oriented in three ways, using the Axis Titles drop-down on the Layout tab.

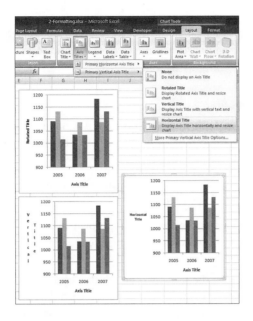

Formatting a Legend

My favorite legend trick is more difficult in Excel 2007 than in previous versions. Although it takes a few more clicks now than it used to, you can still float a legend in an unused portion of the plot area.

The built-in choices for the legend include having the legend outside the left, right, bottom, or top of the plot area. If you move the legend to the top or the bottom, Excel rearranges the legend in a horizontal format, as shown in Figure 2.8.

Figure 2.8
The built-in choices include moving the legend to the top or bottom, which works well in this chart.

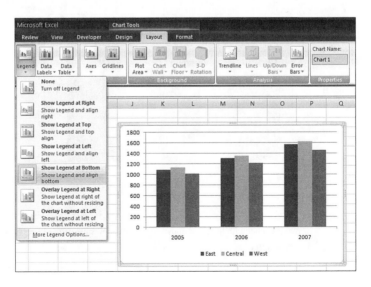

Floating a Legend in the Plot Area

I recommend going outside the built-in legend options. Although the legend usually starts on the right side of the chart, you can often find a corner of the plot area that has white-space.

Due to the yearly growth of the data in Figure 2.8, there is room above the 2005 columns for the legend. You follow these steps to move the legend there:

1. From the Layout ribbon, select the Legend drop-down and then Overlay Legend at Right. This keeps the legend in a vertical arrangement and stretches the plot area out to the right edge of the chart.

2. Carefully click on an edge of the box surrounding the legend. When the mouse pointer is a four-headed arrow, drag the mouse and drop the legend in a free spot on the chart. A new problem in Excel 2007 is that the legend has a transparent fill, so the underlying gridlines may tend to show through.

3. While the legend is still selected, click the Format ribbon tab. Choose Shape Fill, White to convert the transparent fill to a solid fill. The fill prevents gridlines from overwriting your legend titles.

4. Choose Format, Shape Outline, Black to add a border around the legend.

Figure 2.9 shows the legend floating over a vacant area of the plot area. Notice that this allows the plot area to extend nearly to the right edge of the chart area.

Figure 2.9
You can drag the legend over the chart and then format the legend so it has a border and no transparency.

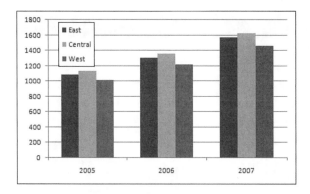

Changing the Arrangement of a Legend

In the top-left chart in Figure 2.10, a new series is added to the chart. This causes the floating legend to obscure part of the columns. To fix this problem, you click the Legend to activate the resizing handles. Then you drag the bottom-right corner of the legend up and out to produce a legend with the labels arranged in a 2-by-2 grid, as shown in the lower-left chart in the figure.

If you keep dragging, the legend becomes a 1-by-4 arrangement, as shown in the top-right chart in the figure.

Figure 2.10
You have some control over the arrangement of the labels in the legend when you resize the legend border.

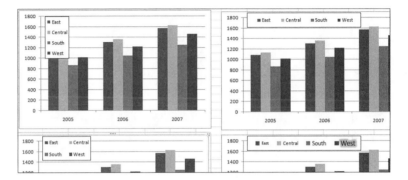

Formatting Individual Legend Entries

A new feature in Excel 2007 is the ability to format or resize the individual legend entries. This is particularly useful when one entry is longer than the others.

To format an individual legend, you follow these steps:

1. Click the legend, and the entire legend is selected.
2. Click the legend entry you want to change.
3. To change the font size, right-click the text and use the options in the mini toolbar. To change anything else, use the Home ribbon or the Format ribbon.

In the chart at the bottom right of Figure 2.10, each legend entry is a different font size. You can also apply effects such as glow to the legend entries.

You can also remove certain legend entries. When an individual legend entry is selected, press the Delete key. This becomes useful when you are using extra series to add elements to a chart. Several examples in Chapter 7, "Advanced Chart Techniques," utilize this method.

Using the Format Legend Dialog

To use the Format Legend dialog, you choose More Legend Options from the Legend drop-down on the Layout ribbon. This dialog allows you to change the fill color, the border color, the border styles, and the shadow behind the legend.

Adding Data Labels to a Chart

The reader of your chart might be able to discern whether one of two adjacent columns is taller than the other. However, it is difficult to compare a column in the center of a chart with numbers along the left axis. That's where data labels can be an advantage. This feature works best if you have only a few data points on the chart.

Traditionally, data labels for a single-series column chart would appear above each column. In Excel 2007, this choice is known as Outside End. The other built-in choices on the Data Labels tab are Center, Inside End, Inside Base, and None (see Figure 2.11).

Figure 2.11
Data labels look best when placed above the bars in a column chart.

The three "inside" choices are useful when you have a stacked column chart. Rather than placing the label for the bottom column inside the top column, the inside choices keep each label inside the appropriate bar.

Figure 2.12 compares the Inside End, Inside Base, and Center options on a single chart.

Figure 2.12
When you have multiple series in a stacked column chart, you should use one of the inside locations for the data label.

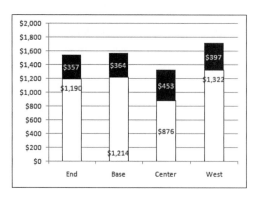

Charting gurus suggest that you should have either numeric labels along the axis or data labels, but not both. Numeric labels along the value axis allow the reader to get a general feel for the location of a marker. A data label allows the reader to know the exact location of a marker. After you add data labels, you can remove the axis labels.

Nudging a Label to Avoid a Gridline

If your chart has dark gridlines, you may find that the data label appears to be crossed out by the gridline. It is a slightly tedious process to fix the labels, but doing so ensures that your data labels are readable. You follow these steps to nudge a data label out of the way of the gridline:

1. Click a data label in the chart. Excel selects all the labels for that particular series.
2. Again click the data label to be moved. Excel now selects just that data label (see Figure 2.13).

Figure 2.13
A second click selects just one data label.

3. Carefully position the mouse pointer over the border of the label. When the mouse pointer changes to a four-headed arrow, click and drag the data label above or below the gridline.
4. Repeat steps 1-3 for any other labels that are running into the gridlines. (If the next label is in the same series, you can skip step 1.)

Using the Format Data Label Dialog

There are many important settings you can access in the Format Data Labels dialog to customize data labels on a chart:

■ On the Label Options tab, you can change the content of the label. In Figure 2.14, for example, the pie chart is labeled with the category name and the value. For other pie charts, you might want the percentage instead.

- On the Number tab, you can change the number format or simply choose to have the format be the same format as in the original dataset.

Figure 2.14
You can control the text in the data labels by using the Format Data Labels dialog.

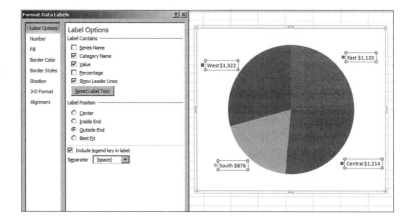

> **TIP**
> In all cases, the Format dialog box contains the built-in choices on the Layout ribbon menus, plus many more options. As I create more charts, I find myself often automatically heading to the Format dialog box so that I have full control over the format of the selected element.
> After you have selected an element in the chart, pressing Ctrl+1 takes you to the appropriate Format dialog box. Further, when a Format dialog box is displayed, you can click a new element in the chart. The Format dialog box will change to reflect the properties available for the newly selected element.

Adding a Data Table to a Chart

A data table is a mini-worksheet that appears below a chart. In it, Excel shows the values for each data point in the table. One advantage of a data table is that you can show the numbers that would normally be shown with data labels without adding any elements to the plot area.

There are two built-in options in the Data Table drop-down on the Layout ribbon: you can show the data table with legend keys or without legend keys.

The data table takes up a fair amount of space at the bottom of the chart. Putting the legend keys in the table allows you to regain some of that space by eliminating the legend element from the chart.

In the chart on the left in Figure 2.15, the legend keys appear in the chart. In the chart on the right in Figure 2.15, the data table appears without legend keys, requiring a separate legend element to appear—in this case, above the chart. This causes the plot area to shrink and makes it more difficult to interpret the data on the chart.

Figure 2.15
A data table provides a concise grid for the actual values without adding extra data to the plot area itself.

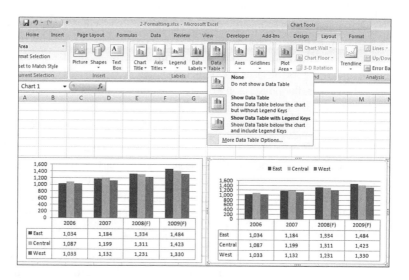

Special Options for Data Tables

If you select the More Data Table options in the Data Table drop-down, you have the usual options for fill, border color, border styles, shadow, and 3-D format, plus special data table options. You can decide to hide or show the horizontal or vertical gridlines in the table and to show or hide the outline around the data table. In Figure 2.16, the outline and horizontal gridlines are turned off, which gives the data table a cleaner look.

Figure 2.16
Special options in the Format Data Table dialog allow you to turn on or off various elements of a data table.

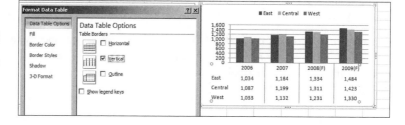

Formatting Axes

Unlike the previously described elements, which are fairly cosmetic, the axis options have major ramifications on the display of data and the ability of the chart reader to interpret data in a chart.

The built-in choices in the Axes drop-down of the Layout ribbon do not begin to touch on the powerful choices in the Format Axis dialog box. To start with, there are four kinds of axes, although the most that you will find in a single chart is three. A pie chart actually has no axes. A radar chart has one axis. A surface chart has three axes. An X-Y chart has two axes. All other charts have two axes, with the possibility of adding an optional third axis.

The horizontal axis contains the category labels. In most charts, it appears along the bottom of the chart. In most programs, this axis is also referred to as the x-axis. (Note that in a bizarre twist, Microsoft calls this axis the primary vertical axis in a bar chart.) Your most important choice for this axis is whether it should be time based or text based. In a chart with a text-based axis, the points along the axis are equally spaced. In a chart that uses a time-based axis, the points are spaced based on the relative time distance between the points. Other choices include selecting whether the data should be plotted left to right or right to left.

The vertical axis contains the scale for the numbers plotted in the chart. The primary vertical axis generally appears along the left side of the chart. In a bar chart, this axis appears along the bottom of the chart and is called a horizontal axis. Choices for this axis include scaling of the axis, the minimum and maximum value for the axis, and the distance between tick marks on the axis. If your data has numbers of different scales, you should specify a logarithmic axis.

In some charts, where one data series is of a vastly different order of magnitude than the others, you may want to plot that series on a secondary vertical axis. This axis has the same choices as the primary vertical axis. It usually appears along the right side of a chart or the top of a bar chart.

The depth axis is a special axis that appears in 3-D surface charts.

Built-in Axis Choices for the Horizontal Axis and Depth Axis

Excel 2007 provides a few built-in options on the Layout ribbon for each axis. As mentioned previously, these options are a tiny fraction of the ones available. It is interesting to note that the options chosen for the built-in menus are a few of the obscure options that you may not have discovered before.

For the horizontal axis, the built-in menu choices allow you to specify that the data should be plotted left to right or right to left. The other choice is for the horizontal axis to appear without any tick marks or labeling. This choice seems remarkably similar to the choice None (see Figure 2.17).

Figure 2.17
The choices in the Primary Horizontal Axis menu are interesting but obscure.

This is one of the few built-in charting menus where you can choose one item and then alter that selection by choosing another menu item. If you choose Show Right-to-Left Axis and then Show Axis Without Labeling, you get a right-to-left axis without labeling. If you reverse those choices, however, the axis labels reappear.

The choices for the depth axis in a surface chart are similar to those for the horizontal axis. Instead of calling the choices Left-to-Right and Right-to-Left, however, the depth axis menu offers the options Normal Axis and Reverse Axis.

Built-in Choices for the Vertical Axis

For the vertical axis, Excel offers the choices None, Default, Thousands, Millions, Billions, and Logarithmic.

The different scales are interesting and allow you to prevent having excess zeros along the vertical axis. In the bottom chart shown in Figure 2.18, there are so many zeros that it is difficult to figure out the numbers at a glance. In the top chart, the zeros are reduced, and a label indicates that the numbers are in billions.

Figure 2.18
Rather than fill your chart area with zeros, you can use an axis scaling factor.

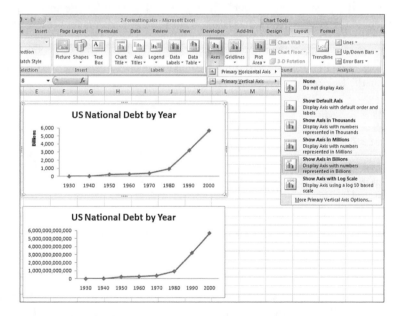

If you access the Format Axis dialog, the Display Units drop-down offers nine scaling options instead of Thousands, Millions, and Billions. You can use Hundreds, Ten Thousands, or even Trillions, which would have been the appropriate scaling factor in Figure 2.18.

> **NOTE**
>
> You can also achieve this effect by using a custom number format with commas at the end of the code. Each comma at the end of the number format divides values by 1,000.

Logarithmic is a useful choice when you need to compare numbers of different scales along the same series. This is described in the next section.

Using a Logarithmic Axis

While the concept of logarithmic axes sounds scary, there is a simple use for logarithmic axes. (A *logarithm* is the power to which a base, such as 10, must be reduced to produce a given number.)

Say that you have a series of data with both large and small data values (for example, sales by model line). Your company probably has the high-flying models that account for 80% of your revenue and then some older-model lines that you are still hanging around. When you try to plot these items on a chart, Excel must make the axis scale large enough to show the sales of the best-selling products. This causes the detail for the smaller product lines to become lost because the values are a small relative percentage of the entire scale.

In Figure 2.19, there is important data regarding the first three product lines, but no one will be able to tell when they look at the chart whether the sales of these products were near the forecast.

Figure 2.19
It's impossible to make out the detail of the smaller product lines because they are relatively too small compared to the largest product line.

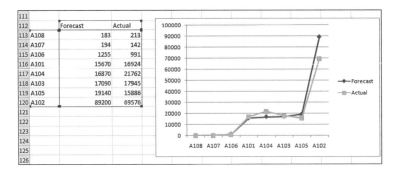

The solution is to convert the axis to a logarithmic axis. In a logarithmic axis, the distance from 1 to 10 is the same as the distance from 10 to 100, and so on. This allows you to easily see detail of the product selling a few hundred units as well as the products selling 100,000 units.

To convert to a logarithmic scale, you choose Layout, Axes, Primary Vertical Axis, Show Axis with Log Scale. The result is a chart such as the one in Figure 2.20. Notice how you can now see that the actual sales were lower than the forecast in the A107 and A106 product lines.

Figure 2.20
If you convert to a log scale, you can see detail for small items as well as large items.

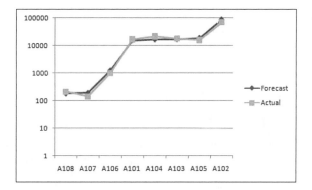

You cannot use the log scale if your data contains negative numbers. There is no way to raise 10 to a power and get a negative number. It would actually be cool if Excel could use the log concept in order to show negative numbers—sort of a pseudo-log scale. Maybe Microsoft will add this in Excel 2009.

Considering Date Versus Text-Based Axes

In most Excel charts, the points along the horizontal axis are equidistant. This makes sense when you are comparing departments or regions or even when you are comparing months of the year.

Other times, your horizontal axis might be based on dates, and these points may not be equally spaced. Figure 2.21 shows the results of random quality control audits. Because the audits are supposed to be a surprise, they do not happen at regular periods. In the top chart, the axis uses a text-based setting and shows the points at equal distances from each other. In the bottom chart, the axis uses a date-based setting, and you can see that certain audits happened closer to or farther away from each other.

Figure 2.21
You can explicitly control whether the horizontal axis is equally spaced, as in the text-based axis here, or if it is date based.

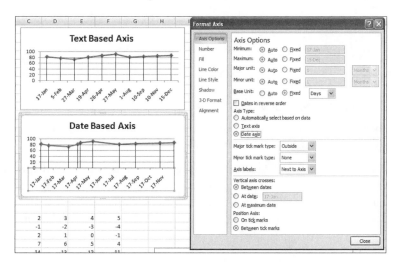

Excel often auto-selects which type of axis to use. To control the axis setting, you can select Layout, Axes, Primary Horizontal Axis, More Primary Horizontal Axis Options, Axis Options, and choose Text Axis or Date Axis from the Axis Type section.

CASE STUDY

Using a Date-Based Axis to Represent Time

Frustratingly, Excel does not offer a time-based axis. If you wanted to plot values that occur at certain times of day, there is no automatic method for achieving this effect. To create the chart in Figure 2.22, for example, you follow these steps:

1. Convert your time values to whole numbers, using =HOURS(A2)*60+MINUTES(A2). Use this column as your category values.

2. Create a line chart.

3. Change the horizontal axis to a date-based axis.

4. Using the built-in styles on the Layout ribbon, turn off the horizontal and vertical axes.

5. Turn on data labels for all points. Specify that the data labels should be above the point. Turn off the labels.

6. Find individual points that represent key times. (For example, Figure 2.22 uses 7 a.m., noon, 5 p.m., and 10 p.m.) Click twice to select the corresponding data point. Right-click and choose Add Data Label. This adds a silly label such as 459 to the point; you will fix this in the next step. Repeat this step for the other three key points in the day.

7. Click a data label, and all labels are selected. Click a second time to select the individual label. Type a new value for the label, such as 7AM, and press Enter. The label changes to the text you typed. (Note that while you are typing, you cannot see the value being typed. You have to wait until you press Enter to see the value.) Repeat this step for the other visible data labels.

Figure 2.22
Creating a time-based axis require a massive kluge.

Changing the Scale of an Axis

Typically, a chart has a vertical axis that runs from zero to a value larger than the largest value in the dataset. This is not ideal for some datasets.

The chart in Figure 2.23 shows daily changes in a measurement that typically fluctuates from 802 to 804. If you use a zero-based vertical axis, as in the top chart, you cannot make out any variability. If you instead change the vertical axis to run from 801 to 804.5, you can see the daily fluctuations in the value, as shown in the bottom chart in the figure.

Figure 2.23
Altering the scale of the axis allows you to see detail in certain datasets.

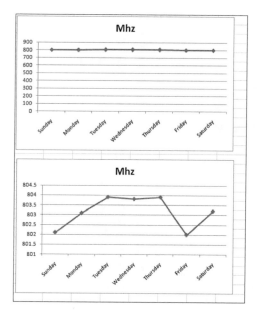

Clearly, altering the axis in Figure 2.23 makes sense. If you didn't change the axis, the chart reader would not be able to make out the variability in a value that is clearly fluctuating wildly within the expected range of values.

In other cases, altering the axis is a great way to mislead people. For example, the top chart in Figure 2.24 shows a 50% increase from 1997 to 2006. If someone wants to manipulate the reader's opinion, he or she can change the minimum and maximum values along the vertical axis. The bottom chart contains the same data as the top chart, but the increase looks far more severe because the scale has been adjusted to focus on values between 5 and 9.

The spin-meisters behind political candidates are experts at manipulating the vertical axis in order to lie or mislead with charts.

When you create a chart, Excel automatically decides whether the vertical axis should reach to zero. The rule is fairly simple: If the range between the lowest and highest values in the dataset is less than 20% of the lowest value, Excel automatically chooses a scale that is not zero based. For example, say that you are plotting data that ranges from 100 to 198. This is a range of 98. Because 98 is almost 50% of the lowest value, Excel automatically creates a vertical axis that extends to 0. As another example, say that you are plotting data that ranges from 1,000 to 1,098. This is a range of 98, but 98 is less than 10% of the lowest value. Excel creates a vertical axis that brackets the range—perhaps 950 to 1,150.

Figure 2.24
Two charts of the same data paint different pictures when the range of the vertical scale is adjusted. (The single vertical line between '99 and '00 is actually drawn in using Insert, Shapes.)

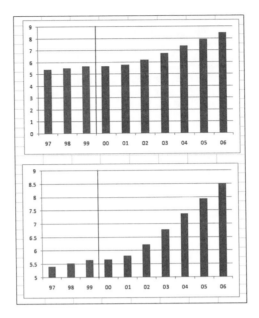

If you are not trying to mislead with your chart, you can usually accept Excel's decision on the vertical axis scale. However, if you need to override the setting, you follow these steps:

1. Select the chart.

2. Choose Layout, Axes, Primary Vertical Axis, More Primary Vertical Axis Options. Excel displays the Format Axis dialog. The axis scale options are in the Axis Options category.

3. To override the minimum value on the axis, choose the Fixed option button for Minimum. You can then type a value for the minimum value to show on the axis.

Figure 2.25 shows the options that are available in the Format Axis dialog.

In Figure 2.25, note the settings Major Unit and Minor Unit. These values are used to control the placement of horizontal gridlines on the chart.

Figure 2.25
You can control the minimum and maximum values along the vertical axis by using this dialog.

Displaying and Formatting Gridlines

Gridlines help the reader to locate data on a chart. Without gridlines, it is difficult to follow the plotted points over to the vertical axis in order to figure out the value of a point.

Gridlines work in conjunction with the Major Unit and Minor Unit settings in the Format Axis dialog (refer to Figure 2.25). The built-in options in the Layout ribbon allow you to turn on major, minor, major and minor, or no gridlines.

Figure 2.26 shows four versions of the same chart. In this chart, the major axis unit is 50 and the minor axis unit is 10.

Figure 2.26
The built-in choices allow you to display major gridlines, minor gridlines, both, or none.

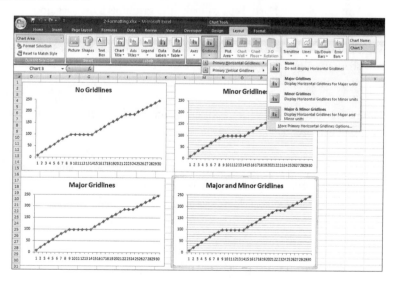

Choosing to display minor gridlines, as in the chart shown in the upper right of Figure 2.26, causes Excel to draw 25 horizontal lines on the chart. This seems like overkill as it is difficult to follow the gridlines across the chart.

Initially, both major and minor gridlines are formatted as 0.75-point lines. This means that selecting Major & Minor Gridlines looks the same as choosing just Minor Gridlines. To make the major gridlines stand out, as in the lower-right chart in the figure, you have to format the major gridlines.

Creating Unobtrusive Gridlines by Using Format Gridline

Gridlines start out as 0.75-point lines. If you plan to display major and minor gridlines on a chart, you likely want to format the gridlines differently.

> **CAUTION**
>
> Using the More Primary Horizontal Gridline Options selection in the built-in menu on the Layout ribbon always leads to a dialog to format the major gridlines. This is particularly frustrating when your chart displays only the minor gridlines. For trouble-free access to the Format Minor Gridlines option, you select Vertical (Value) Axis Minor Gridlines from the drop-down in the Current Selection group of the Layout ribbon. After you have selected the minor gridlines, you click the Format Selection button, which is immediately below the drop-down.

Each Format Gridlines dialog box has three tabs:

- **Line Color**—You can choose a solid-color line in any color, a gradient line in a variety of colors, or an automatic line. When you choose a gradient, Excel applies a slightly different shade to each gridline.
- **Line Style**—You can control the width of each gridline, in 0.25-point increments. You can choose Dash Type to make the gridlines appear as dots, dashes, or various combinations.
- **Shadow**—You can add a shadow to your gridlines. Settings allow you to change the shadow color, transparency, size, blur, angle, and distance. Nothing shouts "chartjunk" more than a shadow on gridlines.

Figure 2.27 shows four varieties of horizontal gridlines and the Line Style tab of the Format Gridlines dialog box.

> The best gridlines are unobtrusive and accent your message instead of overpowering it. Using a dashed thin gridline in a subtle color allows someone to use the gridlines if necessary but makes sure that the gridlines do not overpower the message.

Figure 2.27
You can make the grid-lines as subtle or prominent as you wish.

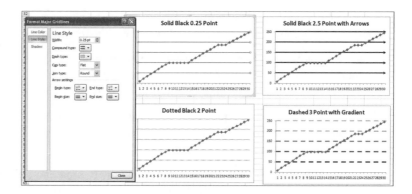

Controlling Placement of Major and Minor Gridlines

You can use the settings in the Format Axis dialog to control the placement of major and minor gridlines. For the vertical axis, you can change the Major Unit and Minor Unit settings to control the spacing of the horizontal gridlines. Although you are allowed to choose something else, for best results, the major unit should be a multiple of the minor unit.

In Figure 2.28, the top and left charts show various settings for the major and minor units and their impact on the gridlines.

Figure 2.28
By changing the units on the Format Axis dialog, you can control the spacing between horizontal gridlines.

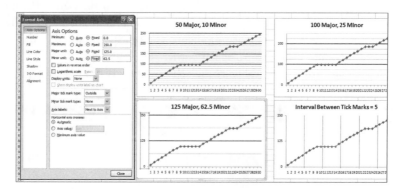

In order to control the placement of vertical gridlines, you have to format the horizontal axis. There is a setting called Interval Between Tick Marks. In the lower-right chart shown in Figure 2.28, the interval has been increased to 5. This causes Excel to display a vertical gridline after every five points.

Formatting the Plot Area

Thankfully, Excel 2007 creates a simple white plot area as the default. In previous versions of Excel, the plot area always started as a gray background, which looked horrible when the chart was printed on a monochrome printer.

When the plot area was gray, I almost always customized the plot area, simply to do away with the gray. Now it is your call if you want to change the white to something a bit more fancy.

The built-in choices on the Layout menu are to either turn off the plot area, resulting in a white background, or to use a fill of the default color, as defined by the chart style chosen on the Design ribbon. In many cases, this default is white, so both choices lead to the same result.

To have better control over the plot area, you have to choose the More Plot Area Options from the built-in menu. Format Plot Area allows you to choose either No Fill, Solid Fill, Gradient Fill, or Picture or Texture Fill.

Some of the cool plot area options involve changing the transparency of the plot area. This actually works in conjunction with the formatting of the chart area. If you make the plot area 90% transparent, then you can see the formatting of the chart area. If you format the chart area to be transparent, then you actually see through to the spreadsheet.

Using a Gradient for the Plot Area

Setting up a simple two-color gradient has become far more difficult in Excel 2007 than it used to be. Microsoft offers many more choices for controlling the gradient, but this causes the process of setting up the gradient to be much more difficult.

The first set of choices involves choosing whether the gradient should be linear, radial, or rectangular, or whether it should follow a predefined path. Within the linear gradients, you can specify a direction, such as 90 degrees for top to bottom, or 180% for right to left. With the radial and rectangular gradients, you can specify whether the gradient radiates from the center or from a particular corner. The path type creates a shape similar to using Rectangular, from Center. Figure 2.29 shows a variety of gradient types.

Figure 2.29
The gradient types can be linear, radial, or rectangular.

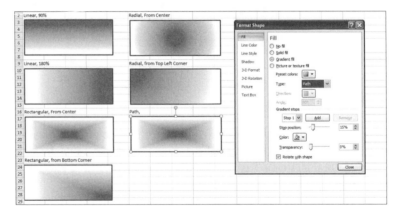

The next choices involve the number of colors. You can either choose a predefined color scheme from the Preset drop-down, or you can specify your own color scheme by defining a number of gradient stops. Each stop is assigned a color, a transparency, and a position ranging from 0% to 100%. You can edit only one gradient stop at a time.

CASE STUDY

Creating a Custom Gradient

Say that you want the plot area to contain a two-color gradient, flowing from green on the top to white on the bottom. This was simple in Excel 2003. It is difficult to set up in Excel 2007 for the first chart. However, if you have many charts to format in the same Excel session, the settings from the first gradient will remain in the Format Plot Area dialog box, making it easier to format subsequent charts. You might decide that the top 5% of the chart should be solid green, the bottom 5% of the chart should be solid white, and everything in between should be a gradient from green to white. The first gradient stop would indicate a color green and 5% as the position. The second gradient stop would indicate a color of white and 95% as the position. Everything from 5% to 95% would be a blend from green to white. To use a lighter color green, you can increase the transparency of the green stop.

If you have previously created a chart with a predefined gradient, you might find that the default gradient has 3 through 6 stops already defined. If this is the case, you select the later stops and click Remove to remove them.

To set up a two-color gradient, you follow these steps.

1. Select a chart. From the Layout tab, choose Plot Area, More Plot Area Options.
2. Change the Fill setting from Automatic to Gradient Fill.
3. Choose Linear gradient.
4. Change the angle to 90 degrees.
5. Open the Gradient Stops drop-down. If there are more than two stops, select the last stop and click Remove. Continue removing any stops higher than Stop 2.
6. Choose Stop 1 from the drop-down. Choose a green color. Set the stop position at 5%. Set the transparency to 25% to make a lighter green.
7. Choose Stop 2 from the drop-down. Choose white as the color. Set the stop position at 95%.

The result is a two-color gradient ranging from dark green at the top to white at the bottom. Figure 2.30 shows the gradient and the setting for Stop 2.

Figure 2.30
Creating a simple two-color gradient requires far more steps in Excel 2007 than in previous versions.

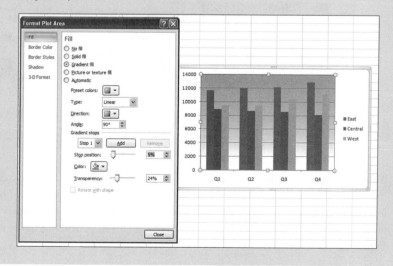

> **NOTE**
>
> After you have created a gradient, Excel remembers the settings and automatically applies them to future gradients that you set up.

Using a Picture or Texture for the Plot Area

You now have many more options available when you want to use a texture or a picture for the plot area. When you choose Picture or Texture Fill, a Texture drop-down appears, with the same two dozen textures that have been in Office for years. To use a picture instead, you click the File button and browse your drives to locate a picture to insert.

When you choose a picture, it is stretched or shrunk to completely fill the plot area. This might end up causing your logo to be a little squashed, as in the top-left chart in Figure 2.31. To make your picture keep its correct aspect ratio, you choose the Tile Picture as Texture check box in the Format Plot Area dialog.

When you choose to tile the picture, you have a number of choices available in the Tiling Options section. In the top-center chart in Figure 2.31, the Scale X and Scale Y options are set to 10% in order to create a repeating pattern of logos. The first logo is aligned with the top left of the plot area.

Figure 2.31
When you choose a picture, clip art, or texture, you can choose to show a single stretched image or to tile the image at various sizes.

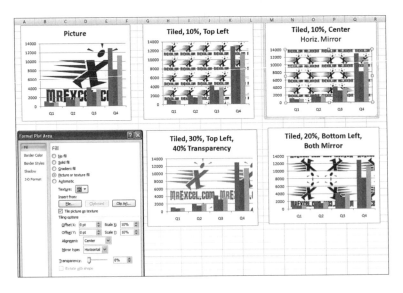

Although it is not appropriate with logos, you can choose for alternating tiles of the image to be mirror images of the first. You can have every other column show horizontal mirror images, as in the top-right chart, have every other row show vertical mirror images, or turn on both horizontal and vertical mirror images, as in the bottom-right chart shown in Figure 2.31.

To lighten the picture, you adjust the Transparency slider to the right. The bottom-center chart in Figure 2.31 has a 40% transparency.

Mixing the Plot Area Color with the Chart Area Color

The Transparency slider on the Format Plot Area dialog allows you to see through the plot area to view whatever formatting has been applied to the chart area.

You may notice that there is not an icon on the Layout ribbon for formatting the chart area. Select the chart area by clicking any white space just inside the border of the chart. Click Format Selection in the Layout ribbon, press Ctrl+1, or choose Format from the right-click menu to access the Format Chart Area dialog.

In the top three charts in Figure 2.32, the chart area includes the default opaque white formatting. If you specify that the black formatting of the plot area be 75% transparent, you have a plot area that is 25% black and 75% white. If you choose a black plot area that is 100% transparent, you see through the plot area, to the white chart area background.

Figure 2.32
Increasing the transparency of the plot area allows the formatting of the chart area to show through.

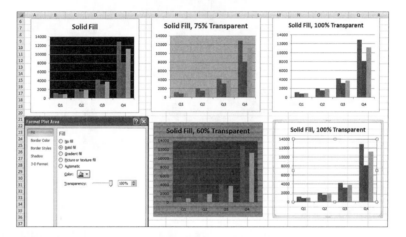

The transparency options become more interesting if you first format the chart area. In the bottom-center chart in Figure 2.32, the chart area has been formatted with a wood grain effect. You achieve this by making the plot area black, with a 60% transparency.

In the bottom-right chart in Figure 2.32, the chart area has been formatted with the None option or using a solid color with 100% transparency. When the plot area is formatted as 100% transparent, you can see through the plot area and the chart area to the underlying cells in the spreadsheet.

Formatting the Chart Walls and Floor of a 3-D Chart

With a 3-D chart, you can format the chart wall and chart floor instead of the plot area. Drop-downs on the Layout ribbon offer built-in choices to turn on the formatting of either the chart wall or the chart floor. Three different components can be formatted: the back wall, the side wall, and the chart floor.

If you use the Current Selection drop-down on the left side of the Layout ribbon, you can select the floor, back wall, side wall, or walls. Selecting Walls is the same as selecting both the back wall and the side wall.

After you have selected an element, you can use the Format Selection button under the drop-down to format the element. As with the plot area, you can specify a solid fill, a gradient, a texture, or a picture.

Figure 2.33 illustrates the various elements that can be individually formatted.

Figure 2.33
In a 3-D chart, you can format the walls individually or as a single unit.

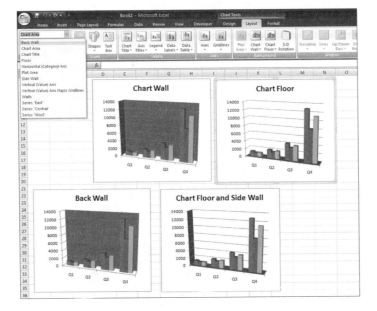

Controlling 3-D Rotation in a 3-D Chart

You have a number of options for rotating a 3-D chart. Of the available options, you are most likely to change the X rotation and leave the other angles alone:

- **X rotation**—You can choose a value from 0 to 359.9 degrees to rotate the floor of the chart counterclockwise. The chart at the top-right of Figure 2.34 has been rotated 30 degrees from the default rotation. This rotation forces the series names to move clockwise to the left. In some cases, you might be able to better see a short series by rotating the x-axis.

- **Y rotation**—You can choose a value from –90 degrees to 90 degrees to change the height of the viewer with respect to the chart. In the default 15% Y rotation, it appears that the reader is slightly above the chart. For a 0-degree rotation, the view appears as if you are at about eye level with the chart, as shown in the chart at the top left of Figure 2.35. At a 90-degree rotation, you appear to be looking straight down on the chart, making it impossible to judge the height of any columns, as shown in the chart at the bottom right of Figure 2.35. Negative rotations create a view where you are actually looking up at the chart from underneath a transparent floor, as shown in the bottom-left chart in Figure 2.35. For best results, you should stick with values from 0 to 20 degrees for the Y rotation.

Figure 2.34
Rotating the x-axis turns the floor of the chart clockwise.

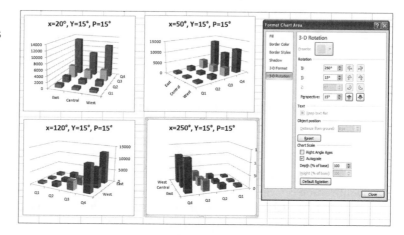

Figure 2.35
You can change your angle of view by using the Y rotation.

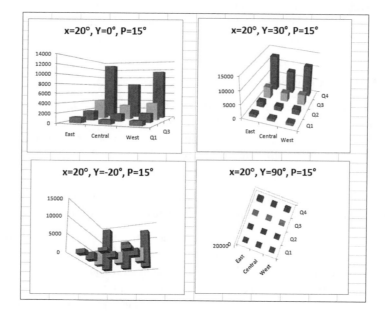

- **Perspective**—You can choose a value from 0 to 120 in order to further distort a chart. If you have ever used a wide-angle lens on a camera, you might have noticed that items in the foreground appear unusually large, while items in the background appear unusually small. Increasing the perspective is similar to using a wide-angle camera. The chart at the top right of Figure 2.36 has an increased perspective. Note how the Q4 bars seem to shrink in this view.

Figure 2.36
Settings for perspective, depth, and height let you twist and stretch a chart.

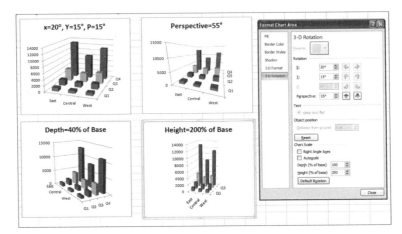

■ **Depth**—You can choose a value from 0% to 2000% of the base. Decreasing the ratio of depth to the base creates a chart where the columns become wide rectangles, as shown in the chart at the lower left of Figure 2.36.

■ **Height**—You can uncheck the Autoscale check box to enable the Height setting. You can choose a value from 0% to 500% of the base. The bottom-right chart in Figure 2.36 shows a chart with an increased height:width ratio.

Forecasting with Trendlines

A trendline attempts to fit existing data points to a formula and extend that formula into the future. When you add a trendline to a chart, Excel uses least-squares regression to find the best line to represent the data points. Excel can either draw the trendline for existing points to indicate whether the points are trending up or down, or it can extend the trendline into the future to project whether you will meet a goal.

In Figure 2.37, actual progress toward a goal is tracked in column B. Note that because the project is in process, several points in the dataset are not yet filled in.

Adding a trendline allows you to project where the project will finish if you continue working at the current pace. To add a trendline, you select Layout, Trendline, Linear Trendline. Excel asks to which series it should add a trendline. If you choose the actual series, Excel adds a new virtual series to the chart. This series is plotted out to the end of the data series. In Figure 2.38, you can see that the linear trendline is projecting that you will have only 50 units complete by the 20th day.

Although creating a trendline requires only a few clicks, there are several trendline options worth learning. These are described in the following sections.

Figure 2.37

This chart shows the actual points and a goal line that indicates how much progress should be made each day in order to reach the project completion.

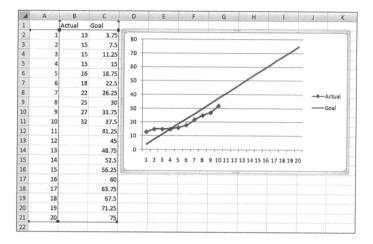

Figure 2.38

The trendline says that, based on your current run rate, you will severely miss the deadline.

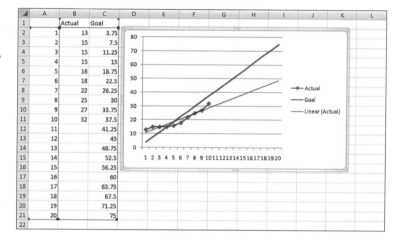

Formatting a Trendline

To format a trendline, you right-click the trendline and choose Format Trendline. Options in the Format Trendline dialog allow you to change the line color and the line style. I usually change the dash type on the Line Style category to show a dashed line. This indicates that it is not actual data but is a computer projection. I also change the color, often to red. When a project is falling behind schedule, the red dashed trendline becomes a call to action. The trendline says, "You need to pick up the pace of production—not just for one day, but for several sustained days."

Say that you suddenly do 10 units of production on the 11th day. Even though this brings the project back on track with 42 units complete and 41.25 needed to stay headed toward the goal, the trendline looks at your average daily production, sees that you spend 10 days only averaging 3 a day, and is not convinced that just because you had 1 good day, you will make the final goal. In this case, the trendline adjusts the projection from 50 to about 57.

This makes the trendline seem like a bit of a cynic, when in reality, it is just using simple math to analyze your behavior thus far in the project.

Adding the Trendline Equation to a Chart

To help understand how a trendline is calculated, you can display the equation on the chart.

> **CAUTION**
>
> While you can usually click the More item from most Layout drop-down menus in order to format an item, this does not work with a trendline. If you click the More button, Excel adds a second trendline to your chart. Instead, you should select Series "Actual" Trendline from the Current Selection drop-down on the left side of the Layout ribbon and then choose Format Selection to access the dialog box.

In the Trendline Options category of the Format Trendline dialog, you choose Display Equation on the Chart. For a linear trendline, Excel displays a trendline in the form of y = mx + b.

You can optionally choose to force the y-intercept to be zero or display the R-squared value on the chart. R-squared is a measure of how closely the trendline fits the existing points. While R-squared can range from 0 to 1, values closer to 1 indicate that the trendline is doing a good job of representing the data points.

In Figure 2.39, the equation predicts that you magically started with 6.8 units done on Day 0 and then have averaged 2.5 units a day since then. This is pretty good because in this case, several units were finished in the previous month but did not make up a full case pack, so their totals were added to Day 1 of the current month. The R-squared of 0.85 says that the trendline is a pretty good fit. The bottom line is that you need to focus on production for the next nine days if you want to make the goal.

Figure 2.39
You can add an equation to a chart to see how Excel is fitting the chart to the line.

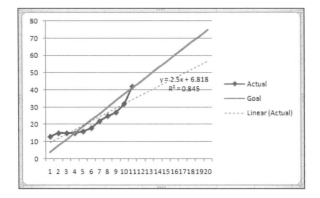

Choosing a Forecast Method

In business, you most often use a linear trendline, which assumes a constant rate of progress throughout the life of the chart. Several other forecast methods are available for trendlines:

- **Exponential**—An exponential trendline, most often found in science, describes a population that is rapidly increasing over successive generations, such as the number of fungi in a Petri dish over time.

- **Logarithm**—A logarithmic trendline results when there is an initial period of rapid growth that levels off over time.

- **Polynomial**—This trendline can describe a line that undulates due to two to six external factors. When you specify a polynomial trendline, you have to specify which order of polynomial. For example, in a third-order polynomial, the line is fit to the equation $y = b + c_1x + c_2x^2 + c_3x^3$.

- **Power**—A power trendline fits the points to a line, where $y = cx^b$. This describes a line that increases at a specific exponential rate over time.

- **Moving average**—A moving average trendline is used to smooth out data that fluctuates over time. A typical trendline would use a three-month moving average.

Adding Drop Lines to a Line or Area Chart

Area and line charts are great at showing trends, but it is often difficult for the reader to figure out the exact values for data points. Because the line is floating in space, you are counting on the viewer's eye being able to travel from the horizontal axis straight up to the data series line.

A *drop line* is a vertical line that extends vertically from a line or area chart and extends down to the horizontal axis. As shown in the lower chart in Figure 2.40, the drop lines help you see that the March point is exactly at 300. This would be difficult to discern in the chart shown at the top of the figure.

To add a drop line, you select the chart and then choose Layout, Lines, Drop Lines.

Figure 2.40

Drop lines help you visualize the exact value of each point along the horizontal axis.

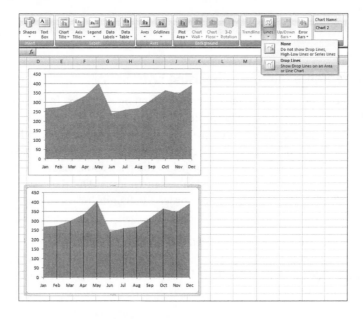

Adding Up/Down Bars to a Line Chart

If you have a line chart with two different data series, you might want to compare those series at each point along the horizontal axis. There are two different options for this, available in two locations along the Layout tab of the ribbon.

In the lower chart in Figure 2.41, high-low lines extend from one line to the other line. These are created using Layout, Lines, High-Low Lines.

In the chart at the right in Figure 2.41, up/down bars extend from one line to the other line. These bars appear in contrasting colors, depending on which line is higher at that particular point. To add up/down bars, you choose Layout, Up/Down Bars, Up/Down Bars.

Figure 2.41
High-low lines and up/down bars help show the relationship between two series at specific points along the x-axis.

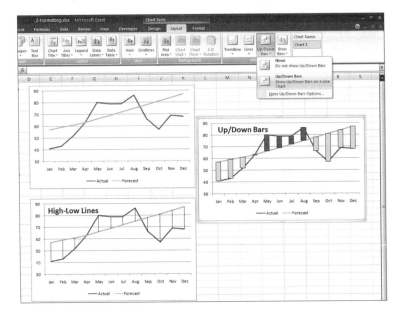

Showing Acceptable Tolerances by Using Error Bars

I used to run monthly sales and operations planning meetings. In these meetings, the leaders of the sales, marketing, engineering, and manufacturing departments would meet in order to decide on the production plan for each sales model. During the next month's meeting, a chart would compare the previous month's forecast to actual demand. If the demand was more than 20% above or below the plan, someone had to present the root causes for that variance. The discussion was often lively: Did the east region really have no clue that Customer XYZ was about to order 1,000 units, or was it sand-bagging so that it could have a lower quota?

To figure out which products required this scrutiny, both the forecast and actual performance were plotted for each product line. Error bars showing the acceptable 20% tolerance were added to the forecast line. If the actual line was within the 20% tolerance, no discussion was needed.

Excel 2007 makes it easy to add error bars: You select one series in the chart and choose Layout, Error Bars, More Error Bar Options. In the Format Error Bars dialog, you can choose whether the error bars should extend up, down, or both from the line. You can add a cap or have no cap. In the lower section, you can specify one of five methods for calculating the size of the error bar. You can specify that the error bars should extend a fixed number of units, base this on standard deviation, and so on. In the sales and operations planning meetings, it was appropriate to add an error bar that was 20% of each data point. Thus, if someone had forecast 200 units of a product, anything from 160 to 240 was an acceptable demand, and for the products with a forecast of 8,000, the acceptable tolerance was 7,400 to 9,600.

Figure 2.42 shows a chart with 20% error bars.

Figure 2.42
The error bars show an acceptable tolerance, or a margin of error around each point.

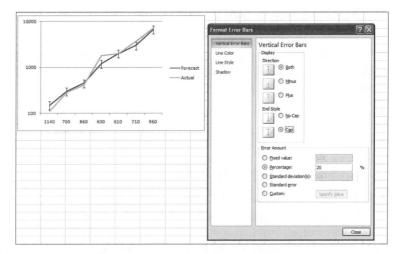

Formatting a Series

It is somewhat strange that there is not a button on the Layout ribbon for the most popular charting element—the Series element.

In order to format the series, you use the Current Selection drop-down on the left side of either the Layout or Format ribbon. Choose the appropriate series from the list to select the series. Click the Format Selection button to access the Format Data Series dialog.

> **NOTE**
> There are alternate ways to format the data series. If you can click on an element in the chart to select it, you can type Ctrl+1 or right-click and choose Format. Using the Current Selection drop-down is usually more reliable. If several data series are plotted as lines that are very close together, it is often difficult to select the correct line.

The Series Options category allows you to plot a series on a secondary axis. This is useful if your one data series contains data that is of a different order of magnitude than the other series. For example, you might chart revenue and gross profit percent. By moving the gross profit percent to the Secondary Axis, you can see detail of revenue in millions and gross profit percentages in the 50% range.

Using the remaining categories, you can edit the Marker style for a series, including the marker color, the line color, the line style, shadow, and 3D formatting.

Formatting a Single Data Point

The first click on a data series selects the entire series. If you pause for a moment and then perform a second click on a data point, the Current Selection drop-down indicates that you have selected an individual data point. The drop-down might say Series "Profit" Point "2006".

It is interesting that the only way to perform this selection is by performing two single clicks on the chart. The Current Selection drop-down does not offer a list of all the data points.

After selecting a data point, use the Format Selection button located on the left side of the Layout or Format ribbon. You can then change the color or marker style of a single point.

Using the Format Ribbon

When you first install Excel 2007, all the new chart options allow you to create fresh and new-looking charts. If you stay on the Design ribbon, you can easily create 21,600 different charts. If you expand to the Layout ribbon, you can create 601 billion different charts. If you include the 20 themes on the Page Layout ribbon, you can create 12 trillion different chart types. If this is not enough variability for you, if you ever get tired of these built-in options, you can head to the Format ribbon and have micro-control over the formatting for any element of the chart.

There actually are a few really cool settings on the Format ribbon. If you venture there, you can create amazing translucent charts to wow your co-workers who have become bored with the standard Excel 2007 charts.

Converting Text to WordArt

You use the WordArt Styles group on the Format ribbon to apply WordArt styles to any text on a chart. You are not allowed to use the type-twisting options in the Transform menu, but you can add shadow, glow, or reflection to the 20 styles in the WordArt menu.

Using the Shape Styles Gallery

The Shape Styles gallery contains 36 built-in styles that can be applied to any shape. There are really six styles for each of the six accent colors in the current theme. The six styles progress from simple on the first row of the gallery to extreme on the last row of the gallery.

To quickly format a particular element, you click that element and choose a new style from the gallery.

When using the Shape Styles gallery, keep these tips in mind:

- The colors and effects available in the gallery change if you select a new theme from the Page Layout ribbon.
- The first time you click a column, you select the entire series. A second click selects only one column or data point.
- If you find it difficult to select a particular item on a chart, you can select the item from the Current Selection drop-down at the left edge of the Format ribbon.
- Live Preview works in this gallery. Although you see the effect after hovering over a tile in the gallery, you actually have to click the tile to apply the style.

Figure 2.43 shows the Shape Styles gallery and six charts that represent the six styles available when the Office theme is active.

Figure 2.43
The Shape Styles gallery offers six effects for each of six accent colors.

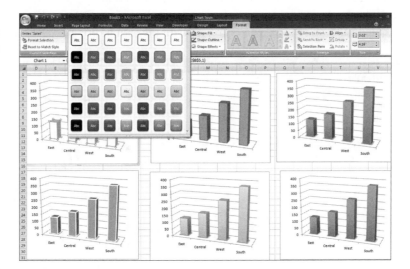

Using the Shape Fill and Shape Effects

Some of the best effects don't seem to be available in the built-in charts. You can access a myriad of other effects by using the Shape Fill, Shape Outline, and Shape Effects drop-downs on the Format ribbon. Figure 2.44 shows a chart in which each bar has a different effect from these drop-downs applied.

Figure 2.44
These effects are available on the Format ribbon.

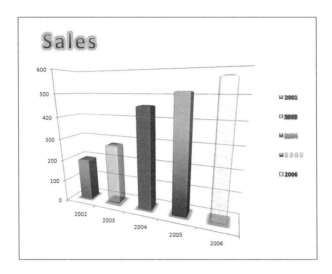

Using Preset Shape Effects

The Preset menu on the Shape Effects drop-down offers 12 built-in combinations of shadow, reflection, glow, soft edges, bevel, and rotation. Figure 2.45 shows the 12 preset thumbnails, plus several charts created with the various presets.

Figure 2.45
The 12 charts on the sheet match the sequence of built-in presets on the menu.

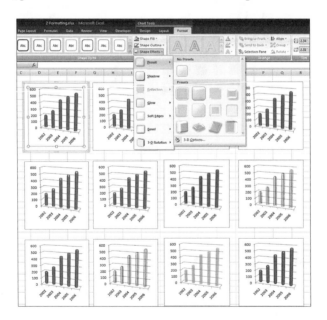

For more control of the effects, you can choose the 3-D Options selection at the bottom of the menu. In the 3-D Format category, the Material drop-down offers 11 textures. The final three textures are translucent textures that give a glass appearance when applied to a bar.

In Figure 2.46, the five bars are formatted as wire frame, powder, translucent powder, clear, and plastic.

Figure 2.46
These bars were formatted by changing the surface material in the Format Data Point dialog.

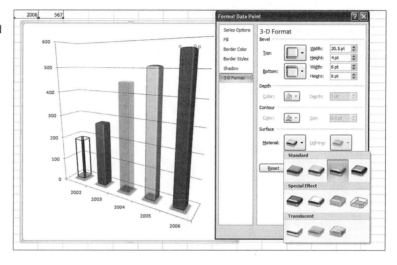

Replacing Data Markers with Clip Art or Shapes

Rather than using columns or cylinders for your data markers, you can use a different shape, such as a Shape or clip art. To achieve this effect, you can change the fill of a data series and then turn off the border around the data point.

Using Clip Art as a Data Marker

Office Online offers thousands of free clip art images. If you have an Internet connection, you can easily insert any of these images in a chart to replace the data markers. Follow these steps to create a pictograph:

1. In a 2-D column chart, select a data series. Right-click the data series and choose Format Data Series.

2. In the Format Data Series dialog that appears, choose the Fill category in the left panel. In the right panel, choose Picture or Texture Fill.

3. Click the Clip Art button. Excel displays a shortened version of the clip art pane, called Select Picture.

4. Select the Include Content from Office Online check box.

5. In the Search Text box, type a keyword to describe the clip art and then click Go.

6. Browse through the returned images. You are looking for something that is cartoonish and, preferably, narrow. Rather than clip art with a detailed background, look for clip art where only the character appears. When you find an acceptable image, click OK.

7. Click the Border Color category and choose No Line.

8. Click Close to close the Format Data Series dialog.

The result is a chart similar to the bottom chart in Figure 2.47. The clip art is stretched to indicate the height of the bar.

Figure 2.47
You can replace the data markers with shapes or clip art for visual interest.

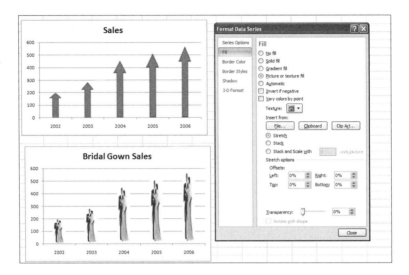

For best results, don't combine a picture with translucent surfaces.

Fans of Edward Tufte may point out that he rails against pictographs in his books. However, what Tufte complained about was both the width and height of the clip art changing in response to increased numbers. Microsoft does not increase the width of the bars, only the height, ensuring that the area of the image stays roughly proportional to the data that it is representing.

Using a Shape in Place of a Data Marker

Replacing a data marker with one of the 175 shapes in the Shape dialog box is slightly more difficult than replacing a data marker with clip art. The fill settings on the Format Data Series dialog do not allow you to specify a shape. However, they allow you to import a shape from the Clipboard.

The AutoShapes from Excel 97 through Excel 2003 have been renamed *shapes* in Excel 2007.

You follow these steps to create the top chart in Figure 2.47:

1. Create a 2-D column chart.
2. Select a cell in the worksheet. From the Insert menu, choose an upward arrow from the Shapes drop-down.

3. Click and drag to draw an arrow on the worksheet.

4. Right-click the shape and choose Copy

5. Click the data series in the chart. Right-click and choose Format Data Series.

6. In the Format Data Series dialog that appears, choose the Fill category in the left panel. In the right panel, choose Picture or Texture Fill.

7. In the Insert From section, click the Clipboard button. Excel replaces the columns with the arrows.

8. Click Close to close the Format Data Series dialog.

This technique works best with 2-D charts. If you attempt to apply a shape to a 3-D column, the shape is pasted to each vertical face of the column.

CASE STUDY

Creating a Chart Template

Say that you need to create a series of charts. You like the look of the translucent glass effect available in Excel 2007. There is not a built-in style for this effect, but you would like to be able to create charts quickly using the glass effect.

The solution is to build one chart and then save that chart as a template. If you then indicate that the template is the default chart type, you can quickly create new charts simply by using the Alt+F1 keyboard shortcut.

You follow these steps to create the template:

1. Create a chart. Use a 3-D column chart as the chart type.

2. Using the tools on the Layout ribbon, remove the legend.

3. Click one of the columns in the chart to select the data series.

4. On the Format ribbon, choose Shape Effects, Bevel, Soft Round.

5. Choose Shape Effects, Bevel, 3-D Options. In the Format dialog, in the 3-D Options category, open the Material drop-down and choose Clear.

6. On the Design ribbon, choose Save As Template. Give the template a name, such as 3DGlass.

7. On the Design ribbon, choose Change Chart Type. Click the Templates category. Click 3DGlass icon in the My Templates window. Choose Set as Default Chart.

After completing these steps, you can create a 3-D glass chart by simply selecting the data to be charted and pressing Alt+F1. Excel creates a chart modeled on your glass chart.

Next Steps

In Chapter 3, "Creating Charts That Show Trends," you will see examples of charts that show trends, such as column and line charts. You will also learn how to use a trendline to project a trend into the future.

Creating Charts That Show Trends

3

Choosing a Chart Type

You have two excellent choices when creating charts that show the progress of some value over time. Because Western cultures are used to seeing time progress from left to right, you are likely to choose a chart where the axis moves from left to right—whether it's a column chart, line chart, or area chart.

If you have only a few data points, you can use a column chart. Column charts work easily for 4 quarters or 12 months. Within the column chart category, you can choose between 2-D and 3-D styles. If you want to highlight one component of a sales trend, you can use a stacked column chart.

> **NOTE**
>
> This book recommends not using pyramid charts or cone charts because they distort your message. For an example, see "Lying with Shrinking Charts" in Chapter 14.

When you get beyond 12 data points, you should strongly consider switching to a line chart. A line chart can easily show trends for hundreds of periods. Line charts can be designed to show only the data points as markers or to connect the data points with a straight or smoothed line.

Figure 3.1 shows a chart of 9 data points. This is few enough data points that a column chart is meaningful. Figure 3.2 shows a chart of 100+ data points. With this detail, you should switch to a line chart in order to show the trend.

Figure 3.1
With 12 or fewer data points, column charts are viable and informative.

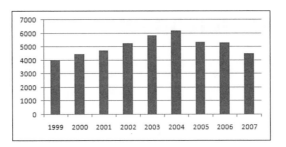

Figure 3.2
When you go beyond 12 data points, it is best to switch to a line chart without individual data points. The bottom chart in this figure shows the same data set as a line chart.

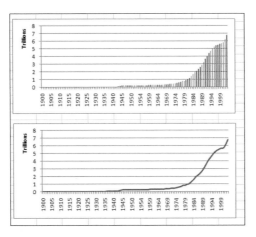

An area chart is a line chart where the area under the line is filled with a shading or color. This can be appropriate if you want to highlight a particular portion of the time series. If you have fewer data points, adding drop lines can help the reader determine the actual value for each time period.

If you are plotting stock market data, you can use stock charts to show the trend of stock data over time. You can also use high-low-close charts to show the trend of data that might occur in a range (for example, if you have to track a range of quality rankings for each day).

You might think that a bar chart could be used to show time trends. However, that would confuse your readers because they expect time to be represented from left to right. In very rare cases, you might use a bar chart to show a time trend—for example, if you had 40 or 50 points, all with very long category labels, and you needed a printed chart to legibly show detail for each point. As an example, Figure 3.3 shows sales for 45 daily dates. The chart would not work as a PowerPoint slide, but if it were printed as a full page on a letter-size piece of paper, the reader could analyze sales by weekday. Note that in the chart in Figure 3.3, weekend days are plotted in a different color than weekdays.

Pie charts are great for comparisons. If you are thinking about using a series of pie charts to show changes over time, however, you should instead use a 100% stacked column chart. Consider the charts in Figure 3.4. It is difficult for the reader's eye to compare the pie wedges from year to year. Did market share increase in 2005?

Figure 3.3
Although time series typically should run across the horizontal axis, this chart allows 45 points to be compared easily.

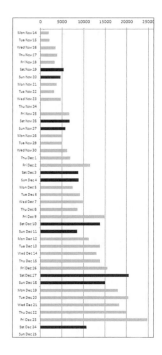

Figure 3.4
It is difficult to compare one pie to the next.

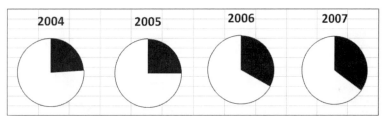

In Figure 3.5, the same data is plotted as a 100% stacked bar chart. Series lines guide the reader's eye from the market share from each year to the next year. The stacked bar chart is a much easier chart to read than the series of pie charts.

Figure 3.5
In a 100% stacked bar chart, the same data from Figure 3.4 is easier to read.

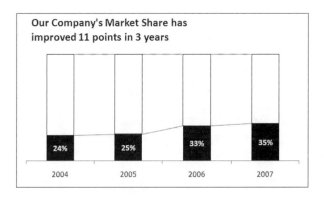

3

Understanding a Date-Based Axis Versus a Category-Based Axis

Excel offers two types of horizontal axes in a trend chart. Having the proper setting can ensure that your message is accurate.

If the spacing of events along the time axis is uniform, it does not matter whether you choose a date-based axis or a text-based axis. The results will be the same. In this case, it is fine to allow Excel to automatically choose the type of axis.

However, if the spacing of events along the time axis is haphazard, you definitely want to make sure that Excel is using a date-based axis.

CASE STUDY

Accurately Representing Data Using a Time-Based Axis

Figure 3.6 shows the spot price for a certain component used in your manufacturing plant. To find this data, you downloaded past purchase orders for that product. Your company doesn't purchase the component on the same day every month; therefore, you have an incomplete dataset. In the middle of the dataset, a strike closed one of the vendors, spiking the prices from the other vendors. Your purchasing department had stocked up before the strike and was able to dramatically slow its purchasing during the strike.

Figure 3.6
The top chart uses a text-based horizontal axis: Every event is plotted an equal distance from the next event. This leads to the shaded period being underreported.

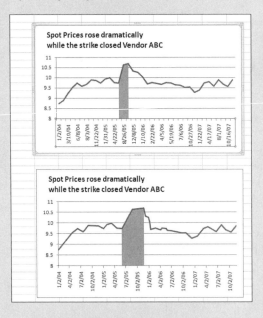

In the top chart in Figure 3.6, the horizontal axis is set to a text-based axis, and every data point is plotted an equal distance apart. Because your purchasing department made only two purchases during the strike, it appears as if the time affected by the strike is very narrow. The bottom chart uses a date-based axis. In this axis, you can see that the strike actually lasted for half of 2005.

NOTE To learn how to highlight a portion of a chart as shown in Figure 3.6, see "Highlighting a Section of Chart by Adding a Second Series," later in this chapter.

Usually, if your data contains dates, Excel defaults to a date-based axis. However, you should explicitly check to make sure that Excel is using the correct type of axis. A number of potential problems force Excel to choose a text-based axis instead of a date-based axis, such as dates that are stored as text in a spreadsheet and dates represented by numeric years. (See the list following Figure 3.7 for other potential problems.)

To explicitly choose an axis type, you follow these steps:

1. Right-click the horizontal axis and choose Format Axis.

2. In the Format Axis dialog box that appears, choose the Axis Options category.

3. Choose either Text Axis or Date Axis, as appropriate, from the Axis Type section (see Figure 3.7).

Figure 3.7
You can explicitly choose an axis type rather than letting Excel choose the default.

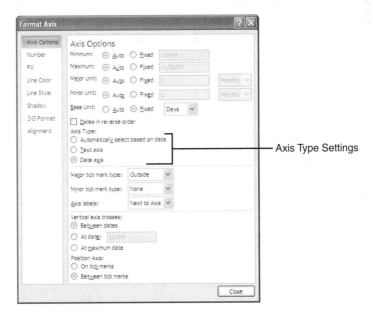

Axis Type Settings

A number of complications that require special handling can occur with your date fields. The following are some of the problems you might encounter:

- **Dates stored as text**—If your dates are stored as text dates instead of real dates, a date-based axis will never work. You have to use date functions to convert the text dates to real dates.

- **Dates represented by numeric years**—All your trend charts may have category values of 2005, 2006, 2007, and so on. Excel doesn't naturally recognize these as dates, but you can trick it into doing so.

- **Dates before 1900**—If your company has been around long enough that you are charting historical trends before January 1, 1900, you are sunk. In Excel's world, there are no dates before this time period.

- **Dates that are really time**—It is not difficult to imagine charts in which the horizontal axis contains periodic times throughout a day. You might want to use such a chart to show the number of people entering a bank. For such a chart, you need a time-based axis, but Excel will group all of the times from a single day into a single point. See "Using a Workaround to Display a Time-Scale Axis" for the rather complex steps needed to plot data by periods smaller than a day.

- **Dates that you need to appear as text in order to draw in a decorative element**—The case study, "Using a Decorative Element in a Chart," later in this chapter, shows a chart by designer Kyle Fletcher in which the dates are forced to be text.

Each of these situations is discussed in the following sections.

Converting Text Dates to Dates

If your cells contain text that looks like dates, the date-based axis will not work. In Figure 3.8, the data came from a legacy computer system. Each date was imported as text instead of as dates.

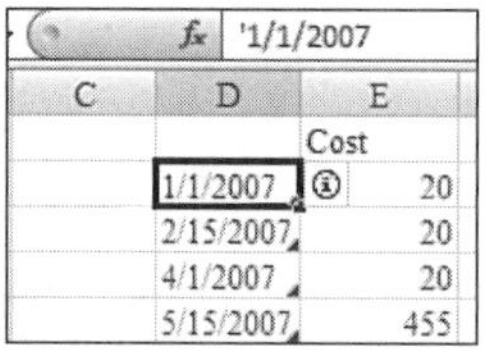

Figure 3.8
These dates are really text, as indicated by the apostrophe before the date in the formula bar.

This is a frustrating problem because text dates look exactly like real dates. You may not notice that they are text dates until you see that changing the axis to a date-based axis has no effect on the axis spacing.

If you select a cell that looks like a date cell, look in the formula bar, and see an apostrophe before the date, you know you have text dates (refer to Figure 3.8). This is Excel's arcane code to indicate that a date or number should be stored as text instead of a number.

> **CAUTION**
>
> Selecting a new format from the Format Cells dialog does not fix this problem, but it may prevent you from fixing the problem! If you import your data from a .txt file and choose to format that column as text, Excel changes the numeric format for the range to be text. After a range is formatted as text, you can never enter a formula, a number, or a date in the range. People try to select the range, change the format from text to numeric or date, and hope that this will fix the problem, but it

doesn't. After you change the format, you still have to use a method described in the section "Converting Text Dates to Real Dates," later in this chapter, to convert the text dates to numeric dates.

However, it is still worth changing the format from a text format to anything else. If you do not change the format, and you then insert a new column to the right of the bad dates, the new column inherits the text setting from the date column. This causes your new formula (the formula to convert text to dates) to fail. So, even though it doesn't solve your current problem, you should select the range, click the Dialog Launcher icon in the lower-right corner of the Number group on the Home ribbon, and change the format from Text to General. Figure 3.9 shows the More icon.

Dialog Launcher Icon

Figure 3.9
Many groups on the ribbon have this tiny More icon in the lower-right corner. Clicking this icon leads to the legacy dialog box.

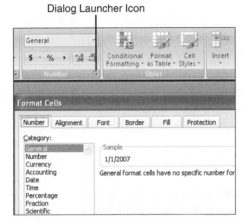

Understanding How Excel Stores Dates and Time

On a Windows PC, Excel stores dates as the number of days since January 1, 1900. For a date such as 9/15/2007, Excel actually stores the value 39,340, but it formats the date to show you a value such as 09/15/2007.

On a Mac running Mac OS, Excel stores the dates as the number of days since January 1, 1904. The original designers of the Mac OS were trying to squeeze the OS into 64K of ROM. Since every byte mattered, it seemed unnecessary to add a couple lines of code to handle the fact that 1900 is not a leap year. Excel for the Mac adopted the 1904 convention. Excel for Windows, which needed to be compatible with Lotus 1-2-3, adopted the 1900 convention. As you will read in the next case study, the 1900 convention incorrectly made 1900 a leap year.

CASE STUDY

Comparing Date Systems

To see firsthand how important this information really is, try the following:

1. Enter the number 1 in cell A1.

2. Select cell A1. Press Ctrl+1 to access the Format Cells dialog. Change the numeric formatting to display the number as a date, using the *Wednesday, March 14, 2001 type. On a PC, you see that the number 1 is January 1, 1900.

3. Type 2 in cell A1. The date changes to January 2, 1900.

> **NOTE**
> If you type 60 in cell A1, you see Wednesday, February 29, 1900—a date that did not exist! When Mitch Kapor was having Lotus 1-2-3 programmed in 1982, the programmers missed the fact that there was not to be a leap year in 1900. Lotus was released with the mistake, and every competing spreadsheet had to reproduce exactly the same mistake to make sure that the billions of spreadsheets using dates produced the same results. While the 1900 date system works fine and reports the right day of the week for the 39,000 days since March 1, 1900, it reports the wrong day of the week for the 59 days from January 1, 1900, through February 28, 1900.

Now try this:

1. Select cell B5. Press Ctrl+; to enter today's date in the cell.

2. Again select cell B5. Press Ctrl+1 to display the Format Cells dialog. Change the number format from a date to a number.

Your date changes to a number in the 39,000 range (assuming that you are reading this in the 2007–2009 time frame).

This might sound like a lot of hassle, but it is all worth it. If you store your dates as real dates (that is, numbers formatted to display as a date), Excel can easily do all kinds of date math. You can figure out, for example, how many days exist between a due date and today by simply subtracting one date from another. Or you can use the WORKDAY function to figure out how many workdays have elapsed between a hire date and today.

Excel provides a complete complement of functions to deal with dates, including functions that convert data from text to dates and back.

Excel stores times as decimal fractions of days. For example, you can enter noon today as =TODAY()+0.5. You can enter 9 a.m. as =TODAY()+0.375. Again, the number format handles converting the decimals to the appropriate display.

Converting Text Dates to Real Dates

The DATEVALUE function converts text that looks like a date into the equivalent serial number. You can then use the Format Cells dialog to display the number as a date.

The text version of a date can take a number of different formats. Say that your international date settings call for a month/day/year arrangement of the dates; Figure 3.10 shows a number of valid text formats that can be converted with the DATEVALUE function.

Figure 3.10

The *DATEVALUE* function can handle any of the date formats in column J.

	J	K	L	M
	Text Date	Date Value	Date Value formatted as a Date	
	1/2/2006	38719	Monday, January 02, 2006	
	2-Jan-2006	38719	Monday, January 02, 2006	
	01/15/06	38732	Sunday, January 15, 2006	
	01-15-2008	39462	Tuesday, January 15, 2008	
	2/Jan/2006	38719	Monday, January 02, 2006	

fx =DATEVALUE(J46)

After using the DATEVALUE function, you need to format the result as a date in order to display the numbers as dates.

Figure 3.11 shows a column of text dates. You follow these steps to convert them to real dates:

Figure 3.11

You need to convert these text dates to real dates before creating a chart.

	A	B	C	D
1		Cost		
2	1/1/2007	20		
3	2/15/2007	20		
4	4/1/2007	20		
5	5/15/2007	455		
6	6/1/2007	45		
7	6/8/2007	45		
8	6/15/2007	145		
9	6/22/2007	45		
10	6/29/2007	45		
11	7/4/2007	45		
12	7/06/2007	45		

1. Insert a blank column B by selecting cell B1 and then choosing Insert, Insert Sheet Columns on the Home ribbon. (Alternatively, use the Excel 2003 shortcut Alt+I+C.)

2. In cell B2, enter the formula =DATEVALUE(A2). Excel displays a number in the 39,000 range in cell B2. You are halfway to the result (see Figure 3.12).

Figure 3.12

The result of the *DATE-VALUE* function is a serial number. You still have to format the result as a date.

B2   *fx* =DATEVALUE(A2)

	A	B	C	D
1			Cost	
2	1/1/2007	39083	20	
3	2/15/2007		20	
4	4/1/2007		20	
5	5/15/2007		455	
6	6/1/2007		45	
7	6/8/2007		45	
8	6/15/2007		145	

3. Select cell B2. On the Home ribbon, select the drop-down at the top of the Number group and choose either Short Date or Long Date. Excel displays the number in cell B2 as a date (see Figure 3.13). (Alternatively, press Ctrl+1 and select any date format from the Number tab.)

Figure 3.13
You can choose a date format from the Number drop-down on the Home ribbon.

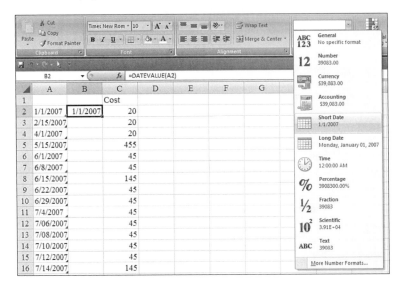

4. Double-click the fill handle in the lower-right corner of cell B2. (The fill handle is the square dot in the lower-right corner of the active cell indicator.) Excel copies the formula from cell B2 down to your range of dates.

5. If some of the dates appear as ########, you need to make the column wider. To do so, double-click the border between the column B and column C headings.

6. To convert the live formulas in column B to be static values, while the range of dates in column B is selected, press Ctrl+C to copy and then on the Home ribbon, select Paste, Paste Values to convert the formulas to values. (Alternatively, you could use this shortcut: Right-click the right border of the selected range and hold the mouse button down as you drag right one column and then back to the original location. When you release the mouse button, choose Copy Here as Values Only from the contextual menu.)

7. Delete the original column A.

After you have converted the text dates to real dates, you can insert a line chart with markers. Excel automatically formats the chart with a date-based axis. In Figure 3.14, the top chart reflects cells that contain text dates. The bottom chart uses cells in which the text dates have been converted to numeric dates.

Figure 3.14
When your original data contains real dates, Excel automatically chooses a more accurate date-based axis. The bottom chart reflects a date-based axis.

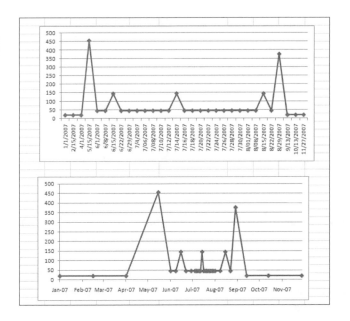

> **TIP**
>
> There are other methods for converting the data shown in Figure 3.11 to dates. Here are some examples:
>
> - Select any empty cell. Press Ctrl+C to copy. Select your dates. On the Home ribbon, select Paste, Paste Special. In the Paste Special dialog, choose Values in the Paste section and Add in the Operation section. Click OK.
> - Select the text dates and then, on the Data ribbon, select Text to Columns, Finish.

Converting Bizarre Text Dates to Real Dates

When you rely on others for your source data, you are likely to encounter dates in all sorts of bizarre formats. While gathering data for this book, for example, I found a dataset where each date was listed as a range of dates. Each date was in the format 2/4-6/06, indicating that the data was collected from February 4 through the 6, 2006.

A number of functions, used in combination, can be useful when you're converting strange text dates to real dates:

- `=DATE(2006,12,31)`—This returns the serial number for December 31, 2006.
- `=LEFT(A1,2)`—This returns the two leftmost characters from cell A1.
- `=RIGHT(A1,2)`—This returns the two rightmost characters from cell A1.
- `=MID(A1,3,2)`—This returns the third and fourth characters from cell A2. (You read the function as "return the middle characters from A1, starting at character position 3, for a length of 2.")
- `=FIND("/",A1)`—This finds the position number of the first slash within A1.

You follow these steps to convert the text date ranges shown in Figure 3.15 to real dates:

Figure 3.15

A mix of *LEFT*, *RIGHT*, *MID*, and *FIND* functions parse this text to be used in the *DATE* function.

	A	B	C	D	E	F
1	Date		Year	Month	Day	Date	
2	2/1-4/01		2001	2	1	2/1/2001	
3	2/9-11/01		2001	2	9	2/9/2001	
4	2/10-12/01		2001	2	10	2/10/2001	
5	12/19-21/02		2002	12	19	12/19/2002	
6	B2: =RIGHT(A2,2)+2000						
7	C2: =LEFT(A2,FIND("/",A2)-1)						
8	D2: =MID(A2,FIND("/",A2)+1,FIND("-",A2)-FIND("/",A2)-1)						
9	E2: =DATE(B2,C2,D2)						
10							

1. Because the year is always the two rightmost characters in column A, in cell B2, enter the formula =RIGHT(A2,2).

2. Because the month is the leftmost one or two characters in column A, ask Excel to find the first slash and then return the characters to the left of the slash. Enter =FIND("/",A2) to indicate that the slash is in second character position. Use =LEFT(A2,FIND("/",A2)) to get the proper month number.

3. For the day, you can either choose to extract the first or last date of the range. To extract the first date, ask for the middle characters, starting one position after the slash. The logic to figure out if you then need one or two characters is a bit more complicated. You need to find the position of the dash, subtract the position of the slash, and then subtract 1. Therefore, use this formula in cell D2:
   =MID(A2,FIND("/",A2)+1,FIND("-",A2)-FIND("/",A2)-1)

4. Use the DATE function, as follows, in cell E2 to produce an actual date:
   =DATE(B2,C2,D2)

> **NOTE**
> Alternatively, you could use =DATEVALUE(LEFT(A2,FIND("-",A2)-1)&RIGHT(A2,3)).

Dates Not Recognized as Dates: Numeric Years

If you are plotting data where the only identifier is a numeric year, Excel does not automatically recognize this field as a date field.

In Figure 3.16, for example, data is plotted once a decade for the past 50 years and then yearly for the past decade. Column A contains four-digit years, such as 1955, 1965, and so on. The default chart shown in the top of the figure does not create a date-based axis. You know this to be true because the distance from 1955 to 1965 is the same as the distance from 1995 to 1996.

Figure 3.16
Excel does not recognize years as dates.

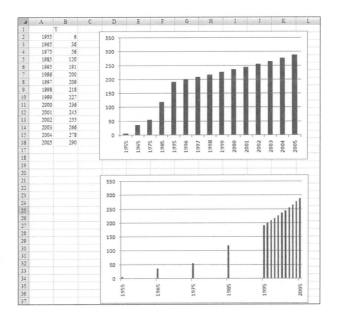

There are two solutions to this problem:

- Convert the years in column A to dates by using =YEAR(A2,12,31). Format the resulting value with a yyyy custom number format. Excel then displays 2005 but actually stores the serial number for December 31, 2005.

- Convert the horizontal axis to a date-based axis. Excel then thinks that your chart is plotting daily dates from May 8, 1905, through June 27, 1905. Because no date format has been applied to the cells, they show up as the serial numbers 1955 through 2005. Excel displays the chart properly, even though the settings show that the base units are days.

Dates Not Recognized as Dates: Dates Before 1900

In Excel 2007, dates from January 1, 1900, through December 31, 9999, are recognized as valid dates. If you happen to be a company that was founded more than a demisesquicentennial before Microsoft was founded, however, you will potentially have company history going back before 1900.

Figure 3.17 shows a dataset stretching from 1787 through 1959. The accompanying chart would lead the reader to believe that the number of states in the United States grew at a constant rate, a statement that would cause Mr. Kessel, my eighth-grade geography teacher, to give me an F for this book.

Figure 3.17

Dates from before 1900 are not valid Excel dates. A date-based axis is not possible in this case.

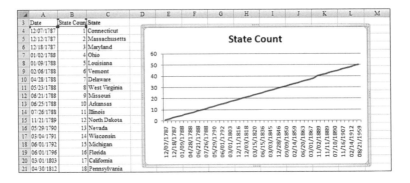

Formatting the chart to have a date-based axis does not work because Excel does not recognize dates before 1900 as valid dates. The next two sections discuss possible workarounds.

Using a Date-Based Axis with Dates Before 1900 Spanning Less Than 100 Years

In Figure 3.18, the dates in column A are text dates from the 1800s. Excel cannot automatically deal with dates from the 1800s, but it can deal with dates from the 1900s.

Figure 3.18

Transforming the 1800s dates to 1900s dates and using clever formatting allows Excel to plot this data with a date axis.

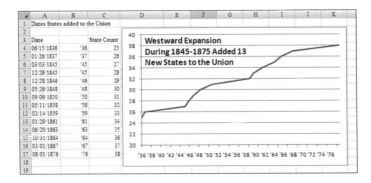

One solution is to transform the dates to be dates in the valid range of dates that Excel can recognize. You can use a date format with two years and a good title on the chart to explain that the dates are from the 1800s.

To create the chart in Figure 3.18, you follow these steps:

1. Insert a blank column B to hold the transformed dates.

2. Enter the formula =DATE(100+RIGHT(A4,4),LEFT(A4,2),MID(A4,4,2)) in cell B4. This formula converts the 1836 date to a 1936 date.

3. Select cell B4. Press Ctrl+1 to open the Format Cells dialog. Choose the date format 3/14/01 from the Date category on the Number tab. This formats the 1936 date as 6/15/36. (You will later add a title to indicate that the dates are in the 1800s.)

4. Double-click the fill handle in cell B4 to copy the formula down to all cells.

5. Select the range B3:C17.

6. From the Insert ribbon, choose Charts, Line, 2-D Line, Line.

7. From the Layout ribbon, choose Legend, No Legend.

8. Right-click the vertical axis along the left side of the chart and choose Format Axis from the context menu.

9. In the Format Axis dialog that appears, on the Axis Options page, choose the Fixed option button next to Minimum and enter a fixed value of 20.

10. Without closing the Format Axis dialog, click the dates in the horizontal axis in the chart. Excel automatically switches to formatting the horizontal axis, and the settings in the Format Axis dialog redraw to show the settings for the horizontal axis. In the Axis Type section, choose Date Axis. Click Close to close the dialog box.

11. From the Layout ribbon, choose Chart Title, Centered Overlay Title.

12. Click the State Count title. Type the new title Westward Expansion<enter>During 1845-1875 Added 13<enter>New States to the Union. Click outside the title to exit Text Edit mode.

13. Click the title once. You should have a solid selection rectangle around the title. On the Home ribbon, click the Decrease Font Size button. Click the Left Align button.

14. Carefully click the border of the title. Drag it so it appears in the top-left corner of the chart.

15. Select the dates in B4:B17. Press Ctrl+1 to access the Format Cells dialog. On the Number tab, click the Custom category. Type the custom number format 'yy. This changes the values shown along the horizontal axis from m/d/yy format to show a two-digit year preceded by an apostrophe.

The result is the chart shown in Figure 3.18. The reader may believe that the chart is showing dates in the 1800s, but Excel is actually showing dates in the 1900s.

This method fails when you are trying to display more than 100 years of data points.

Using a Date-Based Axis with Dates Before 1900 Spanning More Than 100 Years

If you attempt to use the technique described in the preceding section on a chart that contains more than 100 years' worth of dates, the technique will fail.

Microsoft Excel 2007 doesn't do well with large datasets that span 100+ years. While I managed to create a date-based axis covering 630 years with 10 data points, a dataset covering 102 years and 40 points cannot display a date-based axis. As Figure 3.19 shows, however, it is possible to create this chart. To do so, you must transform your date axis into a scale that shows months, hide the axis, and add your own axis, using text boxes. These steps are not for the faint of heart.

You first need to transform the dates from the 1800s to the 1900s. You then transform the dates spanning 172 years into a range where each month in real time is represented by a single day. This results in a time span of six years. You then need to use care to completely hide the labels along the horizontal axis and to replace them with text boxes showing the centuries. You then add a new data series to draw vertical lines at the change of each century.

To create the chart in Figure 3.19, you follow these steps:

Figure 3.19
This chart appears to show a date-based axis that spans 200+ years.

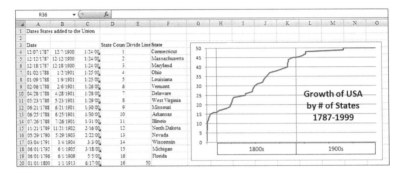

1. Insert new columns B and C.

2. In cell B4, enter the formula =DATE(113+RIGHT(A4,4),LEFT(A4,2),MID(A4,4,2)). This transforms the dates from 1787 to a valid Excel date in 1900. Format this cell with a short date format.

3. In cell C4, type the formula =(YEAR(B4)-1899)*12+MONTH(B4) to calculate a number of months. Format this cell as a short date. This formula now reduces 172 years into 172×12 into 2,064 days, where each day represents 1 month of real time.

4. Select cells B4:C4 and double-click the fill handle to copy the formula down to your range of data. The dates in column B span 1900 to 2072. The dates in column D span 1900 to 1907. Although the relative position of the data points is correct, you have to hide the axis labels that Excel draws in for the horizontal axis. It would therefore be helpful to draw in vertical lines to show where the axis switches from the 1700s to the 1800s and another line to show where the axis switches from the 1800s to the 1900s.

5. Insert a new column E to hold the data for the second series. This series contains just two nonzero points: one at 1800 and one at 1900. Enter the heading Divide Line in cell E3.

6. Look through the dates in column A. Insert a new row before the first date in the 1800s. In this new row, enter 01/01/1800 in column A. Copy the formulas in columns B and C. In column D, copy the point from the row above. In column E, enter the value 50. This draws a single vertical bar from the horizontal axis up to a height of 50.

7. Repeat step 6 to add a new data point for January 1, 1900, and January 1, 2000.

8. Select C4:E55.

9. From the Insert ribbon, choose Charts, Line, Line.

10. On the Layout ribbon, choose Legend, None.

11. Right-click the numbers along the vertical axis and choose Format Axis. Change the Maximum option button to Fixed and enter the value 50. This changes the vertical axis to show from 0 to 50.

12. On the Layout ribbon, use the Current Selection drop-down to select Series. There are now only two data points selected in the chart.

13. On the Design ribbon, choose Change Chart Type. Select the first icon in the column section—for a clustered column chart. This draws narrow columns—actually lines—at 1800 and 1900 on the chart. Note that the chart type change affects only the second series because you selected the Divide Line series in step 12.

14. Click the labels along the horizontal axis. These labels show wrong dates such as 1/23/02. On the Home ribbon, from the Font Color drop-down choose a white font. This causes the axis labels to disappear.

15. On the Insert ribbon, click the Text Box icon. On the chart, draw a text box from the 1800 line to the 1900 line, just below the horizontal axis. The mouse pointer changes into a crosshairs as you draw. You can make sure the vertical line in the crosshairs corresponds to the vertical dividing lines. After you create the text box, a flashing cursor appears inside the text box.

16. Type 1800s. Click the edge of the text box to change it from a dashed line to a solid line.

17. While the text box is selected, choose Center Align from the Home ribbon. Choose Vertical Center Align. Choose Increase Font Size from the Home ribbon.

18. While the text box is still selected, choose Format, Shape Outline, Black on the Layout ribbon in order to outline the text box.

19. Click the text box and start to drag to the right. After you start to drag, hold down the Shift key to constrain the movement to the right. Hold down the Ctrl key to make an identical copy of the text box. When the left edge of the new text box is aligned with the vertical line at 1900, release the mouse button. (Note that you must start dragging before you hold down the Ctrl+Shift keys. Microsoft interprets Ctrl+Click as the shortcut to select an object's container.)

20. Click in the text box and change the text from 1800s to 1900s.

21. On the Layout ribbon, choose Chart Title, Centered Overlay Title. The title Chart Title appears, and it is selected.

22. Click inside the Chart Title text area to enter Text Entry mode. Overwrite the default text in the title by typing Growth of USA, pressing Enter, typing by # of States, pressing Enter, and typing 1787-1999.

23. Click on the border of the chart title to exit Text Entry mode.

24. Drag the chart title to a new location in the lower-right corner of the chart.

The result is a chart that appears to show a line chart that spans 217 years. The line is appropriately scaled, using a date-based axis.

Using a Workaround to Display a Time-Scale Axis

The developers who create Microsoft Excel are careful in the Format Axis dialog box to call the option a *date axis*. The technical writers who write Excel Help refer to a *time-scale axis*. The developers get a point here for accuracy because Excel absolutely cannot natively handle an axis that is based on time.

The data in Figure 3.20 is used to analyze queuing times. In column A, it logs the time that customers entered a busy bank. Times range from when the bank opened at 10 a.m. until the bank closed at 4:00 p.m.

After you enter planned staffing levels in column C, the model calculates when the customer will move from the queue to an open teller window and when he or she will leave, based on an average of three minutes per transaction.

Data in columns I:M record the number of people in the bank every time someone enters or leaves. This data is definitely not spaced equally. Only a few customers arrive in the 10:00 hour, while many customers enter the bank during the lunch hour.

The top chart in Figure 3.20 plots the number of customers on a text-based axis. Because each customer arrival or departure merits a new point, the one hour from noon until 1 p.m. takes up 41% of the horizontal width of the chart. In reality, this one-hour period merits only 16% of the chart. It sounds like a perfect use for a time-series axis, right?

The bottom chart is an identical chart where the axis is converted to show the data on a date-based axis. This is a complete disaster. In a date-based axis, all time information is discarded. The entire set of 300 points is plotted in a single vertical line.

Figure 3.20

Excel cannot show a time-series axis that contains times.

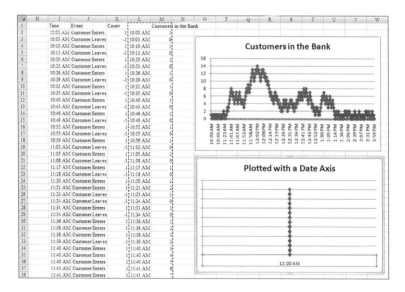

The solution to this problem involves converting the hours to a different time scale (similar to the 1800s date example in the preceding section). Perhaps each hour could be represented by a single year. The 10:00 hour could be represented by 2010, and the 3:00 hour could be represented by 2015 (because 3:00 is the 15:00 hour on a 24-hour clock).

In this example, you manipulate the labels along the vertical axis using a clever custom number format. A few new settings on the Format Axis dialog ensure that an axis label appears every hour.

You follow these steps to create a chart that appears to have a time-based axis:

> **NOTE** In the original chart, a time appeared in column I, and a formula in column L simply copied this time so that it would be adjacent to the customer count in column M. In step 1, the transformation formula is applied to column L.

1. In cell L2, enter the following formula to translate the time to a date:
   `=ROUND(DATE(HOUR(I2)+2000,1,1)+MINUTE(I2)/60*364,0)`

   Because each hour will represent a single year, the years argument of the DATE function is `=HOUR(I2)+2000`. This returns values from 2010 through 2013. The other arguments in the date function are 1 and 1 to return January 1 of the year. Outside the date function, the minute of the time cell is scaled up to show a value from 1 to 365, using `MINUTE(I2)/60*36`. The entire formula is rounded to the nearest integer because Excel would normally ignore any time values.

2. Select cell L2. Double-click the fill handle to copy this formula down to all the data points. The results of this formula ranges from January 1, 2010 (representing the customer who walked in at 10 a.m.), to 12/25/2015 (representing the customer who walked in at 3:57 p.m.).

3. Select cells L1:M303.

4. From the Insert ribbon, choose Charts, Line, Line with Markers.

5. On the Layout ribbon, choose Legend, None. (I hope that after studying Software Quality Metrics (SQM) data for Excel 2007, Microsoft finally realizes that 500 million people instantly turn off the legend in every chart that has a single data series.)

6. Right-click the labels along the horizontal axis and choose Format Axis to display the Format Axis dialog box, where you make the following selections:
   - In the Axis Type section, choose Date Axis.
   - For Major Unit, choose Fixed, 1 Years.
   - For Minor Unit, choose Fixed, 1 Days.
   - For Base Unit, choose Fixed, Days.

   Click Close to close the Format Axis dialog.

7. Return to the transformed dates in column L. Select L2:L303.

8. Press Ctrl+1 to display the Format Cells dialog. On the Number tab, choose the Custom category. A custom number format of yy would display 10 for 2010 and 15 for 2015. Instead, use a custom number format of yy":00". This causes Excel to display 10:00 for 2010 and 15:00 for 2015. This is fairly sneaky, eh?

As you can see in Figure 3.21, the chart now allocates one-sixth of the horizontal axis to each hour. This is an improvement in accuracy over either of the charts in Figure 3.20. The additional chart in Figure 3.21 uses a similar methodology to show the wait time for each customer who enters the bank. If my bank offered 12-minute wait times, I would be finding a new bank.

Figure 3.21
These charts show the number of customers in the bank and their expected wait times.

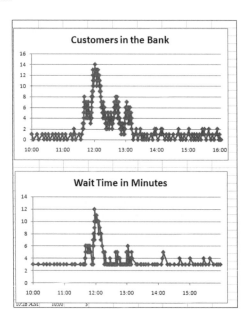

Converting Dates to Text to Add a Decorative Chart Element

There are times when you want to force the category axis to be a text-based axis so that you have a bit more control.

In the following case study, professional designer Kyle Fletcher used Adobe Illustrator to produce a chart for a music industry publication. Kyle needed to separate sales before and after a specific event. Using Illustrator, Kyle drew his chart and created a gap between the pre-event and post-event columns. In order to replicate this effect in Excel, you need to use a text-based axis.

DESIGNING CHARTS LIKE THE PROS

Kyle Fletcher: Using a Decorative Element in a Chart

When commissioned to create a chart for a record industry publication, designer Kyle Fletcher (of www.KyleFletcher.com) created the chart shown in Figure 3.22 using Illustrator. This chart is mostly devoid of chartjunk; it has no gridlines and no axis lines. The only extra element is a separator line used to break the chart into two sections. This separator line takes up the width of an entire column and serves to break the single chart into two charts.

Figure 3.22
This chart from a magazine article uses a vertical element to break the sales trend into two sections.

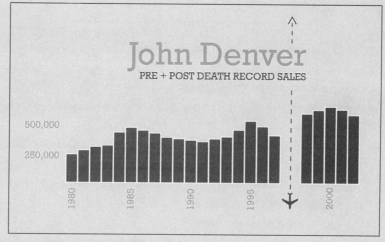

©2005 Kyle Fletcher. Used with Permission.

You follow these steps to create a chart like this one:

> **NOTE**
> The original dataset has year-ending dates in column A and sales in column B.

1. Insert a blank column to the right of the year-ending dates. Enter the formula =**YEAR(A2)** in cell B2. (Converting from dates to numbers ensures that Excel chooses a text-based axis.)

2. While B2 is selected, choose the number format from the drop-down in the Number group on the Home ribbon. Click the Decrease Decimal icon twice to remove the decimals.

3. Insert a blank row between 1997 and 1998. For the year, enter a space. For the sales column, leave the column blank.

4. Change the Sales heading in C1 to John Denver. This will be the start of the title.

5. Select cells B1:C25.

6. On the Insert ribbon, choose Charts, Column, Clustered Column. The initial chart appears as shown in Figure 3.23.

Figure 3.23
The default chart created by Excel.

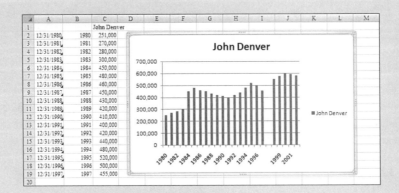

7. On the Layout ribbon, choose Legend, None. Then choose Gridlines, Primary Horizontal Gridlines, None.

8. Left-click the numbers in the vertical axis. On the Layout ribbon, choose Format, Shape Outline, No Outline. This removes the vertical line next to the numbers.

9. With the axis still selected, use the Font drop-down on the Home ribbon to choose the Rockwell font. Change the font color to orange.

10. Right-click a number along the vertical axis and choose Format Axis. In the Format Axis dialog that appears, specify the following:

    • For Minimum, select Fixed, 0.

    • For Maximum, select Fixed, 600000.

    • For Major Unit, select Fixed, 250000.

    Click the Close button. Excel now displays only 0, 250,000, and 500,000 along the vertical axis.

11. Left-click one of the columns to select the data series. On the Layout ribbon, choose Format, Fill, Tan, Darker 50%. Right-click a column and choose Format Data Series. Change the gap width from 150% to 37%. This makes the columns wider, with less of a gap between them.

12. Select the title. Click at the right end of the title to put the title in Text Edit mode. Press the Enter key and then type **PRE + POST DEATH RECORD SALES.**

13. Use the mouse to highlight the characters in the first line of the title. On the Home ribbon, choose Rockwell from the font drop-down. Choose an orange color for the font. Change the font size to 36.

14. Use the mouse to highlight the characters in the second line of the title. Move the mouse cursor up and to the right to activate the mini toolbar. Select Rockwell Condensed as the font. Turn off bold. Choose a tan color as the font color. Choose 18 point.

15. Resize the overall chart to extend from E2 to O24.

16. Left-click one of the years along the category axis. On the Format ribbon, choose Shape Outline, No Outline to remove the line in the x-axis. In the Home ribbon, choose the orange font color. Choose the Rockwell font. The labels along the x-axis remain a source of difficulty. In Kyle's chart, he only showed labels for 1980, 1985, 1990, 1995, and 2000. If you tried to turn on every fifth label, your gap column between 1997 and 1998 would throw off the label for 2000.

17. Go back to the source data and clear the year entries for 1981 through 1984, 1986 through 1989, and so on. As you clear an entry in the worksheet, the corresponding entry along the chart axis disappears.

18. Reselect the chart. On the Insert ribbon, choose Shapes. In the Shapes gallery that appears, choose a line with a single arrow. Start drawing just below the baseline, in between the 1997 and 1998 bars. Hold down the Shift key and draw upward, toward the top of the chart.

19. From the Format ribbon, select Shape Outline, Weight, 2$\frac{1}{4}$ point. Next choose Shape Outline, Dashes and then select the fourth dash type. Choose Shape Outline, Tan Background 2, Darker 50%.

20. With the chart selected, choose Insert, Clip Art. In the Clip Art pane, choose Clip Art on Office Online. Search for `airplane`. For Filter by Type, choose Clip Art. Page through until you find a suitable shape and then click the check box under that shape. In the header above the clip art, you now have the link Download 1 Item. Click that link and then click Download Now. If prompted to do so, choose Open with Clip Organizer. When the clip appears in Microsoft Clip Organizer, choose the drop-down next to the clip and choose Copy.

21. Return to Excel, select the chart, and press Ctrl+V to paste. The clip is initially too large. Use the resizing handles to shrink the airplane. Drag the airplane into position beneath the baseline. Use the green rotate handle to change the orientation of the airplane.

Figure 3.24 shows the final chart in Excel.

Figure 3.24
The chart produced in Excel resembles the original chart from Illustrator.

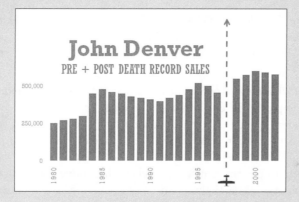

While this chart is close to the original, there are a few elements of the Excel chart that cannot exactly match the chart drawn in Illustrator:

■ The Excel chart shows a value of 0 along the y-axis, whereas the Illustrator chart does not. You could remove this 0 by adding a rectangular shape on top of the 0 and formatting it as white with no border or by using a custom number format of #, ##0;;.

■ In Kyle's chart, the dashed arrow line actually goes behind the title. In Excel, any drawing objects appear on top of the title, and the Send to Back option is grayed out on the Drawing Tools Format ribbon. I chose to move the title out of the way rather than have the arrow cross the title. If you eliminated the title and replaced it with a text box, you could format the text box with a solid white fill and no outline in order to have the arrow appear behind the text box.

It requires more than 20 steps, but with Excel, you can emulate a chart designed with professional design tools. The chart in this example clearly shows the trend of record sales before and after the event. Anyone who is remotely news savvy will understand the meaning of the chart without needing any additional text or title.

NOTE Kyle Fletcher is fresh out of design school and available for hire. Check out his witty annual report at www.KyleFletcher.com.

Using a Chart to Communicate Effectively

A long time ago, in a past job, a McKinsey & Company team investigated opportunities for growth at the company where I was employed. I was chosen to be part of the team because I knew how to get the data out of the mainframe.

The consultants at McKinsey & Company knew how to make great charts. Every sheet of grid paper would be turned sideways, and they would build a landscape chart that was an awesome communication tool simply by using a pencil. After drawing the charts by hand, they would send off the charts to someone in the home office who would generate the charts on a computer. This was a great technique. Long before touching Excel, someone would sit down to figure out what the message should be.

You should do the same thing: Even if you have data in Excel, before you start to create a chart, it's a good idea to analyze the data to see what message you are trying to present.

The McKinsey & Company group used a couple of simple techniques to always get the point across:

- To help the reader interpret a chart, include the message in the title. Rather than use an Excel-generated title such as "Sales," you can actually use a two- or three-line title such as "Sales have grown every quarter except for Q3, when a strike impacted production."

- If the chart is talking about one particular data point, draw that column in a contrasting color. For example, all the columns might be white, but the Q3 bar could be black. This draws the reader's eye to the bar that you are trying to emphasize. If you are presenting data on screen, use red for negative periods and blue or green for positive periods.

The following sections present some Excel trickery that allows you to highlight a certain section of a line chart or to highlight a portion of a column chart. In these examples, you will often be spending some time up front in Excel, adding formulas to get your data series looking correct before creating the chart.

> **TIP**
> If you would like a great book about the theory of creating charts that communicate well, check out Gene Zelazny's *Say It with Charts Complete Toolkit*. Gene is the chart guru at McKinsey & Company who trained the consultants who taught me the simple charting rules. While Say It with Charts doesn't discuss computer techniques for producing charts, it does challenge you to think about the best way to present data with charts and includes numerous examples of excellent charts at work. Visit www.zelazny.com for more information.

Using a Long, Meaningful Title to Explain Your Point

If you are a data analyst, you are probably more adept at making sense of numbers and trends than are the readers of your chart. Rather than hoping that the reader will discover the message you are trying to make, why not add the message as the title of the chart?

Figure 3.25 shows a default chart in Excel. Both the legend and the title use the "Market Share" heading from cell B71. You certainly don't need those words on the chart twice.

Figure 3.25
By default, Excel uses an unimaginative title taken from the heading of the data series.

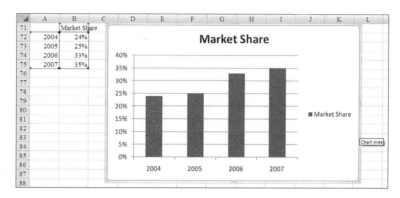

You follow these steps to remove the legend, add data labels, and add a meaningful title:

1. From the Layout ribbon, choose Legend, None and then choose Data Labels, Outside End.

2. Click the title in the chart. Click again to put the title in Edit mode.

3. Backspace to remove the current title. Type **Market share has improved**, press Enter, and type **13 points since 2002**.

4. To format text while in Edit mode, you would have to select all the characters with the mouse. Instead, click the dotted border around the title. The border becomes solid. You can now use the formatting icons on the Home ribbon to format the title.

5. On the Home ribbon, choose left-justified and then click the Decrease Font Size button until the title looks right.

6. Click the border of the chart title and drag it so the title is in the upper-left corner of the chart.

The result, shown in Figure 3.26, provides a message to assist the reader of the chart.

Figure 3.26
You can tell the reader the point of the chart with the title.

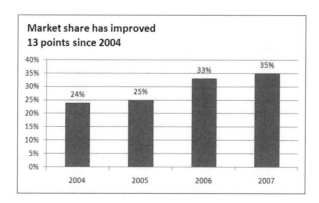

Resizing a Chart Title

When you click a chart title to select it, a bounding box with four resizing handles appears. At least they look like resizing handles; actually, they are not. You do not have explicit control to resize the title. It feels like you should be able to stretch the title horizontally or vertically, as if it was a text box, but you cannot. The only real control you have to make a text box taller is by inserting carriage returns in the title, but you can only type carriage returns when you are in Text Edit mode.

The first click on a title selects the title object. A solid bounding box appears around the title. At this point, you can use most of the formatting commands on the Home ribbon to format the title. You click the Increase/Decrease Font Size buttons to change the font of all of the characters. Excel automatically resizes the bounding box around the title. If you do not explicitly have carriage returns in the title where you want the lines to be broken, you are likely to experience frustration at this point.

When you have the solid bounding box around the title, you could carefully right-click the bounding box and choose Edit Text. However, simply left-clicking a second time inside the bounding box also puts the title in Text Edit mode, as indicated by a dashed line in the bounding box. In Text Edit mode, you can select specific characters in the title and then move the mouse pointer up and to the right to access the mini toolbar and the formatting commands available there. You can edit specific characters within the title in order to create a larger title and a smaller subtitle, as shown in Figure 3.27.

Figure 3.27
By selecting characters in Text Edit mode, you can create a title/subtitle effect.

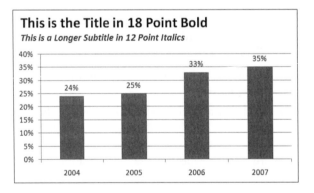

You cannot move the title when you are in Text Edit mode. To exit Text Edit mode, you right-click the title and choose Exit Edit Text or simply left-click the bounding box around the title. When the bounding box is solid, you can click anywhere on the border except the resizing handles and drag to reposition the title.

Deleting the Title and Using a Text Box

If you are frustrated that the title cannot be resized, you can delete the title and use a text box for the title instead. The title in Figure 3.28 is actually a text box. Note the eight resizing handles on the text box instead of the four resizing handles that appear around a title.

Thanks to all these resizing handles, you can actually stretch the bounding box horizontally or vertically.

Figure 3.28
Instead of a title, this chart uses a text box for additional flexibility.

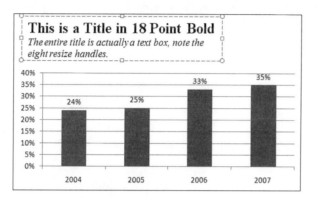

To create the text box shown in Figure 3.28, you follow these steps:

1. Delete the original title by choosing Chart Title, None from the Layout ribbon. Excel resizes the plot area to fill the space that the title formerly occupied.

2. Select the plot area by clicking some whitespace inside the plot area. Eight resizing handles now surround the plot area. Drag the top resizing handle down in order to make room for the title.

3. On the Insert ribbon, click the Text Box icon.

4. Click and drag inside the chart area to create a text box.

5. Click inside the text box and type a title. Press the Enter key to begin a new line. If you don't press the Enter key, Excel word-wraps and begins a new line when text reaches the right end of the text box.

6. Select the characters in the text box that make up the main title and use either the mini toolbar or the tools on the Home ribbon to make the title 18 point, bold, and Times New Roman.

7. Select the remaining text that makes up the subtitle in the text box and use the tools on the Home ribbon to make the subtitle be 12 point, italics, Times New Roman.

Microsoft advertises that all text can easily be made into WordArt. However, when you use the WordArt drop-downs in a title, you are not allowed to use the Transform commands found under Text Effects on the Drawing Tools Format ribbon. When you use the WordArt menus on a text box, however, all the Transform commands are available (see Figure 3.29).

Figure 3.29
Using a text box instead of a title allows more formatting options.

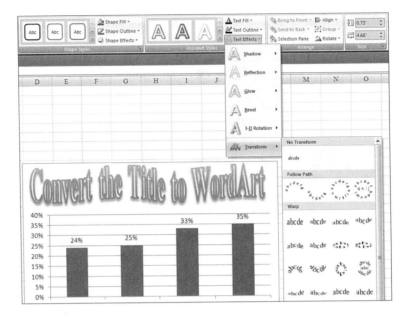

Because a text box is resizable and that you can use WordArt Transform commands, a text box works perfectly: You can move or resize the chart, and the text box moves with the chart and resizes appropriately.

Highlighting One Column

If your chart title is calling out information about a specific data point, you can highlight that point to help focus the reader's attention on it. While the tools on the Design ribbon don't allow this, you can easily achieve the effect quickly by using the Format ribbon.

Figure 3.30
The column for Friday is highlighted in a contrasting color, and it is also identified in the title.

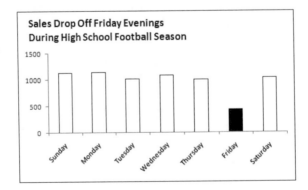

To create the chart in Figure 3.30, you follow these steps:

1. Create a column chart by choosing Column, Clustered Column from the Insert ribbon.

2. Click any of the columns to select the entire series.

3. On the Format ribbon, choose Shape Fill, White. At this point, the columns are invisible. (Invisible bars are great for creating waterfall charts, discussed in Chapter 4, "Creating Charts That Show Differences.") However, in this case, you want to outline the bars.

4. From the Format ribbon, choose Shape Outline, Black. Choose Shape Outline, Weight, 1 point. All your columns are now white, with black outline.

5. Click the Friday column in the chart. The first click on the series selects the whole series. A second click selects just one data point. (If you accidentally click outside the series, you might inadvertently deselect the series.) If all the columns have handles, click Friday again.

6. From the Format ribbon, choose Shape Fill, Black.

7. On the Layout ribbon, turn off the legend and the gridlines.

8. Type a title, as shown in Figure 3.30, pressing Enter after the first line of the title. On the Home ribbon, change the title font size to 14 point, left-aligned.

9. Right-click the numbers along the vertical axis and choose Format Axis. Change Major Unit to Fixed, 500.

The result is a simple chart that calls attention to Friday sales.

Replacing Columns with Arrows

You can use columns shaped like arrows to make a special point. For example, if you have good news to report about consistent growth, you might want to replace the columns in the chart with arrow shapes in order to further indicate the positive growth.

You follow these steps to convert columns to arrows:

1. Create a column chart showing a single series.

2. In an empty section of the worksheet, insert a new block arrow shape. From the Insert ribbon, choose Shapes, Arrows, Up Arrow. Click and drag in the worksheet to draw the arrow.

3. Select the arrow. Press Ctrl+C to copy the arrow to the Clipboard.

4. Select the chart. Click a column to select all the columns in the data series.

5. Press Ctrl+V to paste the arrow. Excel fills the columns with a picture of the block arrow.

6. If desired, choose Format Selection from the Format ribbon. Reduce the gap setting from 150% to 75% to make the arrows wider.

The new chart is shown in the bottom half of Figure 3.31. After creating the chart, you can delete the arrow created in step 2 by clicking the arrow and press the Delete key.

Figure 3.31
Arrows further emphasize the upward growth of sales.

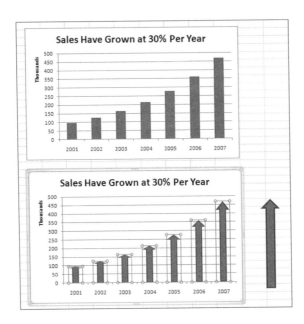

Highlighting a Section of Chart by Adding a Second Series

The chart in Figure 3.32 shows a sales trend over one year. The business was affected by road construction that diverted traffic flow from the main road in front of the business.

Figure 3.32
It would be best to highlight the road construction months in the chart to further emphasize the title.

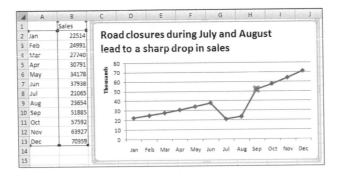

The title calls out the July and August time period, but it would be cool to actually highlight that section of the chart. You follow these steps to add an area chart series to the chart:

1. Begin a new series in column C, next to the original data. To highlight July and August, add numbers to column C for the July and August points, plus the previous point, June. In cell C7, enter the formula of =B7. Copy this formula to June, July, and August.

2. Click the chart. A blue bounding box appears around B2:B13 in the worksheet. Drag the lower-right corner of the blue bounding box to the right to extend the series to include the three values in column C. Initially, this line shows up as a red line on top of a portion of the existing blue line.

3. On the Layout ribbon, use the Current Selection drop-down to choose Series 2. This is the series you just added.

4. While Series 2 is selected, choose Design, Change Chart Type. Select the first area chart thumbnail. Click OK. Excel draws a red area chart beneath the line segment of June through August.

5. On the Format ribbon, use the Current Selection drop-down to reselect Series 2. Then choose Shape Fill, White, Background 1, Darker 25%.

The top chart in Figure 3.33 shows the gray highlight extending from the horizontal axis up to the data line for the two line segments.

Alternatively, you could replace the numbers in column C with 70,000 in order to draw a gray rectangle behind the months, as shown in the bottom chart in Figure 3.33.

Figure 3.33
A second series, with only three points, is used to highlight a section of the chart.

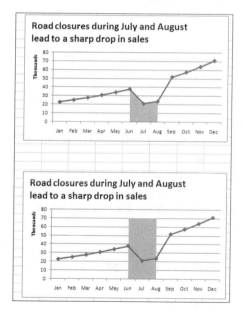

Changing Line Type Midstream

Consider the top chart in Figure 3.34. The title indicates that cash balances improved after a new management team arrived. This chart initially seems to indicate an impressive turn-around. However, if you study the chart axis carefully, you see that the final Q3 and Q4 numbers are labeled Q3F and Q4F to indicate that they are forecast numbers.

Figure 3.34

It is not clear in the top chart that the last two points are forecasts.

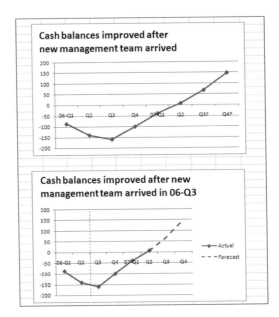

It is misleading to represent forecast numbers as part of the actual results line. It would be ideal if you could change the line type at that point to indicate that the last two data points are forecasts. To do so, you follow these steps:

1. Change the heading above column B from Cash Balances to Actual.

2. Add the new heading Forecast in column C.

3. Because the last actual data point is for Q3 of 2007, move the numbers for Q3 and Q4 of 2007 from column B to column C.

4. To force Excel to connect the actual and the forecast line, copy the last actual data point (the 7 for Q2) over to the Forecast column. This one data point—the connecting point for the two lines—will be in both the forecast and actual columns.

5. Change the last two labels in column A from Q3F to just Q3 and from Q4F to just Q4.

6. Click the existing chart. A bounding box appears around B2:B9. Grab the lower-right blue handle and drag outward to encompass B2:C9. A second series is added to the chart as a red line.

7. On the Layout ribbon, choose Legend, Legend at Right.

8. Click the red line. In the Format ribbon, you should see that the Current Selection drop-down indicates Series "Forecast."

9. Select Format, Shape Outline, Dashes and then select the fourth dash option. The red line changes to a dashed line.

10. While the forecast series is selected, choose Design, Change Chart Type. Choose a chart type that does not have markers.

11. Because the chart title indicates that a new management team arrived, but it does not indicate when the team arrived, change the title to indicate that the team arrived in Q3 of 2006.

12. On the Insert ribbon, select Shapes, Line. Draw a vertical line between Q2 and Q3 of 2006, holding down the Shift key while drawing to keep the line vertical.

13. While the line is selected, on the Format ribbon, choose Shape Outline, Dashes and then select the fourth dash option to make the vertical line a dashed line. Note that this line is less prominent than the series line because the weight of the line is only 1.25 point.

The final chart is shown at the bottom of Figure 3.34.

Adding an Automatic Trendline to a Chart

In the previous example, an analyst had created a forecast for the next two quarters. Sometimes, however, you might want to allow Excel to make a prediction based on past results. For just such situations, Excel offers a trendline feature. Excel can draw a straight line that fits the existing data points. You can either ask Excel to extrapolate the trendline into the future, or, if your data series contains blank points that represent the future, Excel can automatically add the trendline. I regularly use these charts to track my progress toward a goal or trendline.

The easiest way to add a trendline is to build a data series that includes all the days that the project is scheduled to run. In Figure 3.35, column A contains the days of the month. Column B contains 125 for each data point; Excel therefore draws a straight line across the chart, showing the goal at the end of the project. Column C shows the writing progress I should make each day. In this particular month, I am assuming that I would write an equal number of pages six days per week. Column D is labeled Actual; this is where I record the daily progress toward the goal.

The chart is created as a line chart. Gridlines are removed. The legend is removed. The trendline is formatted as a lighter gray. The actual line is formatted as a thick line. The top chart in Figure 3.35 shows the chart before the trendline is complete. You can see that the thick line is not quite above the progress line.

Figure 3.35
In the top chart, the actual line is running behind the trendline, but it seems close.

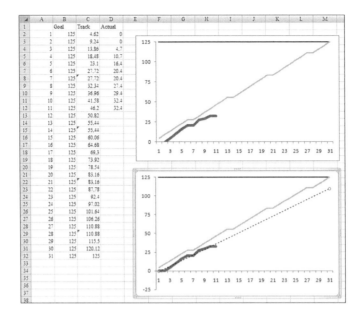

To add a trendline, you follow these steps:

1. Right-click the series line for the Actual column. Choose Add Trendline.

2. The Format Trendline dialog offers to add exponential, linear, logarithmic, polynomial, power, or moving average trendlines. Choose a linear trendline.

3. In the Trendline Name section, either leave the name as Linear (Actual) or enter a custom name, such as Forecast.

4. For the settings where you can forecast forward or backward a certain number of periods, because this chart already has data points for the entire month, leave both of those settings at 0. There are also settings where Excel shows the regression equation on the chart. Add this if you desire.

5. Right-click the trendline to select it. On the Format ribbon, choose Shape Outline, Dashes and then select the fourth dash option. Also choose Shape Outline, Weight, ¼ point.

The trendline is shown in the bottom of Figure 3.35. In this particular case, the trendline extrapolates that if I continue writing at the normal pace, I will miss the deadline by 15 pages or so.

CAUTION

Excel's trendline is not an intelligent forecasting system. It merely fits past points to a straight line and extrapolates that data. It works great as a motivational tool. The current example shows, for example, that it would take a few days of above-average production before the trendline would project that the goal would be met.

Showing a Trend of Monthly Sales and Year-to-Date Sales

In accounting, you generally track sales every month. But in the big picture, you are interested in how 12 months add up to produce annual sales.

The top chart in Figure 3.36 is a poor attempt to show both monthly sales and the accumulated year-to-date (YTD) sales. The darker bars are the monthly results. The lighter bars are the accumulated YTD numbers through the current month. In order to show the large YTD number for November, the scale of the axis needs to extend to $400,000. This makes the individual monthly bars far too small for the reader to be able to discern any differences.

Figure 3.36
The size of the YTD bars obscures the detail of the monthly bars.

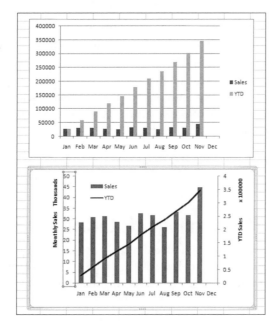

The solution is to plot the YTD numbers against a secondary vertical axis. My preference is that after you change the axis for one series, you should also change the chart type for that series. You follow these steps to create the bottom chart in Figure 3.36:

1. Left-click one of the YTD bars to select the YTD series. Right-click the selected series and choose Format Data Series. Excel displays the Format Data Series dialog.

2. In the Format Data Series dialog, choose Secondary Axis in the Plot Series On section of the Series Options page. Click Close. Excel creates a confusing chart, where the YTD numbers appear directly on top of the monthly numbers, obscuring any monthly numbers beyond August.

3. Excel deselects the series when you change the chart type. Reselect the YTD series by clicking the YTD line.

4. On the Format dialog, choose Shape Outline, Black to change the YTD line to black.

5. Turn off the gridlines by selecting Gridlines, None from the Layout ribbon.

6. Select Axes, Primary Vertical Axis, Show Axis in Thousands from the Layout ribbon.

7. Select Axis Titles, Primary Vertical Axis Title, Rotated Title from the Layout ribbon. Type Monthly Sales and press Enter.

8. Select Axis Titles, Secondary Vertical Axis Title, Rotated Title from the Layout ribbon. Type YTD and press Enter.

9. Right-click the numbers on the secondary vertical axis. Choose Format Axis. In the Scaling section, choose 100,000.

10. Click the legend and drag it to appear in the upper-left corner of the plot area.

11. Click the plot area to select it. Drag one of the resizing handles on the right side of the plot area to drag it right to fill the space that used to be occupied by the title.

12. If you want to present your charts in color, change the color of text in the primary vertical axis to match the color of the monthly bars. To do so, click the numbers to select them. Use the Font Color drop-down on the Home ribbon to select this color (for example, blue). This color cue helps the reader realize that the blue left axis corresponds to the blue bars.

The resulting chart is shown at the bottom of Figure 3.36. The chart illustrates both the monthly trend of each month's sales and the progress toward a final YTD revenue number.

Understanding the Shortcomings of Stacked Column Charts

In a stacked column chart, Series 2 is plotted directly on top of Series 1. Series 3 is plotted on top of Series 2, and so on. The problem with this type of chart is that the reader can tell if the total is increasing or decreasing. The reader might also be able to tell if Series 1 is increasing or decreasing. Because all the other series have differing start periods, it is nearly impossible to tell whether sales in Series 2, 3, or 4 are increasing or decreasing. In the top chart in Figure 3.37, which regions are responsible for the increase from 2001 to 2006? It is nearly impossible to tell.

Stacked column charts are appropriate when the message of the chart is about the first series. In the lower chart in Figure 3.36, the message is that the acquisition of a new product line saved the company. If this new product line hadn't grown quickly, the company would have had to rely on aging product lines that were losing. Because the message here is about the sales of the new product line, you can plot this as the first series, and the reader of the chart will be able to see the impact from that series.

Figure 3.37
In the top chart, no one will draw any conclusions about the West, Central, or South regions.

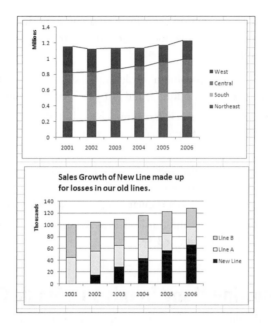

Using a Stacked Column Chart to Compare Current Sales to Prior-Year Sales

The chart in Figure 3.38 uses a combination of a stacked column chart and a line chart. The stacked column chart shows this year's sales, broken out into same-store sales and new-store sales. In this case, the same-store sales are plotted as the first series in white. The new-store sales are the focus and are plotted in black.

The third series, which is plotted as a dotted line chart, shows the prior-year sales. While the total height of the column is greater than last year's sales, there is some underlying problem in the old stores. In many cases, the height of the white column does not exceed the height of the dotted line, indicating that sales at same store are down.

Figure 3.38
The current-year sales are shown as a stacked column chart, with last year's sales as a dotted line.

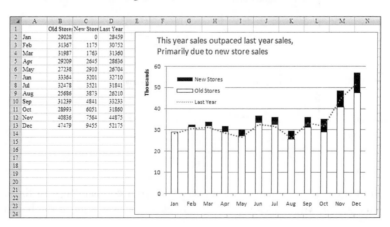

The process of creating this combination chart involves a few steps during which the chart looks completely wrong. You need to overlook the chart in those steps and keep progressing through the steps, as follows:

1. Set up your data with months in column A, old-store sales for this year in column B, new-store sales for this year in column C, and last year's sales in column D.

2. Select cells A1:D13 and create a stacked column chart. Initially, Excel stacks prior-year sales on top of the other sales, and you have a chart that is not remotely close to the expected outcome.

3. Click the top bar to select the third series. Choose Design, Change Chart Type, Line Chart. An important distinction here is that the first two series are plotted as stacked charts. The third series is plotted as a regular line, not as a stacked line.

4. Use the Format ribbon to format the third series as a dotted line. Format the colors of the first two series as shown in Figure 3.38.

Shortcomings of Showing Many Trends on a Single Chart

Instead of using a stacked column chart, you might try to show many trendlines on a single line chart. This approach often leads to confusion. In the top chart in Figure 3.39, for example, the sales trends of five companies create a very confusing chart.

Figure 3.39
Instead of using a single chart with five confusing lines, you can compare your company to each other competitor in smaller charts.

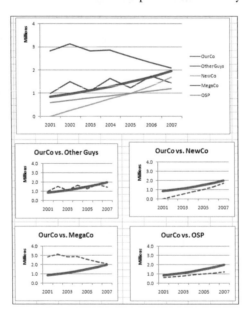

If the goal is to compare the sales results of your company against those of each major competitor, why not show four individual charts, as is done at the bottom of Figure 3.39?

In these charts, the reader can easily see that your company is about to overtake the long-time industry leader MegaCo, but that quick growth from NewCo might still cause you to stay in the second position next year.

Using a Scatter Plot to Show a Trend

Typically, trends are shown with line or column charts. One popular chart from the blogosphere is bucking this trend. This chart, which shows a trend using a combination of two scatter plots, has been published in the blog of professor Charles H. Franklin from the University of Wisconsin (see http://politicalarithmetik.blogspot.com/2005/11/approval-of-president-bush-2001.html).

The advantage of this chart is that the solid line in the chart shows the trend of an average score from month to month. The individual dots in the scatter chart show the individual scores. The degree of scatter in the gray dots gives you an idea of the variation in the individual scores.

As shown in Figure 3.40, my Excel replica of this chart is based on data that I scraped from www.pollingreport.com/BushJob1.htm.

Figure 3.40
This trendline is backed by a scatter plot showing the degree of scatter of individual results.

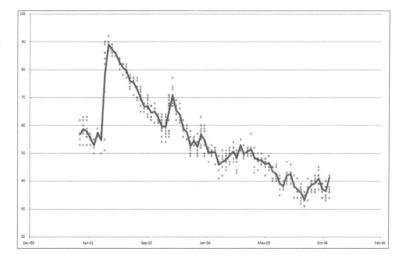

The process of creating this chart involves these steps:

1. Collect all the individual results. Column A contains the month, stored as a real date. Column B contains the individual score that will be shown as the dots in the chart. If you have 60 months of data, this dataset might include hundreds of rows of data.

2. Build a pivot table to summarize the original dataset, by month. The pivot table should have month in the row area and average of score in the data area.

3. In column C, build a formula that gathers the average score for each month. The goal is to report the average month in the first row for each month and then use #N/A values for the remaining rows for that month. If the dates start in A2, the formula is `=IF(A2=A1,NA(),VLOOKUP(A2,$V$4:$W$74,2,FALSE))`. Figure 3.41 shows a few rows of the dataset. Dot scores appear in the second column, and line scores appear once per month in the third column. The results of the pivot table appear in the fourth and fifth columns.

Figure 3.41
The underlying detail used to create the chart in Figure 3.40.

Date	Score	Score2		
Jan-01	57	56.8	Average of Y	
Jan-01	57	#N/A	Date	Total
Jan-01	53	#N/A	Jan-01	56.8
Jan-01	62	#N/A	Feb-01	58.71428571
Jan-01	55	#N/A	Mar-01	58
Feb-01	57	58.71429	Apr-01	55.4
Feb-01	62	#N/A	May-01	53

4. Build a chart based on the first two columns. Select Scatter Chart with Only Markers.

5. Format the data series to use a light-colored marker of a small size.

6. Select the chart. A blue outline appears around the data in the second column. Grab the top-right handle on the blue outline and drag to the right to incorporate the data in the third column.

7. In the Layout ribbon, select the new series from the Current Selection drop-down.

8. In the Design ribbon, change the chart type to a scatter chart with straight lines. Format the line series as a thicker line.

Although Professor Franklin's innovative chart and blog feature mostly political charts, you can easily adapt this concept to your business.

My coauthor on *Excel for Marketing Managers*, Ivana Taylor of Third Force Marketing, is a huge proponent of asking your customers how you are doing. Ivana provides a service whereby she randomly calls 20 customers each month to get a feel for how your customers approve of your service. This data would be a perfect dataset to port to Professor Franklin's chart. Rather than showing only a "consensus" quality score, you could easily see the degree of scatter around the average score.

Next Steps

In Chapter 4, you will learn about charts used to make comparisons, including pie, radar, bar, donut, and waterfall charts.

Creating Charts That Show Differences

4

Comparing Entities

Whereas Chapter 3, "Creating Charts That Show Trends," is concerned with the progression of a trend over time, this chapter focuses on demonstrating the differences between entities. For example, you could use Excel charts to compare each sales region versus the others or your company versus the competitors.

When you want to compare the differences among a handful of entities, a bar chart is the perfect choice. The reader can easily see the differences between the entities.

The only time you should use a pie chart is when you want to show how components add up to a whole entity. Pie charts are vastly overused, and many guidelines contraindicate their use. You should often instead consider 100% stacked column charts, bar of pie charts, or pie of pie charts. These last charts are a bit tricky to master but have some amazingly cool flexibility.

Finally, in this chapter you will learn how to use some more Excel trickery to build a waterfall chart. This type of chart is perfect for telling the story of how a whole entity breaks down into components.

Using Bar Charts to Illustrate Item Comparisons

Bar charts are perfect for comparing items. Bar charts offer a few advantages over column charts for comparing sales of various items:

- People tend to associate column charts—or any other chart in which the data progresses from left to right—as having a time-based component. When you turn the columns on their sides and make them horizontal bars, people tend not to read time into the equation.

- With a column chart, the category names can appear in a horizontal orientation, giving plenty of room for longer names. In the chart shown in Figure 4.1, for example, the category names take almost half the chart, but there is still room to get the point across that the "Excel for" series is not selling as well as the general-purpose Excel books.

Figure 4.1
A bar chart allows for lengthy category names and a comparison of different product lines.

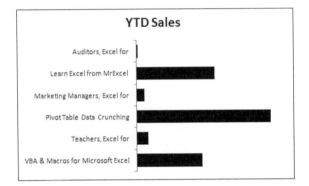

Bar charts are oriented with the first item in the list closest to the bottom of the chart. If you expect people to read a chart from top to bottom, you should sort the categories into descending alphabetical sequence (by clicking the ZA button in the Data ribbon). The bar chart in Figure 4.1 compares sales of six different product lines. It is easy to spot the winners in the chart. The original dataset is sorted to have the VBA title at the top of the spreadsheet.

Figure 4.1 uses a clustered bar chart type, although it has only one series to report. Other alternatives are the clustered bar in 3-D, clustered horizontal cylinder, clustered horizontal cone, or clustered horizontal pyramid. As mentioned in Chapter 3, cone and pyramid charts are bad because they misrepresent data; the same advice applies here. For proof, see the section titled "Lying with Shrinking Charts" on page 425 in Chapter 14, "Knowing When Someone Is Lying to You with a Chart."

For a more powerful arrangement of data, you can sort these categories into ascending sequence, by sales. Excel then plots the largest category at the top of the chart. Even more than the chart in Figure 4.1, the chart shown in Figure 4.2 depicts a clear delineation between the winners and losers.

Figure 4.2
You can sort the data by ascending sales in order to show the largest bars at the top of the chart.

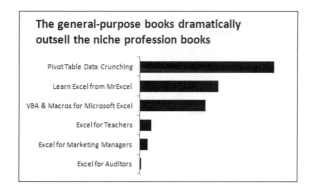

If you think it is silly to have to sort your data into the reverse order from which you want to present it in the chart, there is a setting buried deep in the ribbon that you can use to correct this logic: you can choose Layout, Axes, Primary Vertical Axis, Show Right to Left Axis in order to show the first row in your dataset at the top of the chart. Alternatively, you can right-click the category labels, choose Format Axis, and choose the Categories in Reverse Order check box (see Figure 4.3).

Figure 4.3
Instead of sorting your data in reverse order, you could sort the data in normal order and then specify reverse order for the categories.

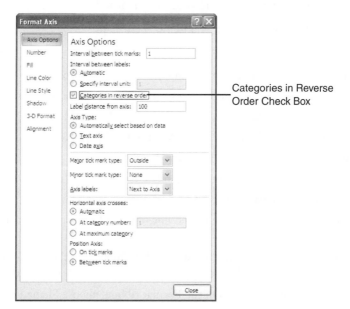

Adding a Second Series to Show a Time Comparison

In Figure 4.4, two series are plotted on the bar chart. The original series presents sales data from this year. This data was moved to Series 2 in order to continue to be plotted as the top bar. The new Series 1 contains sales data from last year, for reference.

Figure 4.4
In this chart, the sales for this year are moved to Series 2. A new Series 1 shows sales from last year; a bit of additional data to show whether sales are increasing or decreasing.

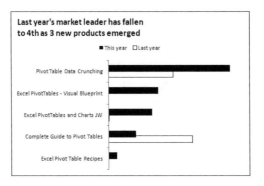

Because the main message is current-year sales, those bars are formatted with a black fill to draw attention to them. The bars for last year are shown with white outlines.

The addition of data from the previous year adds a bit of context to the chart. The reader can tell that Products 2, 3, and 5 are new this year and have no sales history from the previous year. Product 4 was the previous market leader, but its sales have fallen off sharply. Product 1 has experienced good year-to-year growth; it will be interesting to see if the newly emerging products show similar growth in Year 2.

To create the chart in Figure 4.4, you follow these steps:

1. Enter product names in column A.

2. Enter last-year sales in column B and this-year sales in column C.

3. Sort the data so that the largest sales from this year are at the bottom of the chart.

4. From the Insert ribbon, choose Bar, 2-D Bar, Clustered Bar.

5. Choose Layout, Gridlines, Primary Vertical Gridlines, None.

6. Choose Layout, Axes, Primary Horizontal Axis, None.

7. Choose Layout, Legend, Show Legend at Top.

8. Choose Layout, Chart Title, Above Chart.

9. Click in the title area. Type the first line of the title, press Enter, and type the second line of the title.

10. Click the outline of the title to exit Text Edit mode. On the Home ribbon, click the Left Align button and the Decrease Font Size button. Drag the title to the left.

11. Click a bar from this year. On the Format ribbon, choose Shape Fill and then select black.

12. Right-click the black bar and choose Format Data Series. Change the Series Overlap setting to 25%.

13. Click one of the bars for last year. On the Format ribbon, choose Shape Fill, White. On the Format ribbon, choose Shape Outline and then select black.

14. Grab one of the resizing handles in the corner of the chart and drag outward to resize the chart.

Subdividing a Bar to Emphasize One Component

Excel offers a stacked bar chart type. This type allows you to break a bar, such as total sales, to show components.

In the top chart in Figure 4.5, only one component is called out. The subject of the chart is this one component of product cost, showing how Company A has a significant cost advantage. You should use this chart type sparingly. The reader of the chart is able to make a judgment about the size of the black bar for the major subcomponent. The reader of the chart is also able to make a judgment about the total size of the bar. It is difficult to make a judgment about the size of the white component of the bars. Can you tell which company has the lowest "other cost"? (It is Company B.)

Figure 4.5
A stacked bar chart allows the reader to judge the size of the total bar and the first component bar. Beyond that, it's difficult to make a comparison from one bar to the next.

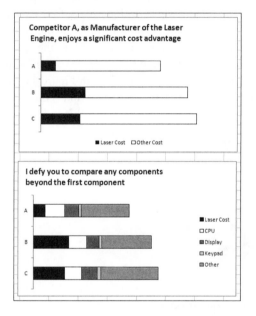

The problem becomes worse if you try to show more than two components in the stacked bar chart. The bottom chart in Figure 4.5, for example, is trying to compare the costs of four major components, but the reader won't be able to learn anything about the additional components.

> **NOTE**
> The charts in Figure 4.5 were created using Insert, Bar, 2-D Bar, Stacked Bar selection. The individual segments of each bar were formatted using Format, Shape Fill.

Showing Component Comparisons

A component comparison chart is useful when you want to show several parts that add up to a whole. You can use this type of chart to show these concepts:

- The market share of several competitors in a market
- The cost breakdown of a product by subcomponent
- The breakdown of time spent in a day
- The relative size of five major customers and all other customers as a group

These are also all great concepts to show using a pie chart or a 100% stacked bar/column chart. Unfortunately, pie charts are overused in business today. People try to use pie charts to compare items that don't add up to a whole. In Figure 4.6, for example, someone tried to use a pie chart to compare product prices. Without reading the individual prices labeling each pie slice, you would be hard pressed to figure out whether the Hummer H3 or the Ford Escape hybrid costs more. As discussed in the previous section, using a bar chart is best when you're trying to compare items. The bottom chart in Figure 4.6 shows the same data as the pie chart, but in this case, it's plotted on a bar chart and is much easier to understand.

Figure 4.6

An attempt to use a pie chart to compare prices is misguided. The bar chart in the lower half of the figure is more effective.

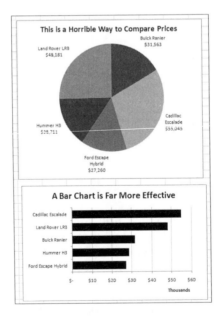

Some of the frustrations with pie charts are humorously summarized by Dick DeBartolo, Mad's Maddest Writer, in this chart that he prepared for this book shown in Figure 4.7.

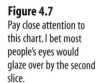

Figure 4.7
Pay close attention to this chart. I bet most people's eyes would glaze over by the second slice.

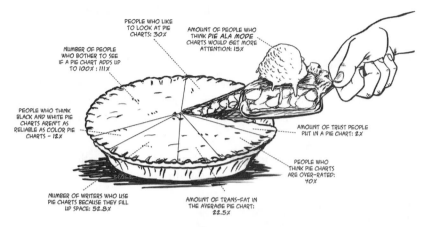

NOTE Dick Debartolo has been writing for *MAD Magazine* for over 40 years. If you are a fan of MAD, check out his book, *Good Days and MAD: A Hysterical Tour Behind the Scenes at MAD Magazine*. Dick also hosts the Daily Giz Wiz podcast—a review of the latest gadgets and those gadgets that once seemed like a good idea but are now collecting dust in Dick's Gadget Warehouse.

When you are performing component comparisons, the following chart types are effective:

- A pie chart is appropriate when you're comparing 2 to 5 components.
- A pie of pie chart is appropriate for comparing 6 to 10 components.
- A bar of pie chart can handle 6 to 15 components.
- You should use a 100% stacked column chart when you want to have two or more pies (for example, comparing market share from this year vs. last year). The 100% stacked bar, 100% stacked line, and 100% stacked area are all variations of the 100% stacked column chart.
- A donut chart is a strange chart that might occasionally be able to compare two pie charts, although a 100% stacked column chart is usually better for this sort of comparison.

The following sections describe the ins and outs of using pie, 100% stacked column, and the other previously mentioned charts.

Using Pie Charts

Pie charts are great for comparing two to five different components. You typically select a range containing category labels in column A and values in column B. Often, the categories are sorted so that the largest value is at the top and the remaining categories are sorted in descending order.

To create a pie chart, from the Insert ribbon, you select the Pie drop-down, as shown in Figure 4.8. There are six icons in this drop-down:

Figure 4.8
You commonly use the first icon to create a 2-D pie chart.

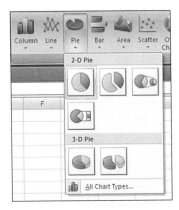

- **2-D Pie**—This is the type that you use most frequently.
- **2-D Exploded Pie**—There is no need to choose this because you can easily explode a pie or a slice of pie later. This technique is discussed later in this chapter, in the section "Highlighting One Slice of a Pie by Exploding."
- **Pie of Pie or Bar of Pie**—Both of these chart types are effective for dealing with datasets that have too many slices and when you care about the small pie slices.
- **3-D Pie**—This is a regular pie chart tipped on its side so that you end up seeing the "edge" of the pie. This is a cool effect when you are trying to decorate a PowerPoint chart. It is not as effective if you actually want someone to read your charts to understand the data.
- **Exploded Pie in 3-D**—Again, this is an option you probably don't want to choose because you can easily explode a pie by using techniques discussed later in this chapter.

The default pie chart has no labels and includes a legend on the right side to help identify the pie slices. Initially, the first data item appears starting at the 12 o'clock position, and additional wedges appear in a clockwise direction, as shown in Figure 4.9.

In black and white especially, it is difficult to match up the tiny color swatches used in the legend with the pie slices. You almost always want to delete the legend and add data labels, as discussed in the next section.

Excel offers seven built-in layouts for a pie chart. All the layouts that include labels add them inside the pie slices. In the current example, the black font on the dark pie slices disappears.

Figure 4.9
The default pie chart uses a legend that is too small and too far from the chart to be effective.

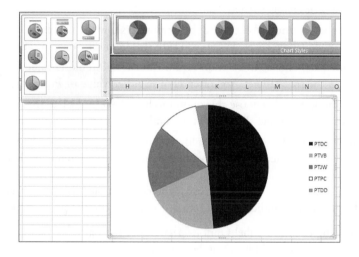

Labeling a Pie Chart

Because a pie chart does not have a lengthy axis running along one edge of the chart, choosing the data labels is an important consideration.

Rather than using the built-in Data Label choices on the Layout ribbon, you choose More Data Label Options from the Data Labels drop-down on the Layout ribbon. Excel displays the Label Options page of the Format Data Labels dialog, as shown in Figure 4.10.

Figure 4.10
You use the More Data Labels option in the Layout ribbon to reach this dialog, where you can build effective pie chart labels.

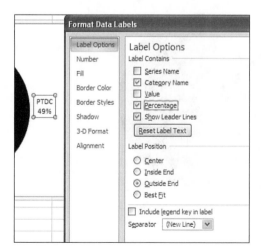

You have options for what the label should contain. You can choose more than one of the following options:

- **Series Name**—This option doesn't make sense in a pie chart because every slice would have a series name such as "Sales."

- **Category Name**—You choose this option to show the names of items represented by the individual pie slices. When you turn this item on, you can set Legend to None.

- **Value**—You choose this option to show the actual numeric value for this slice from the cells in the spreadsheet. You often choose either Value or Percentage.

- **Percentage**—You choose this option to have Excel calculate the percentage of the pie allocated to each pie slice. This is a number that is not typically in your spreadsheet.

- **Show Leader Lines**—You should leave this setting on. If you later reposition a label, Excel draws a line from the label to the pie slice associated with that label.

For the Label Position option, the usual choices for a pie chart are either to show the label outside the pie slice, indicated by Outside End, or inside the pie slice, indicated by Center.

The final choice in the Label Options page of the Format Data Labels dialog is the Separator drop-down. This option becomes important when you have chosen two items in the Label Contains section. If you have chosen Category Name and Percentage, for example, Excel's default choice for a comma as the separator shows the label East, 33%. To remove the comma from the pie chart labels, you choose either (space) or (New Line) from the Separator drop-down.

Figure 4.11 shows a pie chart with category names and percentages at the outside end of each slice. The data label is separated by a new line character.

Figure 4.11
Displaying the labels at the outside end ensures that the labels can be read.

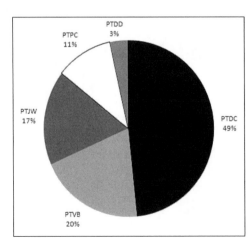

Rotating a Pie Chart

There is an ongoing argument about the rotation of a pie chart. Many people say that the first pie slice should start at the 12 o'clock position, and subsequent pie slices should appear in a clockwise direction. I disagree with this philosophy, from a purely practical point of view. I think that the smallest pie slices should be rotated around so that they appear in the lower-right corner of the pie. This location provides the most room for the labels of the small pie slices to appear without overlapping.

You have control over the rotation of a pie chart. You can right-click a pie chart and choose Format Data Series. On the Options dialog that appears, you can change the setting for Angle of First Slice. In Figure 4.12, for example, the bottom pie chart has been rotated 195 degrees, preventing labels from appearing on top of each other.

Figure 4.12
You can change the angle of first slice to rotate the pie until the data labels have the most room to appear without overlapping each other.

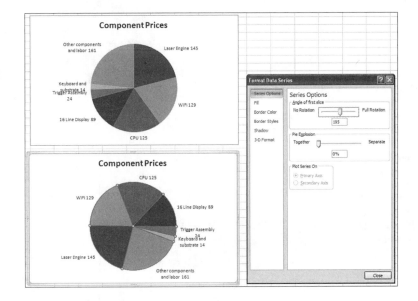

Moving an Individual Pie Slice Label

In a pie chart that has long category names and many slices, you may not be able to find an angle of rotation that enables all the labels to have sufficient room. In this case, you need to move an individual pie slice label.

The first time you click a data label, all the data labels are selected, as shown in Figure 4.13. At this point, you can use icons on the Home ribbon to change the font or font size.

A second click on a data label selects only that particular label. You can click the border of the label and drag it to a new position. If the Leader Lines option remains selected (refer to Figure 4.10), Excel automatically connects the label and the pie slice with a leader line.

In Figure 4.14, the label for the keyboard has been moved so that it does not crash into the label for the trigger assembly.

Figure 4.13
After the first click on a data label, all labels are selected. You can use the Home ribbon icons to format all labels.

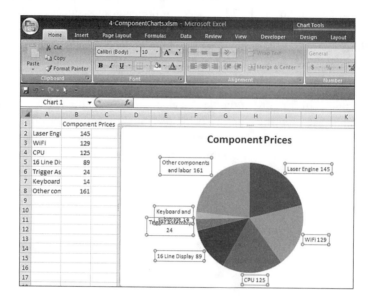

Figure 4.14
After a second single-click, only one label is selected. You can drag an individual data label into a new position.

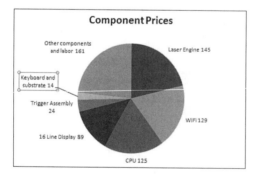

Highlighting One Slice of a Pie by Exploding

The first click on a pie selects the data series (that is, it selects all the pie slices). If you then drag outward from the center of the pie, you explode all the slices of the pie.

> **CAUTION**
>
> If you want to explode the whole pie, you have to be fairly deliberate about it. If you click once to select all the slices and then click again to drag the slices outward, the second click selects only a single slice. Click outside the pie to select the entire chart, and then click on the pie and drag outward. This action will select the pie and explode it in a single step.

The charts in Figure 4.15 show various levels of explosion. The top-left chart uses a 15% explosion factor. Excel allows you to specify up to a 400% explosion factor, which really looks pretty silly.

Figure 4.15
You drag outward while a data series is selected to select the entire pie.

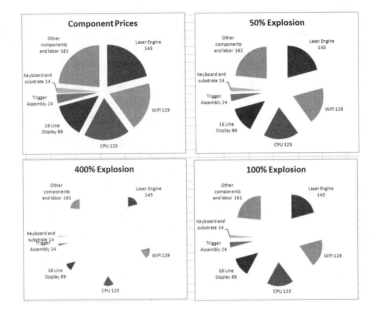

A better technique is to explode just the one slice that is the subject of the pie. In Figure 4.16, a large order could not ship because of shortages of a tiny assembly. The plant managers had previously decided to cut safety stock on this component. To illustrate that this might have been a poor decision, you can explode just that slice of the pie.

Figure 4.16
You can explode one piece of the pie to call attention to that piece.

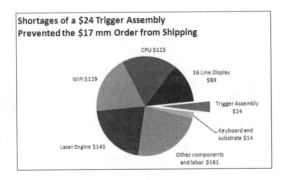

You click once on the pie to select the entire series. Then you click the slice in question one more time to select only that slice. You drag the individual slice outward to explode only that slice, as shown in Figure 4.16.

Highlighting One Slice of a Pie with Color

Instead of exploding a slice of a pie, you can highlight that slice using a contrasting color. A single black pie slice in an otherwise white pie instantly draws the reader's eye, as shown in Figure 4.17.

Figure 4.17
You can plot one slice of the pie in a contrasting color to draw attention to that slice.

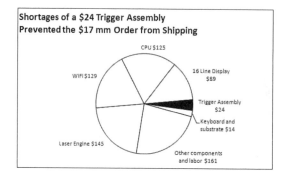

To format the chart as shown in Figure 4.17, you follow these steps:

1. Click anywhere on the pie to select the entire pie.
2. On the Format ribbon, choose Shape Fill, White. The entire pie disappears.
3. On the Format ribbon, choose Shape Outline and then select black. The pie is now a white pie outlined in black.
4. Click the one pie slice that you want to highlight.
5. On the Format ribbon, choose Shape Fill and then select black. The single pie slice now stands out from the other slices.

Switching to a 100% Stacked Column Chart

It is very difficult for a reader to track the trends from one pie to the next when you are trying to show a trend by using multiple pie charts, as shown in Figure 4.18.

Figure 4.18
It is very hard to track trends by looking at multiple pies.

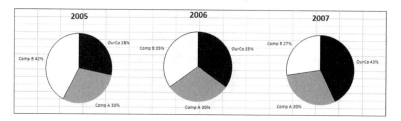

Instead of using pie charts, you can switch to one of Excel's 100% charts. For example, in the 100% stacked column chart, Excel stacks the values from Series 1, Series 2, Series 3, and so on but scales the column so that each column is exactly the same height. This gives the effect of dividing a column into components, just as a pie chart would do.

Excel offers 100% versions of column charts, bar charts, area charts, and line charts. To find them, in the Insert Chart dialog, you look for charts where both the left and right elements are the same height (see Figure 4.19).

Figure 4.19
These icons all create 100% stacked charts.

Figure 4.20 shows examples of 100% stacked column, area, bar, and line charts. The 100% stacked column chart is probably the easiest to interpret. In a 100% stacked chart, the reader is able to judge the growth or decline of both the first series and the last series.

Figure 4.20
For year-over-year comparisons, a 100% stacked column chart is easier to read than multiple pie charts.

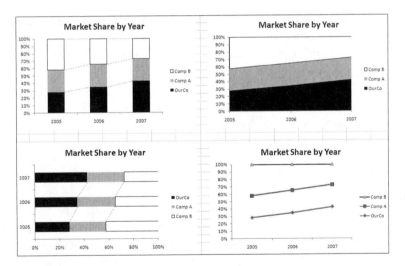

Using a Doughnut Chart to Compare Two Pies

Excel offers another chart type—the donut chart—that attempts to compare multiple pies. In a donut chart, one pie chart encircles another pie chart.

A reader of the chart in Figure 4.21 can see that the market share for OurCo increased between 2006 and 2007 and that the market share for Comp B decreased between 2006 and 2007. It is unlikely that the reader could draw any conclusions about Comp A based on this chart.

Figure 4.21
Doughnut charts are generally difficult to read, although this one does effectively communicate some information.

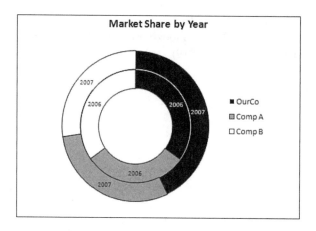

In creating the chart in Figure 4.21, you would have to go through a number of maddening steps, including these:

- You need to select Layout, Data Labels, More Data Label Options and choose to show only the series name as the label. You almost need to leave the legend turned on with this chart because there isn't space to fit OurCo 2006 in the thin ring of the pie.

- Changing the colors using the Format ribbon is a tedious process. You cannot format both OurCo sections at once. You have to click the 2006 ring, then 2006 OurCo, then Format, Shape Fill, and then select black. You then have to repeat these steps for the other five pieces of the doughnut chart.

- To make some data labels white, you have to select the labels for Series 1, then just one label, then use the Font Color drop-down on the Home ribbon. You repeat this step for OurCo for Series 2.

One interesting setting for the doughnut chart is the doughnut hole size. When you right-click the inner series of the doughnut chart and choose Format Data Series, the Format dialog box appears, where you can change the doughnut hole size (valid values range from 10% to 90%). The doughnut chart in Figure 4.22 uses a hole size of 10%. Reducing the hole size makes the chart more readable in this case.

Figure 4.22
Reduce the doughnut hole size to allow more room for labels on the chart.

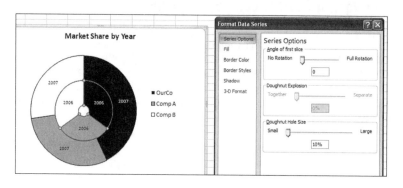

Dealing with Data Representation Problems in a Pie Chart

The 80/20 rule comes into play with pie charts. In many component comparisons, 20% of the categories make up 80% of the pie. In this case, the tiny pie slices at the end of the pie contain too much detail and are not useful. If you attempt to leave these slices in the pie, the labels needlessly complicate the chart, as shown in Figure 4.23.

Figure 4.23
The 20 pie slices make this chart difficult to read.

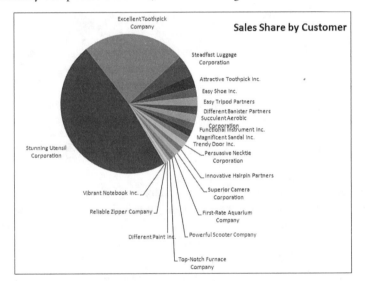

As noted in the earlier section, "Using Pie Charts," there are several methods discussed, such as rotating a pie chart and moving individual pie labels, which enable you to create the chart shown in Figure 4.23. However, with this amount of data, the process is tedious.

Plus, the data used in Figure 4.23 may not be entirely realistic. Usually, a company has a few major accounts and dozens of minor accounts. If you need a list of all your accounts, you should really show it in a table that lists the customers, sorted in descending sequence.

Usually a pie chart is focused on the top four to five accounts. The message for the reader of the chart in Figure 4.23 is that two major accounts make up 75% of the revenue stream. If anything would happen to either of those accounts, this company would be in for tough times. To communicate this message, you can simply replace the last 16 pie slices with a single slice labeled 16 Other Accounts.

If you instead need to show the detail of the small accounts (perhaps in order to grow some new mega-customers), you need to switch to a bar of pie or pie of pie chart. These options are discussed in the next sections.

Replacing Smaller Slices with an Other Customer Summary

Replacing smaller slices with an Other Customer summary requires no charting magic. You simply look through your customer list and figure a logical breakpoint between major customers and customers that should be listed as "other."

The example shown in Figure 4.24 includes two customers that are not exactly major to help communicate how quickly sales fall off.

Figure 4.24
The low-tech solution is to add a formula to the worksheet to total all the smaller accounts.

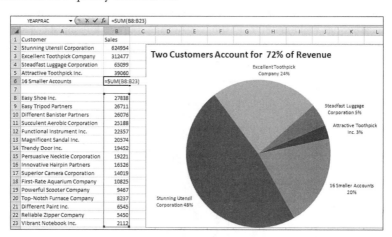

To create this chart, you insert a few blank rows to separate the major accounts from the other accounts. In the worksheet, you add the label 16 Smaller Accounts. Then you enter a SUM function to total all the smaller customers. Finally, you change the chart range to include only the major customers and the Other line.

> **TIP**
> You don't have to re-create the chart to specify a new data range. If you click once on the chart, Excel draws a blue rectangle around the data included in the chart. You grab the blue resizing handle at the bottom of the data range and drag upward to include only the major customers and the Other Total row.

In Figure 4.24, the chart is less busy than in Figure 4.23. The title has been improved, and each data label now includes both the category name and percentage.

Using a Pie of Pie Chart

A pie of pie chart shows the smallest pie slices in a new, secondary pie chart. The true volume of the small slices is shown in a slice marked Other in the original pie. Series lines extend from the Other slice to the secondary pie.

You use this chart type when the focus of your chart is the small slices. In Figure 4.25, for example, the focus is on the emerging markets. Together, the five markets account for a 19% share, but the markets are not doing equally well. The pie of pie chart shows which of the new markets are growing the fastest.

Figure 4.25
A secondary pie shows the detail of the emerging markets.

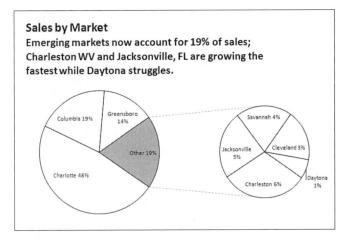

Several interesting settings are available in the "of pie" charts. In both the pie of pie and bar of pie charts, you can control the size of the secondary plot compared to the primary pie. You can control the gap between the plots and choose whether the series lines extend from one chart to the next. To access these settings, you click inside the chart but outside the pie to deselect the pie. Then you right-click the pie and choose Format Data Series; the Format Data Series dialog appears, as shown in Figure 4.26.

Figure 4.26
The pie of pie and bar of pie charts offer new settings in the Series Options tab of the Format Data Series dialog.

> **NOTE**
> Creating the chart in Figure 4.25 requires some tricky steps, as described later in this chapter, in the section "Customizing the Split in the 'Of Pie' Charts."

In the Format Data Series dialog, you can set the gap between the pies from 0% to 500%. The gap size is expressed as a percentage *of the radius* of the main pie. In other words, when you choose 100%, the gap between the pies is equal to the radius of the main pie, which is 50% of the main pie.

You can also set the secondary plot size to be anywhere from 5% to 200% of the main pie chart. The default setting is 75%.

CAUTION

A very annoying bug currently exists in Excel 2007. The Format Data Series dialog reports the initial secondary plot size setting as 5%. When you touch the slider to change the secondary plot size, Excel actually sets the real secondary plot size to 5%. Normally, you can slide a bit to the left and then back to the original position in order to leave the setting unchanged. However, if you want to leave this setting unchanged, you actually have to move it up to 75%.

Adjusting either the gap setting or the secondary plot size changes the size of both pies. If you make either the gap or the secondary plot size larger, Excel has to make the main pie smaller in order to fit all three elements into the same plot area. This requires a little bit of high school algebra. Say that the plot area is 500 pixels wide. And say that the width of the main pie is a variable n. You might encounter these settings:

- With a gap of 100% and a secondary plot size of 75%, the original pie is n pixels wide, the gap is $0.5n$ pixels wide, and the secondary pie is $0.75n$ pixels wide. This means the total width is $2.25n=500$, so n is 222. This results in a main pie width of 222 pixels, a gap of 111 pixels, and a secondary plot size of 166.50.

- If you increase the secondary plot size to 100% and increase the gap to 150%, the original pie is n pixels wide, the gap is $0.75n$ pixels wide, and the secondary pie is n pixels wide. This means the total width is $2.75n=500$. The main pie is 181 wide, the gap is 136 wide, and the secondary pie is 181 pixels wide.

Basically, as you increase the size of either setting, the main pie gets smaller. Table 4.1 shows the horizontal size of the main pie, the gap, and the secondary pie for various combinations of gap width and secondary plot size. For example, the main pie could occupy as much as 83% of the plot area width if you choose a 0% gap and a secondary plot size of 20%. As you increase the gap and secondary plot size, you might end up with a main pie that occupies as little as 18% of the width of the plot area.

Table 4.1 Width of Main Pie/Gap/Second Pie

Secondary Plot Size	Gap Size				
	0%	50%	100%	250%	500%
20%	83%/0%/17%	69%/17%/14%	59%/29%/12%	41%/51%/8%	27%/68%/5%
50%	67%/0%/33%	57%/14%/29%	50%/25%/25%	36%/45%/18%	25%/63%/13%
75%	57%/0%/43%	50%/13%/38%	44%/22%/33%	33%/42%/25%	24%/59%/18%
100%	50%/0%/50%	44%/11%/44%	40%/20%/40%	31%/38%/31%	22%/56%/22%
150%	40%/0%/60%	36%/9%/55%	33%/17%/50%	27%/33%/40%	20%/50%/30%
200%	33%/0%/67%	31%/8%/62%	29%/14%/57%	24%/29%/47%	18%/45%/36%

Figure 4.27 shows the extremes for the gap size and secondary plot size settings.

Figure 4.27
Changing the gap width and secondary plot size can create vastly different looks for the chart.

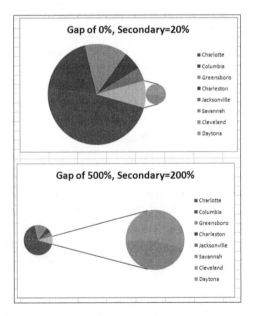

Excel also offers a robust system for choosing which slices should be in the secondary plot. The following section applies to both pie of pie and bar of pie charts.

Customizing the Split in the "Of Pie" Charts

With an "of pie" chart, you have absolute control over which slices appear in the main pie and which slices are sent to the secondary plot. Excel offers a surprising array of ways to control this setting.

When you right-click the pie and choose Format Data Series, the Format Data Series dialog appears. The top setting in the dialog is the drop-down Split Series By, which offers the following options:

- **Split Series By Position**—You can change the spin button to indicate that the last n values should be shown in the secondary pie. Excel then uses the last n values from the original dataset in the secondary pie.

- **Split Series By Value**—When you enter a value in the text box, Excel moves any slices with a value less than the entered value to the secondary pie.

- **Split Series By Percentage Value**—You can use the spin button to enter a value from 1% to 99%. Any slices smaller than the entered percentage move to the secondary plot. Note that if there are no slices smaller than that value, the secondary plot appears as an empty black circle.

- **Split Series By Custom**—This is a flexible setting where you can choose which slices to send to the secondary pie. After choosing Custom from the drop-down, you click on an individual slice in the chart. Then, in the Format Data Point dialog, you indicate that the point belongs to the second plot or the first plot. You continue selecting additional slices in the chart and indicating the location for those points.

CASE STUDY

Creating a Pie of Pie Chart

At this point, you have enough information to create the chart shown previously in Figure 4.25. You follow these steps to create that chart:

1. Enter markets in column A and sales in column B.

2. Sort in descending order, by sales.

3. Select the markets and sales cells.

4. From the Insert ribbon, select Pie, 2-D Pie, Pie of Pie. Excel creates a pie with three items in the secondary plot, a legend, and no labels.

5. From the Layout ribbon, choose Legend, None.

6. Right-click the pie and choose Format Data Labels. Choose Split Series by Position. Choose Second Plot Contains the Last 5 Values.

7. With the entire pie still selected, choose Shape Outline from the Format ribbon and then select black. Choose Shape Fill, White to outline all the pie slices but fill them with white.

8. From the Layout ribbon, choose Data Labels, More Data Label Options. Choose Category Name and Percentage. Uncheck the Value check box. Change the separator from a comma to a space.

9. Click the Other slice in the left pie. If the current selection drop-down in the Layout or Format ribbon does not indicate that you have select "Series x, Point n," click the Other slice again.

10. From the Format ribbon, choose Shape Fill and then select light gray.

11. In the Current Selection drop-down of the Format ribbon, choose Series Lines 1. In the Format ribbon, choose Shape Outline and then select gray. Choose Shape Outline, Dashes and then select the fourth dash choice.

12. Enlarge the chart by clicking one of the resizing handles in the border around the chart. Drag out from the center to enlarge the chart.

13. If a chart title is not visible, on the Layout ribbon, select Chart Title, Above Chart.

14. Click in the chart title twice. Select the characters and type a new title, such as `Sales by Market`, and then press the Enter key. Type the remaining three lines of the title.

15. Select the characters in the top line of the title. On the Home ribbon, choose 20 Point. Select the remaining lines of the title. On the Home ribbon, choose 18 Point.

16. Click the border of the title. On the Home ribbon, click Left Align. Drag the title so that it is left-justified above the chart.

Using a Bar of Pie Chart

The bar of pie chart is similar in concept to the pie of pie chart. In the case of bar of pie, the large slices are plotted on a main pie. The smaller slices are moved over to a column chart on the right side of the chart area. All the settings for gap width, series lines, secondary plot size, and which slices move to the second plot area are valid for the bar of pie chart.

Figure 4.28 shows a bar of pie chart. Technically, this should be called a column of pie chart, shouldn't it?

Figure 4.28
In a bar of pie chart, the smaller slices are grouped into Other, and the detail is shown in a column chart.

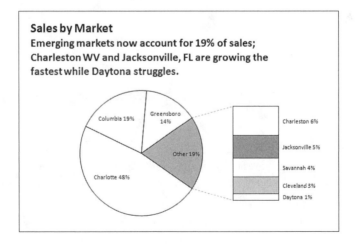

Using a Waterfall Chart to Tell the Story of Component Decomposition

As mentioned in Chapter 3, I spent a few months as a team member of a McKinsey & Company consulting gig when they were brought in to turn around the company where I used to work. McKinsey consultants were experts at creating cool charts and the waterfall chart is closely associated with that firm.

The waterfall chart is a great chart because it tells a story. If you are an NPR fan, you might have encountered Ira Glass's *This American Life* weekly radio show. Glass describes the show as a series of stories: "This happens, and then this happens, and then this happens, and then this happens…". Similarly, a waterfall chart makes a simple table into a story.

I used to use waterfall charts to analyze the profitability of a proposal. The chart would start with a tall column on the left side to show the total list price of the products we were selling. The next column appeared to float in midair, dropping down from the total list price column to show the total discount that the sales team was proposing. The next column showed net revenue. The rest of the chart was a series of floating columns that showed where all that revenue went. A tiny column on the right side showed the profit from the deal (see Figure 4.29).

4

Figure 4.29
A waterfall chart breaks a single component chart out over several columns.

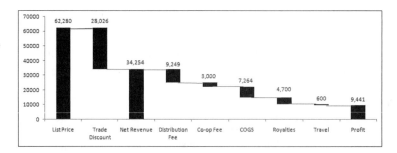

CASE STUDY

Creating a Waterfall Chart

The trick to making the middle columns float is to use a stacked column chart. The second series is the actual columns that appear on the chart. The first series is changed into an invisible color without any lines in order to make the bars in the second series appear to float.

You might start with values such as those shown in columns A and B of Figure 4.30. The trick to creating a waterfall chart is to move those values into two series. The second series is the height of each column that is actually seen. The first series is an invisible column that makes the other bars appear to float.

Figure 4.30
You break the series in column B into two series in E and F.

▲	A	B	C	D	E	F	G
1					Invisible	Visible	
2	List Price	62,280		**List Price**	0	**62,280**	
3	Trade Discount	28,026		Trade Discount	34,254	28,026	
4	Net Revenue	34,254		**Net Revenue**	0	**34,254**	
5	Distribution Fee	9,249		Distribution Fee	25,005	9,249	
6	Co-op Fee	3,000		Co-op Fee	22,005	3,000	
7	COGS	7,264		COGS	14,741	7,264	
8	Royalties	4,700		Royalties	10,041	4,700	
9	Travel	600		Travel	9,441	600	
10	Profit	9,441		**Profit**	0	**9,441**	
11							
12							

You follow these steps to create the chart shown in Figure 4.30:

1. For the three columns in the chart that touch the horizontal axis, set the invisible column to zero and the visible column to the number from column B.

2. The goal for trade discount is to have a floating bar that extends from 62,280 down to 34,254. In order to have the bar float at this level, you need an invisible bar that is 34,254 tall. Therefore, in cell E3, enter the formula =F4.

3. The height of the floating bar needs to extend from 34,254 to 62,280, so enter the formula =F2-E3 in cell F3.

4. After the Net Revenue bar are all the SG&A expenses. The height of each floating bar should be the amount of the expense. Therefore, in cell F5, enter the formula =B5. Copy this down to cells F6:F9.

5. The formula for the invisible portion of the bars is often difficult to figure out. In this case, starting at the final bar might make this easier. The Travel bar representing $600 needs to float just above the Profit bar of 9,441. Thus, enter the formula =F10 in cell E9.

6. The Royalties bar of 4,700 needs to float just above the level of the Travel bar. The height of the Travel bar is the height of the invisible bar (9441 in E9) and the height of the visible bar (500 in F9). Therefore, in cell E8 enter =E9+F9. You now have a formula that can be copied.

7. Copy cell E8 to the blank cells in E7:E5.

8. Select the range D1:F10. From the Insert ribbon, choose Column, Stacked Column.

9. Turn off the legend by selecting Legend, None from the Layout ribbon.

10. Click the lower Trade Discount bar. On the Format ribbon, choose Shape Fill, White. The lower columns disappear.

11. Select the top column. On the Format ribbon, choose Shape Fill and then select black.

12. Turn off the gridlines by selecting Gridlines, Primary Horizontal Gridlines, None on the Layout ribbon.

13. Right-click a top column and choose Add Data Labels. (Normally, you would choose to put the data labels at the outside end. However, because this is a stacked column chart, the outside end is not an option in the Format Data Labels dialog.)

14. Individually grab each label and move it to the top of the column.

15. To finish the waterfall chart, you need to draw connecting lines from the bottom of one column to the next column. Therefore, on the Insert ribbon, choose Shapes, Line. While holding down the Shift key, draw a line from the top of the first column to the top of the next column. Select Format, Shape Outline and then select black to darken the line. Repeat this step to connect all the columns.

4

A waterfall chart can be used in many situations to turn a single component column chart into a whole-page chart. These charts present a dramatic picture of all the components in a process.

Next Steps

In Chapter 5, "Creating Charts That Show Relationships," you'll learn how to create charts that highlight relationships. Although scientists often make use of scatter charts, you will see that you can use them in a variety of ways in business when you want to demonstrate a correlation (or the lack of a correlation). In addition, radar charts are appropriate for conducting annual performance reviews. Chapter 5 also takes a look at surface charts and frequency distributions.

Creating Charts That Show Relationships

Comparing Two Variables on a Chart

The chart types discussed in this chapter are unusual: Scatter, radar, bubble, and surface charts are probably the least understood Excel charts.

Both scatter and bubble charts show the interplay between two or three different variables. They require a bit of care in setting up the data. A scatter chart can help you to figure out whether there is a correlation between two variables. A bubble chart has the unique ability to provide data about a third dimension. The first section in this chapter covers the mechanics of creating scatter charts.

When you are thinking about creating scatter charts to show a relationship, you might need to consider alternative charts, such as a paired bar chart, a paired chart, or a frequency distribution. The second section in this chapter compares the message that you convey with the various chart types. That section describes charts created by charting celebrities such as Gene Zelazny, Kathy Villella, and Alfred E. Neumann.

Radar charts are rarely seen but are great for providing performance reviews. A radar chart can show, for example, how a person scored on 5 to 10 key indicators as spokes emanating from a central point.

Surface charts actually attempt to show a 3-D surface floating above an x,y grid. It is difficult to find a dataset that looks cool with a surface chart, and after you've found an appropriate dataset, it is often difficult to actually make out the valleys that might occur within the dataset.

The first part of this chapter discusses scatter charts in detail. Although it is easy enough to create a simple scatter chart, many annoying complications can occur when you want to add new data series to the chart or when you want to try to label the chart.

Using XY Scatter Charts to Plot Pairs of Data Points

Figure 5.1 shows a table of average January temperatures for selected U.S. cities. There is no trend or pattern to this data.

Figure 5.1
When this data is plotted on a column chart, there is no pattern to the data.

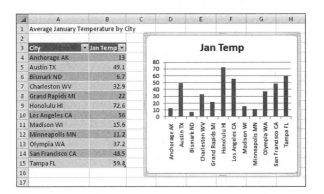

What are the likely causes of variability in January temperature? You might theorize that the most likely cause would be distance from the equator. In Figure 5.2, a new column B shows the latitude of each city. This dataset is perfect for an XY scatter chart. The latitudes in column B represent an independent variable. The temperatures in column C represent a dependent variable. A scatter chart plots one data marker for every pair of latitude and temperature data. In this case, the latitude will be plotted along the x-axis, and the temperature will be plotted along the y-axis.

Figure 5.2
You can plot latitude and temperature on a scatter chart to understand the relationship between the values.

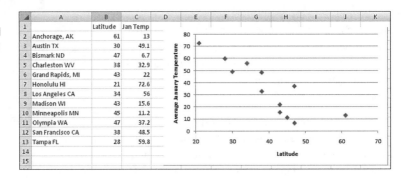

The chart in Figure 5.2 shows a relationship between latitude and temperature: as latitude increases, temperature decreases. You can therefore say that latitude and temperature are inversely related.

> **TIP** If your data is not sorted, you should be sure to choose Scatter with Only Markers as the chart type.

Adding a Trendline to a Scatter Chart

To add a tight grid and a trendline to a scatter chart, you choose Layout 3 from the Chart Layouts gallery on the Design ribbon. The trendline represents the best-fit line, given the data points. If the trendline is angled diagonally from bottom left to top right, it indicates that the x and y variables appear to be directly related. If the trendline is angled from top left to bottom right, it indicates that the x and y variables appear to be inversely related. In Figure 5.3, the trendline confirms that there is an inverse relationship between temperature and latitude.

Figure 5.3
You can add a trendline to confirm the inverse relationship.

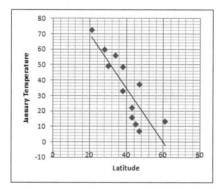

Excel uses a best fit to draw the trendline. Even when there is absolutely no correlation at all between the columns of data, Excel forces a line to fit. In Figure 5.4, the x and y data is random. A horizontal trendline basically represents the average of all the dots, but it does not indicate any correlation.

In Figure 5.4, Excel has added the equation for the trendline and the R-squared value. An R-squared value close to 1 indicates a near-perfect correlation. An R-squared value of 0 confirms that there is not a correlation between the x and y values. To add this equation to your chart, you follow these steps:

1. Select the chart.
2. On the Layout ribbon, choose Trendline, More Trendline Options.

3. In the Format Trendline dialog that appears, choose Display Equation on Chart and Display R-squared Value on Chart. Both settings are near the bottom of the dialog, as shown in Figure 5.5.

Figure 5.4
Although a scatter chart of random data might produce a trendline, there is no correlation.

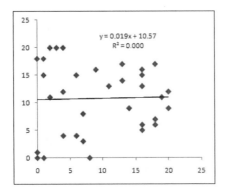

Figure 5.5
You can add a trendline formula to the chart by using this dialog.

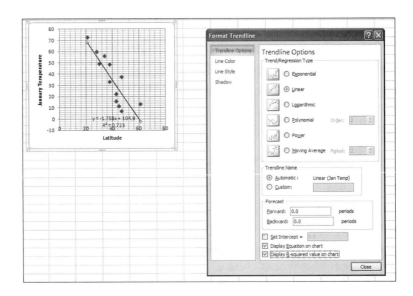

Adding Labels to a Scatter Chart

When you create most other charts in this book, the first column contain labels. In Figure 5.2, there are city names in column A, but they are not part of the dataset. This is annoying. When you click a data point and choose to display the label, you can see that the data point is at 47 latitude and has an average temperature of 37.2. However, you have to scan through the original dataset to see that the data point in question is from Olympia, Washington (see Figure 5.6).

Figure 5.6
It would be good if you could change the label from the x and y values to the label in column A.

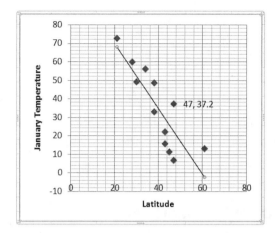

One solution is to write a tiny bit of VBA macro code:

```
Sub AttachLabelsToPoints()
   Dim Counter As Integer, ChartName As String, xVals As String

   'Store the formula for the first series in "xVals".
   xVals = ActiveChart.SeriesCollection(1).Formula

   'Extract the range for the data from xVals.
   xVals = Mid(xVals, InStr(InStr(xVals, ","), xVals, _
      Mid(Left(xVals, InStr(xVals, "!") - 1), 9)))
   xVals = Left(xVals, InStr(InStr(xVals, "!"), xVals, ",") - 1)
   Do While Left(xVals, 1) = ","
      xVals = Mid(xVals, 2)
   Loop

   'Attach a label to each data point in the chart.
   For Counter = 1 To Range(xVals).Cells.Count
     ActiveChart.SeriesCollection(1).Points(Counter).HasDataLabel = _
         True
     ActiveChart.SeriesCollection(1).Points(Counter).DataLabel.Text = _
         Range(xVals).Cells(Counter, 1).Offset(0, -1).Value
   Next Counter

End Sub
```

If you select the chart and then run this macro, Excel displays the label next to each data point, as shown in Figure 5.7. This is a useful addition to the chart.

> **TIP**
> If you are not comfortable with VBA, you can download a free add-in, the XY Chart Labeler, from Rob Bovey, at www.appspro.com/Utilities/ChartLabeler.htm.

Figure 5.7
Relevant labels for XY charts are an asset. Why does Microsoft make it so hard to add them?

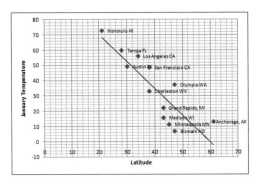

Joining the Points in a Scatter Chart with Lines

Of the five types of scatter chart types in the Change Chart Type dialog shown in Figure 5.8, four are dots joined using lines.

Figure 5.8
Most of the scatter charts are dots joined with lines.

However, whereas the dot version of a scatter chart can be sequenced in any order, chaos results if you try to join the dots with lines. In Figure 5.9, a familiar curve turns to spaghetti when the dots are joined with lines.

Figure 5.9
Chaos results when an unsorted XY chart is joined with lines.

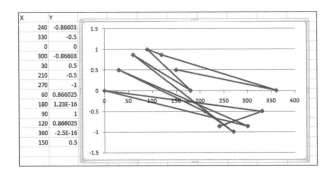

In Figure 5.10, using a line to join exactly the same dataset as in Figure 5.9 appears orderly. If you plan on joining points with a line, you need to sort the underlying data into ascending sequence by the x value.

Figure 5.10
If your data is sorted into ascending sequence by the x value, either a straight line or smooth line will work.

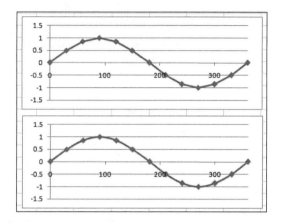

The bottom chart in Figure 5.10 uses Scatter with Smooth Lines and Markers. The top chart in Figure 5.10 uses Scatter with Straight Lines and Markers. The difference is barely perceptible: The line in the bottom chart is just slightly smoother.

If you use Scatter with Straight Lines and Markers when fewer data points are available, the curve is not as well defined (see the top chart in Figure 5.11). You can use Scatter Chart with Curved Lines and Markers to have Excel extrapolate and fill in the curve (as in the bottom chart in Figure 5.11).

Figure 5.11
A smoothed line is particularly important with sparse data.

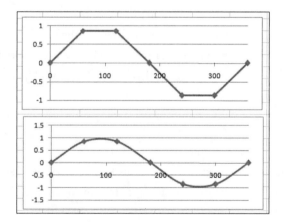

Adding a Second Series to an XY Chart

It is fairly unintuitive to plot a pair of XY series on a single chart: you create a chart for a single series and then use the Select Data icon to add the second series.

You follow these steps to create an XY chart with two series:

1. Start with an XY series in two columns. In Figure 5.12, for example, the XY series is in columns B and C.

Figure 5.12
You can create a chart with an XY series.

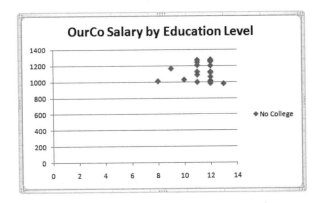

2. Add the label for this series in the cell above the y points column (for example, the No College heading in C1).

3. Create an XY chart from the data in B1:C24. The initial legend is No College. Leave this legend as it is.

4. Change the title from No College to a title that covers both series.

5. Enter a new series in columns F:G. Enter the label for the second series in cell G1.

6. Click the chart to select the chart and bring back the Charting Tools ribbon.

7. From the Design ribbon, click the Select Data icon. Excel displays the Select Data Source dialog.

8. Click the Add button in the Legend Entries section of the dialog. Excel displays the Edit Series dialog.

9. Click in the Series Name box and choose cell G1.

10. Click in the Series X Value box. Highlight cells F2:F15 in the worksheet.

11. Click in the Series Y Values box and backspace to remove the default value of 1. Click the Refers To box and highlight G2:G15. Excel adds sheet names and the dollar signs to make the references absolute, as shown in Figure 5.13.

12. Click OK to close the Edit Series dialog. Click OK to return to the worksheet.

The final chart is shown in Figure 5.14.

Figure 5.13
You specify the new series in the Edit Series dialog.

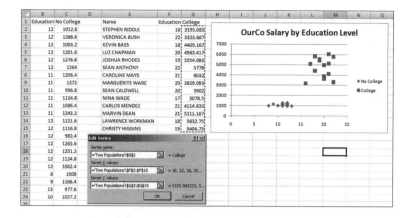

Figure 5.14
This chart compares two XY series.

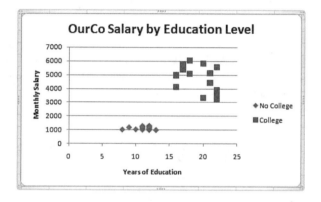

Drawing with a Scatter Chart

An unusual use for XY scatter charts with straight lines is to make crude drawings on a chart.

To create a drawing, it helps to trace your drawing onto quadrille graph paper first. You need to choose a point where the left edge and bottom edge cross. This will be the (0,0) point. For every point in the drawing, you enter the x and y location. The x location is the number of gridlines from the left edge of the chart to that point. The y location is the distance from the bottom of the chart to the point.

If you need to draw a curve, you can choose as many points as possible around the perimeter of the curve. The more points you can plot, the smoother the curve.

Figure 5.15 shows an x and y dataset.

Figure 5.15
You can transfer points from a drawing into columns for x and y.

	A	B
1	X	Y
2	0	3
3	5.5	7
4	5	11
5	7.5	11
6	8	9
7	10.8	11
8	13.5	11
9	8.2	6.7
10	8.8	3
11	11.5	2.7
12	6.25	0.5
13	5.9	4.7
14	3.5	2.5
15	3.7	0
16	0	3

Next, you select the data from A2:B16. From the Insert ribbon, you choose Insert, Scatter, Scatter with Straight Lines (that is, the thumbnail with straight lines and no markers). Excel creates the chart shown in Figure 5.16.

Figure 5.16
Excel connects the x and y points to create a simple drawing. See Figure 7.46 in Chapter 7, "Advanced Chart Techniques," for an over-the-top example of this technique.

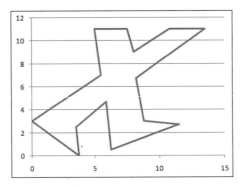

Using Charts to Show Relationships

There are several types of charts that can be used to illustrate the relationship between two variables.

- **Scatter charts** are particularly well suited to comparing two variables that you think might be related. While you can use scatter plots with large datasets, they are limited in that it is very difficult to label the points without using some VBA or an add-in. If you have a small dataset, you can use a paired bar chart to see the same information, and this chart also adds a label so that you can see which records are not in line with the others.

- In some cases, a **pair of matching charts** allows the reader to compare two variables to see if there is a relationship.

- In the real world, it is rare to find a value that is influenced by only one variable. Usually, a whole host of factors contribute to a result. A **bubble chart** is a special type of XY scatter chart that attempts to show the interplay between three variables. Bubble charts are best used with small datasets.

- **Radar charts** are rarely used charts that allow you to see the relationship between four to six variables.

- In some cases, you might have a population of results and be trying to figure out whether any patterns exist in one variable. In these cases, use of the FREQUENCY function allows you to make sense of the data by grouping members into similar categories and then comparing the categories.

Testing Correlation Using a Scatter Chart

The dataset for a scatter chart is composed of two variables for every row in the dataset. The values in the first column are plotted along the horizontal axis. The values in the second column are plotted along the vertical axis. The heading for the second column becomes the name of that series.

In Figure 5.17, the data in B2:B15 represents a price survey of regional car dealerships for a particular model of vehicle. Each pair of numbers in a row represents the data for a single car. Mileage is in the first column, and price is in the second column. In theory, you would expect that as the miles go up on a car, the price would come down.

Figure 5.17
The default scatter chart at the top requires some formatting before it can be useful.

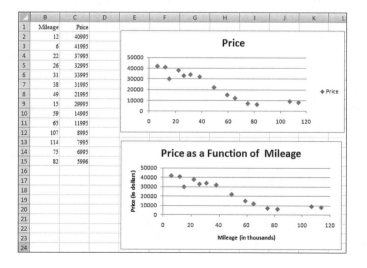

If you select the data from B1:C15 and insert a scatter chart, Excel provides the chart shown in the top of Figure 5.17. The chart needs some labels to tell the complete story. You follow these steps to format the chart to look like the bottom chart in Figure 5.17:

1. From the Layout ribbon, choose Legend, None to remove the legend.
2. From the Layout ribbon, choose Axis Titles, Primary Horizontal Axis Title, Title Below Axis to add the words Axis Title below the horizontal axis.
3. Click Axis Title and type the new axis title `Mileage (in thousands)`.
4. From the Layout ribbon, choose Axis Titles, Primary Vertical Axis Title, Rotated Title to add the words "Axis Title" to the left of the vertical axis.
5. Click the Axis Title and type the new axis title of `Price (in dollars)`.
6. Click the title and type a more descriptive title, such as `Price as a Function of Mileage`.

In Figure 5.17, it definitely appears that there is a fairly strong relationship between mileage and price. Because the dots slant from top left to bottom right, the variables have an inverse relationship.

You can ask Excel to do a least-squares regression and fit a trendline to the points plotted on the chart. One of the trendline options is to display the regression equation and the R-squared value on the chart. (Remember that R-squared is a measure of how well a trend-line matches the points. R-squared ranges from 0 to 1, with 1 meaning a nearly perfect correlation.)

Figure 5.18 shows three different scatter charts. The top chart has a perfect correlation and an R-squared value of 1. The next chart has just a small bit of variation. Individual points appear close to the trendline but are sometimes a bit above or below it. This provides an R-squared value of 0.995. The bottom chart looks like a shotgun blast. There doesn't appear to be any correlation between those variables, and Excel reports an R-squared value of 0.003. If the dataset is truly random, the trendline is often a straight horizontal line, drawn through the value that marks the average of all of the points.

5

Figure 5.18
R-squared is a measure of how well a trendline fits the points in a chart.

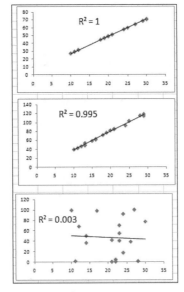

There are a few different ways to add a trendline and the R-squared value to a chart. One way is to follow these steps:

1. Select the chart.

2. From the Layout ribbon, choose Trendline, More Trendline Options.

3. Choose Linear as the trend/regression type.

4. In the bottom of the Format Trendline dialog, choose either Display Equation on Chart or Display R-squared Value on Chart.

5. If you want only the R-squared value on the chart, choose the Line Color style and move the Transparency slider to 100%.

In Figure 5.19, the R-squared value has been added to both charts. Price and mileage have an R-squared value of 0.849. Price and age have an R-squared value of 0.944. While both sets have correlations, the age of the car seems to have more of an impact on price than does mileage.

Figure 5.19
Based on the R-squared values, age is a better predictor of price than is mileage.

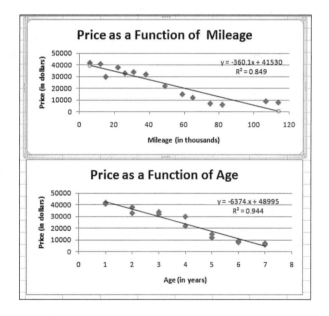

Using Paired Bars to Show Relationships

A scatter chart lacks any easy ability to label the points with identifying names. If you need to compare two variables and have around a dozen points, a paired bar chart can be more effective than a scatter chart. For example, Figure 5.20 shows a preference for ice cream, based on a survey of two groups, kids and adults.

The chart is sorted by the kids' preference. Any bars toward the bottom of the chart that have a sizable presence on the right are flavors that grow in popularity as the respondents mature.

Figure 5.20
A paired bar chart allows you to compare values for two populations.

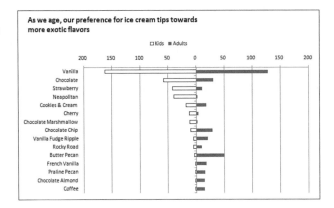

To create this chart in Excel, you need to use a little trickery in several steps. This is a stacked bar chart. The values for the left bar have to be in the Excel table as negative in order to force them to stretch leftward from the axis.

You follow these steps to create the chart in Figure 5.20:

1. Sort your original data so that it is in descending order, by the first series.

2. Copy the dataset to the right of the original dataset. In the copy of the dataset, enter the formula -B2 in cell F2 to create a negative value for the first series (see Figure 5.21).

Figure 5.21
You can use a formula to make the first series negative.

F2		f_x =-B2	

	A	B	C	D	E	F	G
1	Flavor	Kids	Adults		Flavor	Kids	Adults
2	Vanilla	162	128		Vanilla	-162	128
3	Chocolate	58	31		Chocolate	-58	31
4	Strawberr	42	11		Strawberr	-42	11
5	Neapolita	40	2		Neapolita	-40	2
6	Cookies &	18	18		Cookies &	-18	18
7	Cherry	12	4		Cherry	-12	4
8	Chocolate	11	2		Chocolate	-11	2
9	Chocolate	10	29		Chocolate	-10	29
10	Vanilla Fu	5	21		Vanilla Fu	-5	21
11	Rocky Roa	5	10		Rocky Roa	-5	10
12	Butter Pec	3	50		Butter Pec	-3	50
13	French Va	1	18		French Va	-1	18
14	Praline Pe	1	16		Praline Pe	-1	16
15	Chocolate	1	15		Chocolate	-1	15
16	Coffee	1	15		Coffee	-1	15

3. Select the data for your chart. Press Ctrl+1 to display the Format Cells dialog box. On the Number tab, choose the Custom category and type the custom number code 0;0. Click OK. The negative numbers in column F are now displayed without the minus sign.

> **NOTE**
> While you are likely to type only a single format as your custom number format, the field is allowed to have up to four "zones," separated by semicolons. If you have two zones, the first format is for positive numbers, and the second format is for negative numbers. For example, the code 0; -0 would display numbers as positive and negative. The code 0; (0) would display the negative numbers in parentheses. The code 0; would hide the negative numbers. The code 0;0 would actually force the negative numbers to display without the minus sign and without parentheses. It is difficult to imagine why anyone would want to show negative numbers without the minus sign, until you consider our current example, where it certainly comes in handy.

4. From the Insert ribbon, choose Bar, Stacked Bar. Excel creates the chart shown in Figure 5.22. Note that the custom number format from step 3 carries through to the horizontal axis labels. Even though the kids' numbers are stored as negative, the numbers to the left of the midpoint are shown as positive.

Figure 5.22
Excel displays the start of a paired bar chart.

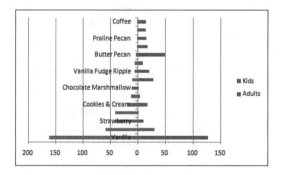

5. From the Layout ribbon, choose Legend, Top to move the legend to the top. Moving the legend changes the legend to a landscape orientation, with the first series on the left and the second series on the right. This arrangement matches the data in the chart.

6. Resize the chart vertically to allow enough room for each category name to appear along the axis.

7. Choose Vertical (Value) Axis from the Current Selection drop-down on the Layout ribbon. Then choose the Categories in Reverse Order check box (the fourth selection in the Axis Options panel).

N O T E Steps 8 and 9 are both optional, but they both involve the horizontal axis. If you plan to do either step, choose Horizontal (Category) Axis from the Current Selection drop-down and choose Format Selection.

8. (Optional) The initial chart is not quite symmetrical, running to 200 on the kids' side and to only 150 on the adults' side. To correct this, specify a fixed minimum of –200 and a fixed maximum of 200.

9. (Optional) Initially, the category labels overwrite the left bars. You have to decide how annoyed you are by this. It might be best to keep the labels there. If you want to move them to the left, select Low from the Axis Labels drop-down.

This example creates a chart that plots a frequency distribution for two populations. While it allows you to compare the preferences of the populations, the case study that follows provides another example of a paired bar chart that lets you examine the correlation between two variables, just as you would do in a scatter chart.

CASE STUDY

Comparing the Relationship Between Discount and Sales

OurCo employs a staff of 10 sales reps. The sales reps are given a fair amount of discretion in offering sales discounts. A rep is authorized to offer a new customer discount in order to secure a deal. A rep can also offer a large volume discount in order to get the customer to increase the size of an order. Over the years, some of the veteran sales reps have created their own discounts. As long as the order comes in with some reasonable explanation of why the customer was offered a discount, the order is approved. In reality, no one in order processing has ever questioned any discount. There are no checks and balances.

The sales manager defends the discounting practice, asserting that discounting leads to larger sales volumes. While this could be true, it could also be that less savvy sales reps are using the discount as a crutch when they should be selling on value.

You produce the table in Figure 5.23. If you print this out and take it to the sales manager and, worse, his boss, their eyes will glaze over.

Figure 5.23
This table doesn't reveal many trends.

	A	B	C
1	REP	List Price	Revenue
2	Anita	167835	125876
3	Chad	121842	112095
4	Clara	137095	116531
5	Jessica	90943	84577
6	Marlene	85823	74666
7	Nathan	117112	111256
8	Roy	125019	98765
9	Terry	93104	79138
10	Travis	112962	85851
11	Viola	127573	105886
12			

A better presentation for the same data would be the chart in Figure 5.24. If higher discounts lead to higher sales, then the revenue bars on the right would also be sorted from longest to shortest. However, the rep with the lowest discount (Nathan) happens to have one of the highest sales volumes.

Figure 5.24

If higher discounts lead to higher sales, the bars on the right would be sorted from longest to shortest.

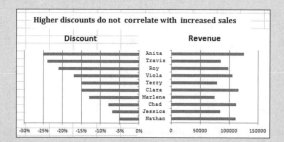

You follow these steps to build a paired bar chart to compare discount with revenue:

1. In cell D1, enter the heading Rep. In cell D2, enter =A2. Select D2. Double-click the fill handle to copy the formula down to D11.

2. In cell E1, enter the heading Revenue. In cell E2, enter the formula =C2 in order to copy revenue over to column E.

3. Repeat step 1 in column F to build rep names in column F.

4. Enter the heading Discount in cell G1. Enter the formula =(C2/B2)-1 in cell G2 to calculate discount from a list as a percentage. Select cell G2 and double-click the fill handle to copy the chart down to G11.

5. Select one cell in column G. Choose ZA ↓ from the Data ribbon to sort the data with the smallest discount at the top.

6. Select cells D1:E11. Next, you are going to create the left and right halves of the chart in different steps. The data in cells D1:E11 will be used for the Revenue side of the chart.

7. From the Insert ribbon, choose Bar, 2-D Bar, Clustered Bar. Excel creates a bar chart for revenue. You want to completely format this chart first.

8. From the Layout ribbon, choose Legend, No Legend.

9. Click the border of the chart to select the chart area. From the Format ribbon, choose Shape Outline, None. This will allow you to later arrange the two charts without anyone knowing that they are not the same chart.

10. Drag the chart to the lower-right corner of your screen.

11. Click the border of the chart. Start to drag to the left. After you start to drag, press and hold down Ctrl+Shift. The Ctrl key tells Excel that you want to make a copy of the object. The Shift key constrains the movement in one direction. If you move to the left, the copy will be exactly the same vertical location as the original.

12. Click outside the new chart and then click in the new chart.

13. You don't need the names along the vertical axis. From the Layout ribbon, choose Axes, Primary Vertical Axis, No Axis.

5

14. You should see a blue box around the revenue cells in column E. Click the border of the blue outline and drag it to the right so that it surrounds the discounts in column G. Because those values are negative, the chart flips around, and the bars extend left from an axis on the right side of the chart.

> **NOTE** It is worth noting that if both of your series were positive, you would need to convert the series for the left chart to be negative. For this, you would use the custom format code 0;0 discussed earlier in this chapter.

15. Drag the green box around Revenue in E1 over to the Discount heading in G1.

16. Click the border of the chart on the left. From the Format ribbon, choose Shape Fill, None to make the area outside the plot area transparent. Doing this allows you to move the chart on the left very close to the axis labels of the chart on the right.

There is one remaining problem: The names along the vertical axis of the right chart are right-aligned. To center-align these labels between the two charts, one approach is to add extra spaces to the right side of the short names in order to move them away from the axis. This trick works best when the labels are in a fixed-width font, such as Courier New. To center the names, you follow these steps:

1. Enter this formula in cell D2:

   ```
   =A2&REPT(CHAR(160),ROUNDUP(4-LEN(A2)/2,0))
   ```

   Copy this formula down to the other rows.

2. Click the labels along the vertical axis. On the Home ribbon, choose Courier New from the Font drop-down.

3. If necessary, drag the chart on the left into position. Remember to hold down the Shift key while you drag the chart to constrain the movement in only one direction. This enables you to move the chart sideways without moving it up or down.

Several important steps are necessary to pull off the chart trick. By making one chart and then copying it, you are sure that both charts have the same height and scale. By using No Line on both charts and No Fill on the left chart, you remove many of the clues that this is really two charts.

The title above the chart in Figure 5.24 is a text box. To create the text box, you follow these steps:

1. On the Insert ribbon, choose the Text Box icon.

2. Drag in the spreadsheet above the charts and type a title.

3. Click the border of the text box and use the formatting tools on the Home ribbon to adjust the font size.

The following section describes an example of a paired bar chart.

DESIGNING CHARTS LIKE THE PROS

Kathy Villella: Comparing Three Variables with a Paired Bar Chart

The paired bar chart discussed here is particularly difficult to emulate in Excel. It is a chart from Kathy Villella, the founder of PowerFrameworks.com. Kathy shows this chart in PowerPoint, but it is created using a custom template.

Kathy emphasizes that you should always have the larger numbers on the left of a chart. The chart in Figure 5.25 compares the revenue of one company to the revenue of an entire industry. The numbers for the entire industry should appear on the left.

Figure 5.25
This paired bar chart compares one company to the entire industry, providing information for both industry segment and region.

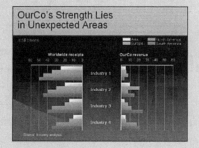

To emulate this chart in Excel, you follow these steps:

1. Set up the data in A2:E6 of Figure 5.26 to create the chart shown on the right in Figure 5.25. Put the industry labels across cells B2:B6. Put the regions in cells A3:A6. (The title in cell A1 is there for convenience only.)

2. Copy cells A1:E6 to A8. Change the second dataset to include data to create the chart on the left in Figure 5.25.

3. Select cells A2:E6. From the Insert ribbon, choose Bar, 2-D Bar, Clustered Bar.

4. In the Design ribbon, open the Chart Styles gallery. Choose one of the styles that show various shades of blue.

5. Initially, the chart shows a scale from 0 to 30. You need to make this large enough to match the chart on the left side. Right-click the numbers along the horizontal axis and do the following:
   - Choose Format Axis.
   - Choose Maximum, Fixed, 60.
   - Choose Major Unit, Fixed, 10.

6. Right-click the labels along the vertical axis and then choose Format Axis. Click Categories in Reverse Order.

7. From the Layout ribbon, choose Legend, Show Legend at Top.

8. Click the resizing handle for the chart on the right side and drag to the left to make the chart more like a square than a rectangle.

5

Figure 5.26
The final Excel chart emulates Kathy Villella's chart.

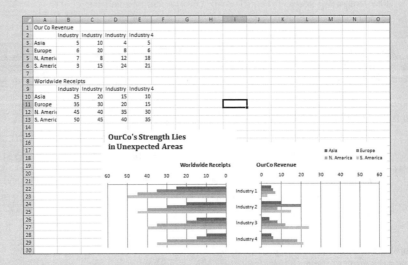

9. From the Layout ribbon, choose Chart Title, Above Chart. Excel adds a chart, centered above the left chart, above the legend, and a bit too large. Click the Chart Title and type the new title OurCo Revenue. Click the border of the title to select it. From the Home ribbon, click the Decrease Font Size button until the title is about 12 point. Drag the title so that it appears flush with the left vertical axis. This causes the title to overlay part of the legend.

10. Drag the legend to the upper-right corner of the chart. The legend will be one row tall by four columns wide. Resize the legend, making it about half as wide and more than twice as tall. This action should convince Excel to show the legend in a two-by-two arrangement. If you see only two of the four parts of the legend, click the Decrease Font Size button on the Home ribbon until the legend appears in a two-by-two arrangement.

11. Click the chart area. From the Format ribbon, choose Shape Outline, No Outline. This removes the line from around the entire chart. Because the final product actually contains two charts, you don't want a border around just one of the charts.

12. Make a copy of the original chart. Click the border of the chart and drag it to the left. After you start to drag, hold down Ctrl+Shift. Drop the new chart just to the left of the original chart. The copy of the chart still points at B2:E7.

13. While the new chart is selected, there is a blue border around B3:E7. Click this border and drag it down so that it encompasses B10:E12. The green border automatically moves to A10:A13. However, the purple border stays around B2:E2. This is okay.

14. Right-click the values along the top of the chart. Choose Format Axis. Choose Values in Reverse Order and click OK to reverse the direction of the bars so that they run from right to left. You still have to remove the vertical axis labels from the left chart and the legend from the left chart. This will cause the perfectly sized plot area on the left chart to resize.

15. Click the Legend in the chart on the left and press the Delete key.

16. Click the labels along the vertical axis in the chart on the left and press the Delete key.

17. Click the plot area. Use the top resizing handle to pull the top of the chart down so that it is even with the top of the chart on the right. As you are dragging, there are two dotted rectangles. You want to focus on the top of the inner rectangle to line it up with the top of the plot area on the right chart.

18. In the chart on the left, change the OurCo Revenue title to `Worldwide Receipts`. Click the border of the title. Hold down the Shift key while you drag this title so that it is flush with the right side of the axis. After you have deleted the axis labels from the chart, Excel stretches the plot area to fill the entire chart area.

19. Resize the plot area either with VBA or by selecting Shapes, Lines, Line from the Insert ribbon. Draw a horizontal line below the chart on the right. The line is a measuring tool; draw it from the left baseline to the right plot area. It is important that this line be outside the chart area; you want to draw the line on the spreadsheet.

20. Move the line so that it is under the chart on the left. The right side of the line should line up with the right edge of the plot area. This line provides a guideline in step 21. As you are resizing the chart, keep adjusting until the plot area is the correct size.

21. Click the chart area of the chart on the left. Drag the left resizing handle toward the center of the chart. Release the handle and see if the plot area is about the same size as the line underneath the chart. This is a trial-and-error method. Keep resizing until the plot area and the line are roughly the same size.

22. From the Insert ribbon, click the Text Box icon. Drag to draw a new text box above the charts. In the text box, type the title `OurCo's Strength Lies`, press Enter, and type `in Unexpected Areas`. Click the border of the text box to select the text box. From the Home ribbon, change the font to Cambria, change the size to 16 point, and click the Bold button. From the Format ribbon, choose Shape Outline, None. Drag the title into position so that it appears that it is lined up with the left edge of the chart on the left.

The final chart is shown in Figure 5.26.

> **NOTE** Kathy Villella offers templates to help you communicate effectively with PowerPoint and charts at www.PowerFrameworks.com. Thanks to Kathy for donating this chart!

Using Paired Matching Charts

Since 1950, the "usual gang of idiots" have been satirizing popular culture at *MAD Magazine*. Writers Dan Birthcer and George Woodbridge inadvertently came up with an interesting way of comparing two independent variables in the October 1991 panel described in the following section.

DESIGNING CHARTS LIKE THE PROS

MAD Magazine: Creating a Paired Comparison Chart

A *MAD Magazine* article titled "Cause or Coincidence" in October 1991 fictitiously tried to show a relationship between two variables. The writers would hypothesize that the rise in missing person reports happened to coincide with the increase in David Copperfield performances. Of course, not all of the charts were exactly politically correct. Figure 5.27 shows a modern-day version of a *MAD* chart illustrated by Bob D'Amico.

> **NOTE**
> If you are a fan of *MAD*, check out issue 306, pp 30-31, to see all nine of the chart comparisons. A DVD of every *MAD* published from 1950 through 2005 was published in 2006.

Figure 5.27
These chart pairs ponder if there is a causal relationship between two variables.

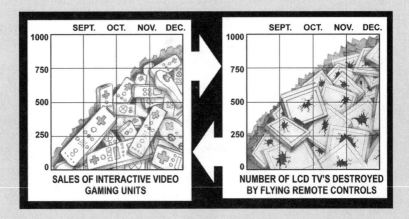

Figure 5.28 shows a similar pair of charts in Excel. To create this illustration, you use two series in each chart. The first series provides a solid background and a line for the area chart. The second series provides the illustration for the area chart.

You follow these steps to create a paired comparison chart in Excel:

1. Set up a dataset in A1:B6 with the information for the left chart. Copy the data in B2:B6 to C2. Add the heading `Football 2` in C1. The data in C1 will become the second series that is used to hold the graphic to fill the area underneath the line.

2. Select A1:C6. From the Insert ribbon, choose Area, 2-D Area, Area.

3. Add vertical gridlines by choosing Gridlines, Primary Vertical Gridlines, Major Gridlines on the Layout ribbon.

4. Add a title by choosing Chart Title, Above Chart on the Layout ribbon. Type a title such as `Football Wins`.

Figure 5.28
This Excel chart approximates the *MAD* chart.

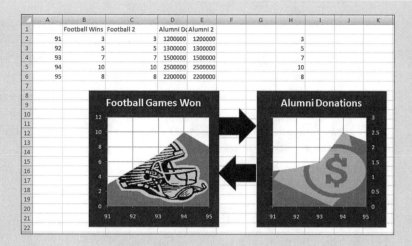

5. Click the area chart. To select the second series, from the Insert ribbon, choose Clip Art to display the Clip Art pane. Search clips for football. When you find a suitable one, click the arrow for the drop-down list to the right of that clip and then choose Copy. Press Ctrl+V to paste the clip art into your chart. Most of the Microsoft clips have transparent backgrounds. The Series 1 area, which is the same size and shape as Series 2, will provide a colored background for the transparent clip art.

6. Remove the Legend by choosing Legend, None on the Layout ribbon.

7. Click on the chart area (that is, the area inside the chart border but outside the plot area). From the Format ribbon, choose Shape Fill and choose a light blue fill. You will actually use a dark fill later, but the light blue provides the necessary contrast for step 8.

8. Click the title. From the Home ribbon, choose a white font. Click the vertical axis labels and choose white from the font color drop-down. Do the same for the horizontal axis labels.

9. Click the chart area and then choose Format, Shape Fill and select either a black or dark blue fill.

10. Because the chart is wider than it is tall, shrink the width of the chart so that the chart is just slightly taller than it is wide by dragging a resize handle.

11. You can now make a copy of the chart. Click the chart border and drag to the right. After you start to drag, hold down Ctrl+Shift. Drag the chart far enough that you have about a one-column split between the charts.

12. Set up a column for alumni donations in column D and a column with identical numbers but the heading `Alumni2` in column E.

13. Click the plot area of the second chart (being careful not to select gridlines or the data series). Excel draws a blue border around cells B2:C6. Grab the edge of the blue border and drag to the right so that it surrounds D2:E6. The green outline in B2:B6 also gets copied to D1:E1.

14. Change the title of the second chart to `Alumni Donations`.

15. Notice that the plot area on the right side is a bit smaller than the plot area on the left. This is because the numeric labels are longer on the right chart. Choose the labels along the vertical axis. Right-click and choose Format Axis. For Display Units, choose Millions. For the Axis Labels drop-down, choose High. Click Close. The axis labels move to the right side of the chart.

16. In the Clip Art pane, search for Dollar or Money. Choose one of the clip art icons and choose Copy from the drop-down list on the right. Click the football helmet in the new chart. From the Layout ribbon, the Current Selection drop-down indicates that Series Alumni 2 is selected. Press Ctrl+V to paste the money clip art into that chart. The final steps are to draw in the arrows.

17. From the Insert ribbon, choose Insert, Shapes, Block Arrow, Right Arrow. From the Format ribbon, choose Shape Fill and then choose a black fill. Choose Shape Outline, Black.

18. To add a second arrow, press Ctrl+C when the first arrow is selected. Click a new cell and press Ctrl+V to paste a new arrow. While holding down the Shift key, use the green outline to spin the arrow so it is pointing left.

19. If necessary, nudge the charts so that the arrows touch each chart.

Thanks to the usual gang of idiots at *MAD Magazine* for providing the concept for this chart.

Adding a Third Dimension with a Bubble Chart

A bubble chart attempts to add a third piece of information to each point in an XY scatter chart. In a bubble chart, the size of the marker varies, based on the third data point for each marker.

The best time to use a bubble chart is when you have a sparse dataset. The size of the bubbles makes it difficult to read the chart when you have too many data points on the chart.

Figure 5.29 shows a bubble chart. The size of each bubble is based on the selling price for a particular model of car. The location of the bubble along the horizontal axis indicates the age of the car. The location of the bubble along the vertical axis shows the mileage of the car.

In theory, cars that are older or have higher mileage should have lower prices. However, you can find some bubbles where the seller of an older car is asking for more money.

Here are some tips for creating bubble charts:

- You should always leave the heading off the top-left cell in the data range. This rule applies any time you have numbers as the first column of your dataset. It is particularly important with bubble charts.

- The initial size of the bubbles is always too large (initially scaled to 100%). If you see too much overlap in the bubbles, you can right-click a bubble and choose Format Data Series. In Figure 5.29, the bubbles are scaled down to 30% in order to prevent excessive overlapping.

- There is an option in the Format Series dialog to have the size data translated into the area of the bubble or the width of the bubble. You should always choose the area of the bubble.

Figure 5.29
This bubble chart shows the relationship between age, mileage, and price.

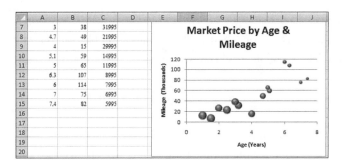

In both charts shown in Figure 5.30, each bubble is two times larger than the previous bubble. The top chart includes the option that the size of data in the third column affects the area of the bubble. This is the default setting, and it is the correct setting. If you instead decide to tie the data in the table to the width of the bubble, you violate the pictograph rule. When you are using pictures for markers, you should increase the marker in only one dimension, not in both dimensions.

Figure 5.30
The width setting in the bottom chart creates the false impression that the bubble is four times larger than the previous bubble.

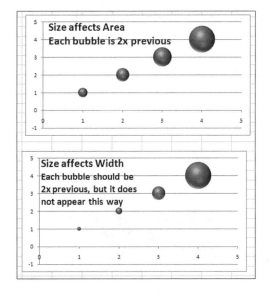

The area of a circle is determined with the formula `PI()` * `Radius^2`. If you have one bubble that is double the size of another and you attempt to demonstrate this by doubling the radius, the actual area of the circle increases geometrically. This is misleading.

To create the chart in Figure 5.29, you follow these steps:

1. Set up your data with age in column A, mileage in column B, and price in column C. It is okay to have headings above the data in columns B and C.

2. Select cells A1:C15.

3. From the Insert ribbon, choose Other Charts, Bubble, Bubble with a 3-D Effect.

4. Right-click one bubble and choose Format Series. Change the Scale Bubble Size value from 100 to 30.

5. Right-click the numbers along the vertical axis and choose Format Axis. Change Minimum to Fixed, 0.

6. From the Layout ribbon, choose Legend, None.

7. From the Layout ribbon, choose Chart Title, Above Chart. Click the title and type a new title.

8. From the Layout ribbon, choose Axis Titles, Primary Horizontal Axis Title, Title Below Axis. Click the axis title and type the new title `Age (Years)`.

9. From the Layout ribbon, choose Axis Titles, Primary Vertical Axis Title, Rotated Title.

When you need to show the relationship between three variables and you have only a few points to compare, a bubble chart will create an effective presentation of the data.

Using a Frequency Distribution to Categorize Thousands of Points

Suppose your dataset had results of 30,000 trials. Figuring out how to present this data is fairly difficult. The chart in Figure 5.31 is a first attempt. The data is sorted by the trial number in column A, and a line chart is based on columns A and B. You can't really tell anything from this chart. Well, you can tell that the range is basically from 20 to 100, but that is about it.

Figure 5.31
This can't be the best way to plot this data.

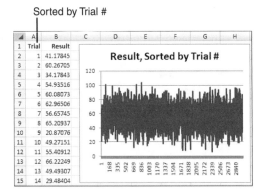

If you sort the data by the result field in column B, the chart changes into a smooth line, as shown in Figure 5.32. Again, you can tell that the range is from 20 to 100. In addition, you can tell that for 60% of the chart, the data ranges from 40 to 60.

To create a more useful chart with this data, you need to use a fairly obscure function. You use the FREQUENCY function to group the data into bins. This function is one of the few functions that returns several different answers all at once. These functions, called *array functions*, require special care and handling.

Figure 5.32
Some might be able to draw conclusions from this, but this chart is not obvious.

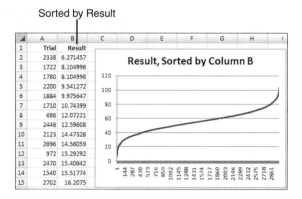

Sorted by Result

Creating Bins

To make sense of the data in column B in Figure 5.32, you need to group the results into equal-sized bins. You need to type limits for each bin in a range, going down a column of the worksheet.

If your first bin is the number 0, the FREQUENCY function shows all the trial results less than 0 next to that bin. If the next bin is the number 15, the FREQUENCY function shows all the trial results from the last bin (0) to the current value (15).

To create bins that contain ranges of 15 units each, you follow these steps:

1. Type **0, 15, 30, 45, 60, 75, 90, 105**, in cells E2:E9. Remember that this range contains eight cells.

2. Because the FREQUENCY function returns one more value than the number of bins that you have, select the empty cells F2:F10, as shown in Figure 5.33. The additional bin is for any results larger than your last bin value.

Figure 5.33
It might feel strange, but you are entering one formula in this range.

E	F	G
0		
15		
30		
45		
60		
75		
90		
105		

3. Type **=FREQUENCY(**.

4. When Excel asks for the data array, enter the trial results from B2:B3001. Type a comma.

5. When Excel asks for the Bins array, enter the values from E2:E9.

> **NOTE**
>
> If you were actually entering nine copies of this formula, you would have to put dollar signs in all those references. However, this is one single formula that will return nine results, so you don't need dollar signs.

   6. Type the closing parenthesis but do not press Enter (see Figure 5.34).

Figure 5.34
It might feel strange, but you are entering one formula in this range.

	A	B	C	D	E	F	G	H
2	2338	6.271457				0	=FREQUENCY(B2:B3000,E2:E9)	
3	1722	8.104998				15		
4	1780	8.104998				30		
5	2200	9.541272				45		
6	1884	9.975647				60		
7	1710	10.74399				75		
8	686	12.07221				90		
9	2446	12.59608				105		
10	2123	14.47328					8R x 1C	
11	2696	14.56059						

   7. Hold down Ctrl+Shift while pressing Enter. Excel returns all nine answers at once. You now have one formula entered in nine cells.

   Take a look at the results of the formula shown in Figure 5.35.

Figure 5.35
These results make sense only if you understand how the bins work.

fx {=FREQUENCY(B2:B3000,E2:E9)}

D	E	F	G
	0	0	
	15	10	
	30	130	
	45	607	
	60	1149	
	75	826	
	90	243	
	105	34	
		0	

You have to "know the code" in order to figure out what is going on here. There is a 0 next to the 0, and there is a 10 next to the 15. This means that none of the results were less than 0 and 10 of the results were between 0 and 15. At the other end of the range, there is a 34 next to the 105, and there is a 0 below that. This means that there are 34 results between 90 and 105. The final 0 means that there were no results above 105. When you set up the bin range, you should always bracket the expected results with one bin above and below your expected results. Having a 0 end up as the first and last result means that you have accurately captured all your results.

> If you can't remember if the 10 means that there were numbers below 15 or above 15, you can always sort the results and count the number that appears in the first range. If the process of creating bins seems extremely confusing, you are not alone. Microsoft hopes to make frequency distribution charts much easier in a future version of Excel.

Creating the Frequency Distribution Chart

The results in column F in Figure 5.35 are somewhat difficult to decode, but you can improve the appearance of the labels along the axis of the chart.

In Figure 5.36, the formulas in H3:H9 concatenate the bins so that they make more sense. The formula =E2&" - "&E3 concatenates the bin in the previous row, a dash, and the bin in the current row. The formulas in column I simply copy the results from the current row of the array formula in F.

Figure 5.36
You can use formulas to build a table that makes more sense than the previous results.

H3				*f_x* =E2&"-"&E3		
	D	E	F	G	H	I	J
2		0	0			
3		15	10		0-15	10
4		30	130		15-30	130
5		45	607		30-45	607
6		60	1149		45-60	1149
7		75	826		60-75	826
8		90	243		75-90	243
9		105	34		90-105	34
10			0			

To create the Frequency Distribution chart, you follow these steps.

1. Select cells H3:I9.
2. From the Insert ribbon, choose Column, 2-D, Clustered Column.
3. From the Layout ribbon, choose Legend, None.
4. Normally, there is a fair-sized gap between the columns. If you prefer that the columns touch each other, or even that there be less of a gap, you can change the gap width by right-clicking a column, choosing Format Data Series, and then dragging the Gap Width slider to 0%.
5. Resize the chart so that it is narrower.

5

Figure 5.37
Frequency charts typically eliminate the gap between columns. This is strictly your preference.

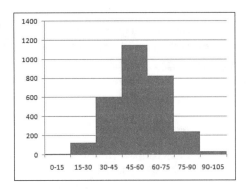

Using Radar Charts to Create Performance Reviews

Radar charts are designed for showing a person's or a company's rating along several performance areas. Here are some typical usages:

- **Employee performance review**—a manager might rate an employee using a one- to five-point rating scale in areas such as efficiency, accuracy, timeliness, and so on. While this data can be presented in a table, a radar chart provides an interesting presentation alternative.

- **Customer satisfaction results**—a marketing manager could use a radar chart to summarize the results of a customer satisfaction survey. In this case, one line could be used to show customer satisfaction along rating areas such as speed, accuracy, and value.

If you wanted to summarize customer satisfaction results for two companies, you could present the results as two charts, as shown in Figure 5.38, or as two series on a single chart, as shown in Figure 5.39.

You can choose to fill in the chart area or to show the series as a line. You should leave the chart unfilled when you put two series on one chart.

Figure 5.38
With only one series, you can choose to fill in the series.

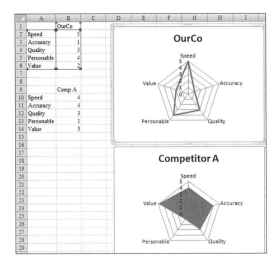

Figure 5.39
When you have two series, you should not fill in the lines so the reader can see the overlap.

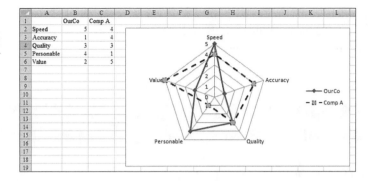

You can use a radar chart to compare some kind of results from this year versus the same kind of results from last year. In Figure 5.40, for example, the line for last year is dark black, and the line for this year is a dashed line in a lighter color.

Figure 5.40
Radar charts can compare several values from last year to this year.

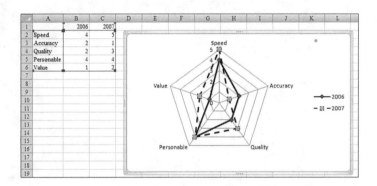

To create the performance review chart shown in Figure 5.40, you follow these steps:

1. Using the information in Figure 5.40, enter the categories in column A, starting in A2. The category in A2 will appear at 12:00 on the chart. The remaining categories will be arranged in clockwise order.

2. In cells B1 and C1, enter the headings for last year and this year.

3. Enter the 1–5 ratings in B2:C6.

4. Select cell A1:C6. From the Insert ribbon, choose Other Charts, Radar, Radar with Markers.

5. Click the line from this year. From the Format ribbon, choose Shape Outline, Dashes, and then select the fourth choice, called Dash.

All the examples so far show measures that are of similar scale. If you needed to show a series that is of a different order of magnitude, you could plot the series on a secondary axis. To do this, you select the axis and choose Format Axis and then choose Secondary Axis.

5

In the celebrity chart described in the following section, the designer used a radar chart for something that is not quite typical. In this case, the designer solves the order-of-magnitude problem by using a logarithmic scale.

DESIGNING CHARTS LIKE THE PROS

Manoj Sharma: Radar Charts

The radar chart in Figure 5.41 shows four rating metrics for 24 different individuals. This is an unusual use for a radar chart.

Figure 5.41
Radar charts can compare several values from last year to this year.

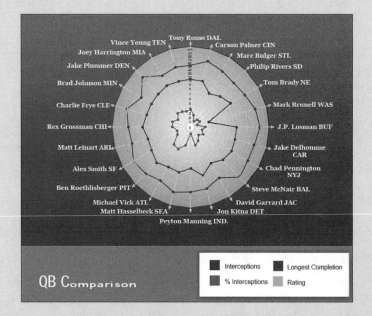

This chart packs a lot of information into a small space. You can spot anomalies within the data. For example, you can see that Mark Brunell had significantly lower interceptions than other quarterbacks. However, with this chart, it is difficult to figure out exactly what is happening. To a certain extent, a particular point looks interesting only if a neighboring point is higher or lower. For example, several quarterbacks on the right side of the chart have longer receptions than others, but because they are all higher than normal, it is difficult to detect an issue.

Figure 5.42 shows a similar chart, created in Excel.

Sorting the players in alphabetic sequence allows some variability to appear. If you sorted the players in descending sequence by passing yards, that line would gently spiral in, and the change would be barely perceptible.

Figure 5.42
This radar chart does an average job of approximating the designer chart.

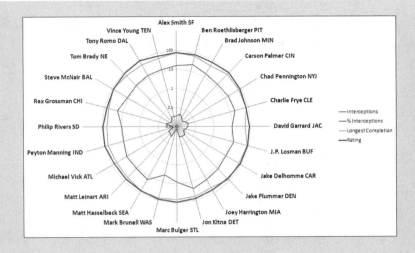

Figure 5.43
To set up a radar chart, put the names of each spoke in the first column, and then values for each series in subsequent columns.

	A	B	C	D	E
1		Passing Yards	Attempts	Cmp	Touchdown Passes
2	Tom Brady NE	3529	516	319	24
3	Drew Brees NO	4418	554	356	26
4	Mark Brunell WAS	1789	260	162	8
5	Marc Bulger STL	4301	588	370	24

To create the radar chart, follow these steps:

1. Start with player names in column A, and then four measures in columns B through E (Figure 5.43).
2. Select the range A1:E25. From the Insert ribbon, choose Other Charts, Radar. Excel creates a chart that is very small.
3. Use the zoom slider to reduce the worksheet zoom to 80%. This allows you to resize the chart to cover a larger area of the worksheet.
4. Enlarge the chart—for example, a chart from G2:AB48 is large enough to allow all of the player names to appear at the end of each spoke.
5. Right-click on the axis numbers and choose Format Axis. Check the box for Logarithmic Scale. Click OK to close the Format Axis dialog. You will now be able to see the smallest series—% Interceptions on the chart.
6. On the Layout ribbon, choose Gridlines, Primary Horizontal Gridlines, More Primary Horizontal Gridlines Options. Change the line color from Automatic to Sold Line. Choose a light grey color so that the gridlines do not overpower the series lines.
7. Click on one data label to select all of the data labels. Use the Increase Font Size icon on the Home ribbon to enlarge the labels. Use the Bold icon on the Home ribbon to change the labels to Bold.
8. Sort the data into alphabetic sequence. Select one player name in the worksheet. Use the AZ button on the Data ribbon to sort the players. This allows some variability to appear. If you sorted the players in descending sequence by rating, that line would gently spiral in, and the change would be barely perceptible.

The designer chart has a better legend than the built-in legend in Excel. You would have to replace the built-in legend with a series of shapes in Excel 2007 to approximate the legend in Figure 5.41.

> **NOTE** This chart in Figure 5.41 was designed in AutoCAD by Manoj Sharma. He can be found doing custom design work as ThePrintGuru on www.elance.com.

A Chart from Gene Zelazny

Gene Zelazny is the director of visual communications for McKinsey & Company. His books on charting and presentations are filled with ideas for effectively communicating information visually.

I asked Gene if he would contribute a chart that doesn't look like a typical Excel chart. He contributed the chart described in the following section.

DESIGNING CHARTS LIKE THE PROS

Gene Zelazny: Zelazny Chart

A number of retirees were surveyed about their impressions of certain types of companies to provide retirement advice. The resulting data is shown in the table in Figure 5.44. A typical approach to this analysis, a 100% stacked bar chart, is shown at the bottom of Figure 5.44.

Figure 5.44
Most people would present this data with a 100% stacked bar chart.

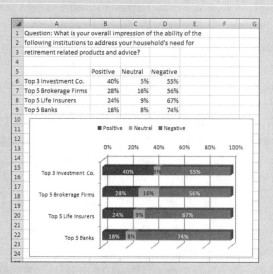

Gene's version of the chart, shown in Figure 5.45, minimizes the neutral answers. All the neutral answers are shown along an imaginary baseline, in equal-size markers. The positive answers are shown as yellow upward-facing arrows. The neutral markers are blue. The negative answers are shown as red downward-facing arrows (see Figure 5.45).

Figure 5.45
Gene's chart will be moderately difficult to re-create in Excel.

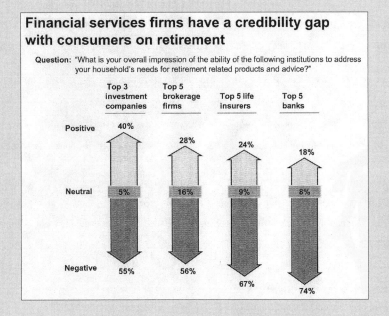

To create this chart in Excel, you follow these steps:

1. Set up data labels in column A for the four types of institutions.
2. Type the heading `Negative` in cell B1. Enter negative percentages in B2:B5. For example, the value for investment companies should be entered as `-55%`. This forces the bar to be drawn below the axis.
3. Type the heading `Neutral` in cell C1. Enter `0%` in C2:C5.
4. Type the heading `Positive` in cell D1. Enter the positive values from the original table.
5. Make sure that columns C and D are formatted as percentages with 0 decimal places.
6. Format column B with a custom numeric code of `0%;0%`. This forces negative values to show as positive.
7. Select cells A1:D5. From the Insert ribbon, choose Column, 2-D Column, Stacked Column.
8. Resize the chart using the resize handles so that it is larger—perhaps as large as cells A7:J34.
9. Carefully right-click one of the labels along the axis. Choose Format Axis. In the Format Axis dialog, choose Axis Labels as High. The titles move so that they are above the chart.
10. Right-click the columns above the axis. Choose Add Data Labels. From the Format ribbon's Shape Fill drop-down, choose a yellow color.
11. Click the data labels. Choose a size of 14 point from the Home ribbon.

12. Click a data label and move it on top of the appropriate column. Repeat for each of the other data labels.

13. Right-click the columns below the axis. Choose Add Data Labels. From the Format ribbon's Shape Fill drop-down, choose a red color.

14. Click the lower data labels. On the Home ribbon, choose 14 point for the font size.

15. Click a data label and move it to below the appropriate bottom column. Repeat for each of the other data labels.

16. From the Format ribbon's Current Selection drop-down, choose Series Neutral. Then choose Shape Fill, Green to make the legend entry green.

17. Choose the legend by clicking it. On the Home ribbon, increase the font size to 14.

18. Choose the Axis labels. Change the font size to 14.

19. From the Insert ribbon, choose Shapes, Block Arrows, Upward Facing Arrow. Draw an arrow next to the chart.

20. From the Format ribbon, choose Shape Outline, No Outline to remove the border. Then choose Shape Fill, Yellow. Choose a yellow to match the upper columns.

21. With the arrow selected, press Ctrl+C to copy the arrow.

22. Click one of the top columns in the chart. Press Ctrl+V. Excel replaces the columns with a block arrow.

23. Select the arrow. From the Format ribbon, choose Rotate, Flip Vertical and then choose Format Shape Fill, Red.

24. Press Ctrl+C to copy the arrow.

25. Click the lower bars in the chart. Press Ctrl+V to paste. The lower bars are replaced by red arrows.

26. Delete the arrow on the worksheet.

27. Right-click any bar and choose Format Data Series. Change the gap width to 30%.

28. From the Insert ribbon, choose Text Box. Draw a text box for the neutral labels on the first arrow. The text box should be as wide as the arrow. It should extend equally above and below the horizontal axis.

29. With the text box selected, choose Shape Fill, Green on the Format ribbon. Choose Shape Outline, No Outline.

30. Press Ctrl+1 to access the Format Shape dialog. Choose Text Box from the categories on the left. Change the Internal Margin to 0 inches on the left, right, top, and bottom. Close the Format dialog.

31. From the Home ribbon, choose 14 point, black font, center align, and middle align.

32. Type 5% in the text box.

33. Click the border of the text box. Start to drag right. After you start to drag, hold down Shift+Ctrl to make a copy of the text box and constrain the movement to only horizontal. Drop the text box on the second column and type 16%.

34. Repeat step 33, using 9% for the third column and 8% for the fourth column.

35. Add a title above the chart in the worksheet cells.

The final chart is shown in Figure 5.46.

Figure 5.46
The final Zelazny chart in Excel.

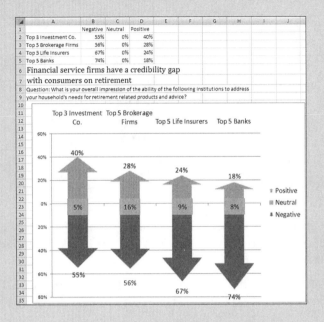

NOTE Thanks to Gene Zelazny for contributing this original chart to the book. For more information about Gene and his excellent *Say It With Charts* book, visit www.zelazny.com.

Using Surface Charts to Show Contrast

Not many datasets can be plotted as surface chart, which look like topographic maps. Because you use a surface chart to represent a 3-D surface on a 2-D piece of paper, it is particularly important that your surface be generally sloping toward the front of the chart. Otherwise, you will never see the details hidden by the hill at the front of the chart.

Before you start to build a dataset, you should look at Figure 5.47. The data for the chart is in C3:L12. Each data point requires two headings. Headings for the front axis are in C2:L2. Headings for the side axis are in B3:B12.

Figure 5.47
You should study this table and chart to understand how surface charts work.

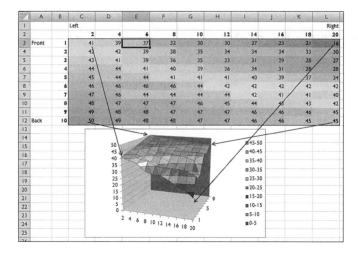

Data at the top of the table appears at the front edge of the chart. Data in the last row of the table appears at the back of the chart. The Front and Back labels in column A are there to help you keep track of this.

Data in the left column of the table appears in the left side of the chart. The four arrows point out where each corner of the data table ends up in the chart.

To create this chart, you select cells B2:L12. From the Insert ribbon, you choose Other Charts, Surface, 3-D Surface.

Many datasets are not designed to have the smallest numbers at the front of the chart. In Figure 5.48, for example, the top-left chart has the highest numbers along the front wall of the chart.

Figure 5.48
All four charts represent the same data. Each chart provides a different view angle.

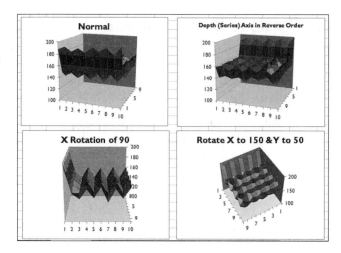

When the front wall of the surface chart is higher than the other points, you can use the techniques that follow to create the other three charts.

Using the Depth Axis

One element unique to surface charts is the depth axis. This is the axis that falls along the right side of the chart in the default orientation.

In the top-right chart in Figure 5.48, the chart has been turned around by having the orientation of the depth axis changed. You follow these steps to create this effect:

1. From the Layout ribbon, choose Current Selection, Depth (Series) Axis.
2. Click Format Selection.
3. Choose Series in Reverse Order.

Because the depth axis is treated as a category axis, you do not have control over the minimum or maximum values along the axis. The Format dialog box is limited to settings for the interval between tick marks and labels and where the tick marks and labels appear.

Controlling a Surface Chart Through 3-D Rotation

You can spin a surface chart by rotating it. To access the rotation settings, you choose 3-D Rotation from the Layout ribbon. This takes you to the 3-D Rotation category of the Format Chart Area dialog, which has the following settings:

- **X Rotation**—This setting ranges from 0 degrees to 359.9 degrees. It rotates the floor of the chart in a clockwise direction (looking down at the chart from above).

- **Y Rotation**—This setting starts at +15 degrees. It is your viewing angle in relation to the baseline of the chart. With an angle of 15 degrees, you are looking slightly down at the chart. With an angle of 0 degrees, a lot of the 3-D effects disappear. As you increase from 10 to 80 degrees, you have slightly different views of the chart. At 90 degrees, the chart becomes flat, as you are looking directly down from above. You can also enter negative values from 0 to –90. As you move from –10 to –80, you look at the chart from underneath. This might allow you to see better detail. When you reach –90, the chart turns flat again, as you are looking directly up at the chart from below.

Perspective ranges from 0 to 120. A value of 0 creates the least distortion. As you increase to 120, the foreshortening increases, creating distortion similar to what you get with an ultra-wide-angle lens on a camera.

Next Steps

In Chapter 6, "Creating Stock Analysis Charts," you will learn about the process of creating charts to show the performance of stocks and securities. While Excel offers four types of built-in stock charts, they appear dated in light of modern stark charts available on numerous web sites. Chapter 6 shows you how to go beyond the four built-in charts to create modern-looking stock charts.

5

Creating Stock Analysis Charts

Overview of Stock Charts

Excel provides four basic types of stock analysis charts: High-Low-Close, Open-High-Low-Close, Volume-High-Low-Close, and Volume-Open-High-Low-Close. These built-in charts are helpful when you need to display a stock trend for use in an executive dashboard.

Unfortunately, like the old charting in Excel 2003, the stock charts are showing signs of age. If you are used to the charts in *The Wall Street Journal* or on http://finance.yahoo.com, you can see that charting technology has definitely left Excel 2007 behind.

This chapter guides you on how to coax acceptable results out of the Excel charting engine. Sometimes, though, it is easier to ditch the Excel stock charts and design your own chart, using a line chart.

If you are planning on doing dashboard reporting, this chapter gives you a few tips for making your charts much smaller than usual but still keeping them readable.

Typically, stock charts in the newspaper or online are represented by one of three chart types: line charts, open-high-low-close (OHLC) charts, and candlestick charts.

Line Charts

A line chart shows the closing price of a security every day for a month, quarter, half year, year, or longer. A line chart may show a second series of volume represented as a column chart at the bottom of the chart. To create a line chart in Excel, you don't have to use stock chart types at all; you can simply choose a line chart.

One advantage of line charts is that it is very easy to add a second security to a line chart to show how the original security is doing compared to an index or a competitor. In Figure 6.1, for example, a line chart shows the closing price for a security for one year. A volume chart at the bottom shows unusually high activity for the security in April.

Figure 6.1
A line indicates the closing price of the security each day for a year. The column chart at the bottom shows the volume of shares traded each day.

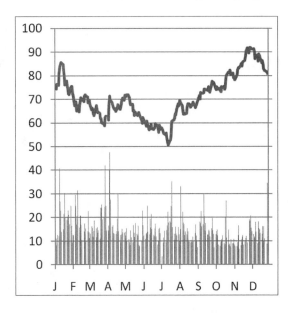

OHLC Charts

An OHLC chart shows a vertical line extending from the low price to the high price for a given period. A dash on the left side of the line indicates the opening price. A dash on the right side of the line indicates the closing price. For example, the chart in Figure 6.2 shows that January opened at 72, the price ranged from 71 to 86, and January closed at 76.

Figure 6.2
This is a true OHLC chart. Excel's built-in types omit the marker for the opening price.

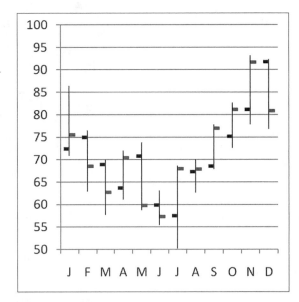

Excel does not have a built-in style for OHLC charts, but it can create a variant of this chart: Excel's high-low-close chart shows the vertical line and the closing line on the right side of the line but is missing the marker for the opening price. (If you desperately need to show the opening price, see "Creating OHLC Charts" later in this chapter.) Excel's volume-high-low-close chart is a variant of the OHLC chart that is coupled with a volume chart showing trading volume.

Candlestick Charts

A candlestick chart has a vertical line that indicates the range of low to high prices for a security. A thicker column indicates the opening and closing prices. If the price of the security closed up, the thicker column appears in white or green. If the price of the security closed down, the thicker column appears in black or red.

The candlestick chart is so named because each shape appears as a candle with a wick sticking out of the top and the bottom. In Figure 6.3, for example, the security enjoyed five months of gains from July through November, before falling in December. Excel easily creates these charts using the Open-High-Low-Close chart type. In another variant, volumes for each period are plotted on a second axis. You can quickly scan this type of chart to see if the stock has had more winning periods than losing periods.

Figure 6.3
The thicker column indicates the open and closing prices. The thinner line indicates the high-to-low range.

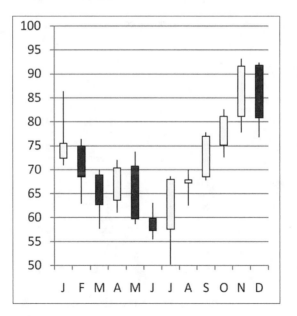

Obtaining Stock Data to Chart

There are plenty of free sources of historical data to chart. To obtain stock data to chart, go to http://finance.yahoo.com or another of these sites and follow these steps:

1. If you don't know the stock ticker symbols for the company of interest, use the Symbol Lookup link that appears next to the Go button in the top navigation bar of the page.

2. Enter a stock ticker symbol in the Get Quotes text box and press the Go button. Yahoo returns a table and a chart showing information about the current day.

3. Click Historical Prices in the left navigation bar. Enter a starting date and an ending date and choose whether you want the data summarized daily, weekly, or monthly. Click Get Prices to generate new results. Yahoo shows columns for date, open, high, low, close, volume, and adjusted close. A minor annoyance is that it shows about 50 dates on a page and then offers a Next link.

4. Instead of copying a page at a time, scroll down and choose the Download to Spreadsheet link that appears below the results.

5. In the File Download dialog that appears, click Save. An imaginative name of `table.csv` is proposed. Save using this name of something such as `MSFTDaily2006.csv`.

6. In Excel 2007, select Office icon, Open. In the Open dialog that appears, in the Files of Type drop-down, select Text Files (*.prn, *.txt, *.csv).

7. Browse to the downloaded `.csv` file and click Open. Excel opens the file. Column A, which contains dates, is typically too narrow, as shown in Figure 6.4. Double-click the border between the column A and B column headings to make column A wider.

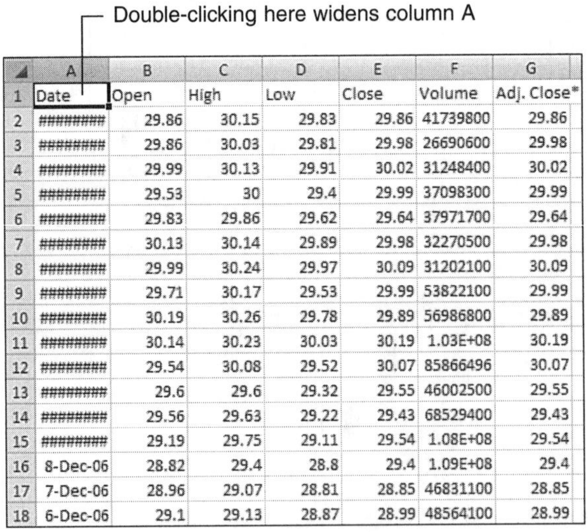

┌─ Double-clicking here widens column A

Figure 6.4
The `.csv` file opens in Excel, but you need to adjust the column widths.

	A	B	C	D	E	F	G
1	Date	Open	High	Low	Close	Volume	Adj. Close*
2	########	29.86	30.15	29.83	29.86	41739800	29.86
3	########	29.86	30.03	29.81	29.98	26690600	29.98
4	########	29.99	30.13	29.91	30.02	31248400	30.02
5	########	29.53	30	29.4	29.99	37098300	29.99
6	########	29.83	29.86	29.62	29.64	37971700	29.64
7	########	30.13	30.14	29.89	29.98	32270500	29.98
8	########	29.99	30.24	29.97	30.09	31202100	30.09
9	########	29.71	30.17	29.53	29.99	53822100	29.99
10	########	30.19	30.26	29.78	29.89	56986800	29.89
11	########	30.14	30.23	30.03	30.19	1.03E+08	30.19
12	########	29.54	30.08	29.52	30.07	85866496	30.07
13	########	29.6	29.6	29.32	29.55	46002500	29.55
14	########	29.56	29.63	29.22	29.43	68529400	29.43
15	########	29.19	29.75	29.11	29.54	1.08E+08	29.54
16	8-Dec-06	28.82	29.4	28.8	29.4	1.09E+08	29.4
17	7-Dec-06	28.96	29.07	28.81	28.85	46831100	28.85
18	6-Dec-06	29.1	29.13	28.87	28.99	48564100	28.99

8. The data is always sorted with the most recent data first, so click a cell in column A and choose Data, AZ to sort the date into ascending sequence by column.

9. If you have more than one screen of data, from the View ribbon, choose Freeze Panes, Freeze Top Row to ensure that you can always see the headings at the top of the screen.

10. `.csv` files are not good places to store Excel charts. Before creating any charts, select Office icon, Save As. Choose to save as an Excel 2007 macro-enabled workbook.

Rearranging Columns in the Downloaded Data

If you are using one of the Excel built-in stock charts, you should know that Excel 2007 is very particular about the sequence of the columns. In a high-low-close chart, for example, the date should be in the first column, followed by a High column, a Low column, and a Close column. This does not match the sequence of the data downloaded from Yahoo.com. You need to be prepared to insert new columns and then cut and paste data from one column to another in order to sequence your data as necessary. The following list shows the required sequence of columns for each chart type:

- **Line Chart**—Date in column A and Close in column B.
- **Line Chart with Volume**—Date in column A, Close in column B, and Volume in column C.
- **High-Low-Close**—Date in column A, High in column B, Low in column C, and Close in column D.
- **Volume-High-Low-Close**—Date in column A, Volume in column B, High in column C, Low in column D, and Close in column E.
- **Open-High-Low-Close as Candlestick**—Date in column A, Open in column B, High in column C, Low in column D, and Close in column E.
- **Open-High-Low-Close as OHLC**—Date in column A, High in column B, Low in column C, Close in column D, and Open in column E.
- **Volume-Open-High-Low-Close as Candlestick**—Date in column A, Volume in column B, Open in column C, High in column D, Low in column E, and Close in column F.
- **Volume-Open-High-Low-Close as OHLC**—Date in column A, Volume in column B, High in column C, Low in column D, Close in column E, and Open in column F.

> **TIP**
> Although you might be tempted to delete the unused columns, it is better to leave them out to the right of the data to be charted. This way, if you decide to later add a series to the chart, it is easy to do so.

Dealing with Splits Using the Adjusted Close Column

Before charting data, you should look at the last row of data and compare the Close column to the Adjusted Close column. If they are different, you know that one of two events happened during the time period in question:

- The company declared a dividend. For example, if the company pays out 3 cents per share, the adjusted price is reduced by 3 cents for all months that occurred earlier than the dividend.
- If the company declares a stock split, then the adjusted close shows the closing price, pretending that the split had previously occurred.

6

Figure 6.5 shows an example of a stock split. Apple Computer stock began February 1, 2005, at a price of $77.05 and closed the month at a price of $44.86. The stock did not really incur a huge drop during the month.

Figure 6.5
At first glance, it appears the Apple stock took a nose-dive in February 2005.

◢	A	B	C	D	E	F	G
1	Date	Open	High	Low	Close	Volume	Adj. Close*
21	2-May-05	36.21	40.94	33.11	39.76	22555271	39.76
22	1-Apr-05	42.09	44.45	34	36.06	34093790	36.06
23	1-Mar-05	44.99	45.11	38.83	41.67	24857231	41.67
24	1-Feb-05	77.05	90.88	43.96	44.86	41542400	44.86
25	3-Jan-05	64.78	77.89	62.6	76.9	48909540	38.45
26	1-Dec-04	67.79	67.95	61.6	64.4	26342863	32.2
27	1-Nov-04	52.5	69.57	52.04	67.05	31408371	33.53

Apple had declared a two-for-one stock split on February 28, 2005. Every person who had 100 shares on that day was given 200 shares. The value of each share was cut in half at the time of the split. So in this case, you might have started the month with 100 shares of Apple, valued at $7,705. You would have ended the month with 200 shares of Apple, valued at $8,972. With this information, you can see that instead of losing value, Apple shares actually gained value during February.

To learn when the split or dividend occurred, you actually have to look through the table on http://finance.yahoo.com, which shows splits and dividends. This information is not downloaded in the .csv file.

If you are plotting a line chart showing the closing price, you can deal with the split by simply using the Adjusted Close column. Notice in Figure 6.6 that the Adjusted Close column for January 2005 is $38.45, half the real closing price of $76.90. Yahoo goes to the trouble of adjusting the closing price to provide a comparable view of the closing price.

If you are plotting a chart showing high, low, and close, you have to add some additional calculations. To do so, you follow these steps:

1. Add the new column headings Date, High, Low, Close to H1:K1.

2. Copy the formula =A2 from cell H2 down to all rows. (This formula is for the date.)

3. Copy the formula =G2 from cell K2 down to all rows. (This formula is for the adjusted close.)

4. Copy the formula =C2*($G2/$E2) from cell I2 down to all rows. (This formula adjusts the high price from column C by the same ratio as adjusted close to close.) You might change it in some rows. The dollar signs before columns G and E allow you to copy the formula to column J for the adjusted low as well.

5. Manually fix any dates where a split occurred. The original data showed a high price of $90.88 for February 2005. You can assume that this high happened before the split. In cell I24, divide C24 by 2 to adjust the high to $45.44. The original data showed a low price of $43.96 for February 2005. Again, you can assume that this happened on February 28, 2005, after the split. The opening price of $77.05, if divided by 2, would indicate an adjusted low price of $38.25. It is possible the stock price went even lower.

If you need the chart to be exactly correct, go back to http://finance.yahoo.com and run a daily report for February 2005. You find that the actual low before the split was $76.58. Divide this by 2 to show a low of 38.29.

6. Create your stock charts from the data in columns H:K as shown in Figure 6.6.

Figure 6.6
Most of the adjusted columns are a formula, but you need to use special care in the months in which a stock split occurred.

	A	B	C	D	E	F	G	H	I	J	K
	Date	Open	High	Low	Close	Volume	Adj. Close*	Date	High	Low	Close
18	1-Aug-05	42.57	48.33	42.02	46.89	15223234	46.89	1-Aug-05	48.33	42.02	46.89
19	1-Jul-05	36.83	44.38	36.29	42.65	19029154	42.65	1-Jul-05	44.38	36.29	42.65
20	1-Jun-05	39.89	40.76	35.52	36.81	19067509	36.81	1-Jun-05	40.76	35.52	36.81
21	2-May-05	36.21	40.94	33.11	39.76	22555271	39.76	2-May-05	40.94	33.11	39.76
22	1-Apr-05	42.09	44.45	34	36.06	34093790	36.06	1-Apr-05	44.45	34	36.06
23	1-Mar-05	44.99	45.11	38.83	41.67	24857231	41.67	1-Mar-05	45.11	38.83	41.67
24	1-Feb-05	77.05	90.88	43.96	44.86	41542400	44.86	1-Feb-05	45.44	38.29	44.86
25	3-Jan-05	64.78	77.89	62.6	76.9	48909540	38.45	3-Jan-05	38.945	31.3	38.45
26	1-Dec-04	67.79	67.95	61.6	64.4	26342863	32.2	1-Dec-04	33.975	30.8	32.2
27	1-Nov-04	52.5	69.57	52.04	67.05	31408371	33.53	1-Nov-04	34.7902	26.0239	33.53
28	1-Oct-04	39.12	53.2	37.65	52.4	28749295	26.2	1-Oct-04	26.6	18.825	26.2

J27 formula: =+D27*($G27/$E27)

Creating a Line Chart to Show Closing Prices

A line chart is the easiest type of stock chart to create. You don't have to use Excel's built-in stock charting types; you will simply use a line chart. You follow these steps to create a line chart:

1. Download data for the security from http://finance.yahoo.com.

2. Sort the data into ascending sequence by date.

3. Insert a blank column B after the Date column.

4. Copy the Adjusted Close column from column H to the new column B.

5. Delete the extra column H.

6. Clear cell A1. (Whenever your row labels contain dates, the top-left cell of the chart range should be blank.)

7. Select your data in columns A and B.

8. On the Insert ribbon, choose Line, 2-D Line, Line. Excel creates the chart shown in Figure 6.7.

Figure 6.7
Excel creates a line chart showing closing prices.

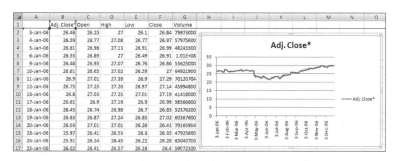

6

9. On the Layout ribbon, choose Legend, None. Excel removes the legend from the chart.

10. Click the chart title. Type a new title, such as `Microsoft 2006 Closing Prices`.

11. The value axis currently runs from a low of 0 to a high of 35. During 2006, the security closing prices ran from a low of $21.36 to a high of $30.19. If you want to show more detail in the chart, right-click the value axis and choose Format Axis. Change the Minimum setting to Fixed, 20.

12. The dates in the horizontal axis are trying to show month, day, and year, as in the original dataset. To display one label for each month, do the following:

    • Right-click the labels along the horizontal axis and choose Format Axis.

    • On the Axis Options dialog, choose Major Unit, Fixed, 1, Month.

    • Choose Axis Type, Date Axis.

    • Click the Number category in the left navigation bar.

    • Click the Custom category.

    • Type a custom format of mmmmm. Click Add.

    • Uncheck the Linked to Source check box.

    • Select mmmmm from the Type box. Click OK. The mmmmm custom type displays a single letter for each month. In the English version of Excel, it displays JFMAMJJASOND, a format regularly seen in *The Wall Street Journal*.

13. Resize the chart so it is narrower than the default chart. Click the chart border to select the chart. Drag the right resizing handle to the left.

The resulting chart is shown in Figure 6.8.

Figure 6.8
When you zoom in on the $20–$30 price range, more details are visible.

Adding Volume as a Column Chart to the Line Chart

A popular option in stock charts is to add a column chart that shows volume of shares traded. This chart usually appears at the bottom of the trend chart.

Continuing with the example from the preceding section, to plot prices in the $20–$30 range with volumes in the 50–100 million range, the volumes have to be plotted on a secondary axis. One trick is to artificially inflate the maximum for the secondary axis by a factor of three or four in order to keep the volume chart in the lower portion (that is, the lower quarter to third) of the chart.

You follow these steps to create a chart that shows closing prices and volume:

1. Download data from http://finance.yahoo.com.
2. Sort the data into ascending sequence by date.
3. Insert blank columns B and C after the Date column.
4. Copy the Adjusted Close column from column I to the new column B.
5. Copy the Volume column from column H to the new column C.
6. Delete the extra columns H and I.
7. Select your data in columns A:C.
8. Choose Line, 2-D Line, Line from the Insert ribbon. Excel creates the chart shown in Figure 6.9.

Figure 6.9
Don't be alarmed that you can see only volumes.

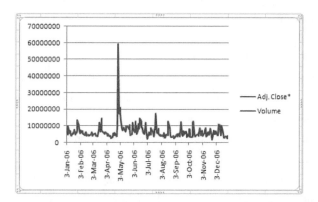

9. On the Layout ribbon, choose Layout, Legend, None. Excel removes the legend from the chart.
10. Choose Series Volume from the Current Selection drop-down.
11. On the Design ribbon, click Change Chart Type. Select the first column chart type. Click OK. (Any time you change the chart type, Excel annoyingly unselects the data series.)
12. On the Layout ribbon, choose Series Volume from the Current Selection drop-down. Click the Format Selection button. Excel displays the Format Data Series dialog.
13. In the Series Options panel of the Format Data Series dialog, change the Plot Series On value from Primary Axis to Secondary Axis. Click Close to dismiss the Format dialog box. For the first time, you can see both the closing price and the volume.

6

14. On the Layout ribbon, choose Chart Title, Centered Overlay. Type `MSFT 2006` and press Enter to change the title.

15. The value axis currently runs from a low of $0 to a high of $35. Although prices of Microsoft (MSFT) stock never dipped below $20 in 2006, you can leave that space to hold the volume portion of the chart. The highest volume was about 600 million shares traded. If you scale the secondary axis to have a maximum value of 1,200 million shares traded, the volume portion of the chart occupies the lower half of the chart. Right-click the secondary value axis and choose Format Axis. Change Maximum to Fixed, `1.2E9`. The tallest column in the volume area of the chart stays below the gridline for $20.

16. Usually, the analyst doesn't care how many shares are traded; he or she is interested in the relative scale of the shares being traded. From the chart, you can tell that something remarkable happened when Microsoft traded six times more shares than usual. Thus, you don't need to have any volume numbers along the right side of the chart, so right-click the numbers along the right value axis and choose Format Axis. Click the Number category in the left navigation bar of the Format Axis dialog. In the Category column, choose Custom. Type a new custom format of ; ; ; and then click Add. In the Type box, choose the ;;; entry. This custom format code is the code to hide the values, and Excel removes the numbers from the right side of the chart.

17. The dates in the horizontal axis are trying to show month, day, and year, as in the original dataset. To display one label for each month, do the following:

- Right-click the labels along the horizontal axis and choose Format Axis.
- On the Axis Options dialog, choose Major Unit, Fixed, 1, Month.
- Choose Axis Type, Date Axis.
- Click the Number category in the left navigation bar.
- Click the Custom category.
- Type a custom format of mmmmm. Click Add.
- Uncheck the Linked to Source check box.
- Select mmmmm from the Type box. Click OK. The mmmmm custom type displays a single letter for each month. In the English version of Excel, it displays JFMAMJJASOND, a format regularly seen in *The Wall Street Journal*.

18. Resize the chart so that it is narrower than the default chart. Click the chart border to select the chart. Drag the right resizing handle to the left.

The resulting chart is shown in Figure 6.10.

The process of creating line charts is fairly straightforward. Although a certain amount of tweaking needs to happen, it is about normal for a chart. In contrast, to create OHLC charts, you must jump through more hoops, as described in the next section.

Figure 6.10
The final chart shows closing price as a line chart and volumes as columns at the bottom of the chart.

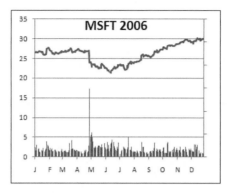

Creating OHLC Charts

Excel offers two built-in chart types that come close to the OHLC chart shown in Figure 6.2. The built-in types both ignore the left-facing dash used to indicate the opening price each day.

Microsoft isn't being dense here; a fundamental flaw in the underlying chart engine makes it hard to show the left-facing marker. This is why Microsoft doesn't support the open marker in the built-in charts. As you will see in the sections that follow, you can work around this.

Producing a High-Low-Close Chart

Before progressing to a true OHLC chart, it is easiest to start with Excel's built-in high-low-close chart. You follow these steps to produce a high-low-close chart in Excel 2007:

1. Download data from http://finance.yahoo.com. Since you cannot save a chart in a csv file, use the Save As command to save the file as an Excel 2007 file type.

2. Move the Open data from column B to the blank column H. Delete the now-empty column B. This leaves you with dates in column A, High in column B, Low in column C, and Close in column D.

3. Select your data in columns A:D.

4. On the Insert ribbon, select the Other Charts icon. In the Other Charts menu, the first four thumbnails are the four built-in stock charts (see Figure 6.11). Choose the first stock icon—High-Low-Close. Excel creates the default chart shown in Figure 6.12.

Figure 6.11
The four built-in stock charts are hidden under the Other Charts icon.

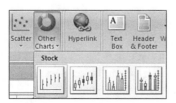

Figure 6.12
The default stock chart has formatting problems that make it difficult to see the close icons.

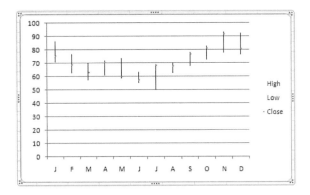

The default chart leaves a lot to be desired. You can see the vertical line extending from low to high. However, the marker for the close is impossibly hard to see. The legend on the right side adds no useful information to the chart.

If you turn to the Chart Layouts gallery on the Design ribbon, you face a perplexing selection. Layouts 1 and 3 appear to be identical. Layout 2 attempts to add data points for high, low, and close, making it impossible to see anything. The gray plot area in Layout 5 is not actually a gray plot area; instead, it is Microsoft trying to draw in 100 gridlines. The only interesting layout is Layout 4, where Excel adds a data table; this layout works for the charts in Figure 6.13 because they have only 12 months.

Figure 6.13
None of the built-in layouts improve the stock chart.

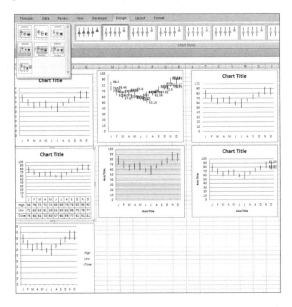

If you dare to choose any of the layouts from the Chart Styles gallery, the close markers change from being imperceptibly small to being far too large. Because Close is the third series, the markers are automatically upward-pointing triangles. This leads to the mistaken impression that the stock was trending up at the time the market closed (see Figure 6.14).

Figure 6.14
If you try to assign a style from the Design ribbon, you automatically get triangles, which are the markers traditionally used for the third series.

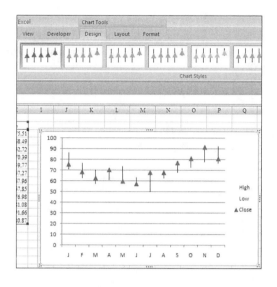

Customizing a High-Low-Close Chart

It is possible to make an acceptable high-low-close chart in Excel 2007. After getting rid of extraneous chart elements and zooming in, you need to format and change the marker style for the Close series. Here's how you do it:

1. On the Layout ribbon, choose Legend, None to remove the legend from the chart.

2. In the Current Selection drop-down of the Layout ribbon, choose Vertical (Value) Axis. Click Format Selection to display the Format Axis dialog box.

3. In the Axis Options category in the Format Axis dialog box, choose Minimum, Fixed. Enter a number that is a bit lower than the low value in the chart. In the current example, 50 would be appropriate, as shown in Figure 6.15.

Figure 6.15
You zoom in to show only the relevant price range for the stock by using a fixed minimum value for the vertical axis.

6

4. While the Format dialog box is open, select a new element from the Current Selection drop-down; this prevents you from having to close the Format dialog and then choose Format Selection again. Select the Series "Close" option from the drop-down, as shown in Figure 6.16.

Figure 6.16
New in Excel 2007, the Format dialog box is now modeless, meaning that you can select other items from the ribbon without closing the dialog.

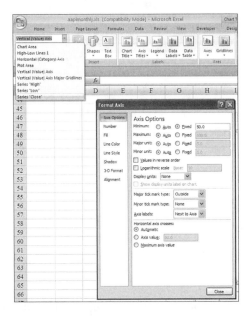

5. Choose the Marker Options category along the left side of the axis.

6. Choose Built-In as the marker type.

7. Increase the Size setting to 9 to ensure that the markers are visible (see Figure 6.17).

Figure 6.17
You can change from Automatic to Built-in and increase the size to 9. The size can be up to 72 points, in case you are ever making a huge chart.

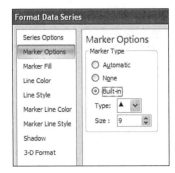

8. In the Type drop-down, choose the sixth marker style, which is a dash that extends from the right of center. This style is perfect for the close marker, which typically extends to the right of the line. As you look through the list of available marker styles, you will see why Excel doesn't offer OHLC charts similar to high-low-close charts: it doesn't include a left-facing dash (see Figure 6.18).

Figure 6.18
You choose the right-facing dash from the drop-down. Note that since Excel doesn't offer a left-facing dash, Microsoft can not easily place the Open Markers to the left of the vertical line.

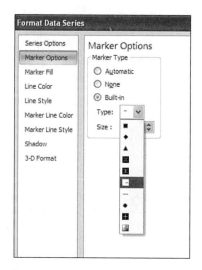

9. Click the Marker Fill category in the Format Data Series dialog box. Select Solid Fill and then choose the black color.

10. From the Current Selection drop-down in the Layout ribbon, choose Vertical (Value) Axis Major Gridlines. The Format dialog box is now called Format Major Gridlines.

11. For Line Color, choose Solid Line. From the Color drop-down, choose gray.

12. Click the Line Style category in the left of the dialog box.

13. Change the width to 0.5 points. Click Close to dismiss the Format dialog box.

14. Click the chart border. Drag the right resizing handle to the left to shrink the chart.

The resulting chart is shown in Figure 6.19.

Figure 6.19
After formatting the high-low-close chart, you can actually see the close markers.

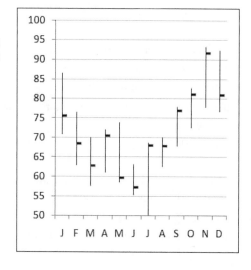

Creating an OHLC Chart

The fundamental barrier to creating a true OHLC chart is that Excel does not offer a left-facing dash as a built-in marker for a chart. You can, however, import your own image as a marker.

For example, I used Photoshop to create a new graphic that is 11 pixels wide and 3 pixels tall. The leftmost five columns of pixels are black, and the remaining pixels are transparent. I saved this file as a .gif image named LeftDash.gif. If you don't want to go to the hassle of creating such an image, you can download it from the webpage of examples for this book (www.MrExcel.com/chartdata.html).

The trick to creating an OHLC chart is to start with a high-low-close chart and add the Open series with a custom marker style. You follow these steps to create an OHLC chart in Excel 2007.

1. Start with data that has Date in column A, High in column B, Low in column C, Close in column D, and Open in column E. Do not include the Open data in the initial selection. Select the data in A:D.

2. From the Insert ribbon, choose Other Charts, Stock, High-Low-Close. Excel draws a chart. A blue box surrounds the charted data in B2:D13.

3. Click the blue handle in cell D13. Drag to the right to include the Open data on the chart. Excel adds the Open data in a format similar to the Close data.

4. On the Layout ribbon, choose Series Close from the Current Selection drop-down. Click Format Selection.

5. For the Marker Options category, leave the marker as the right-facing dash and change the size to 7.

6. For the Marker Fill category, choose Solid Fill. Choose black from the color drop-down.

7. For the Marker Line Color category, choose Solid Line. Choose black from the color drop-down.

8. Without closing the Format dialog box, choose Series Open from the Current Selection drop-down on the Layout ribbon. Again select the Marker Options category.

9. Change the Marker Type setting from None to Built-in.

10. In the Type drop-down, choose the 10th marker, which is a tiny version of the Picture icon that is prevalent throughout Excel.

11. Click the Marker Fill category in the left navigation bar of the Format Data Series dialog.

12. Choose Picture or Texture Fill. Excel updates the chart to show the default brown paper texture. Don't worry, you will fix this.

13. Click Insert from File in the dialog. Navigate to and select LeftDash.gif. Excel automatically adds a line around your marker. Even though the right side of the marker is transparent, Excel outlines the entire marker.

14. For the Marker Line Color category, choose No Line. Click Close to close the Format dialog box.

15. On the Layout ribbon, choose Legend, No Legend.

16. Choose Chart Title, Above Chart. Type the title AAPL 2006.

17. Resize the chart so it is horizontally smaller.

18. Right-click the numbers along the vertical axis, choose Format Axis, and then choose Minimum, Fixed, 50. (If you are going to later add volume to the chart, you could allow the vertical scale to run from 0 to 100. If you are only showing OHLC on the chart, you can scale the vertical axis from 50 to 100.)

The final chart is shown in Figure 6.20.

Figure 6.20
The markers for the Open series are image files created in Photoshop.

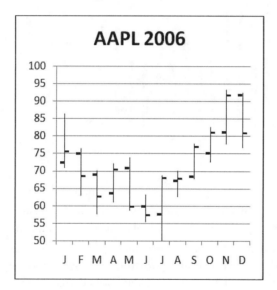

The process of adding the open markers adds complexity to creating this chart. However, if you often need to create OHLC charts, you can save this chart type as a template to streamline the process in the future. To save a chart as a template, select the chart and then chose Save As Template from the Type group on the Design ribbon.

Adding Volume to a High-Low-Close Chart

There are two ways to add a volume column chart to a high-low-close chart. First, Microsoft offers a built-in volume-high-low-close chart; however, this built-in chart automatically moves the prices from the left axis to the right axis. Second, you can add volumes while keeping the prices along the left axis.

Creating a Built-in Volume-High-Low-Close Chart

You follow these steps to create a built-in volume-high-low-close chart:

1. Arrange your data with Date in column A, Volume in B, High in column C, Low in column D, and Close in column E.

2. If you have actual dates in column A, remove the Date heading from the top-left-corner cell.

3. Select the range of data in A:E.

4. On the Insert ribbon, choose Other Charts, Volume-High-Low-Close. Excel creates the chart shown in Figure 6.21. The volume bars are keyed to a different axis than the rest of the chart, but the scale seems a bit wrong; the volume bars obscure the actual OHLC lines.

Figure 6.21
The volume columns hide the high-low-close markers for most of this chart.

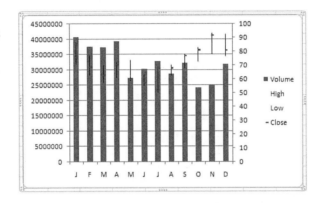

5. Right-click the numbers along the left side of the chart and choose Format Axis.

6. In the Format Axis dialog that appears, click Minimum Fixed and double the value shown in the box. In this example, you double the original value of 4.5E7 to 9E7.

7. To remove the axis labels for the Volume columns, change the Axis Labels drop-down in the center of the Format Axis dialog to None. Change the Major Tick Mark Type drop-down to None. Click Close to close the Format Axis dialog.

8. On the Layout ribbon, choose Legend, None.

9. In the Current Selection drop-down, choose Series Close. Click Format Selection.

10. Click Marker Options in the left navigation bar of the Format Data Series dialog. Increase the size from 5 to 9. Click Close.

11. The gridlines shown in the chart are for the volume columns. You need to remove them and put in gridlines for the prices, so on the Layout ribbon, choose Gridlines, Primary Horizontal Gridlines, None. Then choose Gridlines, Secondary Horizontal Gridlines, Major Gridlines.

12. From the Current Selection drop-down, choose Secondary Vertical (Value) Axis Major Gridlines. Click Format Selection.

13. In the Format Major Gridline dialog that appears, choose Solid Line. In the Color drop-down, choose a light gray color to make the gridlines less obtrusive.

14. On the Layout ribbon, choose Chart Title, Centered Overlay Title. Type `AAPL 2006` and press Enter.

15. Click on the border of the chart to choose the chart area. On the Format ribbon, select Shape Outline, No Outline to remove the extra box around the chart.

16. Reduce the horizontal size of the chart by clicking the right resizing handle and dragging toward the center of the chart.

The resulting chart is shown in Figure 6.22. It is a bit disconcerting to have the axis scale appear on the right side of the chart when 99% of the charts in the Western world have the axis appear on the left side of the chart.

Figure 6.22
After a number of adjustments, the built-in volume-high-low-close chart does the job, although the axis appears on the wrong side.

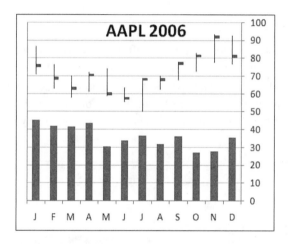

Adding Volume to the Right Axis of a High-Low-Close Chart

Although the method described in this section is a bit more complicated than the method described in the preceding section, it allows you to add the volume to the axis on the right side of the chart. This method completely abandons the built-in stock chart types and shows how the stock chart types are really just an interesting mixture of standard settings.

The following steps add volume to the high-low-close chart shown in Figure 6.19. You could easily expand the concept to add an Open marker as in the chart shown in Figure 6.20.

You follow these steps to create a volume-high-low-close chart:

1. Download data from http://finance.yahoo.com. Rearrange the data to show Date in column A, High in column B, Low in column C, Close in column D, and Volume in column E.

2. Remove the Date heading from the top-left cell in the range.

3. Although you have data in columns A:E, select only the data in columns A:D.

4. On the Insert ribbon, choose Line, 2-D Line, Line. Excel creates the chart shown in Figure 6.23.

6

Figure 6.23
This line chart appears to be a long way from the OHLC format you desire.

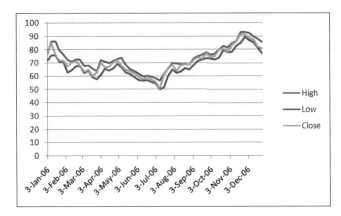

5. On the Layout ribbon, choose Series High from the Current Selection drop-down. Click Format Selection and then choose Line Color, No Line.

6. Without closing the Format Data Series dialog, choose Series Low from the Current Selection drop-down in the Layout ribbon. In the Format Data Series dialog, choose Line Color, No Line. The high and low lines are now completely invisible, as shown in Figure 6.24.

Figure 6.24
Make the high and low lines invisible.

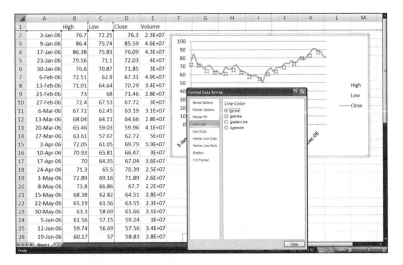

7. Keep the Format dialog open. From the Layout ribbon, choose Lines, High-Low Lines. Excel draws vertical lines between the invisible high and low points, as shown in Figure 6.25.

Figure 6.25
Add High-Low lines to draw the vertical lines from the invisible high and low markers.

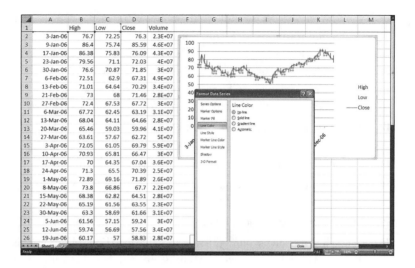

8. Keep the Format dialog open. Choose Series "Close" from the Current Selection drop-down on the Layout ribbon. In the Format dialog, make the following selections:

- Choose Marker Options, Built-In, Type, choose the sixth type, which is a right-facing dash.
- Change the Size setting from 5 to 8.
- Choose Marker Fill, Solid Fill and then select black.
- Choose Line Color, No Line.
- Choose Marker Line Color, Solid Line and then select black.

Click Close to close the dialog box. You have now created a high-low-close style chart from the line chart, as shown in Figure 6.26.

Figure 6.26
The line chart is now a high-low-close style chart. Notice the blue resizing handle in the upper-right corner of D2.

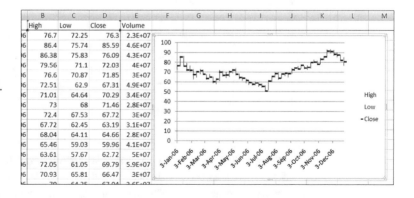

6

9. From the Current Selection drop-down in the Layout ribbon, choose Chart Area. You should notice a blue outline around columns B:D.

10. Grab the blue resizing handle in the upper-right corner of D2. Drag to the right to add column E to the chart. Don't be concerned that you can no longer see the high-low-close markers.

11. From the Current Selection drop-down on the Layout ribbon, choose Series Volume. Click Format Selection. Choose Secondary Axis. Click Close. In a bizarre twist, the columns that appeared in step 10 turn into an invisible line chart.

12. On the Design ribbon, choose Change Chart Type. Select the first column chart icon–Clustered Column. The columns reappear.

13. Right-click the numbers along the right axis of the chart. Choose Format Axis.

14. Click Maximum, Fixed. Double the number in the Fixed text box. Choose Major Tick Mark Type, None. Choose Axis Labels, None. Click Close.

15. Choose Layout, Legend, None.

16. Right-click the labels along the horizontal axis. Choose Format Axis. Choose Axis Options, Major Unit, Fixed, 1, Months. For the Number category, choose the custom type mmmmm. Click Close.

17. Choose Layout, Chart Title, Above Chart. Type the chart title AAPL 2006.

18. Reduce the horizontal size of the chart.

The final chart is shown in Figure 6.27.

Figure 6.27
This volume-high-low-close chart was created from a line chart.

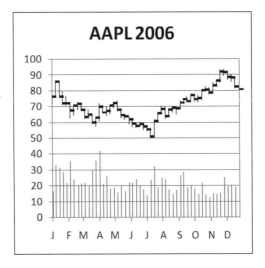

> **NOTE**
> If you try to add volume as a column chart on the secondary axis to one of Excel's built-in stock charts, Excel indicates that certain types cannot be combined and prevents you from producing the chart. As you can see, you can actually skip the built-in stock chart type and build the chart as a line chart.

The next section describes candlestick charts, which require the least customization because Excel actually has good built-in charts to create candlestick charts.

Creating Candlestick Charts

A basic candlestick chart requires a data range with date in the first column, then open, high, low, and close values in the remaining columns. To create a candlestick chart, you follow these steps:

1. Download data from http://finance.yahoo.com. Your data will be in the correct sequence, with Date in column A, Open in column B, High in column C, Low in column D, and Close in column E.

2. Select your data in columns A:E.

3. On the Insert ribbon, select Other Charts, Stock, Open-High-Low-Close. Excel creates the top chart in Figure 6.28.

Figure 6.28
The top chart shows the default chart created in step 3. Minimal formatting changes are required to create the final chart at the bottom of this figure.

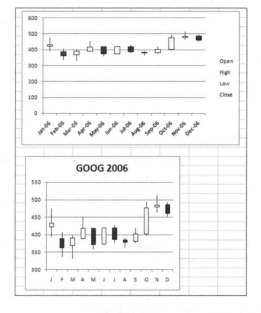

4. Right-click the numbers along the vertical axis and choose Format Axis. Specify a fixed minimum value that is greater than zero but lower than the low value for the range in question.

5. On the Layout ribbon, choose Legend, None.

6. Still on the Layout ribbon, choose Chart Title, Above Chart. Type the title GOOG 2006 and press Enter.

7. Right-click the labels along the horizontal axis and choose Format Axis. On the Number tab, specify the custom formatting code mmmmm.

8. Reduce the horizontal size of the chart.

The final chart is shown as the bottom chart in Figure 6.28.

Changing Colors in a Candlestick Chart

By default, Excel uses white columns to indicate periods in which the stock price increased and black columns to indicate periods in which the stock price decreased. Although that is incredibly convenient for this monochrome book, you are likely to present your charts in color. It is easy to customize the colors in a chart.

To apply an effect to the columns, you use the Design ribbon and select, for example, Layout, Style 28. This applies a beveled effect to the up/down bars.

The white up bars and the black down bars are actually two separate objects in the chart. You have to format the up bars and then the down bars. To change the color of the bars, you follow these steps.

1. On the Format ribbon, select Current Selection, Up Bars 1.

2. Select Format, Shape Fill and then select green. (In color stock charts, up periods are typically shown in green.)

3. On the Format ribbon, select Current Selection, Down Bars 1.

4. Select Format, Shape Fill and then select red. (In color stock charts, up periods are typically shown in red.)

Adding Volume to a Candlestick Chart

Excel offers a built-in chart you can use to create a candlestick chart with volume bars. As with the volume-high-low-close chart, the height of the volume bars is often too large.

You follow these steps to create a chart based on the built-in volume-open-high-low-close chart type:

1. Download data from http://finance.yahoo.com. Save the data as an Excel 2007 workbook. Insert a new column B before the Open column. Move the Volume data from column G to the new column B. Delete column G. Your data will be in the correct sequence, with Date in column A, Volume in column B, Open in column C, High in column D, Low in column E, and Close in column F.

2. Remove the Date heading from cell A1.

3. Select your data in columns A:F.

4. On the Insert ribbon, select Other Charts, Stock, Volume-Open-High-Low-Close. This is the fourth stock chart thumbnail. Excel creates the top chart in Figure 6.29.

5. Right-click the numbers along the left vertical axis and choose Format Axis. Specify a fixed maximum value that is about double the original amount. Choose Major Tick Mark Type, None. Choose Axis Labels, None.

6. On the Layout ribbon, choose Legend, None.

7. Choose Chart Title, Above Chart. Type the title `GOOG 2006` and press Enter.

8. Right-click the labels along the horizontal axis. Choose Format Axis. On the Number tab, specify the custom formatting code mmmmm.

9. Reduce the horizontal size of the chart.

The final chart is shown as the bottom chart in Figure 6.29.

Figure 6.29
The top chart shows the default chart created in step 4. The bottom chart shows the result of the remaining formatting.

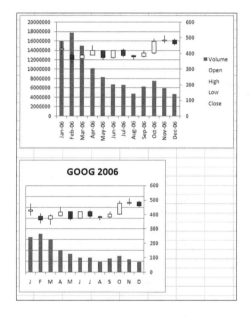

Manually Creating a Candlestick Chart with Volume

The problem with the chart in Figure 6.29 is that the stock prices appear on the right side of the chart. If you would like your stock prices on the left side of the chart, you have to abandon the built-in stock charts. In that case, you need to have a good understanding of how Excel draws in high-low lines and up/down bars.

6

Figure 6.30 shows four line series on a single chart. The first series is the thick solid line from lower left to upper right. The second series is the dotted line at the top of the chart. The third series starts out as the lowest dashed line but crosses to become the second-lowest line late in the chart.

You add high-low lines to a chart by selecting Layout, Lines, High-Low Lines. Figure 6.31 shows that the vertical lines extend from the lowest value at each data point to the highest value at each data point. In February, the line extends from the 1 in series 3 up to the 12 in series 2. In October, the high-low line extends from the 1 in Series 1 to the 12 in Series 2.

Figure 6.30
These four series are used to illustrate the different behavior of high-low lines and up/down bars.

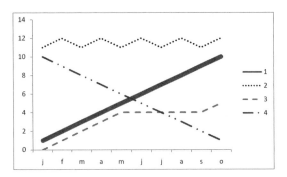

Figure 6.31
High-low lines look at all the line series in the chart and extend from the lowest to the highest at each data point.

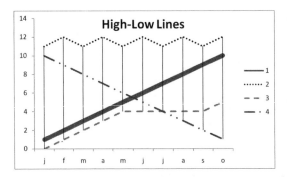

In contrast to high-low lines, up/down bars always extend from the first series line to the last series line. In Figure 6.32, the up/down bars always start at the solid line for Series 1 and extend to the dash-dot line for Series 4. You would think that there would be a setting somewhere that you could use to specify that the up/down bars should extend from one series to another series. Instead, Excel always draws them from the first series to the last series (see Figure 6.32).

Both the high-low lines and up/down bars are valid only for series that are plotted as line charts. If you need to add a series for volume, you need to make sure to plot that series as a column chart so that it does not interfere with your high-low or up/down elements. If you need to add a series to show the price of a competing stock, you can add the series as a scatter chart with a smooth line to prevent that series from interfering with the high-low or up/down elements.

Figure 6.32
Up/down bars always start at the first series and extend to the last series.

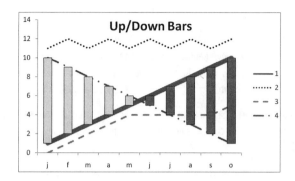

CASE STUDY

Creating a Candlestick Stock Chart Showing Volume and a Competitor

Candlestick charts are popular at http://finance.yahoo.com. In addition to a candlestick chart showing the price of one security, a secondary line chart is often added to show the relative price of another security. The chart is designed to show how equal investments in one security or the other would have fared over time.

In this case study, the chart you'll build compares the performance of Apple versus Microsoft from March 1, 2005, through December 31, 2006.

When you download data from the historical tables at http://finance.yahoo.com, make note of the opening price for both stocks on the starting date of March 1, 2005. (The price for Apple was $44.99, and the price for Microsoft was $25.19.)

In Figure 6.33, the first few columns show Apple data from http://finance.yahoo.com. Date, Open, High, Low, Close, and Volume occupy columns A:F. Column G contains the adjusted closing price for Microsoft for each month. Column F shows the start of the calculation of a MSFT index line. This line shows the closing price of Microsoft multiplied by (44.99/25.19). This calculation adjusts the starting price of Microsoft stock up to the same value as Apple. Say that you had purchased $44.99 of Apple and Microsoft on March 1, 2005. The MSFT index line shows the value of your Microsoft shares.

Figure 6.33
You can build a column that shows the relative value of Microsoft.

	G2	▾	fx	=(44.99/25.19)*H2			
◢	A	B	C	D	E	F	G	H
1		Open	High	Low	Close	Avg Vol	MSFT Index	MSFT Close
2	Mar-05	44.99	45.11	38.83	41.67	24,857,231	42.17	23.61
3	Apr-05	42.09	44.45	34	36.06	34,093,790		24.71
4	May-05	36.21	40.94	33.11	39.76	22,555,271		25.28
5	Jun-05	39.89	40.76	35.52	36.81	19,067,509		24.34
6	Jul-05	36.83	44.38	36.29	42.65	19,029,154		25.1
7	Aug-05	42.57	48.33	42.02	46.89	15,223,234		26.91
8	Sep-05	47	54.56	46.09	53.61	21,903,747		25.29

6

To begin building the chart, you copy the formula from G2 down to all rows of your dataset. Based on how Excel plots high-low lines and up/down bars, you know that the Open column has to be the first series plotted as a line. The Close column has to be the last series plotted as a line. This means you have to manually change the chart type for the volume series to a column and manually change the chart type for the line series to a scatter chart.

If you were starting with a stock chart type, you would have to build the chart with a few series and then add more series later. Because you are building this chart as a line chart, you can add all six series at once. To finish building the chart, you do the following:

1. Select the data in A1:G23. On the Insert ribbon, choose Line, 2-D Line, Line. You see a chart with only one visible line. Because the Volume numbers are so large, this is the only line you can initially see (see Figure 6.34).

Figure 6.34
You initially see only one line on the chart.

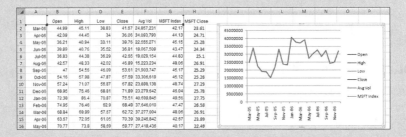

2. On the Layout ribbon, select Series Avg Vol from the Current Selection drop-down. Click Format Selection. Click Secondary Axis. Excel now shows six lines on the chart (see Figure 6.35).

Figure 6.35
After you move the volume to a secondary axis, all six lines appear.

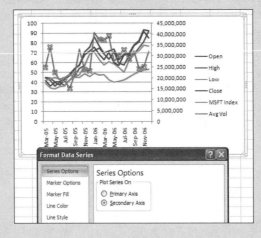

3. Choose Series Avg Vol from the Current Selection drop-down on the Layout ribbon. On the Design ribbon, choose Change Chart Type, Column, Clustered Column. The columns are too large and cover up many of the lines in the chart.

4. Right-click the numbers along the secondary value axis on the right side of the chart. Choose Format Axis. Choose Maximum Fixed. Change the current value for the maximum from 4.5E7 to 1.2E8. (This is about 2.7 times the original size to ensure that the volume bars take up only the lower third of the chart.) In the same dialog box, change Major Tick Mark Type to None and Axis Labels to None.

5. Choose Series MSFT Index from the Current Selection drop-down on the Layout ribbon. On the Design ribbon, choose Change Chart Type, X Y (Scatter), Scatter with Straight Lines. This is the fifth charting thumbnail in the X Y Scatter line. The line for MSFT disappears.

6. Choose Series MSFT Index from the Current Selection drop-down on the Layout ribbon. Click Format Selection. Change the Series Options panel to indicate Primary Axis. Change Line Color to Solid Line and then select red. Change Line Style, Dash Type to a dotted line. Your chart now has four series as line charts, one as a column chart, and one as an X Y scatter chart. It is now appropriate to draw in the high-low lines and up/down bars.

7. Choose Series Open from the Current Selection drop-down on the Layout ribbon. Choose Lines, High-Low Lines. Choose Up/Down Bars, Up/Down Bars.

8. Next, to remove the lines from the first four series, on the Format ribbon, choose Series Open. Choose Format, Shape Outline, No Line.

9. Repeat step 8 for High, Low, and Close lines.

10. Add a title by choosing Chart Title, Centered Overlay Title on the Layout ribbon. Type the title AAPL and press Enter. Drag the title to the top-left corner of the chart.

11. You need a legend in this chart to indicate that the dotted line is a Microsoft index line. While four of the six legend entries are useless because the line is hidden, the legends for Volume and MSFT Index are worthwhile, so, in the original dataset, clear the headings Open, High, Low, and Close in B1:E1. The legend appears, with Volume on the top, then four blank lines, and MSFT Index on the bottom. Use the Layout ribbon to select Legend, Show Legend at Bottom. After moving the legend to the bottom, only the Avg Vol and MSFT Index entries appear.

12. Traditionally, http://finance.yahoo.com shows this chart without any prices along the axis. This is because the Microsoft line is a relative index line and not an actual price line. To remove the prices from the axis, right-click the labels on the left axis. Choose Format Axis, Axis Options, Axis Labels, None. Or, instead of removing the axis labels, you can use the Number tab and format them as currency with no decimal places.

The chart is shown in Figure 6.36.

Figure 6.36
Microsoft was outper-forming Apple during 2005. Since the video iPod (and the "Learn Excel from MrExcel" pod-cast?) debuted in October 2005, Apple has taken off.

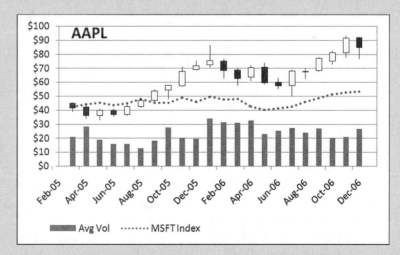

This chart presents a number of interesting concepts:

- Either the candlestick or OHLC charts must be created with series that use a line chart type, although you turn off the line in all cases.
- Any other index lines on the chart must be converted to X Y scatter charts, with a line connecting invisible points. Thus, the only series on the chart that appears as a line really is not a line chart at all.
- You could add additional index lines to the chart, but each would have to be X Y series.
- You can squash the volume column chart into the lower third of the chart by fixing the maximum value for the scale at three times the maximum value.

This case study demonstrates that you can duplicate stock charts without using the Microsoft built-in stock chart types. In fact, using a line chart gives you more flexibility to add additional data series to a chart.

Creating a Live Chart by Using a Web Connection

In public companies, senior management spends a lot of time focusing on the current stock price. This could be because they are truly concerned for the individual investors, or it could be that they are interested in the current value of their stock options.

In the 1980s, an investor relations administrator continually updated a whiteboard showing the stock price of my employer and the two competitors in our industry. Dialing in to a service 24 times a day just to update the whiteboard had to be a horrible chore.

Excel offers fabulous tools that automatically query data from a webpage every minute and refresh data in Excel. It is best if this process is running in its own instance of Excel or, better yet, on a standalone computer. (If you think it is insane to spend $500 on a computer to update the stock price every minute, consider how insane it was to have a person doing this job manually day after day.)

To set up a web query, you need to first move the cell pointer to an out-of-the-way location on the worksheet. The web query returns unformatted data that you almost always want to reformat. You therefore want to locate the query outside the field of view and use formulas or charts to display the data. To build this chart, you then do the following:

1. Select cell A40.
2. From the Data ribbon, choose From Web. A New Web Query dialog box pops up, showing the home page selected in your installation of Internet Explorer. (On my computer, the Google home page displays in a mini browser in Excel.)
3. Use the New Web Query dialog box to navigate to your favorite source of stock quote information. For example, navigate to http://finance.yahoo.com. Click in the Get Quotes box and type the ticker symbols MSFT, AAPL, GOOG and click the Go button. After the webpage finishes loading, Excel draws a series of yellow arrows. Each arrow indicates a table on the webpage.

4. Scroll down to the table that contains the data you would like to import to Excel. While you hover over the yellow arrow, an outline appears, showing the extent of the table. Click the yellow arrow to change it to a green check mark (see Figure 6.37).

Figure 6.37
You choose the table(s) from the webpage to be imported.

Yellow Arrows

Green Checkmark

Extent of Selected Table

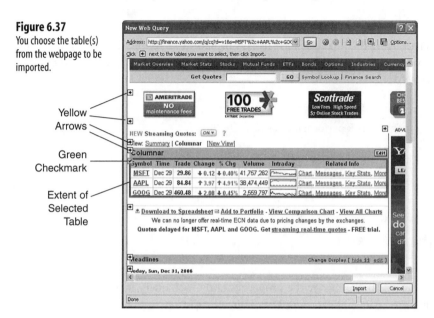

5. Click the Import button. The New Web Query dialog box is dismissed, and the Import Data dialog appears. Confirm the location for the imported data and then click OK. A strange bit of text appears in the active cell. A few seconds later, a text version of the table appears in your spreadsheet. Right now, this is a one-time snapshot of the data. After you build a few formulas and a chart, you can change the properties of the web query to refresh every minute.

> **NOTE**
> You do not want to be working in Excel while the query is set to auto-refresh. It is incredibly annoying to lose focus on the active cell every minute while the web query refreshes. To alleviate this problem, have the web query running in one instance of Excel and work in a second instance of Excel.

6. You want to build formulas that extract the desired information from the imported data. In this case, a simple bar chart with three points will work fine. The formula in I41 builds some text that is used as both the category value and the label for the bar chart. The formula in I41 is `=A41&" "&C41&" "&E41`. The formula in J41 is more complex, as it has to convert the text value of Down 0.40% to a value of -0.4%. The formula in J41 is `=IF(LEFT(E41,1)="D",-1*MID(E41,6,4),1*MID(E41,4,4))/100`. Copy these formulas down for the competitor's stock quotes, as shown in Figure 6.38.

Figure 6.38
You build formulas
that you can use to
create a chart.

◢	A	B	C	D	E	F	G	H	I	J
40	Symbol	Time	Trade	Change	% Chg	Volume	Intr	Related Info		
41	MSFT	29-Dec	29.86	Down 0.12	Down 0.40%	41,757,262		Char	MSFT 29.86 Down 0.40%	-0.4%
42	AAPL	29-Dec	84.84	Up 3.97	Up 4.91%	38,474,449		Char	AAPL 84.84 Up 4.91%	4.9%
43	GOOG	29-Dec	460.48	Down 2.08	Down 0.45%	2,559,797		Char	GOOG 460.48 Down 0.45%	-0.5%
44										

7. Build a chart using the formulas in I41:J43. Format the chart and move it up to occupy a spot in your executive dashboard. In Figure 6.39, a simple bar chart shows the relative increase/decrease of each security.

Figure 6.39
You build a chart
that reflects data
from the web query.

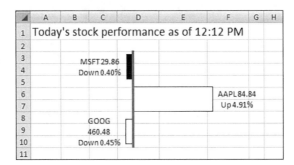

8. After the chart is built, change the properties of the web query by right-clicking a cell in the imported data and choosing Data Range Properties.

9. In the External Data Range Properties dialog that appears, check the Refresh Every box. Change the spin button from 60 minutes to 1 minute. Also choose the box for Refresh Data When Opening the File (see Figure 6.40). When you click OK, the web query begins to refresh every minute, automatically updating your chart in the dashboard.

Figure 6.40
Excel updates the
web query every
minute.

6

It is possible to build a dashboard with many different web feeds and charts that automatically update as long as the Internet connection remains live. You can accomplish this without writing any VBA macros.

Making Charts Small for Use in Dashboards

The goal of creating an executive dashboard is to fit a lot of data into a single screen of data. Fellow Excel MVP Charley Kyd publishes a great e-kit called "Dashboard Reporting with Excel." This is a good kit, with innovative examples of how to fit 100+ charts on a single printed page. When dealing with charts from Excel 97 through Excel 2003, it took Charley 10 pages to explain how to create tiny charts.

Microsoft has added features to Excel 2007 that make it easy to scale charts down until they are very small. In Figure 6.41, it takes only a few steps to modify the default large chart (at the top) to a chart that occupies 1/16 the space (the second chart) and still communicates just as much information.

Figure 6.41
It is now easier to create small charts for dashboards.

You follow these steps to convert the original chart shown in Figure 6.39 into the smaller chart shown as the second chart in the figure.

1. On the Layout ribbon, choose Legend, None.

2. Right-click the labels on the horizontal axis. Choose Format Axis. Click the Number category. Specify the custom number format mmmmm. Click the Axis Options category in the left navigation bar. Choose Major Unit, Fixed, 1, Months. For the Tick Mark Location setting, choose None. Click Close.

6

3. Click the chart border to select the entire chart. On the Home ribbon, change the font size to 8. While the chart area is selected, choose Shape Outline, None from the Format ribbon to remove the border from the entire chart. To have the background of the worksheet's cells show through, choose Shape Fill, None from the Format ribbon.

4. Resize the chart down to seven cells tall by four cells wide.

In just a few steps, you have achieved a 75% reduction in the chart size. If you want to reduce the chart size even more, you can follow these steps to create the third chart shown in Figure 6.39:

1. On the Layout ribbon, choose Chart Title, Centered Overlay Title. Excel now uses 70% of the vertical height of the chart area for the plot area. Grab the title and move it to an out-of-the-way location. In this particular chart, that might be the lower-right corner of the plot area.

2. Right-click the Value axis labels and do the following:
   - Choose Format Axis.
   - Choose Minimum, Fixed, 50.
   - Choose Major Unit, Fixed, 50.
   - Choose Major Tick Mark Type, None.

3. Resize the chart to three columns tall by five cells wide, as shown in the third chart in Figure 6.41.

This is an 86% reduction from the size of the original chart.

The fourth chart in Figure 6.41 is reminiscent of Edward Tufte's sparkline concept. The developers at Microsoft are fans of Tufte and provided one useful layout that gets you to this chart very quickly. In the following steps, you start with the first chart in Figure 6.41 and end up producing the fourth chart in the figure:

1. Right-click the labels along the vertical axis. Choose Format Axis. Choose Minimum, Fixed, 50.

2. On the Design ribbon, open the Chart Layouts gallery and choose Layout 11.

3. Click once on the chart line to select the whole line. Very carefully, click the last point in the line. If you look in the Current Selection box on the Layout ribbon, the selection should be Series AAPL, Point 26-Dec. Right-click the final point and choose Add Data Label.

4. On the Layout ribbon, choose Chart Title, Centered Overlay Title. Type AAPL and press Enter. Drag the title to the lower-right corner of the chart.

5. Resize the chart to three rows tall by two columns wide—a 95% reduction from the original chart. After you have resized the chart, use the Font drop-down on the Home ribbon to select an 8-point font.

Using the steps described here, you can easily fit stock charts for all 30 components of the Dow Jones 30 Industrials Index on half of a printed sheet of paper (see Figure 6.42).

Figure 6.42
These eight charts take up four columns × 13 rows. You can easily fit 30 charts in a single screen of data.

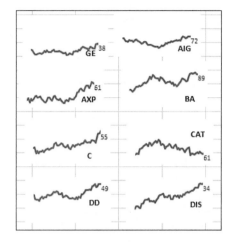

Next Steps

You learned in this chapter that sometimes you need to think creatively to coax an "impossible" chart out of Excel. In Chapter 7, "Advanced Chart Techniques," you will learn how to use Excel's built-in charting tools to create charts that you normally do not see in Excel.

6

Advanced Chart Techniques

A Tool Chest of Advanced Charting Techniques

As the host of MrExcel.com, I get to see a lot of wild spreadsheets that people create. I've seen some amazing things come across my desk. This chapter covers some of the usual advanced charting tricks, and some unusual charts that you don't typically see in Excel. At the end of the chapter are a few examples of some charts that impressed me, so that you can see some of the cool things people can coax out of Excel.

The ideas in this section can be useful on most chart types that you work with. They include many techniques that you will come to realize are the basic, why-didn't-I-think-of-doing-that kind of ideas.

Mixing Two Chart Types on a Single Chart

Although the Chart Type dialog doesn't offer it as a choice anymore, you can represent a chart's series with different chart types. Instead of two lines on a chart, you can show one series as a line and one series as columns. Or you can mix columns and area charts, as shown in Figure 7.1.

To change the chart type for a series, you right-click the series and choose Change Series Chart Type from the context menu.

Figure 7.1
To emphasize one series, you can mix chart types on a single chart.

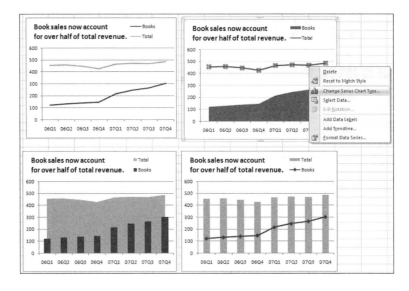

You can mix only certain chart types. For best results when mixing chart types, follow these guidelines:

- You should stick with 2-D chart types. Excel does not let you mix 3-D charts.

- Within the 2-D types, you should mix only clustered chart types. Excel doesn't, for example, stack a stacked area chart on top of stacked columns.

- You can't mix vertical types with horizontal types. You need to keep columns, lines, and area charts together because bar charts don't mix with them.

- You can mix circular charts. You can, for example, change one series of a doughnut chart to a pie chart.

- Remember that in many cases, a line chart can be changed to an XY scatter with line series. The advantage is that up/down bars and hi-lo lines ignore an XY scatter chart line.

Moving Charts from One Worksheet to Another

You can combine charts from many worksheets into a single dashboard by moving the charts from their original locations.

If your sales data is on a sales worksheet, for example, you can build the chart on the sales worksheet. When the chart is selected, you choose Move Chart from the Design ribbon. You can then choose to move the chart to a different worksheet (see Figure 7.2).

Figure 7.2
You use the Move Chart
dialog to build a dash-
board of charts on a
single sheet.

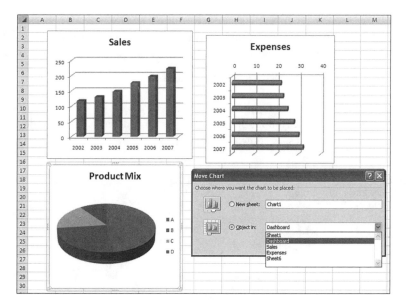

The chart continues to point to data on the original worksheet, but you end up with an uncluttered screen of just charts. Even though the charts are on a new worksheet, they still respond to data changes on the source worksheets.

Using Shapes to Annotate a Chart

Excel offers 165 shapes on the Insert ribbon. Any of these shapes can contain text and can be added to a chart to call attention to certain aspects of the chart. As an example, in the chart in Figure 7.3, a block arrow shape points out reduced revenue levels in July through September. A callout below the chart points to the reduced June profits.

Figure 7.3
Shapes with added text
annotate key points in
this chart.

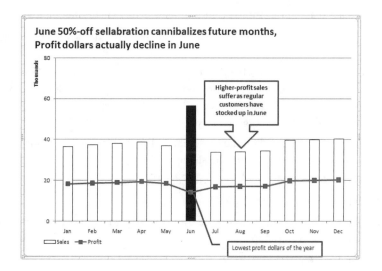

There is one trick to using shapes on your chart: you need to make sure your chart is active before you click a shape in the Insert ribbon. If the chart is not active and you draw a shape over the chart, the shape is actually anchored to a particular cell in the worksheet.

To add a shape to a chart, you follow these steps:

1. Click the chart.

2. On the Insert ribbon, open the Shapes drop-down. This drop-down offers 165 shapes in 8 categories, as shown in Figure 7.4.

Figure 7.4
You can choose from these 165 shapes.

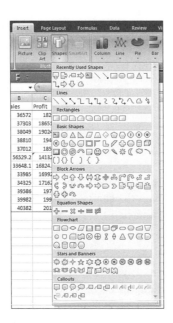

3. Click a shape. Your mouse pointer changes to a small plus sign.

4. Click and drag on the chart to draw a shape. The initial shape is filled with a solid color.

5. Use the white resizing handles to adjust the size of the shape. Use the yellow diamond handles to change the inflection points of the shape. Use the green rotation handle to rotate the shape. All the shapes in Figure 7.5 are right arrow callout shapes that have been modified by dragging the yellow inflection handles.

6. From the Format ribbon, choose Shape Fill, White and then Shape Outline, Black to remove the fill color from the shape.

7. Right-click the shape and choose Edit Text.

8. Type your text in the shape.

9. Use the formatting icons on the Home ribbon to change the alignment and font size of the text in the shape.

Figure 7.5
You can use the handles to resize, reshape, and rotate a shape.

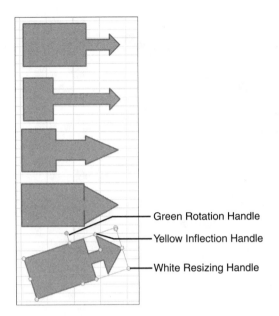

Green Rotation Handle

Yellow Inflection Handle

White Resizing Handle

> **NOTE**
> Because you are planning on adding text to these shapes, you should not plan on rotating the shapes unless you want the text to be rotated as well.

When working with shapes, you'll note that the Shapes drop-down includes a number of lines and arrows. While adding an arrow to a chart, you can hover over an existing shape to reveal four red connector dots. If you start or end an arrow on a connector dot, the arrow automatically moves when the connected shapes move.

Making Columns or Bars Float

In Figure 7.6, the black bars appear to float in midair. This type of chart is good for showing the components of a whole.

The secret is that you plot the floating bars as Series 2. Series 1 is a dummy series that you fill using No Fill in Excel 2007.

There are some interesting settings involved in creating the charts shown in Figure 7.6. You follow these steps to create the top chart in the figure:

1. Set up a data table to split the single series into two series. In Figure 7.7, column B shows the sales for each category. The formulas in column C:E are the data used to create the chart. The formulas in column C copy the values from column A. The formulas in column E copy column B.

7

Figure 7.6
The floating columns or bars demonstrate how components make up a whole.

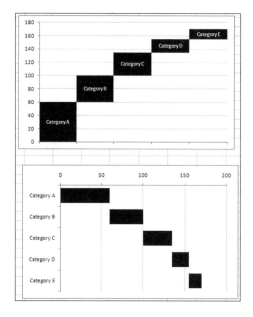

2. Enter 0 in cell D2. This is the "height" of the invisible column. For the first series, the height is therefore 0.

3. In cell D3, enter =D2+E2. This formula adds the starting height of the last column (D2) and the height of the previous column (E2).

4. Double-click the fill handle in cell D3 to copy the formula down to the rest of the series. Your data should now look like the data shown in Figure 7.7.

Figure 7.7
Formulas in column C show the starting point for each column. That series will later become invisible.

D3			f_x =D2+E2		
	A	B	C	D	E	F
1		Sales		Invisible	Sales	
2	Category A	60	Category A	0	60	
3	Category B	40	Category B	60	40	
4	Category C	35	Category C	100	35	
5	Category D	20	Category D	135	20	
6	Category E	15	Category E	155	15	
7						

5. Select cells C1:E6. From the Insert ribbon, choose Column, Stacked Column. Excel creates the chart shown in Figure 7.8.

6. From the Layout ribbon, choose Legend, None.

7. Click any of the lower columns in order to select the first series. From the Format ribbon, choose Shape Fill, No Fill. You might think that Excel is still outlining the first series, but those lines are the selection border. Click away from the series in order to make the selection completely disappear.

Figure 7.8

You can see the Invisible series before it disappears.

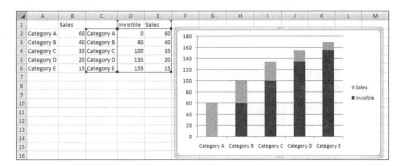

8. Right-click the visible series and choose Format Data Series. In the Series Options category, set Gap Width to No Gap.

9. The second series is whichever color happens to be the second accent color in the current theme. While the series is selected, choose Shape Fill and select a desired color.

10. Right-click the second series and choose Add Data Labels. If your series fill color is dark, you can't see the labels at all. Right-click in the center of one column and if you are lucky, you actually select the label. If you aren't lucky, use the Current Selection drop-down in the Layout ribbon to select Series Sales Data Labels.

11. With the data labels selected, choose Font Color on the Home ribbon and then select a font color that contrasts with the column. You can now see that Microsoft has labeled the columns with the sales value. Click the Bold button on the Home ribbon. After changing the label in step 13, you might come back to the Home ribbon to change the font size so that the labels completely fit in the column.

12. From the Layout ribbon, choose Format Selection. Excel displays the Format Data Labels dialog.

13. In the Format Data Labels dialog, change Label Contains from Value to Category Name. Note that in Label Position, you don't have a choice for Outside End, and that is really the choice you want. Turn toward Redmond and grumble that Microsoft disabled this choice in stacked charts. Click Close to close the dialog. Your chart now has the categories shown as labels on the columns and along the horizontal axis, as shown in Figure 7.9. This is a redundant use of ink.

Figure 7.9

The category labels along the horizontal axis are redundant.

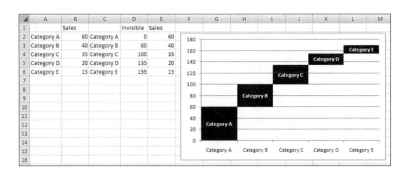

7

14. Right-click the labels along the baseline and choose Format Axis. Change the Axis Labels drop-down to None. Change Major Tick Mark Type to None and then click Close.

15. The last element to format are the gridlines. While having gridlines every 20 units seems to create too many gridlines, those gridlines are very useful for the smaller Category D and Category E columns, which are a long way from the left axis. Still, you can make the gridlines less obtrusive: Right-click a gridline and choose Format Gridlines. Choose Solid Color, and a color drop-down appears. Select a light gray from the color drop-down.

The preceding steps create the column chart shown in the top of Figure 7.6. The steps to create the bar chart in the bottom of Figure 7.6 are similar, with two changes:

- In step 5, choose Bar, Stacked Bar from the Insert ribbon to create a bar chart instead of a column chart.

- In step 8, set the gap width to 43% instead of No Gap. This creates a small vertical gap between the bars.

- Add a new step to reverse the order of the bars. Right-click the category axis, and choose Format Axis. In the Format dialog box, choose the Categories in Reverse Order check box.

Using a Rogue XY Series to Label the Vertical Axis

The chart in Figure 7.10 shows annual scores against a government performance index. The actual index number is not as relevant as the ranges shown in A11:B15. These ratings decide whether a company can continue to do business in a particular segment. It would be better to create arbitrary gridlines in place of the horizontal gridlines.

Figure 7.10

A better chart would have gridlines to correspond to the five performance categories shown in A11:B15.

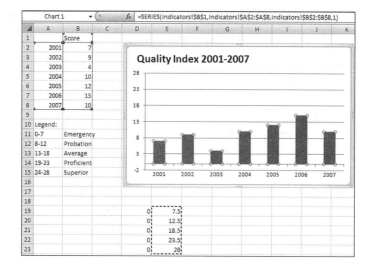

The goal is to draw gridlines at unevenly spaced locations of 3, 8, 13, 18, 23, and 27. There is not a good way to adjust the gridlines to show horizontal lines for each category. The main problem is that Excel treats the collection of horizontal gridlines as a single object. When you format one major gridline, all major gridlines change. If each gridline could be formatted individually, you could draw a gridline every one unit and make most of the gridlines invisible.

The gridlines in Figure 7.10 are actually error bars that are attached to an invisible XY series added to the chart. This solution may seem bizarre. It is not one of those obvious, do-two-steps-and-you-are-done solutions.

CASE STUDY

Converting a Series to Gridlines

This is a fairly complex set of steps, but the results are worth the work. If you actually try it a few times, you will realize how perfectly it works and appreciate the flexibility to both replace the gridlines with new gridlines and to replace the vertical axis labels with new labels. This example includes more figures than usual so you can easily see how it works.

You follow these steps to create arbitrary gridlines and labels:

1. Somewhere on the worksheet, build a table of the locations for each arbitrary gridline. In this case, you want the gridlines to be drawn between 7 and 8, so use numbers such as 7.5, 12.5, and so on in a column.

2. To the left of those labels, fill an identical column with zeros.

3. Select the one-column range that contains the new gridline locations. Press Ctrl+C to copy. Click the chart and press Ctrl+V to paste. Excel adds the data as a new series, as shown in Figure 7.11. Even though this new series has a different number of points than the first series, Excel takes a guess and draws the new series as a clustered column series.

Figure 7.11
When you paste the points to the chart, Excel adds them as a clustered column series.

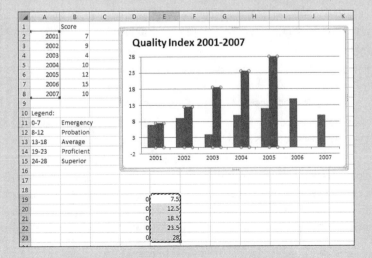

4. Click one of the new columns to select the second series. From the Design ribbon, choose Chart Type, XY (Scatter), Scatter with Only Markers. Because you have mixed a traditional chart with a scatter chart, Excel adds a second horizontal axis at the top of the chart and a second vertical axis at the right of the chart. Out of desperation, Excel applies Series 2 to the secondary axis on both the horizontal and vertical axes.

Figure 7.12
You might be thinking that this series has nothing to do with arbitrary gridlines.

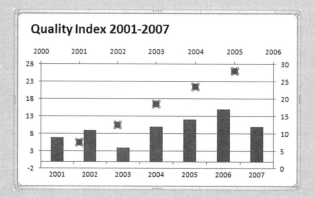

In step 5, you will edit the SERIES function to show Excel where the x values are stored for the second series. If you aren't familiar with the SERIES function, read the sidebar that follows before moving to step 5.

Understanding the SERIES Function

Before proceeding to step 5, you need to understand the SERIES function. If you select a series in a column, line, or bar chart, Excel displays a function in the formula bar. The function has four arguments:

```
=SERIES(Series Name, Labels for Series, Values for Series, Series Sequence)
```

The formula at the top of Figure 7.10, using the SERIES function, looks like this:

```
=SERIES(Indicators!$B$1,Indicators!$A$2:$A$8,Indicators!$B$2:$B$8,1)
```

This means that the series will be known as the score series, based on cell B1. The labels for the horizontal axis are the years in cells A2:A8. The values for each point are in cells B2:B8. The final 1 indicates that this is the first series in the chart.

When you paste new data into the chart, Excel has to guess what you mean. Look at the SERIES function at the top of Figure 7.11:

```
=SERIES(,Indicators!$A$2:$A$8,Indicators!$E$19:$E$23,2)
```

This means that the second series has no name. Excel guessed that the axis labels should be in cells A2:A8. Excel knows that the marker values are in cells E19:E23. The final 2 indicates that this is the second series.

When faced with a problem, computer programmers tend to try to shoehorn a new feature into an old paradigm, and this certainly seems to be the case with the XY charts. In an XY chart, every marker has two locations. You have to specify an x location and a y location. Rather than create a new function to handle XY charts, however, the spreadsheet architects decided that they could replace the labels as the second argument of the SERIES formula and store the x values there. I am sure it made sense at the time, but that is why it is so difficult to label XY charts!

---

5. Click one of the markers for the second series. Wait until Excel displays the SERIES function in the formula bar. Then click in the formula bar and change the second argument of the SERIES formula to point to the zeros in cells D19:D23:

```
=SERIES(,Indicators!$D$19:$D$23,Indicators!$E$19:$E$23,2)
```

> **CAUTION**
>
> Save your workbook before editing the series formula. This is particularly important if you have not updated Excel to Service Release 1 (due out in early 2008). A bug in the initial release of Excel 2007 may sometimes cause a crash when you edit the Series formula.

6. Press Enter to accept this formula. As shown in Figure 7.13, Excel moves the five markers to the left vertical axis, which is the default x location for 0. The secondary horizontal axis at the top of the chart now runs from 0 to 1, in 0.2-unit increments. You will clean all this up later, but it is important to see that the top marker is at that location because it has an x value of 0 and a y value of 28.

Figure 7.13
The second series markers are now glued to the left axis.

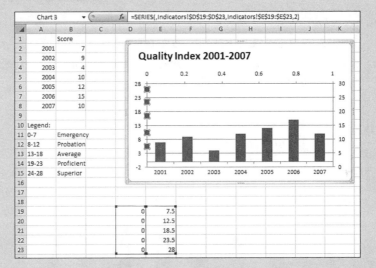

7. To explicitly make sure the scale for the left and right axes match, click the labels along the left axis and press Ctrl+1 to format the primary vertical axis. Make sure the axis shows a fixed minimum of 0 and a fixed maximum of 28. (While you are in the Format Axis dialog, you could make the changes from step 9.) Repeat for the right axis, making sure it runs from a minimum of 0 to a fixed maximum of 28.

8. Format the horizontal axis along the top of the chart. Click the numbers above the chart. Press Ctrl+1 to format the axis. Set a fixed minimum of 0 and a fixed maximum of 1. In Figure 7.14, note that the top marker along the left axis has moved to the top of the chart. This is because you changed the secondary axis maximum from 30 to 28, as shown in Figure 7.14.

9. Go back to the left, top, and right axes and format each axis. Change Axis Labels to None. Change Major Tick Mark Type to None.

10. From the Layout ribbon, choose Gridlines, Primary Horizontal Gridlines, None.

7

Figure 7.14
Make sure that all the axes have fixed upper and lower bounds.

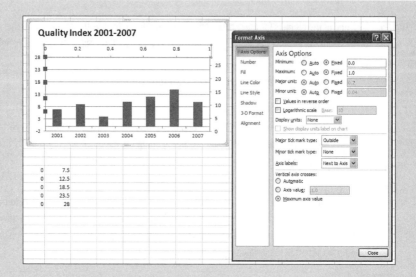

11. Click the border surrounding the plot area. From the Format ribbon, choose Shape Outline, No Outline.

12. Right-click one of the markers along the left vertical axis. Choose Add Data Labels. Excel adds the wrong labels, in the wrong place, as shown in Figure 7.15.

Figure 7.15
You will have to replace those axis labels and move them to a new location.

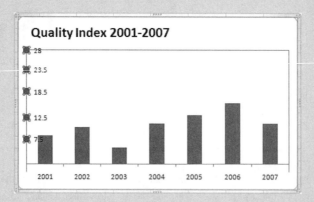

13. Click the top data label (the 28). Initially, all five data labels are selected. Click the data label again, and just that label is selected. Type a new data label, such as 24-28 Superior. Repeat this step for each marker in series 2.

TIP

Chapter 13,"Using Excel VBA to Create Charts," includes a macro that labels all the points in an XY chart. You can use that macro instead of repeating step 13 once for each data label.

14. Click the plot area to deselect the data labels. Again click the data label in order to select all the Series 2 data labels. Right-click the labels and choose Format Data Labels.

15. Choose Left for Label Position. Excel moves the data labels a few millimeters to the left, until they hit the left edge of the chart area.

16. Click the plot area. Grab one of the left resizing handles. Resize the plot area so it is smaller by dragging a left resizing handle to the right. When you have made enough room for the long Series 2 labels, let go of the mouse.

17. From the Layout ribbon, choose Series 2 from the Current Selection drop-down. Also from the Layout ribbon, choose Error Bars, More Error Bars Options. Excel seems to erroneously take you to the Format dialog box for vertical error bars. In reality, though, Excel has added both x and y error bars. It chooses to show you the Format dialog box for the vertical error bars. Close the dialog box.

18. In the Current Selection drop-down, select Series 2 X Error Bars. Click Format Selection. Change Direction to Plus. Change End Style to No Cap. Set Error Amount to Fixed, with a value of 1.0. From the Line Style category, choose a width of 1.5 in order to make the error bars a bit more substantial. Click Close to close the dialog box.

19. In the Current Selection drop-down, select Series 2 Y Error Bars. When those error bars are selected, press Delete to delete the y error bars.

20. Choose Series 2 from the Current Selection drop-down. Click Format Selection. In the Marker Options category, choose None. Excel erases the markers from the y-axis.

21. Type a more descriptive title for the chart.

The final chart is shown in Figure 7.16. This technique is particularly interesting because for many steps, it appears as if you are heading in the wrong direction.

Figure 7.16
The labels along the y-axis look so simple to add, but a casual Excel user would have a difficult time discovering how to put them there.

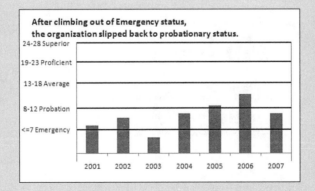

7

If you try the steps a few times, this workaround starts to seem natural and almost poetic. The rogue XY series comes into play in the next example, which involves stacking many charts on a single chart.

> **NOTE**
> I am not sure who was brave enough to discover this technique. Today, many of my fellow Excel MVPs show this tip on their excellent websites. Check out the website of Jon Peltier (www.PeltierTech.com), Andy Pope (www.andypope.info/charts.htm), Charley Kyd (www.ExcelUser.com), and Tushar Mehta(www.Tushar-Mehta.com) for more great examples of charting and all other things Excel.

Showing Several Charts on One Chart by Using a Rogue XY Series

Figure 7.17 shows a single chart that appears to stack up four different charts. This chart is especially useful because one of the middle series, which is the subject of the chart, has a particularly low Q3 value. If you used a series of overlaid area charts, you would never be able to see the Q3 value in question. Note that it is important that all four charts in the stack have the same scale. Even with the current arrangement, it is difficult to compare one year to another. Which Q1 is largest? Without looking at the data, you cannot really tell.

Figure 7.17
This stacked arrangement of charts allows you to compare one year to the next.

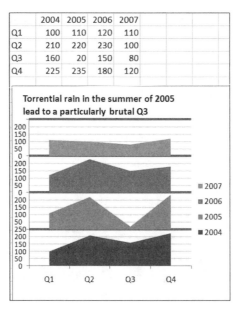

The chart is actually a stack of seven area charts. The second, fourth, and sixth charts are invisible charts that are the complements to the first, third, and fifth charts. For example, if you've decided that the range for each chart should be 0 to 250, then the formula for each point in the second series will be 250 minus the corresponding point in the first series.

You follow these steps to set up the data for this chart stack:

1. Insert blank columns before 2005, 2006, and 2007.

2. The formula in the blank column should be 250 minus the column to the left. Copy to all three blank columns. Your data should like the data shown in Figure 7.18.

Figure 7.18
You can add a series between each year to force the next year to start at an even increment of 250.

	C9			f_x	=250-B9		
◢	A	B	C	D	E	F	G	H
8		2004	blank 1	2005	blank 2	2006	blank 3	2007
9	Q1	100	150	110	140	120	130	110
10	Q2	210	40	220	30	230	20	100
11	Q3	160	90	20	230	150	100	80
12	Q4	225	25	235	15	180	70	120

3. Select the range of data. From the Insert ribbon, choose Area, Stacked Area. Because there are four rows and seven columns, Excel creates the chart with the data reversed: four series with seven points each.

4. From the Design ribbon, choose Switch Row/Column to create the chart as seven series with four points each. The chart appears as shown in Figure 7.19.

Figure 7.19
The chart initially shows seven areas.

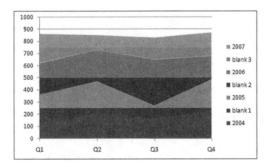

5. In the chart, click series 2. From the Format ribbon, choose Shape Fill, No Fill. Repeat this process for Series 4 and Series 6.

6. Click the numbers along the vertical axis. From the Layout ribbon, choose Format Selection. Then do the following:
   - Choose Maximum, Fixed, 1000.
   - Choose Major Unit, Fixed, 250.
   - Choose Minor Unit, Fixed, 50.
   - Choose Axis Labels, None.
   - Choose Major Tick Mark Type, None.

7

7. Type three columns of data. The first column is the new data labels that you want to appear along the y-axis. This could be four sets of 0, 50, 100, 150, and 200. In the next column, fill zeros down the column for the x location of the XY points. In the next column, type values from 0 to 1,000, in 50-unit increments for the y locations of the XY points.

8. Although the second column contains x locations, you initially add only the y locations to the chart. Select the third column, containing y locations and the heading above the data, as shown in Figure 7.20.

Figure 7.20
After you paste this new series into the chart, the markers provide the locations for new labels.

Value to Appear	Zero	Label Series
0	0	0
50	0	50
100	0	100
150	0	150
200	0	200
0	0	250
50	0	300
100	0	350
150	0	400
200	0	450
0	0	500
50	0	550
100	0	600
150	0	650
200	0	700
0	0	750
50	0	800
100	0	850
150	0	900
200	0	950
250	0	1000

9. Press Ctrl+C to copy the data. Select the chart. Press Ctrl+V to paste the new series to the chart. You now have a complete mess, as shown in Figure 7.21.

Figure 7.21
The new series initially ruins the chart.

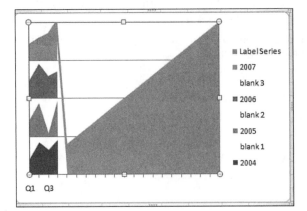

10. Click the new Label series. From the Design ribbon, choose Change Chart Type, XY (Scatter), Scatter with Only Markers.

11. Select Series Label Series from the Current Selection drop-down in either the Layout or Format ribbon.

12. Wait until the formula bar shows the SERIES function. Edit the third argument to point to the column of zeros. Do not include the label for the zero heading (see Figure 7.22):

    =SERIES(Stacked!$L$3,Stacked!$K$4:$K$24,Stacked!$L$4:$L$24,8)

Figure 7.22

After you add the x values as the second argument in the SERIES function, the markers move to the left vertical axis.

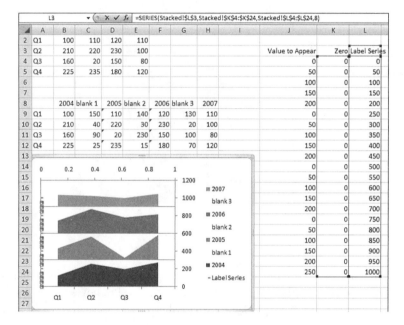

13. Right-click the numbers along the right vertical axis. Choose Format Selection or press Ctrl+1. Then do the following:

    • Choose Maximum, Fixed, 1000.

    • Choose Major Tick Mark Type, None.

    • Choose Axis Labels, None.

    While the Format Axis dialog remains open, click the axis labels along the top of the chart and choose Major Tick Mark Type, None. Then choose Axis Labels, None.

14. Right-click the markers along the left vertical axis. Choose Add Data Labels. Right-click the data labels and then choose Format Data Labels. Choose Label Position, Left.

15. Click the plot area. Grab the bottom-left resizing handle and drag toward the center of the chart until there is enough room for the new labels.

7

16. From the Layout ribbon, choose Primary Horizontal Gridlines, Display Major & Minor Gridlines. Format the major gridlines to have a thicker line weight by selecting Vertical (Value) Axis Major Gridlines from the Current Selection drop-down. Then, from the Format ribbon, choose Shape Outline, Weight and select 2½ point.

17. Choose Series Label Series from the Current Selection drop-down on the Format ribbon. Click Format Series, Marker Options, Marker Type to None. In Figure 7.23, you can see that three issues remain. The legend contains entries for the blank series. The Q1 and Q4 points don't extend to the left and right axes. The labels along the left side of the chart run from 0 to 1,000 instead of 0 to 250 repeatedly.

Figure 7.23
You still have to fix the legend and the labels along the left axis.

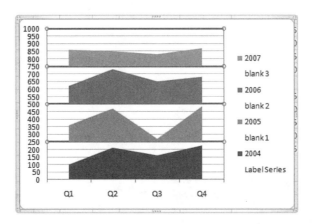

18. Click the Legend to select the whole legend. Click again on the Blank 3 legend entry to select only that entry and press Delete. Excel removes that entry from the legend. Repeat with Blank 2, Blank 1, and Label Series to delete them from the legend.

> **NOTE**
> To fix the labels along the y-axis, you have three choices:
> ■ Write some VBA (see Chapter 13).
> ■ Download Rob Bovey's XY Chart Labeler utility from www.appspro.com/Utilities/ChartLabeler.htm.
> ■ Repeat step 19 several times.

19. To fix the labels manually, click the data labels on the left side of the chart to select all the labels. Click just the 250 label. Type 0 and press Enter. Repeat to change the 300 label to 50, the 350 label to 100, and so on.

20. Add a title, if desired.

21. Notice that there is a gap between the left vertical axis and the Q1 label. To remove this gap, right-click the Q1 label and choose Format Axis. The bottom setting on the Axis Options category is the Position Axis option button. Change from Between Tick Marks to On Tick Marks. In Figure 7.24, the bottom chart is set to On Tick Marks. The top chart is set to Between Tick Marks.

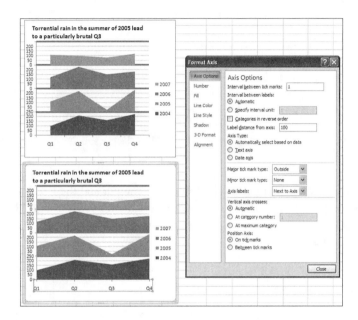

When you distribute this chart to others, they will be wondering how you managed to make Excel put four charts on a single chart. Actually, your manager won't even know this is difficult, but other people who use Excel might be impressed.

Using Multiple XY Series to Create a Trellis Chart

A trellis chart compares values from two series that are usually related. Each series is plotted as dots on a horizontal line in the chart. For maximum effectiveness, the dataset should be sorted in descending sequence.

In Figure 7.25, the companies are sorted in descending order, by revenue. The chart shows revenue and research and development (R&D) expenditures. Any time the R&D dots seem out of sequence, you can figure that the company is either investing unusually high or low amounts in R&D.

Although this chart seems like a bar chart, it is actually produced by creating a chart with three XY series. As in the preceding two examples, the third XY series is used to add the company labels along the left side of the chart.

7

Figure 7.25
Provided that one series in the trellis chart is sorted, you can spot companies whose spending in the R&D series seems out of line with the rest of the industry.

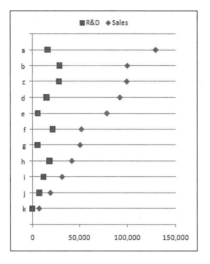

The x portion of the first two series is the Sales amount and the R&D amount. The y portion is a completely artificial series containing the numbers 1 through 11. If you thought about this logically, you might assume that you would arrange your data in pairs of x,y data, as shown in Figure 7.26.

Figure 7.26
Logically, the dots in the chart could be represented by these x,y pairs.

X for R&D	Y for R&D	X for Sales	Y for Sales	X for Labels	Y for Labels
16,508	11	130,000	11	0	11
28,910	10	100,543	10	0	10
28,586	9	99,875	9	0	9
15,364	8	92,838	8	0	8
6,075	7	79,525	7	0	7
21,761	6	52,456	6	0	6
5,603	5	51,046	5	0	5
18,407	4	42,287	4	0	4
12,069	3	32,020	3	0	3
7,497	2	19,772	2	0	2
0	1	7,573	1	0	1

However, creating an XY chart with multiple series is far from logical. Examine Figure 7.27. The data has to be rearranged so that the R&D numbers are in the first selected column. The completely artificial columns of 1 through 11 have to come next, with the important headings R&D, Sales, and Labels. Excel needs this arrangement because it assumes that all XY charts have a single x range and multiple y ranges. When you select the data in cells C39:F50, Excel uses column C as the x labels for all three y series.

In the process of arranging the data in this manner, the true x values for the Sales series, and the zeros that will be used for x values for the Labels series are cast aside—in this case to the left. The actual company labels are moved to the right, if only as a reference.

Figure 7.27
You arrange the data with the first x range and then all other y ranges in sequence.

◢	A	B	C	D	E	F	G
39	Zeroes	Sales	R&D	R&D	Sales	Labels	
40	0	130,000	16,508	11	11	11	a
41	0	100,543	28,910	10	10	10	b
42	0	99,875	28,586	9	9	9	c
43	0	92,838	15,364	8	8	8	d
44	0	79,525	6,075	7	7	7	e
45	0	52,456	21,761	6	6	6	f
46	0	51,046	5,603	5	5	5	g
47	0	42,287	18,407	4	4	4	h
48	0	32,020	12,069	3	3	3	i
49	0	19,772	7,497	2	2	2	j
50	0	7,573	0	1	1	1	k
51							
52			⇧	⇧	⇧	⇧	
53							
54			1st	1st	2nd	3rd	
55			X	Y	Y	Y	
56							
57							

To create the chart, you follow these steps:

1. Select the cells in the range C39:F50.

2. From the Insert ribbon, choose Scatter, Scatter with Markers. Excel creates a chart in which all three markers are plotted at the proper locations for R&D (see Figure 7.28).

Figure 7.28
Initially, all three series appear to be identical.

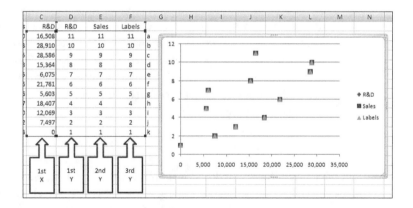

3. From the Layout ribbon, choose Series Sales from the Current Selection drop-down. Excel outlines column E in blue and column C in purple. Grab the border of the purple outline and drag it left so that the purple outline surrounds the sales in column B. This technique is much easier than editing the SERIES function.

4. From the Layout ribbon, choose Series Labels from the Current Selection drop-down. Excel outlines column F in blue and column C in purple. Grab the border of the

purple outline and drag it left so that the purple outline surrounds the sales in column A. As shown in Figure 7.29, you now have a chart that is starting to resemble the final chart.

Figure 7.29
After you specify a different x range for each series, the chart starts to take shape.

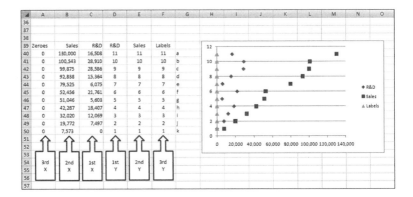

5. From the Format ribbon, choose Current Selection, Vertical Value Axis and then choose Format Selection. Set Major Unit to Fixed Value and 1. This ensures that every company's dots appear on a gridline. Choose Axis Labels, None. Leave the Format dialog box open for steps 6 through 8.

> **NOTE**
> The ability to access the chart and Ribbon without closing the Format dialog box is a cool improvement in Excel 2007. Rather than repeatedly displaying the Format dialog, you can display it once, and then use the Current Selection dropdown in the Ribbon to choose a new item to be formatted. The Format dialog box will change to show settings for the new selected chart component. You can also simply click on a new element in the chart to select that element. The Format dialog box will change to reflect settings for the clicked element.

6. From the Current Selection dropdown on the Format ribbon, select Series Labels. Right-click and choose Add Data Labels. Click the Labels and choose Format Selection. Then choose Label Position Left.

7. On the Format ribbon, open the Current Selection dropdown and select Series Labels. Choose Marker Options, Marker Type, None.

8. Click the Legend. The Format dialog box changes to show settings for the Legend. In the Format dialog box, choose Top.

9. Click the entry in the legend for Labels. Press the Delete key. Close the Format dialog box.

10. Click the Plot Area. Drag one of the left resizing handles to the right to make room for the labels.

NOTE Fixing the labels remains a tedious process. You could switch to VBA or use Rob Bovey's add-in. You could also use the method described in step 11, which is slightly different from step 19 in the previous section.

11. To fix the labels manually, click the data labels on the left side of the chart to select all the labels. Click just the 1 label. This corresponds to the company name in cell G50. While the 1 label is selected, with a solid line surrounding it, type =`'Sheet Name'!G50` and press Enter.

12. Repeat step 11 to change the 2 label to =`'Sheet Name'!G49`. Continue to replace all the labels.

13. Resize the entire chart area so that it is taller than it is wide.

The final chart is shown in Figure 7.30.

Figure 7.30
The final chart uses an XY series for R&D, an XY series for sales, and a hidden XY series to replace the vertical axis labels.

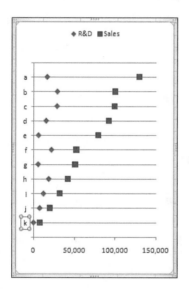

Creating Dynamic Charts

In this section, *dynamic* refers to a chart that expands, contracts, changes, or moves in response to changes in the underlying worksheet.

In many cases, you need to change the SERIES function attached to a data series in order to calculate a series on-the-fly. However, the examples in this section rely on four worksheet functions: VLOOKUP, MATCH, INDEX, and OFFSET. In case you are new to these functions, coverage of each of them follows.

7

Using the OFFSET Function to Specify a Range

The OFFSET function allows you to specify a rectangular range of data. You have to provide five arguments to specify the range:

- **Any starting cell**—An example is Sheet1!A1.

- **A number of rows to move down from the starting cell to the first cell in the range**—If you specify a positive number, the range starts below the starting cell. If you specify 0, the range starts in the same row as the starting cell. If you specify a negative number, the range starts above the starting cell.

- **A number of columns to move right from the starting cell to arrive at the first cell in the range**—You can specify a positive number to move right, 0 to stay in the same column as the starting cell, or a negative number to move to the left.

- **The number of rows in the range**—If you specify 1, you describe a range that is one row tall.

- **The number of columns in the range**—If you specify 1, you describe a range that is one column wide.

To understand the various types of ranges that the OFFSET function can return, consider the shapes in Figure 7.31.

Figure 7.31
Examples of the OFFSET function.

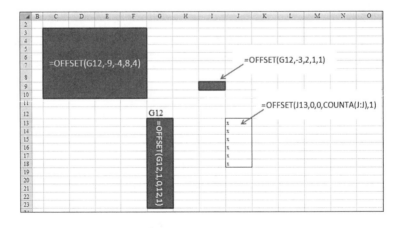

The top-left shape in Figure 7.31 highlights a range that is 8 rows tall by 4 columns wide. If the starting cell is G12, you would have to move 9 rows up from the starting cell and 4 columns left from the starting cell to arrive at the top-left corner cell of the range. The function to refer to this range is =OFFSET(G12,-9,-4,8,4).

The box underneath cell G12 is 12 rows tall by 1 column wide. It starts 1 row from the starting cell of G12 and 0 columns to the right. The function to refer to this range is =OFFSET(G12,1,0,12,1).

The single cell in I9 is 3 rows above the starting cell, 2 columns to the right, 1 row tall, and 1 column wide. The formula is =OFFSET(G12,-3,2,1,1).

Of course, it is silly to write any of these formulas. If you knew that your chart range was always going to be in cells G13:G23, you would simply refer to Sheet1!G13:G23. The power of the OFFSET function is that you can use other functions for some of the arguments. For example, you could count the category labels in your dataset today by using the formula COUNTA($J:$J). The formula =OFFSET(J13,0,0,COUNTA(J:J),1) starts in column J and extends down to include the number of cells with data in column J. This formula counts on the data in column J to not include any blank cells.

Using VLOOKUP or MATCH to Find a Value in a Table

The VLOOKUP function does a vertical lookup. It looks for a particular value in the first column of a lookup table. When the first exact match is found, Excel returns a particular column from that row of the table.

VLOOKUP usually has four arguments: VLOOKUP(lookup_value, table_array, col_index_num, [range_lookup]).

- **Lookup value**—This is the name or value you are trying to find. In Figure 7.32, it is the name in cell A1.

Figure 7.32
Examples of the VLOOKUP and MATCH functions.

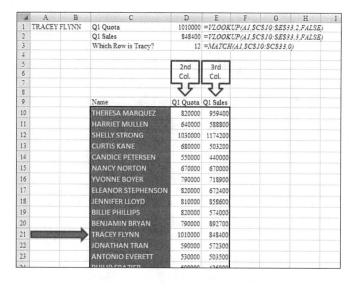

- **Table array**—This is a rectangular range of cells. Excel searches the first column of the table array in an effort to find a cell that has the same value as the lookup value. In Figure 7.32, this is the range C10:E33. If you plan on copying the VLOOKUP formula in either direction to find additional customers or columns, you should use the F4 key to make the table array absolute.

> **TIP**
>
> While editing a formula, pressing the F4 key will toggle a cell reference through the four possible relative/absolute/mixed reference states. The first press of F4 changes A1 to $A$1. The next press of F4 freezes only the row number, A$1. The next press of F4 freezes only the column, $A1. The next press of F4 returns to a relative reference of A1.
>
> How does Excel know which reference to change? If the cursor is inside a reference or immediately to the right of a reference, Excel will change that reference. While entering the previous formula, if you type C10:E33 and then press F4 before typing the comma, Excel will add dollar signs to both C10 and E33 at the same time. If you need to add dollar signs to only C10 or only E33, select the characters in the formula bar before pressing F4.

- **Column index number**—This specifies the column Excel should return as the result of the formula. The columns are numbered 1, 2, 3, and so on, starting with the column that contains the lookup value. In Figure 7.32, specifying 2 would give you the Q1 quota for the person. Specifying 3 would give you the Q1 sales. Note that specifying 1 would give you the person's name again. While this might seem silly, since you already have the person's name as the lookup value, you can sometimes use VLOOKUP to test to see if the lookup value is a valid name in the table array. In this case, it is fine to specify 1 as the column index. Note that if you need to copy this function across several columns in order to return the second, third, fourth, and fifth columns from table array, you can use COLUMN(B1) instead of using 2 as the third argument. As the formula is copied to the right, Excel automatically returns COLUMN(C1), COLUMN(D1), COLUMN(E1), and so on, which then ask for the third, fourth, and fifth columns from the table array.

- **Range lookup**—This is either TRUE or FALSE. You specify FALSE to indicate that you are looking for an exact match. In the FALSE version, the table array can be in any order. If you instead specify TRUE, Excel returns the value of the closest match that is equal to or lower than the lookup value. In the TRUE version, the table array must be sorted in ascending order. If you leave off this parameter, it is the same as specifying TRUE.

VLOOKUP is a workhorse function in Excel. If you've ever dabbled in Access, you might have joined tables in order to bring new columns from a lookup table into a query. The VLOOKUP function allows you to simulate joining tables in Excel.

In Figure 7.32, a VLOOKUP function in cell D1 asks for the second column of the table array and finds the Q1 quota for the sales rep listed in cell A1. A second VLOOKUP in cell D2 asks for the third column of the table array and finds the Q1 sales. The HLOOKUP can do a horizontal lookup, in case your table array has the key values across one row.

There is a curious variant of VLOOKUP called the MATCH function, which looks for a lookup value in a one-column-wide lookup array. When a corresponding value is found in the lookup array, Excel tells you the row number within the lookup array where the match is found. Match can also find a value in a one-row-tall lookup array, similar to the HLOOKUP function.

This seems completely useless, doesn't it? Has your manager ever called you to ask, "By the way, can you tell me in what relative row number within a range that customer is located?" This is a bit of trivia that rarely comes up in conversation. However, bear with me because the MATCH function can be useful when combined with the INDEX function, which is discussed in the next section.

The MATCH function requires arguments that are similar to the first, third, and fourth arguments of the VLOOKUP function:

- **Lookup value**—This is the value that you are trying to find.
- **Lookup array**—This is the first column of the table array range from VLOOKUP. This is the column where Excel looks to find a match for the lookup value.
- **Match type**—This is conceptually similar to using TRUE or FALSE as the fourth argument in the VLOOKUP function. A FALSE in VLOOKUP requires an exact match. In the MATCH function, a 0 requires an exact match. A TRUE in VLOOKUP returns the next-smallest value from a sorted table array. Similarly, a 1 in MATCH returns the next-smallest value. (Remember that spreadsheets store TRUE as a 1.) MATCH offers one more option for match type. If you specify -1, Excel finds the next-largest value from the descending sorted lookup array.

> **TIP**
>
> Did you know that FALSE is equivalent to 0? You can actually specify FALSE as the third argument in MATCH, and it works like a 0.

In Figure 7.32, a MATCH function in cell D3 looks for the sales rep from cell A1 in the range C10:C33. Note that although the match is actually on row 21, this row is the 12th row in the table array. Thus, the MATCH function returns 12.

Both the VLOOKUP and MATCH functions are CPU intensive, particularly when the lookup table contains thousands of records. The lengthy part of the function is finding the matching record from the first column of the lookup table. After Excel locates that value, moving right to grab the second or third column is relatively quick.

Combining INDEX **and** MATCH

Initially, the INDEX function doesn't seem that useful. Its syntax, which is used in a later chart example, is as follows:

```
=INDEX(Rectangular Range, Which Row in the Range, Which Column in the Range)
```

`=INDEX(A1:Z26,5,10)` returns the value at the 5th row and 10th column of the range A1:Z26. There are certainly easier ways to refer to cell J5 (for example, =J5).

> **NOTE**
>
> If the range specified as the first argument contains only one column, you can leave the third argument out of the function. By default, Excel assumes that you are talking about the first column.

The INDEX function becomes powerful when you use a MATCH function as the second argument to specify which range to return.

In Figure 7.33, a processor-intensive MATCH function in cell D1 finds the row number where the sales rep can be found. Relatively fast INDEX functions in cells D2 and D3 then return the value from that row in the quota or sales column.

The next three charting examples make use of the OFFSET, VLOOKUP, INDEX, and/or MATCH functions to change a chart in response to changes in the underlying worksheet.

Figure 7.33
Examples of the MATCH and INDEX functions.

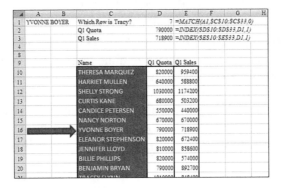

Using Validation Drop-Downs to Create a Dynamic Chart

This example creates a chart that is a bit like a pivot chart, except it uses a drop-down on the worksheet to choose which data to chart.

Figure 7.34 shows a simple chart that compares sales to quota by quarter for a particular sales rep.

Figure 7.34
This simple chart could be part of an executive information system for a vice president of sales.

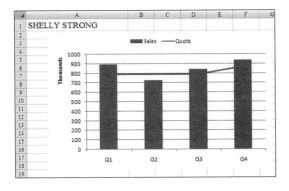

When you click in cell A1 of this chart, a drop-down appears. When you open the drop-down and select a new sales rep, the chart instantly updates to show that particular sales rep's figures (see Figure 7.35).

This chart is not that amazing; it uses just some basic Excel tools that are hiding on the worksheet.

First, hidden out of sight in row 63 is all the data needed to create the chart for any particular sales rep. Sales reps are in A64:A87. Their individual quota and sales figures are in columns B:K (see Figure 7.36).

Figure 7.35

If you choose a new rep from the drop-down in A1, the chart updates.

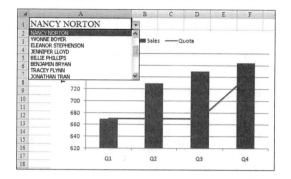

Figure 7.36

The source data for all charts is hidden.

	A	B	C	D	E	F	G	H	I	J	K
63	Name	Q1 Quota	Q1 Sales	Q2 Quota	Q2 Sales	Q3 Quota	Q3 Sales	Q4 Quota	Q4 Sales	Total Quo	Total Sales
64	THERESA MARQUEZ	820000	959400	820000	1066000	820000	959400	900000	1215200	3360000	4200000
65	HARRIET MULLEN	640000	588800	640000	614400	640000	659200	700000	783800	2620000	2646200
66	SHELLY STRONG	1030000	1174200	1030000	1153600	1030000	1287500	1130000	1659700	4220000	5275000
67	CURTIS KANE	690000	503200	680000	537200	680000	530400	750000	1023900	2790000	2594700
68	CANDICE PETERSEN	550000	440000	550000	528000	550000	517000	610000	707200	2260000	2192200
69	NANCY NORTON	670000	670000	670000	730300	670000	750400	740000	764300	2750000	2915000
70	YVONNE BOYER	790000	718900	790000	758400	790000	805800	870000	989300	3240000	3272400
71	ELEANOR STEPHENSON	820000	672400	820000	680600	820000	836400	900000	1137000	3360000	3326400
72	JENNIFER LLOYD	810000	858600	810000	955800	810000	972000	890000	1363600	3320000	4150000
73	BILLIE PHILLIPS	820000	574000	820000	623200	820000	688800	900000	1104400	3360000	2990400
74	BENJAMIN BRYAN	790000	892700	790000	726800	790000	845300	870000	937200	3240000	3402000
75	TRACEY FLYNN	1010000	848400	1010000	989800	1010000	1030200	1110000	1313000	4140000	4181400
76	JONATHAN TRAN	590000	572300	590000	525100	590000	560500	650000	689500	2420000	2347400
77	ANTONIO EVERETT	530000	503500	530000	482300	530000	466400	580000	696100	2170000	2148300
78	PHILIP FRAZIER	600000	426000	600000	408000	600000	402000	660000	436800	2460000	1672800
79	CAROLYN CASH	1050000	787500	1050000	945000	1050000	861000	1160000	1242400	4310000	3835900
80	BRANDY SNIDER	1000000	890000	1000000	1090000	1000000	1030000	1100000	1131000	4100000	4141000
81	DANIEL HERMAN	580000	440800	580000	522000	580000	591600	640000	659000	2380000	2213400
82	BERTHA FAULKNER	510000	438600	510000	423300	510000	489600	560000	759400	2090000	2110900
83	VERA GOODMAN	850000	748000	850000	799000	850000	875500	940000	1102400	3490000	3524900
84	BRADLEY LEBLANC	560000	487200	560000	621600	560000	498400	620000	715800	2300000	2323000
85	JACOB SHANNON	500000	355000	500000	365000	500000	390000	550000	714500	2050000	1824500
86	BRANDY GIBBS	880000	466400	880000	660000	880000	616000	970000	712400	3610000	2454800
87	JEAN PACE	550000	330000	550000	335500	550000	335500	610000	626200	2260000	1627200

Hidden behind the chart are a number of formulas:

- In cell A2, the formula =MATCH(A1,A64:A87,0) indicates the location of the sales rep selected in cell A1.

- In C4:F5, formulas similar to =INDEX($A$64:$K$87,$A$2,2) pull the information for the selected sales rep and format it into two data series. The structure of the original dataset is typical of how accounting keeps track of such data. If the original dataset were in a different format, a simpler formula could be written. As it is, the third argument of this formula had to be edited in each of the other seven cells after being copied to C4:F5. You could also abandon the MATCH formula in cell A2 and build eight VLOOKUP formulas here, and that would be fine; it is a matter of personal preference.

7

To create the drop-down in cell A1, you follow these steps:

1. Select cell A1.

2. From the Data ribbon, click the top half of the Data Validation icon.

3. In the Data Validation dialog that appears, change the Allow drop-down from Any Value to List. New fields appear in the dialog, including a Source field.

4. Click the Reference box at the right side of the Source field and choose the A64:A87 range, which contains names.

5. By default, the In-cell Dropdown check box is checked. Leave it checked. Click OK to close the dialog.

Figure 7.37 shows the structure of the data hidden behind the chart as well as the completed Data Validation dialog box.

Figure 7.37
Formulas convert the name in cell A1 into a chartable dataset. The drop-down in cell A1 appears because of the Data Validation settings.

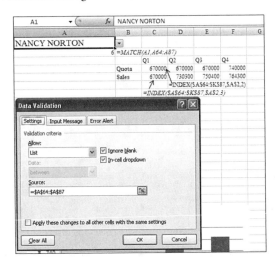

After you set up the formulas, you create a chart from B3:F5. You follow these steps to create the chart:

1. Select the range B3:F5. From the Insert ribbon, choose Column, Clustered Column.

2. Click any column marker in the chart for quota. From the Design ribbon, choose Change Chart Type, Line, Line.

3. From the Layout ribbon, choose Legend, Show Legend at Top.

4. From the Layout ribbon, choose Axes, Primary Vertical Axis, Show Axis in Thousands.

5. Click outside the plot area but inside the chart border to select the chart area. From the Format ribbon, choose Shape Outline, No Outline.

6. Drag the selection border of the chart to move it to cell A2 and then resize the chart so that it covers any of the formulas behind the chart.

As mentioned earlier, this chart is not really dynamic. The worksheet is dynamic and responds using formulas. The chart is always plotting a static range of data. The chart in the next example is truly dynamic, expanding or contracting as data is added or removed from the spreadsheet.

Using Dynamic Ranges in a Chart

A chart based on a dynamic range expands or contracts as new data points are added to a specific range.

The chart in this example requires an understanding of the SERIES function and the OFFSET function. If you are not reading straight through this chapter, you should review the SERIES function discussion (in the section "Using a Rogue XY Series to Label the Vertical Axis," earlier in this chapter) and the OFFSET discussion (in the section "Using the OFFSET Function to Specify a Range," earlier in this chapter).

As shown in Figure 7.38, the data for the chart is initially located in A5:B16. There are headings in cell B4 and cell C5. The COUNTA() function, described later, counts all the entries in column A and subtracts 1 to factor out the heading. This approach requires two assumptions, which you have to work to control:

- There should be no other data anywhere in the million other rows of column A. You shouldn't build new tables down below, and you shouldn't add a title in cell A1. If you are doing either of these things, you will have to adjust the COUNTA() function to subtract more than just the first heading cell.

- Customers should always start in cell A5 and extend in a contiguous range. You shouldn't leave a blank cell in cell A17 and type a new customer in cell A18. This won't work. If you want to delete a customer from the chart, you need to delete the entire row containing the customer. You shouldn't delete the values in row 8, leaving a blank row.

> **NOTE**
> In the example that follows, the sheet name in the sample file is called Dynamic Chart. The workbook name is 7-Dynamic1.xlsm. Sheet names with spaces are more difficult to deal with than sheet names without spaces. The SERIES formula requires you to fully qualify the named ranges. For this example, substitute the appropriate workbook or worksheet range names.

To build this chart, you first build and format a static chart. You then make the chart a chart that will dynamically resize. Here's how you create this chart:

1. Select the data in cells A4:B16. From the Insert ribbon, choose Bar, 2D Bar, Clustered Bar.
2. From the Layout ribbon, choose Legend, None.
3. Right-click the customer names along the left side of the chart and choose Format Axis to open the Format dialog box.
4. Choose Categories in Reverse Order.

5. Choose Specify Interval Unit and make sure the unit is 1. Close the Format dialog box.

6. Resize the chart so that it is taller.

7. Click outside the chart. You now need to define a couple of range names that point to a dynamic range of data.

8. From the Formulas ribbon, choose the Name Manager.

9. Click the New button. Excel displays the New Name dialog.

10. Type a name such as `Customers`.

11. Leave Workbook as the scope.

12. Adding a comment, which is new in Excel 2007, helps when you want to document how a complicated name works. Perhaps the comment here could be "See Chapter 7 of Jelen's *Excel Charting* book."

13. Set Refers to Box to the following:

    ```
    =OFFSET('Dynamic Chart'!$A$5,0,0,COUNTA('Dynamic Chart'!$A:$A)-1,1)
    ```

    This basically says to start in cell A5, move 0 rows down, and 0 rows over but to include as many entries as are found in column A, except for the heading.

14. Click OK to return to the Name Manager dialog. You then see the new name added in the box.

15. Repeat steps 9 through 14 to assign a name to a formula for the sales values. Use the name `Sales`, and use the following formula in step 13:

    ```
    =OFFSET('Dynamic Chart'!$B$5,0,0,COUNTA('Dynamic Chart'!$A:$A)-1,1)
    ```

    Note that the fourth argument is still counting the number of customer names in column A. This allows a new customer to appear but have a blank in column B to indicate zero sales. People should never leave a cell blank to indicate a zero, but this would handle it in case they did.

> **NOTE**
> Once you've set up the relatively complicated Customers named range, you could base the Sales range as being 1 column offset from the first range. A formula of `=OFFSET(Customers,,1)` would achieve the same result as the formula in step 15.

16. Close the Manage Names dialog box.

17. Test whether your range names are working. Click in the Name Box drop-down just to the left of the Formula bar. Type `Customers` and press Enter. Excel highlights the range of customers. Repeat for sales. Type a new test customer in A17. Type `Customers` in the name box again and press Enter. Excel should now highlight a range that has been extended to include the new customer. If this is not working, go back and check the formulas you entered in steps 13 and 15.

18. Click the chart to activate it.

19. Click the data bars in the chart. Wait for Excel to display the SERIES formula in the formula bar, which should initially look like this:

```
=SERIES('Dynamic Chart'!$B$4,'Dynamic Chart'!$A$5:$A$16,
    ➥'Dynamic Chart'!$B$5:$B$16,1)
```

> **NOTE**
> The SERIES formula is too long for the physical constraints of this book. You will not see the continuation arrow at the beginning of the second line in your formula.

The first argument in this formula means that the series name comes from cell B4. The labels along the vertical axis come from cells A5:A16. The values for each bar are located in B5:B16. This is the first (and only) series in the chart.

20. On the Design ribbon, click the Select Data button. Excel displays the Select Data Source dialog.

21. In the left side of the Select Data Source dialog, choose Series1 and click Edit. Excel displays the Edit Series dialog.

22. Assuming that Sales is a workbook-level name, you have to specify the workbook name in apostrophes, an exclamation point, and then the range name as the series values. In my workbook, this is `='7-Dynamic1.xlsm'!Sales`. Click OK.

23. On the right side of the Select Data Source dialog, choose Edit for Axis Labels. Excel displays the Axis Labels dialog.

24. In the Axis Labels dialog, type a similar reference that points to Customer. In my case, this is `='7-Dynamic1.xlsm'!Customers`. Click OK to close the Axis Labels dialog.

25. Click OK to close the Edit Series dialog. In the formula bar, you should see the following new SERIES formula:

```
=SERIES('Dynamic Chart'!$B$4,'7-Dynamic1.xlsm'!Customers,
    ➥'7-Dynamic1.xlsm'!Sales,1)
```

Figure 7.38 shows the final chart and the SERIES formula. Two new test customers have been added to the bottom of the dataset and appear in the chart.

Figure 7.38
As new customers are added to the bottom of the data range, the series formula automatically expands. Customers and Sales are names that are defined using the OFFSET function.

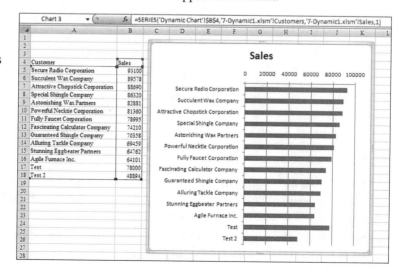

CAUTION

If you are a careful typist, you can edit the SERIES formula in the formula bar in Excel. There is no error checking, however, so if you mistype something, you lose the data for your chart.

This example uses the OFFSET function to automatically expand a chart. The next example uses the OFFSET function to chart a rolling 12 months of data.

Creating a Scrolling Chart

An interesting dynamic chart is a chart that shows a scrolling 12 months of data. In Figure 7.39, 36 months of data are available and are shown in the bottom chart. However, you can show a scrolling 12 months in the top chart. As you move the scrollbar, the top chart shows a closer view of a 12-month segment of the longer chart.

In Figure 7.39, a gray box shades the portion of the bottom chart that is shown in the top chart.

Figure 7.39
When the scrollbar in row 2 is scrolled toward the right, you see recent months.

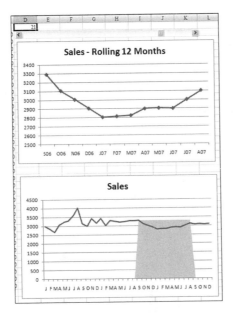

In Figure 7.40, the scrollbar is moved left to show a different portion of the detail.

You follow these steps to create a scrolling chart:

1. Format your dates with a MMMMMYY custom format. The five M's are the code to force the month to be displayed with only the first letter of the month. This allows more dates to fit across the bottom of the chart.

2. Select the data in cells A1:B37. From the Insert ribbon, choose Line, Line. Delete the legend. Excel creates a basic line chart with all 36 months of data.

3. Move the chart so that it starts in row 22. Make a copy of the chart that starts in cell D3.

4. Deselect the chart. Enter a number between 1 and 25 in cell D1.

Figure 7.40
Note the number 9 in cell D1. This cell changes in response to the scrollbar changes.

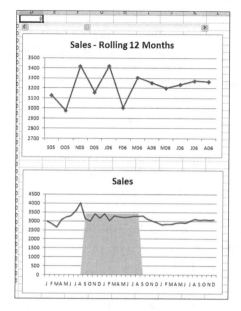

5. From the Formulas ribbon, choose Name Manager. Click the Add button.

6. Type **Months** in the Name field. In the Refers To field, enter:

```
=OFFSET(Scroll!$A$1,Scroll!$D$1,0,12,1)
```

This says to start from cell A1 of the Scroll worksheet, move down the number of rows in cell D1, and then take a range that is 12 rows by 1 column. Click OK to accept the name.

7. Add another name. Type the name SalesByMonth. In the Refers To box, use:

```
=OFFSET(Scroll!$A$1,Scroll!$D$1,1,12,1)
```

The only change is that in the third argument, you move right one column to grab data from column B.

8. Click the line series in the first chart. Wait for the SERIES formula to appear in the formula bar. Edit the formula so that it looks like this:

```
=SERIES(Scroll!$B$1,'7-Dynamic.xlsm'!Months,
   ➥'7-Dynamic.xlsm'!SalesByMonth,1)
```

9. Test the chart. Enter a new number between 1 and 25 in cell D1. The top chart should change. You now need to provide an easy way for the reader to change the number in cell D1. This can be accomplished through a scrollbar.

The icon for adding a scrollbar is located on the Developer ribbon. Open the Insert dropdown and find the Scrollbar icon in the center of the second row of Form Controls. Since many people do not have the Developer tab available in the ribbon, you can use Step 10 to add the scrollbar control to the Quick Access Toolbar.

7

10. From the Office icon menu, choose Excel Options. Choose Customize. In the top-left drop-down, choose Command Not in the Ribbon. Browse through the list box on the left for Scroll Bar (Form Control). Select this item and click the Add>> button to add the control to the Quick Access Toolbar. Click OK to close the Excel Options dialog.

11. Click the newly added scrollbar control in the Quick Access toolbar. (Depending on your computer, the Quick Access toolbar is the row of icons either immediately below or immediately above the ribbon.) After clicking the scrollbar icon, drag to draw a scrollbar control on the worksheet. Drag from the top left of cell D2 to the bottom right of cell K2.

12. Right-click the scrollbar and choose Format Control.

13. Change Minimum Value to 1 and Maximum Value to 25. Set Incremental Change to 1. For Cell Link, click the Refers To button and choose cell D1. Click OK. Click outside the scrollbar to deselect it. To test the scrollbar, drag the slider. The value in cell D1 should change. The top chart should also change.

14. Change the chart title of the top chart to indicate that it is a rolling 12 months. The top chart is now complete. If you want to draw the shaded box on the bottom chart, continue with the following steps.

15. Enter the heading `Shading` in cell C1.

16. Enter the following formula in cell C2:

    `=IF(AND(ROW(A1)>=$D$1,ROW(A1)-$D$1<12),MAX(SalesByMonth),0)`

    Copy this formula down to the other 35 months.

17. Select the range C1:C37. Press Ctrl+C to copy the range. Select the bottom chart. Press Ctrl+V to paste a new series to the chart.

18. Click the line for the second series. From the Design ribbon, choose Change Chart Type, Area Chart.

19. Click the area chart to select the second series. From the Format ribbon, choose Shape Fill and select light gray to make the box less obtrusive.

The scrollbar makes this chart fun to use. People will be encouraged to interact with the chart, which will mean they spend more time with the chart. Perhaps it is a bit gimmicky. Perhaps it makes sense when you have 20 years of monthly data. I can certainly understand the argument that the 12-month chart is less informative than the 36-month chart. However, the scrolling chart is here in this book because it is unusual.

Modifying the Scrollbar Example to Show the Last 12 Months

In the previous section, a scrollbar was used to determine which 12-month range was plotted on a chart. You can use similar concepts without the scrollbar. Say that you always want to display the latest 12 months of data. After you add a new month to the end of the range, and you want the chart to automatically shift to show the last 12 months. This would be the start of the OFFSET formula:

`=OFFSET(A1,Some Number of Rows,0,12,1)`

This formula always grabs 12 rows by 1 column. The trick is figuring out where to start the selection in order to get the last 12 months.

You can figure out how many months are present in column A by using =COUNTA(A:A). When there are 36 months, you want to use the data A26:A37. This means you need to move 25 rows down from a starting position of cell A1. Thus, the Some Number of Rows argument would be =COUNTA(A:A)-11.

To create a chart that shows the latest 12 months, you follow the steps in the previous example except that in step 6, the formula for months should be =OFFSET(Scroll!$A$1,COUNTA(Scroll!$A:$A)-11,0,12,1) and in step 7, the formula for SalesByMonth should be =OFFSET(Scroll!$A$1,COUNTA(Scroll!$A:$A)-11,1,12,1).

Creating Advanced Charts

The last few examples in this chapter are unconventional charts that you can create. Each chart requires a few tricks in order to coax the result out of Excel.

Thermometer Chart

A thermometer chart is a big way to display a single number. It is great for use on a dashboard display where you want everyone to see progress toward a goal.

To create a thermometer chart like the one shown in Figure 7.41, you follow these steps:

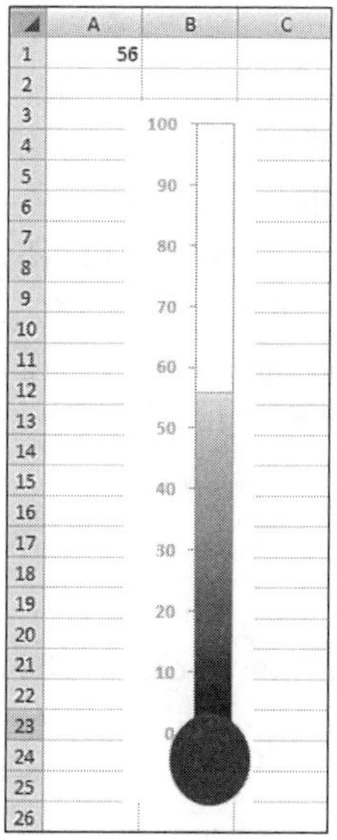

Figure 7.41
This chart is a single column based on the number in cell A1.

1. Enter a number between 0 and 100 in cell A1.
2. Select cell A1. From the Insert ribbon, choose Column, 2-D Column, Clustered Column.

3. From the Layout ribbon, choose Legend, None.

4. From the Layout ribbon, choose Axes, Primary Horizontal Axis, None.

5. From the Layout ribbon, choose Gridlines, Primary Horizontal Gridlines, None.

6. Right-click the single column and choose Format Data Series. Change Gap Width to 0%. For the Fill category, choose Gradient Fill. In the Preset Colors drop-down, choose the ninth thumbnail, a blend from red to orange. For Border Color, choose Solid Line and then choose an orange color from the drop-down. You can leave the Format dialog open while you do steps 7 and 8.

7. Choose Plot Area from the Current Selection drop-down. Format the border color as a solid line and choose an orange color.

8. Choose the chart area and format the border as No Line. Close the Format dialog box.

9. Resize the chart area so that it is narrow and long.

10. Right-click the numbers along the vertical axis. Choose Format Axis. Then do the following:

    • Choose Minimum, Fixed, 0.

    • Choose Maximum, Fixed, 100.

    • Choose Major Unit, Fixed, 10.

    • For the Line Color category, choose Solid Line and then select orange.

    Click OK to close the Format dialog box.

11. With the axis labels still selected, choose Font Color and then select orange on the Home ribbon.

12. Select the plot area. Drag the bottom resizing handles up so that there is space between the bottom of the plot area and the bottom of the chart area.

13. From the Insert ribbon, choose Shapes, Basic Shapes and then select an oval. Hold down the Shift key while you draw a circle at the bottom of the chart. Note that the shift key forces the oval shape to be drawn as a circle.

14. From the Format ribbon, choose Shape Fill and then select a dark orange and then choose Shape Outline and select a dark orange color for the ball at the bottom of the thermometer.

Benchmark Chart

A benchmark chart shows sales for each period as a column chart. The quota, goal, or benchmark for the period is shown as a cap. If the sales exactly meet the quota, the sales column fits perfectly into the cap. If sales fell short of the quota, you see some whitespace between the cap and the column.

You follow these steps to create a benchmark chart like the one in Figure 7.42:

Figure 7.42

The horizontal markers on each column indicate where the quota had been for that month.

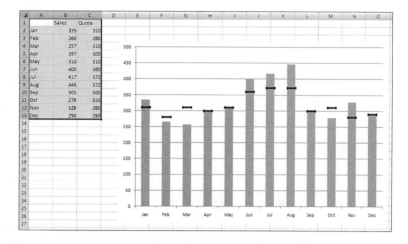

1. Enter Months in column A, Sales in column B, and Quota in column C.

2. Create a clustered 2-D column chart from the data. Delete the legend.

3. Click the Quota series in the chart. From the Design ribbon, choose Change Chart Type and then choose Scatter (XY). Excel automatically moves the series to a secondary axis.

4. Select one of the quota data markers. Right-click and choose Format Data Series. Choose Primary Axis.

5. Make sure the quota series is still selected. From the Layout ribbon, choose Error Bars, More Error Bar Options. Close the Error Bar Format dialog and open the Current Selection drop-down. If you see Series Quota Y Error Bars, select that and press the Delete key. Select Series Quota X Error Bars and click Format Selection. Change Fixed Value from 1.0 to 0.2. For the Line Style category, choose a 3-point width.

6. Choose Series Quota from the Current Selection drop-down. Click Format Selection. For the Marker Options category, choose None.

The horizontal lines in this chart are actually error bars that show the goal or quota for each month.

Delta Chart

You can use a delta chart to plot revenue and a quota as line charts. A special data marker appears halfway between the two lines to show the percentage of quota (see Figure 7.43). The hard part of creating a delta chart is getting the labels to float halfway in between the two lines.

Figure 7.43
The labels automatically float halfway between the two lines.

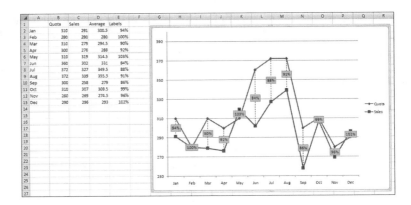

You follow these steps to create a delta chart:

1. Set up a dataset with months in column A, quota in column B, and revenue in column C.

2. In column D, enter the following formula to average revenue and quota:
   =AVERAGE(B2:C2)
   This will be the location point for the data label. Copy the formula down the column.

3. In column E, enter the formula =C2/B2 to hold the label. This formula will show the percentage to quota. Format the results as a percentage with 0 decimal places and copy the formula down the column.

4. Create a chart from cells A1:D13. From the Insert ribbon, choose Line, Line with Markers.

5. Select Value Axis from the Current Selection drop-down on the Layout ribbon. Click Format Selection. Choose a fixed minimum and a fixed maximum that are appropriate to zoom in on the data in the chart.

6. Choose Series Average from the Current Selection drop-down on the Layout ribbon. Click Format Selection. Choose to move the series to the secondary axis. This allows the labels to be adjusted for just this series.

7. Choose Secondary Vertical (Value) Axis from the Current Selection drop-down on the Layout ribbon. Choose the same minimum and maximum as in step 5.

8. Close the Format dialog box.

9. Click the Average series to select it. From the Design ribbon, choose Select Data.

10. Click the Average series on the left side of the Select Data Source dialog. On the right side of the dialog, click the Edit button. Excel displays the Axis Labels dialog, where

you can choose new Horizontal Category Axis Labels. Point to the percentages in column E. Click OK to close the Axis Labels dialog. Click OK to close the Select Data Source dialog.

11. Make sure Average Series is still selected. From the Layout ribbon, choose Data Labels, More Data Label Options. In the Format Data Labels dialog, choose Category Name and deselect Value. Then do the following:

- For Label Position, choose Center.
- For Fill, choose Solid Fill and choose a light color.
- For Border Color, choose Solid Line and choose a dark color.

12. Click the Average series to select it. From the Format ribbon, choose Shape Fill, No Fill. Choose Format, Shape Outline and select No Outline. Close the Format dialog box.

13. From the Layout ribbon, choose Lines, High-Low Lines. Select High Low Lines 1 from the Current Selection drop-down. From the Format ribbon, choose Shape Outline, Dashes and choose the fourth dash selection.

14. From the Layout ribbon, choose Axes, Secondary Value Axis and set it to None.

15. Click the Average entry in the legend. The first click selects the whole legend. The second click selects just the Average entry. Press Delete to remove that entry.

Because the average series was converted to an XY chart, you could have a separate set of category labels for the series. This allows the markers to be at one height while displaying the label from a different value.

Amazing Things People Do with Excel Charts

The last few examples are not charts that you are likely to create. They are simply a few displays that you won't believe are created in Excel. In each case, the author created the display using VBA.

Earl Takasaki submitted the Civil War chart shown in Figure 7.44 as an entry to a MrExcel.com Challenge of the Month as the most innovative use of graphics in Excel. With this chart, you can enter a cannon trajectory in an attempt to hit a target. The trajectory of the shot is graphed at the bottom of the figure.

Earl's workbook and many other entries from this contest are available for download at www.mrexcel.com/pc11.shtml.

Mala Singh of XLSoft Consulting created the chart in Figure 7.45. Mala used a shape to create a cross-section of a river at the proposed location for a bridge.

7

Figure 7.44
The graph at the bottom teaches students about physics.

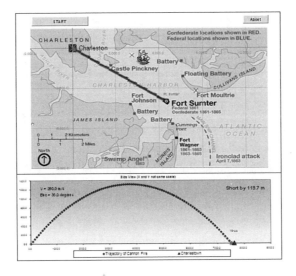

Figure 7.45
Blue shapes create the profile of the river at the bridge location.

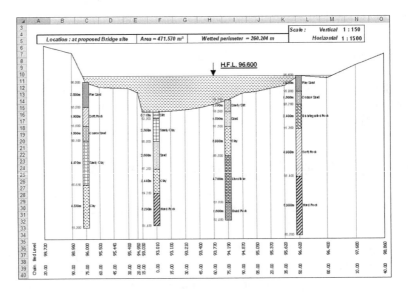

In Figure 7.46, Mala drew the bridge abutment using an XY chart in Excel.

Brett Bernardo sent in the chart shown in Figure 7.47 for his entry in the innovative charts contest at MrExcel.com. The VBA macro in this proprietary system starts with a manifest and actually draws the 3-D bundles in the Excel workbook.

Figure 7.46
Don't have AutoCAD?
This blueprint is actually
an XY chart.

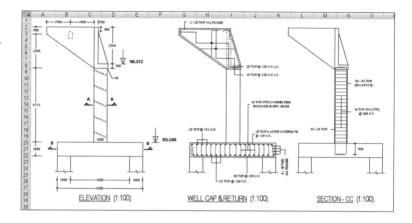

Figure 7.47
VBA macros draw
bundles to scale as they
should be loaded on a
truck.

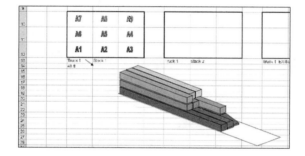

You can read more about innovative chart entries at www.mrexcel.com/pc15.php.

Next Steps

In Chapter 8, "Creating and Using Pivot Charts," you will learn how to summarize thousands of rows of detailed data into a summary chart. Pivot tables are Excel's most powerful feature. The pivot chart feature has been vastly improved in Excel 2007.

7

Creating and Using Pivot Charts

8

Creating Your First Pivot Chart

Pivot tables are the most powerful feature in Excel. A pivot table allows you to summarize a million records of transactional data in Excel with a few mouse clicks. A pivot chart is an extension of the pivot table concept. While building a summary of your data using a pivot table, you can specify that the results be presented in a chart. With the resulting chart, you can quickly filter to see a summary of records that match current criteria. You can also replicate a pivot chart so that you have one chart for each region, product, customer, and so on.

What's New in Excel 2007 Pivot Tables

If you are a pivot table veteran, you will find a few changes in Excel 2007. Rather than dragging and dropping fields on a pivot table or pivot chart, you now build a pivot table by dragging fields to drop zones right in the PivotTable Field List box. This eliminates the chances of dropping a field in the wrong place and the chaos that would normally ensue.

The drop zones have been renamed in Excel 2007. The old Page fields are now named Report Filter fields. The old Data Fields are now named Σ Values fields. When you are creating a pivot chart, Excel further renames the row fields as Axis fields and renames column fields as Legend fields.

By default, a pivot chart is now created on the same worksheet as the underlying pivot table. This is a welcome improvement: You can now easily see the relationship between the pivot table and the pivot chart. If you want to print only the pivot chart, you can either set the print range to include just the chart, or you can select the Charting Tools Layout ribbon and then choose the Move icon to move the pivot chart to a new worksheet.

Another improvement is that you can now apply more logical filters to fields that are in the row or column areas. Whereas previous versions of Excel allowed you to apply the Top 10 AutoShow settings, you can now ask for fields that match a certain pattern, dates that fall in a certain month, and many other options.

> **CAUTION**
>
> The new filtering features are not compatible with Excel 2003 pivot tables. If you have a pivot table that was originally created in Excel 2003, Excel assumes that you might want to be able to save the file with backward compatibility, so it turns off the new features for that pivot table. To overcome this problem, you should save the file as an Excel 2007 file and then re-create the pivot table from your dataset.

Deciding Which Comes First: The Table or the Chart

The examples in this chapter assume that you have set out to create a pivot chart. However, if you have an existing pivot table, you can add a pivot chart by selecting one cell in the pivot table and pressing Alt+F1. Either way, you should follow these simple rules:

- Any fields in the column area (that is, going across the columns at the top of the pivot table) will be converted to series. You should have either one or zero fields in this area.

- Any fields in the row area (that is, going down the left column of the report) will become categories along the horizontal axis.

Rules for Preparing Underlying Pivot Data

Pivot tables work best when they are created from transactional data. Every row in a dataset should represent a detailed transaction. You do not want any sort of a summary in your dataset. If you have months going across the columns, this dataset is not ideal for creating pivot charts. A report with months going across the columns is a cross-tab summary of the detailed records in your dataset. You should go back to the person who provided that dataset and see if you can get the original underlying data that person used to produce the summary.

Your data should have no blank columns or blank rows. An occasional blank cell is not fatal but really compromises the pivot table engine's internal logic. If you have 99,999 cells with numbers and 1 blank cell, Excel assumes that the column contains text and chooses to count the records instead of summing them. If you can, you should fill any blank cells with zeros before you begin.

> **TIP**
>
> To find and fill any blank cells with zeros, you select the cells in your dataset and then choose Home, Find & Select, Go to Special. In the GoTo Special dialog, choose Blanks and then click OK. All the blank cells in your selection are then selected. Next, you type a zero and then press Ctrl+Enter to put the zero in all the cells in the selection.

Every column should have a unique one-cell heading. These headings will appear in the PivotTable Field List box, so they should be relatively short but meaningful.

It is not necessary, but you might want to convert your dataset to a table before creating a pivot table. The advantage is that if you later add new records to the table, you can easily refresh your pivot chart without re-specifying the range of data to be used. To create a table, you select a cell in the dataset and press Ctrl+T.

Creating Your First Pivot Chart

You follow these steps to create your first pivot chart:

1. Select one cell in your dataset and choose Insert, PivotTable, PivotChart, as shown in Figure 8.1.

> **NOTE**
> The leftmost icon on the Insert ribbon is a PivotTable icon; it has a top half and a bottom half. Rather than click the top half of the icon, you need to click the bottom half, where you can access the PivotChart menu item.

Figure 8.1
You use the drop-down at the bottom of the PivotTable icon to access the PivotChart menu item.

2. In the Create PivotTable with PivotChart dialog, Excel guesses about the extent of your dataset. If your dataset is either a table or follows the rules given earlier, Excel guesses correctly. In this dialog, you can choose to create the pivot table on the current worksheet or on a new worksheet. The default is to use a new worksheet. Click OK.

You now have the makings of a blank pivot table and pivot chart. There are four elements visible on the worksheet shown in Figure 8.2.

- Columns A:C contain a blank area where the pivot table will be built.
- Columns E:M contain the area where the chart will be built.
- The PivotTable Field List box contains a list of fields at the top of the dialog and four drop zones at the bottom of the dialog. (If your field list looks different than the one

in Figure 8.2, you can select the drop-down at the top of the list and choose Fields Section and Areas Section Stacked.)

■ The PivotChart Filter Pane box is an abbreviated version of the PivotTable Field List box. You can use the icon in the upper-right corner of this pane to turn on or off the larger field list.

Four new PivotChart Tools ribbon tabs appear. The first three tabs—Design, Layout, and Format—are identical to the charting ribbon tabs that you have been using throughout this book. You can use the Analyze tab to toggle on or off the PivotTable Field List box or PivotChart Filter Pane box or to refresh the pivot chart (see Figure 8.2).

Figure 8.2
You are ready to start building a pivot chart by adding fields to the report.

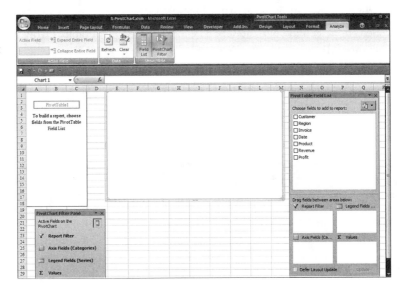

Say that you want to create a chart that summarizes revenue by product. To do so, you follow these steps:

1. Choose the check box next to the Product field in the top of the PivotTable Field List box. Excel shows a unique list of products in column A of the pivot table. The Product field heading appears in the Axis Fields section of the PivotTable Field List box. You do not see a chart yet; you need to specify at least one field in the Σ Values area of the PivotTable Field List box.

2. Click the Revenue field in the top of the PivotTable Field List box. If your data contains no blank cells, the Revenue field appears in the Σ Values area of the field list, and your chart appears as shown in Figure 8.3. If the Revenue field instead moves to the Axis Fields area, you have one or more blank or text cells in your data. In an ideal world, you would fix these. Instead, you can drag the field from the Axis Fields drop zone to the Σ Values drop zone.

Figure 8.3
Excel starts with the default chart, as defined in your copy of Excel.

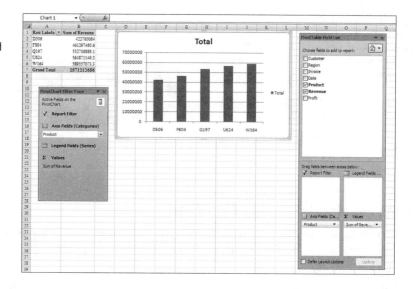

The summary in Figure 8.3 is remarkable. Even if you count clicking the PivotTable icon as two clicks, you need only five mouse clicks to summarize the 100,000+ records of data from Figure 8.1 into the summary chart in Figure 8.3.

Changing the Chart Type and Formatting the Chart

You can use the tools on the Design ribbon to change from a default chart type to almost any other chart type. (However, you cannot use scatter, XY, or bubble charts as pivot charts.) To change the chart type, you choose Design, Change Chart Type and select a chart type from the gallery.

You can use the tools on the Layout ribbon to change elements such as data labels, titles, or the 3-D rotation. Figure 8.4 shows the data from Figure 8.3 recast as a 3-D pie chart. To create this chart, you use the familiar tools on the Design and Layout ribbon tabs:

1. On the Design ribbon, choose Change Chart Type and select a 3-D pie chart.

2. On the Layout ribbon, choose Chart Title, None.

3. Choose Layout, Legend, None.

4. Choose Data Labels, More Data Label Options, Category Name, Percentage, Outside End. Uncheck the Value box.

Figure 8.4
With just a few clicks, you can change the default pivot chart to any other available chart type.

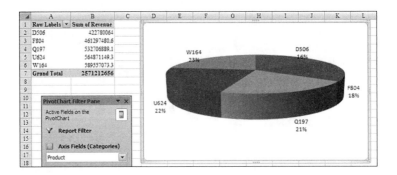

Adding Additional Series to a Pivot Chart

So far, each of the pivot charts in this chapter has plotted a single series. You can easily specify values in another text field that can be used to differentiate the single series into multiple series.

To specify a field as the legend, you need to drag the field from the top of the PivotTable Field List box to the Legend Fields drop zone. To create the chart in Figure 8.5, you follow these steps:

Figure 8.5
You can add a field to the Legend drop zone in order to break the total into multiple series.

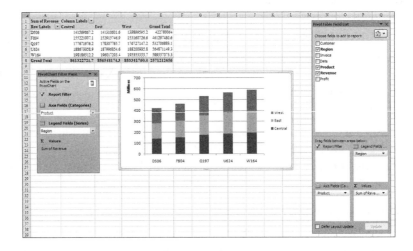

1. Drag the Region field to the Legend Fields drop zone. Excel breaks the total revenue into three series.

2. Choose Design, Change Chart Type, Stacked Column.

3. Choose Layout, Legend, Show Legend at Right.

4. Choose Layout, Axes, Primary Vertical Axis, Show Axis in Millions.

Returning to a Pivot Table for Advanced Operations

Pivot tables are very powerful. A subset of pivot table operations are available in the pivot chart interface. Sometimes, however, you need to return to the pivot table in order to carry out an advanced operation. After you have made the change to the pivot table, you can then click the pivot chart in order to return to the pivot chart interface.

One example of an advanced operation is grouping daily dates up to months and years. Because the underlying data is transactional, it is reported at the daily level. If you build a pivot chart with dates along the Axis Field, your chart will be a confusing mess. In Figure 8.6, for example, Product is moved to the Legend field, and Date is shown in the Axis field. With five years' worth of dates, you cannot make out any details.

Figure 8.6
It is easy to summarize the daily dates to yearly and monthly dates in a pivot table.

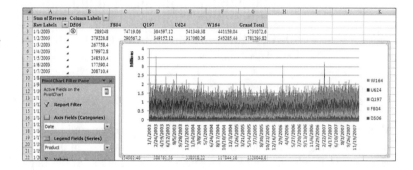

To group the data in the Date field, you follow these steps:

1. Select any date cell, such as cell A3. Excel puts away the Pivot Chart Tools ribbon tabs and adds the PivotTable Tools ribbon tabs.

2. From the Options ribbon, choose Group Field.

3. In the Grouping dialog, Excel defaults to grouping by months. You need to add Years in the Grouping dialog box. Otherwise, Excel will add January of this year and January of last year into a single value called January (see Figure 8.7).

Figure 8.7
You choose Months and Years from the Grouping dialog.

4. Click OK. Excel adds a new virtual field called Years to your field list and adds this field to the Row Labels field. The original field called Date is recast to include months.

5. Click the chart to put away the PivotTable Tools ribbon tabs and bring back the PivotChart Tools ribbon tabs.

After grouping, you can see details by month and year, as shown in Figure 8.8.

Figure 8.8
Excel presents both years and months along the horizontal axis.

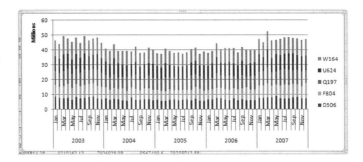

Although the grouping feature initially adds both the year and month information to the same area of the pivot table, you can easily split them apart in order to show year versus year data. In Figure 8.9, the Product field was dragged out of the Legend Fields drop zone, and the Date field was moved to the Legend Fields drop zone. You can now compare monthly sales from one year to the next.

Figure 8.9
You can separate the year and date fields in order to show year-over-year comparisons.

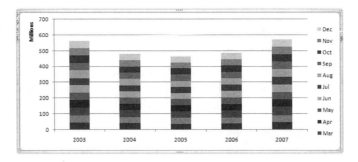

Filtering a Pivot Table

There are two ways to filter a pivot table report. If you have used pivot tables before, you'll find that the Report Filter field works similarly to Page Fields in previous versions of Excel. You can add a field to the Report Filter field and choose to limit the report to one or more values from the filter.

New in Excel 2007, you can also apply logical filters to fields in either the Axis or Legend fields. These filters allow you to specify various ranges. For example, you can select dates that occur in this year or customers that fall alphabetically between A and E.

Filtering Using a Report Filter Field

To add fields to the report filter, you drag them from the top of the PivotTable Field List box to the Report Filter drop zone at the bottom of the PivotTable Field List box.

You can drag multiple fields to the Report Filter section. However, you cannot drag a field that has already been used elsewhere in the pivot table.

For each field you add to the Report Filter section, you have a new drop-down in the PivotChart Filter Pane box. When you initially open this drop-down, you can select only one value from the drop-down. For example, you can select to filter the report to the east region, as shown in Figure 8.10.

Figure 8.10
Initially, each filter field allows you to select a single value.

You can build filters that select multiple items. For example, to create a chart for two related customers, you would follow these steps:

1. Open the Customer drop-down in the Report Filter section of the PivotChart Filter Pane box.

2. In the lower-left corner, choose the Select Multiple Items check box. Then, annoyingly, Excel checks every customer in the list.

3. The top entry in the drop-down is (All). Uncheck this box, and all the other check marks are cleared.

4. Select the customers of interest, as shown in Figure 8.11. Click OK.

The pivot chart is redrawn to show totals for only the selected customers. The Customer field in cell B2 shows the somewhat cryptic (Multiple Items) entry. At this point, you should add a title above the chart, perhaps in cell D2, to identify the customers shown in the chart.

Figure 8.11
By using the
Multiple Items check
box, you can create a
report for related
customers.

Any filters defined in the Report Filter field will persist when you later drop those fields in either the Axis or Legend fields. In Figure 8.12, after pivoting the report, Excel presents a report comparing two customers.

Figure 8.12
After pivoting the
filtered Customer
field, the filters
persist.

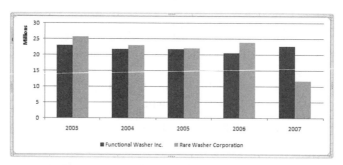

Using the Excel 2007 Filters for Axis and Legend Fields

If your pivot chart was created in a new Excel 2007 worksheet and never existed as an Excel 2003 pivot table, you can try out the new filters available for the Legend and Axis fields.

The drop-downs for the Axis and Legend fields in the PivotChart Filter Pane box offer the same list of items shown previously, as well as new entries for Value Filters, Text Filters, and/or Date Filters.

The new Label Filters list, shown in Figure 8.13, allows you to select customers whose names start with certain letters or that contain certain words.

Figure 8.13
Text filters allow you to filter based on patterns in the items for a field.

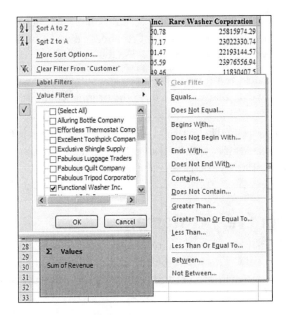

The Date Filters list, shown in Figure 8.14, allows you to select transactions that fall into a number of virtual date periods. These periods recalculate when you open the file in a later month. So, if you select records from last month, the report updates after you refresh the report in a new month.

Figure 8.14
Date filters allow you to select records from a certain quarter, month, or period.

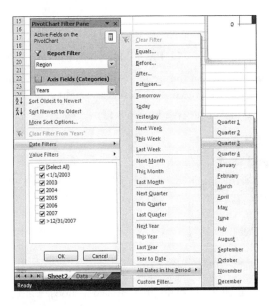

Value filters are more powerful than the other types of filters discussed so far. While label and date filters allow you to filter the items in the list based on the items themselves, value filters allow you to filter the items in the list based on values in other fields. For example, you can choose all customers where the sum of revenue is over $1 million. Or you can use the Top 10 Filter to limit the pivot chart to the top five customers.

Every Axis and Legend field features a value filter. You will also see either label or date filters based on the type of data that Excel finds in the original column.

> **NOTE** In order to see the date filters, all the values in the original column must be formatted as dates when you create the pivot table. One single cell with a text value in a column of one million dates will cause Excel to show a label filter instead of a date filter.

Creating a Chart for Every Customer

The Show Report Filters Pages functionality allows you to copy a pivot table for every value in a Report Filter field. This would be a fantastic bit of functionality to have available for pivot charts. However, when you use this feature, Excel copies the pivot table but not the pivot chart.

You have a couple of choices in solving this problem. First, you could set up a simple looping macro in VBA to print the chart for each value in the report filter. Or, you could follow these basic steps:

1. Set up a pivot chart that has the proper formatting. Make sure the Customer field is in the Report Filter area.
2. Select the pivot chart. Choose Design, Save as Template. Define that template as the default chart type.
3. Select a cell in your pivot table. The PivotTable Tools ribbon tabs appears.
4. Look for the Options button on the far left of the Options tab. Don't click the Options button. Instead, click the drop-down at the right side of this button.
5. Select Show Report Filter Pages (see Figure 8.15).

Figure 8.15
You can choose Show Report Filter Pages.

6. In the Show Report Filter Pages dialog that appears, choose Customer and then click OK. Excel copies the current worksheet once for each customer.
7. Select the worksheet for the first customer. Select a cell in the pivot table. Press Alt+F1. Excel creates a pivot chart on the worksheet.

Repeat step 7 for each additional customer. Every time you press Alt+F1, you can wonder why the fine folks at Microsoft could not have allowed pivot charts to work with the Show Report Filter Pages feature.

CASE STUDY

Stratifying Invoice Amounts

You cannot create a scatter chart based on a pivot table. Although scatter charts are best for stratifying data, you can still achieve the same effect by using a pivot chart.

During the process of building a pivot chart, there are two steps during which you might temporarily have thousands of data points along the axis field. Rather than ask Excel to attempt to render a chart with thousands of data points, it would make more sense to build the analysis as a pivot table first, group the fields, and then convert it to a pivot table.

You follow these steps to analyze invoice sizes for the five largest customers in your dataset:

1. Select one cell in your data.
2. From the Insert ribbon, choose the top half of the PivotTable icon.
3. Click OK to confirm the information in the Create PivotTable dialog.
4. Drag the Revenue field to the Σ Values drop zone.
5. Drag a second copy of the Revenue field to the Row Labels drop zone.
6. Right-click one value in column A of your pivot table and choose Group from the context menu.
7. As shown in Figure 8.16, Excel suggests grouping the data into strange groups, starting at 8002.40. Change those figures to round numbers, perhaps 5000 to 130000, in increments of 5000. Click OK.

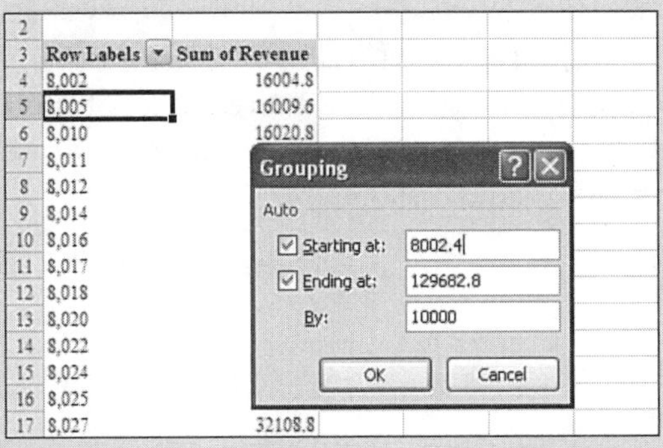

Figure 8.16
When grouping numeric values, Excel suggests strange starting points. You should round them to even ranges.

8. Add Customer as the first Row Labels field. Then move Customer before Revenue by dropping the field slightly above the Revenue button in the Row Labels drop zone.
9. Hover the mouse above the Customer field at the top of the PivotTable Field List. A new drop-down appears. Click this drop-down. Choose Value Filters, Top 10. Choose Top 5 Items by Sum of Revenue. Click OK.
10. Hover the mouse over the Revenue field in the Σ Values area of the PivotTable Field List box. Click the drop-down and Choose Value Field Settings.

11. In the Value Field Settings dialog that appears, change Sum to Count. Click OK.

12. In the Options ribbon, click the PivotChart icon. Choose a Stacked Columns chart. Click OK.

13. In the Layout ribbon, choose Lines, Series Lines.

14. Also in the Layout ribbon, choose Legend, No Legend.

The result is the chart shown in Figure 8.17. For each customer, you can expect the invoices to be grouped around a central value. If you see any invoices that fall far outside the normal range, they might be worthy of audit. In Figure 8.17, for example, you can see that Fabulous Tripod tends to order in the $10,000 to $30,000 range, yet they had at least one invoice in the $125,000 range. This might be the result of a keying error because it is so far outside the norm.

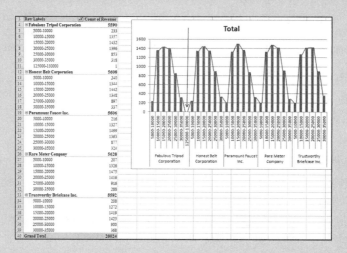

> **TIP**
>
> To find the invoice(s) outside the $10,000 to $30,000 range for Fabulous Tripod, you can go back to the original pivot table and double-click the value next to the 125000-130000 range for Fabulous Tripod. Excel then extracts all the records that make up that data and presents them on a new worksheet for you.

Next Steps

Pivot charts are about as high-tech as you can get. In some cases, you don't need a chart to present your data. Chapter 9, "Presenting Data Visually Without Charts," goes low-tech, showing you how to use various formula tricks to build graphic displays of information right in your spreadsheet cells.

Presenting Data Visually Without Charts

9

Creating Charts in the Worksheet Cells

In many cases, you don't need to create a chart in order to visually communicate data. While prior versions of Excel have included features such as slider controls, text bar charts, and conditional formatting to automatically color in certain cells, Excel 2007 offers three fantastic new data visualization tools under the rewritten conditional formatting logic:

- **Data bars**—This tool offers a tiny, in-cell bar chart for each number in a range. The reader's eye is drawn to the largest numbers because of the size of the bars.

- **Color scales**—Color scales, also called heat maps, color cells in a range of colors. You can use one of six built-in schemes where red is high and blue is low, or green is high and red is low, or you can define your own color scheme.

- **Icon sets**—You can now add a tiny icon next to each number in a range. Icons can use a traffic light metaphor, power bar metaphor, or arrow metaphors to show which data points are the best performers in a dataset.

With each of these new data visualizations, Excel requires only three clicks to get a result. However, each visualization offers advanced settings that give you finer control.

This chapter starts by discussing the new data visualizations on the Conditional Formatting drop-down on the Home ribbon and then describes some of the legacy data visualizations, such as using the REPT function to build bar charts in cells.

Using Data Bars to Create In-Cell Bar Charts

A *data bar* is a semitransparent swath of color that starts at the left edge of a cell. The smallest numbers in a formatted range have just a tiny bit of color in the cell. The largest numbers in the formatted range are 90% filled with color. This creates a visual effect that enables you to visually pick out the larger and smaller values.

Creating data bars requires just a few clicks. You follow these steps:

1. Select a range of numeric data. Do not include the total in this selection. If the data is in noncontiguous ranges, hold down the Ctrl key while selecting additional areas. This range should be numbers of similar scale. For example, you can select a column of sales data or a column of profit data. If you attempt to select a range that contains both units sold and revenue dollars, the size of the revenue numbers will overpower the units sold numbers, and no color will appear in the units sold cells.

2. From the Home ribbon, select Conditional Formatting, Data Bars. You see six built-in colors for the data bars: blue, green, red, orange, bright blue, and pink. Select one of them.

> **NOTE**   If you don't like the six basic colors Excel offers for data bars, you can choose any other color, as described in the next section.

The result is a swath of color in each cell in the selection, as shown in Figure 9.1.

Figure 9.1
After applying a data bar, you can easily see that California is a leading exporter of agriculture products.

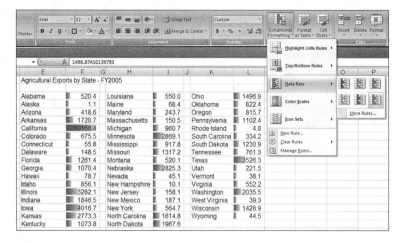

Customizing Data Bars

By default, Excel assigns the largest data bar to the cell with the largest value and the smallest data bar to the cell with the smallest value. You can customize this behavior by following these steps:

1. From the Conditional Formatting drop-down on the Home ribbon, choose Manage Rules.

2. From the Show Formatting Rules drop-down, choose This Worksheet. You now see a list of all rules applied to the sheet.

3. Click the Data Bar rule.

4. Click the Edit Rule button. You see the Edit Formatting Rule dialog, as shown in Figure 9.2.

Figure 9.2
You customize data bars by using the Edit Formatting Rule dialog.

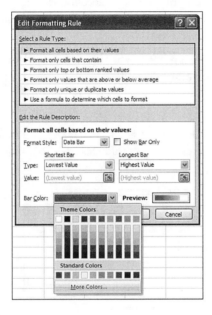

5. To change the color of the data bars beyond the six basic colors, choose the Bar Color drop-down and then choose from the theme colors or standard colors or click More Colors to build any RGB value you like.

6. Select the Show Bar Only check box. Excel hides the numbers in the cells and shows only the data bars. This is an interesting variation, as shown in Figure 9.3.

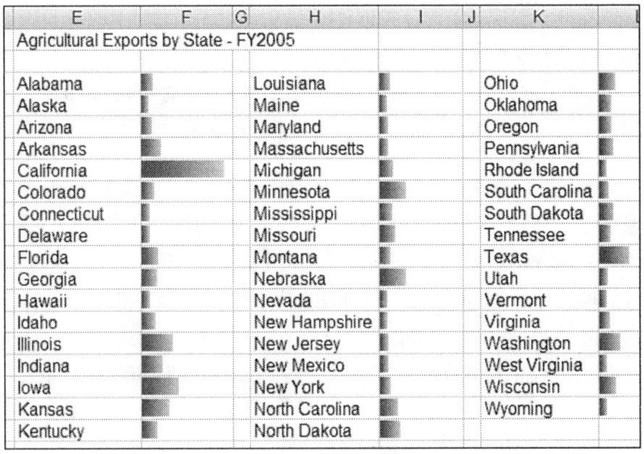

Figure 9.3
Showing only the data bars is an interesting alternative.

E	F	G	H	I	J	K	L
Agricultural Exports by State - FY2005							
Alabama	▮	Louisiana	▮			Ohio	▮
Alaska	▏	Maine	▏			Oklahoma	▮
Arizona	▮	Maryland	▮			Oregon	▮
Arkansas	▮▮	Massachusetts	▮			Pennsylvania	▮
California	▮▮▮▮	Michigan	▮▮			Rhode Island	▏
Colorado	▮▮	Minnesota	▮▮▮			South Carolina	▮
Connecticut	▏	Mississippi	▮▮			South Dakota	▮▮
Delaware	▏	Missouri	▮▮			Tennessee	▮
Florida	▮	Montana	▮			Texas	▮▮▮
Georgia	▮	Nebraska	▮▮▮			Utah	▏
Hawaii	▏	Nevada	▏			Vermont	▏
Idaho	▮	New Hampshire	▏			Virginia	▮
Illinois	▮▮▮	New Jersey	▏			Washington	▮▮
Indiana	▮▮	New Mexico	▮			West Virginia	▏
Iowa	▮▮▮▮	New York	▮			Wisconsin	▮▮
Kansas	▮▮▮	North Carolina	▮▮			Wyoming	▏
Kentucky	▮	North Dakota	▮▮				

There are two Type drop-downs in the Edit Formatting Rule dialog: Shortest Bar and Longest Bar. These drop-downs offer the choices Lowest Value and Highest Value, Number, Percent, Formula, and Percentile, as explained in the following section.

Controlling the Size of the Smallest/Largest Bar

Any dataset is likely to have a few outliers. Say that the vast majority of your customers account for over $10,000 in sales each, but one stray account has sales of just a few dollars. For such situations, Microsoft gives you explicit control over the cell value that gets the smallest bar.

For example, consider column A in Figure 9.4. The values are mostly in the 10,000 to 20,000 range. However, one outlier value of 15 forces Excel to assign a medium-sized data bar to the 10,000 value in cell A1.

For the numbers in column D, the steps in the preceding section were used to edit the rule. In this case, the Shortest Bar Type drop-down is set to 10,000. Excel then treats any value of 10,000 as the value with the shortest bar. Any value less than 10,000 is given the same size bar as the 10,000 bar.

Figure 9.4
You can manage the rules for column D to set the shortest bar to any value of 10,000 or below.

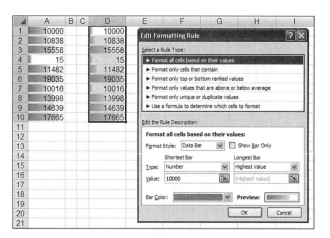

Are Data Bars Truly Evil Incarnate, as Some Suggest?

Using data bars is a way to quickly call attention to the largest and smallest values in a range of data. If your goal is to highlight large customers versus small customers, the visualizations in column D in Figure 9.4 do a better job than the visualizations in column A.

However, many statisticians cry foul when they analyze the new data bars feature. There are two main reasons. First, Microsoft decided that every cell would get a bar. It also decided that the smallest bar would occupy 10% of the cell. This means that the tiny value of 15 in cell A4 is given about 10 pixels of shading. Statisticians complain that when a value of 15,000 is then given 60 pixels of shading, as in cell A9, the data is grossly misrepresented. The ratio of cell A1 to A6 is better. Cell A1 uses 40 pixels for 10,000 and cell A6 uses 72 pixels for 19,000. In both cells, each pixel of shading represents $250–$260.

Second, Microsoft allows the creator of a spreadsheet to control the value for the shortest bar, as in column D. In this case, the 10,000 in cell D1 gets 4 pixels. The 19,000 in cell D6 gets 62 pixels. Edward Tufte and others would argue that the $2,500 per pixel in cell D1 is out of line with the $306 per pixel in cell D6.

Personally, I prefer data bars to color scales and icon sets. Icon sets lump customers into one of three to five buckets. Color scales reproduce horribly in black-and-white printouts and are problematic for people who are color-blind. Data bars allow you to show a graduated indicator in a single color that prints well. You can think of a data bar as an icon set with 70 different icons instead of 5 power bars; data bars do a perfectly acceptable job of allowing the reader to hone in on the largest values in a sea of numbers.

If you feel compelled to do so, you can add notes to your spreadsheets to indicate that the "data bars are not to scale" or, perhaps, "Data bars are scaled from a range of 10,000 (shortest) to 20,000 (longest)."

Because data bars are designed to highlight the relative size of the largest customers, you might try showing data bars for only the top 20% of values. For more information, see "Showing Data Bars for a Subset of Cells," later in this chapter.

You need to keep in mind the following rules for each of the Type options in the Edit Formatting Rule dialog:

- For Lowest Value/Highest Value, Excel evaluates all the values in the range of cells and selects the lowest value as the shortest bar and the highest value as the longest bar. This is the default behavior.

- For Number, you enter the values that should receive the shortest and/or longest bars. For numbers that are more or less than that value, Excel simply draws the shortest or longest bar, as appropriate.

- For Percent, you enter a percentage to associate with the shortest and longest bars. For example, if the values in the selected cells range from 0 to 1,000, a minimum value associated with 10% would be 100. In this example, any cells having values equal to or less than 100 would have the shortest bar drawn in the cell.

- Percentile examines the values in the range of cells, sorts them, and then uses their positions within the sorted list to determine their percentiles. In a set of 20 ordered cells, for example, the 30th percentile would always be the 6th cell, regardless of the value contained within it. If you choose Percentile and enter 10 for the shortest bar and 90 for the longest bar, any outliers below 10 would get the shortest bar assigned to them and any outliers above 90 would get the longest bar assigned to them.

- Formula allows you to enter a formula that is evaluated to determine the value used for the shortest and longest bars. This is useful for developing conditional formats that aren't easily handled by the other four choices.

One frustrating feature with data bars is that you cannot reverse their size, using the smallest bar for the highest number and vice versa. Although in some scenarios, such as top 100 rankings, the lowest score might deserve the largest bar, there is no way to make this happen with data bars. If you need to do this, you should consider using color scales instead.

Showing Data Bars for a Subset of Cells

In the data bars examples given in the previous sections, every cell in the range receives a data bar. But what if you just want some of the values (for example, the top 20%) to have data bars? The process for making this happen isn't intuitive, but it is possible. Basically, you apply the data bar to the entire range. Then you add a new conditional format (a very boring format) to all the cells that you don't want to have data bars. For example, you might tell Excel to use a white background on all cells with values in the lowest 80th percentile. The final important step is to manage the rules and tell Excel to stop processing more rules if the white background rule is met. This requires clever thinking. If you want to apply data bars to cells in the top 20%, you first tell Excel to make all the cells in the bottom 80% look like every other cell in Excel. Turning on Stop if True (in the Conditional Formatting Rules Manager dialog) is the key to getting Excel to not apply the data bar to cells with values in the lower 80%.

Figure 9.5 shows data bars applied to only the top 20% of states.

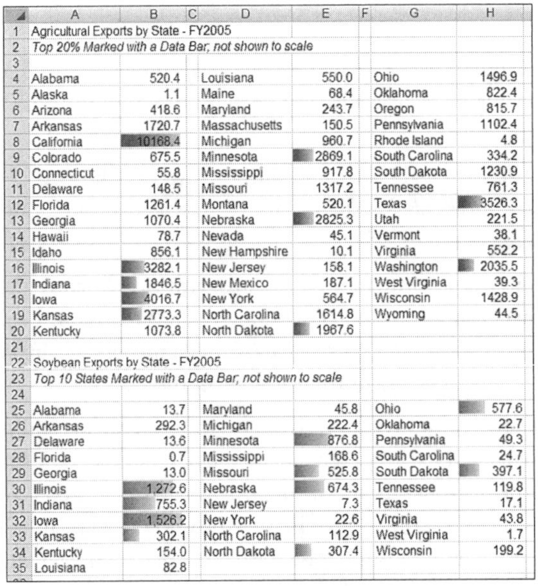

	A	B	C	D	E	F	G	H
1	Agricultural Exports by State - FY2005							
2	*Top 20% Marked with a Data Bar, not shown to scale*							
3								
4	Alabama	520.4		Louisiana	550.0		Ohio	1496.9
5	Alaska	1.1		Maine	68.4		Oklahoma	822.4
6	Arizona	418.6		Maryland	243.7		Oregon	815.7
7	Arkansas	1720.7		Massachusetts	150.5		Pennsylvania	1102.4
8	California	10168.4		Michigan	960.7		Rhode Island	4.8
9	Colorado	675.5		Minnesota	2869.1		South Carolina	334.2
10	Connecticut	55.8		Mississippi	917.8		South Dakota	1230.9
11	Delaware	148.5		Missouri	1317.2		Tennessee	761.3
12	Florida	1261.4		Montana	520.1		Texas	3526.3
13	Georgia	1070.4		Nebraska	2825.3		Utah	221.5
14	Hawaii	78.7		Nevada	45.1		Vermont	38.1
15	Idaho	856.1		New Hampshire	10.1		Virginia	552.2
16	Illinois	3282.1		New Jersey	158.1		Washington	2035.5
17	Indiana	1846.5		New Mexico	187.1		West Virginia	39.3
18	Iowa	4016.7		New York	564.7		Wisconsin	1428.9
19	Kansas	2773.3		North Carolina	1614.8		Wyoming	44.5
20	Kentucky	1073.8		North Dakota	1967.6			
21								
22	Soybean Exports by State - FY2005							
23	*Top 10 States Marked with a Data Bar, not shown to scale*							
24								
25	Alabama	13.7		Maryland	45.8		Ohio	577.6
26	Arkansas	292.3		Michigan	222.4		Oklahoma	22.7
27	Delaware	13.6		Minnesota	876.8		Pennsylvania	49.3
28	Florida	0.7		Mississippi	168.6		South Carolina	24.7
29	Georgia	13.0		Missouri	525.8		South Dakota	397.1
30	Illinois	1,272.6		Nebraska	674.3		Tennessee	119.8
31	Indiana	755.3		New Jersey	7.3		Texas	17.1
32	Iowa	1,526.2		New York	22.6		Virginia	43.8
33	Kansas	302.1		North Carolina	112.9		West Virginia	1.7
34	Kentucky	154.0		North Dakota	307.4		Wisconsin	199.2
35	Louisiana	82.8						

Figure 9.5
Using Stop if True after formatting the lower 80% with no special formatting allows the data bars to appear only on the top states.

In Figure 9.5, the goal is to have the data bars appear only on the top 20% of states. You can use the following steps to create an analysis similar to this:

1. Apply a data bar to the range of cells.
2. With the range of cells selected, from the Home ribbon, select Conditional Formatting, Manage Rules. Excel displays the Conditional Formatting Rules Manager dialog.
3. Click New Rule. Excel displays the New Formatting Rule dialog.

4. In the top of the New Formatting Rule dialog, choose Format Only Top or Bottom Ranked Values. In the bottom of the dialog, change Top to Bottom. Enter 80 in the text box and select the % of the Selected Range check box. Leave the Preview box as No Format Set (see Figure 9.6). Click OK to create the rule.

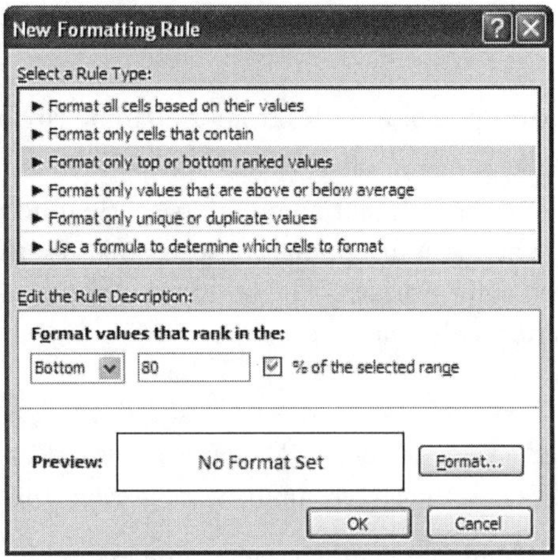

Figure 9.6
You can choose to high-light the bottom 80% with no special formatting.

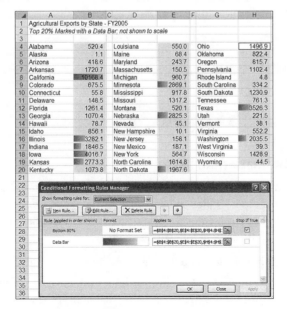

5. In the Conditional Formatting Rules Manager dialog, make sure that the Stop if True box is checked for the Bottom 80% rule. Note that new rules are initially added to the top of the list (see Figure 9.7). Click Close to dismiss the dialog.

Figure 9.7
Using these settings, Excel applies no special formatting to the bot-tom 80% and then stops processing more rules.

Using Color Scales to Highlight Extremes

Color scales are similar to data bars. Instead of having a variable-size bar in each cell, however, color scales use gradients of two or three different colors to communicate the relative size of each cell. Here's how you apply color scales:

1. Select a range that contains numbers. Be sure not to include headings or total cells in the selection.

2. Select Conditional Formatting, Color Scales from the Home ribbon.

3. From the Color Scales fly-out menu, select one of the eight styles to apply the color scale to the range. (Note that this fly-out menu offers subtle differences that you should pay attention to. The top four options are scales that use three colors. These are great onscreen or with color printers. The bottom four options are scales that use two colors. These are better with monochrome printers.)

In a default color scale with a three-color scale, the smallest cells are assigned a value of red. The middle values are assigned a value of yellow. The largest cells are assigned a value of green. Even within the green values, the larger numbers are greener than the other numbers.

In Figure 9.8, a three-color scale highlights the largest numbers in blue, middle numbers in yellow, and the smallest numbers in red.

Figure 9.8
Excel provides a range of shading, depending on the value. When viewed in color, you would see that Carole and John's receivables have been increasing throughout the year.

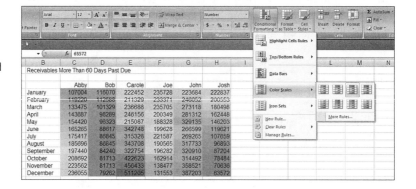

Converting to Monochromatic Data Bars

As you can see from the black-and-white images in this book, color scales do not perform well when printed in black and white. When you know you'll be printing in black and white, one option is to convert a color scale to a monochromatic scale that varies from white to a dark color. To do so, you follow these steps:

1. Select a single cell in your formatted range.

2. From the Insert ribbon, choose Conditional Formatting, Manage Rules. In the Conditional Formatting Rules Manager dialog that appears, the initial drop-down defaults to Current Selection. This works fine as long as your selection is part of the range that has conditional formatting. The dialog shows any conditional formatting rule(s) applied to the current selection.

3. Even if there is only one rule in the dialog, click the rule to select it and then click
Edit Rule. Initially, the Edit Formatting Rule dialog shows the selected yellow–red
scale, as shown in Figure 9.9.

Figure 9.9
You can customize the
settings for a color scale
in the lower half of the
Edit Formatting Rule
dialog.

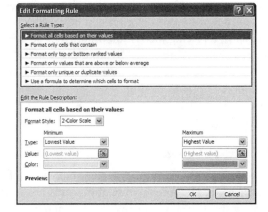

4. For color scales, change any of the settings in the lower half of the dialog box, in the
Edit the Rule Description section. From the Format Style drop-down, choose 2-Color
Scale. (The other options included are 3-Color Scale, Data Bar, and Icon Sets.)

5. For the minimum, select the Color drop-down and choose white. For the maximum,
select the Color drop-down and choose a dark color. Click OK to return to the
Conditional Formatting Rules Manager dialog and then click OK again to complete
the operation.

The new monochromatic color scale is shown in Figure 9.10.

Figure 9.10
Setting up a two-color
gradient from white to
dark works best with a
printed document.

Receivables More Than 60 Days Past Due						
	Abby	Bob	Carole	Joe	John	Josh
January	107004	116070	222452	235728	223684	222837
February	119220	112588	211329	233371	246052	200553
March	133475	101329	236688	235705	273118	180498
April	143687	98289	246156	200349	281312	162448
May	154420	96323	215087	188328	329135	146203
June	165265	88617	342748	199628	266599	119621
July	175417	86845	315328	221587	269265	107659
August	185696	86845	343708	190565	317733	96893
September	197440	84240	322754	196282	320910	87204
October	208692	81713	422623	162914	314492	78484
November	223562	81713	456433	138477	358521	70636
December	236055	79262	511205	131553	387203	63572

Troubleshooting Color Scales

Excel 2007 considers a three-color scale and a two-color scale to be completely different visualizations. This leads to some erratic behavior when you attempt to change the color scale pattern by using the Color Scale icon on the Conditional Formatting drop-down.

Say that you use the Color Scale icon to apply a three-color red–yellow–green visualization. You decide to go back to the icon and instead apply a three-color blue–yellow–red visualization. Excel 2007 is smart enough to convert the red–yellow–green pattern to blue–yellow–red. This behavior is logical enough.

However, say that you decide to choose a visualization from the second row of color scales—perhaps the green–yellow visualization. Even though this is accessed on the same fly-out menu, Excel 2007 considers the two-color scale to be a different visualization from the three-color scale. Instead of replacing the visualization, Excel adds a second rule. This can lead to muting of the colors from both rules. To avoid this problem, when switching from two-color to three-color scales, you need to be sure to use the Manage Rules choice at the bottom of the Conditional Formatting drop-down on the Home ribbon to convert from a three-color to a two-color scale.

Using Icon Sets to Segregate Data

Icon sets, which were popular with expensive management reporting software in the late 1990s, have now been added to Excel. An icon set might include green, yellow, and red traffic lights or another set of icons to show positive, neutral, and negative meanings. With icon sets, Excel automatically applies an icon to a cell, based on the relative size of the value in the cell compared to other values in the range.

> **NOTE** Initially, icon sets look like they will be cool. However, there are a few limitations in Excel 2007 that make them annoying. I suspect that the implementation of icon sets will improve greatly in future versions of Excel.

Excel 2007 ships with icon sets that contain three, four, or five different icons. The icons are always left-justified in the cell. Excel applies rules to add an icon to every cell in the range:

- **Three-icon sets**—For the three-icon sets, you have a choice between arrows, flags, two varieties of traffic lights, signs, and two varieties of what Excel calls "3 Symbols." This last group consists of a green check mark for the good cells, a yellow exclamation point for the middle cells, and a red X for the bad cells. You can either get the symbols in a circle (that is, 3 Symbols(Circled)) or alone on a white background (that is, 3 Symbols). One version of the arrows is available in gray. All the other icon sets use red, yellow, and green.

- **Four-icon sets**—For the four-icon sets, there are two varieties of arrows: a black-to-red circle set, a set of cell phone power bars, and a set of four traffic lights. In the traffic light option, a black light indicates an option that is even worse than the red light. The power bars icons seem to work well on both color displays and monochromatic printouts.

- **Five-icon sets**—For the five-icon sets, there are two varieties of arrows, a five-power bar set, and an interesting set called "5 Quarters." This last set is a monochromatic circle that is completely empty for the lowest values, 25% filled, 50% filled, 75% filled, and completely filled for the highest values.

Setting Up an Icon Set

Given that icon sets are in their first Excel incarnation, they require a bit more thought than the other data visualization offerings. Before you use icon sets, you should consider whether they will be printed in monochrome or displayed in color. Several of the 17 icon sets rely on color for differentiation and look horrible in a black-and-white report.

> **NOTE**
> After creating several reports with icon sets, I have started to favor the cell phone power bars, which look good in both color and black and white.

To set up an icon set, you follow these steps:

1. Select a range of numeric data of a similar scale. Do not include the headers or total rows in this selection.

2. From the Home ribbon, select Conditional Formatting, Icon Sets. Select 1 of the 17 icon sets. Figure 9.11 shows the "5 Ratings" choice selected.

Figure 9.11
You can choose from the 17 icon sets.

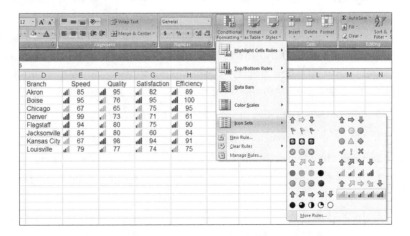

Moving Numbers Closer to Icons

In the top rows of Figure 9.12, the icon set has been applied to a rectangular range of data. The icons are always left-justified. There is no way to center them, and there is no way to have an icon appear to the right of the value. This can be problematic; in Figure 9.11, for example, the icons for column F appear to apply to the numbers in column E.

One way to mitigate this problem is to center all the numbers in the range. This at least puts the value and the icon closer together. Rows 11 through 19 of Figure 9.12 show this solution.

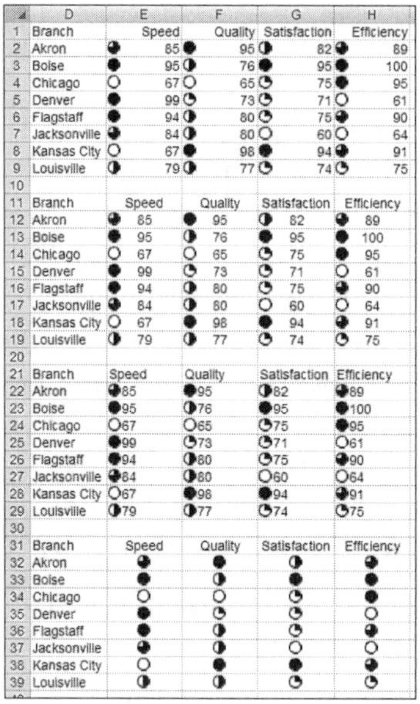

Figure 9.12

Changing the alignment of the numbers moves them closer to the icon.

Choosing left-justified for the numbers is another choice. In this case, the numbers appear adjacent to the icon set, as shown in rows 22 through 29 of Figure 9.12.

If you don't want to show numbers at all, you can edit the conditional formatting rule and choose Show Icon Only. Rows 31 through 39 show this solution. Ironically, when the numbers are no longer displayed, you can position the icons by using the Left Align, Center Align, and Right Align icons.

To show the icons only, as in the last rows of Figure 9.12, you follow these steps:

1. Select one of the cells with the icon set formatting.
2. From the Home ribbon, select Conditional Formatting, Manage Rules.
3. In the Conditional Formatting Rules Manager dialog, click the Icon Set rule and then click Edit Rule.
4. In the lower-right corner of the Edit Formatting Rule dialog, choose Show Icon Only. Click OK twice to close the two dialog boxes.
5. Select all the cells that contain icons and click the Align Center button on the Home ribbon.

Reversing the Sequence of Icons

Say that you have data to track reject rates for several manufacturing lines. You apply an icon set that offers green check marks, yellow exclamation points, and red X icons.

In the default view of the data, Excel always assumes that higher numbers are better. However, that is not the case in this situation, where higher reject rates are bad.

Unlike with color scales or data bars, with icon sets, you can reverse the order. To do so, you follow these steps:

1. Select one cell in your data.
2. From the Conditional Formatting drop-down on the Home ribbon, select Manage Rules.
3. Click Icon Set to select this rule. The rule color changes from gray to blue.
4. Click the Edit Rule button. The Edit Formatting Rule dialog appears.
5. In the Edit Formatting Rule dialog, choose the Reverse Icon Order check box. Click OK twice to close both open dialog boxes.

Creating a Chart Using Conditional Formatting in Worksheet Cells

In the old days, charts were drawn by hand, using a sheet of graph paper and a pencil. Think about the Excel worksheets on your computer. Basically, an Excel worksheet is a very large sheet of graph paper, with 17 billion tiny little boxes.

You can create plenty of charts right on a worksheet, without ever invoking the Excel charting engine. Figure 9.13 shows such a chart. The gray bars in D2:R6 are drawn based on conditional formatting rules in response to data entered in B2:C6. Note how the bars have expanded or contracted in the bottom image when starting or ending years are adjusted.

I created this worksheet for a friend who was trying to visualize the years of production for various models of Mullins Steel Boats. With Excel 2007's limit of only three rules for prior conditional formatting, it was not quite possible to handle every condition by using Excel's conditional formatting. However, it is possible to manually create this type of chart.

The years stretch from cell D1 and would extend as far right as necessary. To make the chart narrow, you can select Vertical Text from the Orientation drop-down in the Home ribbon (see Figure 9.14). You can then resize the columns to a column width of 2.

Figure 9.13
The gray bars are created through a series of conditional formatting rules.

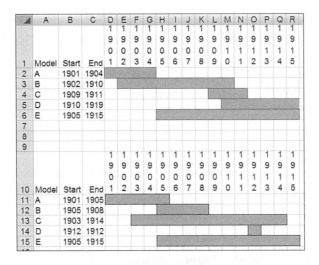

Figure 9.14
The Vertical Text setting is located behind the diagonal-ab icon in the Home ribbon.

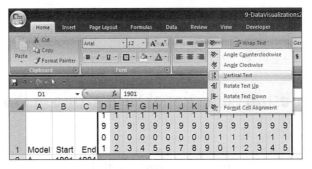

The logic for creating the bars is as follows:

- If the start and end year are equal and they match the year in row 1, color the cell gray, with borders on all four sides.

- If the start year in column B matches the year in row 1, color the cell gray. Include left, top, and bottom borders.

- If the end year in column C matches the year in row 1, color the cell gray. Include right, top, and bottom borders.

- If the year in row 1 is greater than the start year and less than the end year, color the cell gray, with top and bottom borders but no side borders.

You follow these steps to create the conditional formatting rules for this logic:

1. Select the range D2:R6. (Although you have selected many cells, you write the conditional formatting rules as if they applied to the top-left cell, D2.)

2. From the Home ribbon, choose Conditional Formatting, Manage Rules. Excel displays the Conditional Formatting Rules Manager dialog.

3. Click the New Rule button. Excel displays the New Formatting Rule dialog.

4. In the top half of the dialog, choose Use a Formula to Determine Which Cells to Format. The bottom half of the dialog box redraws to show Format Values Where This Formula Is True.

5. Enter the formula =$B2=D$1 for the first condition. This formula checks whether the start year in column B of the current row is equal to row 1 of the current column. It is crucial that you enter dollar signs before the B and 1 but not before the 2 and D.

6. Click the Format button in the dialog. On the Fill tab, choose a fill color for the cell. On the Border tab, click None and then click the Top, Bottom, and Left. Click OK to close the Format Cells dialog. Click OK to close the New Formatting Rule dialog. If you click the Apply button, you should see that the first cell for each bar is drawn in the worksheet.

7. Repeat steps 3 and 4 and then enter the formula =$C2=D$1 for the second rule; this is the formula to format the last cell of the bar. The Format selection is the same color fill as in step 6. On the Border tab, choose None, Top, Bottom, and Right.

8. Repeat step 7 and then enter the formula =AND($B2<D$1,$C2>D$1) for the third rule; this is the formula to format center cells in the bar. The Format selection is the same fill as in step 6. On the Border tab, choose None, Top, and Bottom.

9. Repeat step 7 and then enter the formula =AND($B2=$C2,$B2=D$1) for the last rule; this is the formula to find where the model was only available for a single year. The Format selection is the same fill color as in step 6. On the Border tab, choose Outline. Rules are added to the beginning of the rule list. By entering this rule last, you ensure that it is evaluated first.

At this point, your Conditional Formatting Rules Manager dialog should look similar to the one in Figure 9.15.

Figure 9.15
Four rules create the chart. One drawback: the dot for row 6 appears outside the print area.

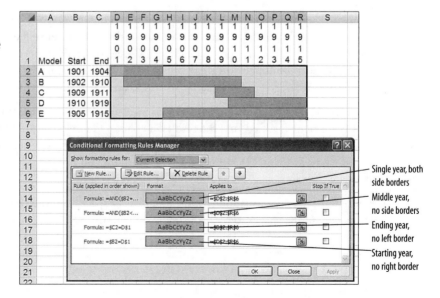

This example is complicated by the fact that you draw borders on the appropriate edges of each cell. If you instead used a solid black fill, you could create the effect with a single rule, using the formula =AND($B2<=D$1,$C2>=D$1), as shown in Figure 9.16.

Figure 9.16

If you aren't concerned with the cell borders, the chart can be reduced to a single conditional formatting rule.

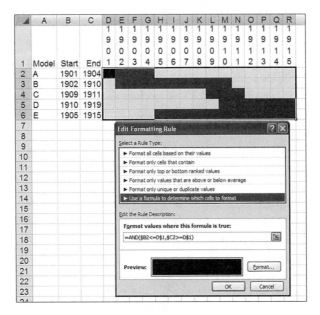

Creating a Chart Using the REPT Function

The REPT function, which has been around since Excel 5, takes two arguments. The first argument is the text to repeat. The second argument is the number of times to repeat the text.

In Figure 9.17, column B shows cotton exports. The numbers range from 1,337 down to 13. You create the bar charts in column C by repeating the | character numerous times. Rather than show a line of 1,337 pipe characters in cell C4, however, the repeat argument in cell B4 is 1,337 divided by 10; cell C4 therefore contains 133 vertical bars. Cell C20 contains 1 vertical bar. (Although 13.7 divided by 10 is 1.3 bars, Excel shows only complete bars.)

The result of the REPT function can be left- or right-justified. In Figure 9.18, the results in column E are right-justified, and the results in column G are left-justified to create a comparative histogram. The formulas on the right side of the chart use a REPT function concatenated with a space and then the value. The formulas on the left side of the chart concatenate the value, a space, and the REPT function.

In Figure 9.19, the REPT function repeats a number of spaces and then concatenates a single dot at the end of the spaces to create a simple dot chart.

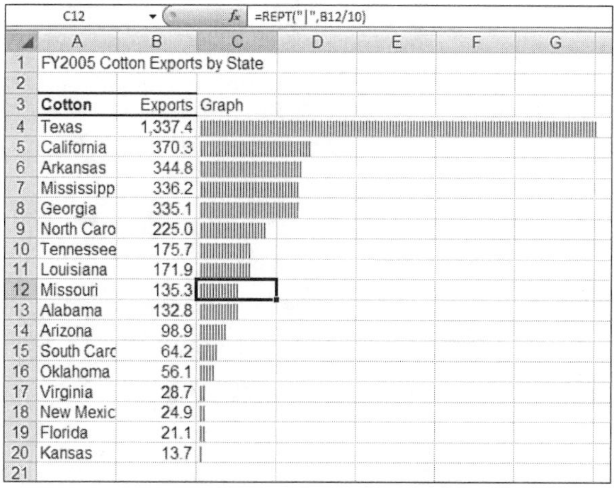

Figure 9.17
Using the REPT function is a quick way to produce a bar chart right in a worksheet. The trick is to use the proper scaling factor.

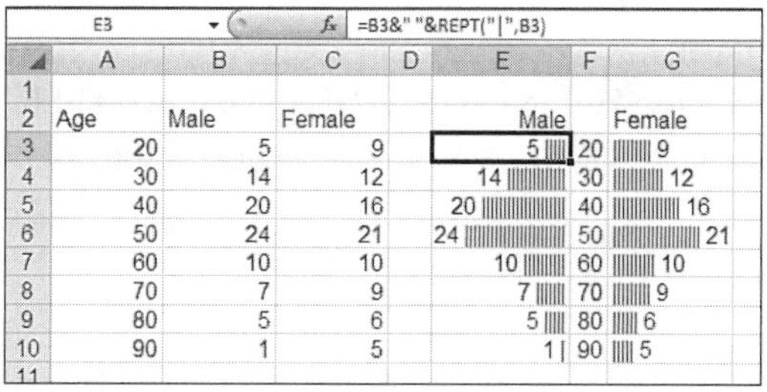

C12 =REPT("|",B12/10)

	A	B	C	D	E	F	G
1	FY2005 Cotton Exports by State						
2							
3	**Cotton**	Exports	Graph				
4	Texas	1,337.4	|||||||||||||||||||||||||||||||||||||||||||||				
5	California	370.3	||||||||||				
6	Arkansas	344.8	|||||||||||				
7	Mississipp	336.2	||||||||||				
8	Georgia	335.1	||||||||||				
9	North Caro	225.0	||||||||				
10	Tennessee	175.7	|||||||				
11	Louisiana	171.9	|||||||				
12	Missouri	135.3	||||||				
13	Alabama	132.8	||||||				
14	Arizona	98.9	|||||				
15	South Carc	64.2	||||				
16	Oklahoma	56.1	||||				
17	Virginia	28.7	||				
18	New Mexic	24.9	||				
19	Florida	21.1	||				
20	Kansas	13.7						
21							

Figure 9.18
Here, pairs of REPT functions create a comparative histogram.

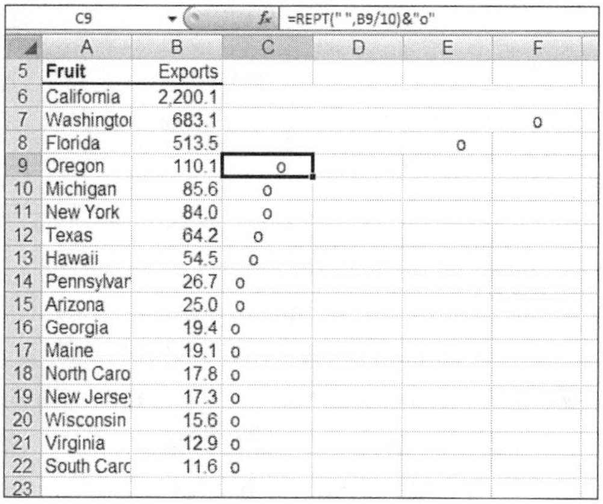

E3 =B3&" "&REPT("|",B3)

	A	B	C	D	E	F	G
1							
2	Age	Male	Female		Male	Female	
3	20	5	9		5					20						9
4	30	14	12		14										30							12
5	40	20	16		20												40									16
6	50	24	21		24															50											21
7	60	10	10		10						60						10
8	70	7	9		7					70					9
9	80	5	6		5					80				6
10	90	1	5		1		90				5
11							

Figure 9.19
Repeating spaces followed by a single lowercase letter o creates a simple dot chart.

C9 =REPT(" ",B9/10)&"o"

	A	B	C	D	E	F
5	**Fruit**	Exports				
6	California	2,200.1				
7	Washingtor	683.1				o
8	Florida	513.5			o	
9	Oregon	110.1	o			
10	Michigan	85.6	o			
11	New York	84.0	o			
12	Texas	64.2	o			
13	Hawaii	54.5	o			
14	Pennsylvar	26.7	o			
15	Arizona	25.0	o			
16	Georgia	19.4	o			
17	Maine	19.1	o			
18	North Caro	17.8	o			
19	New Jerse	17.3	o			
20	Wisconsin	15.6	o			
21	Virginia	12.9	o			
22	South Carc	11.6	o			
23						

Creating a Chart Using Scrollbar Controls

The worksheet in Figure 9.20 uses horizontal scrollbars to produce a chart in the worksheet cells. Setting up this chart requires a bit of up-front work. However, the reader of the worksheet can adjust numbers in the spreadsheet by using the slider on the scrollbars.

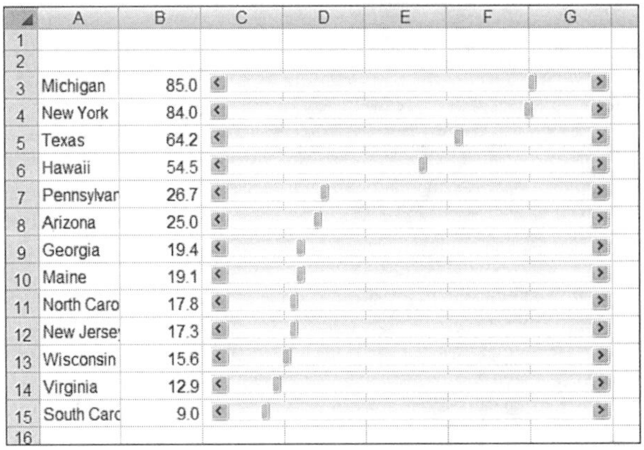

Figure 9.20
A dozen scrollbars comprise this chart.

To create the chart in Figure 9.20, you follow these steps:

1. If you have labels in column A and values in column B, copy the values in column B and move them to column H (see Figure 9.21). (The process of building the scrollbars will destroy the data in column B, so you need a copy of the values to paste back later.)

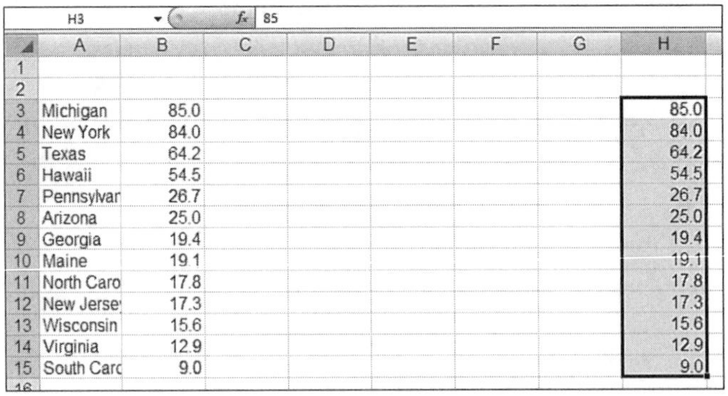

Figure 9.21
You need to make a copy of your original data.

2. Right-click the Quick Access toolbar and choose Customize Quick Access Toolbar. Excel displays the Customize section of the Excel Options dialog.

3. In the left-top drop-down in the dialog, choose Commands Not in the Ribbon.

4. In the left list box in the dialog, find Scroll Bar (Form Control). Note that there are two different scrollbars. You specifically want the Form Control scrollbar for this chart. Click Scroll Bar (Form Control) and then click the Add button in the center of the screen. Click the OK button to return to the worksheet.

5. Select rows 3:15. On the Home ribbon, choose Format, Row Height, type 20 and then click OK.

6. In the Home ribbon, click the Middle Align icon (which is usually the second icon in the top row of the Alignment group). The icon moves the numbers to the vertical middle of each cell.

7. Click the Scrollbar control in the Quick Access toolbar. Click and drag to draw the first scrollbar, starting just inside the top-left corner of cell C3 and dragging to the bottom-right corner of cell G3. It is very important that neither corner extends outside row 3.

8. Right-click the scrollbar and choose Format Control. Excel displays the Format Control dialog. Choose the Control tab in the dialog. You see that the scrollbar is set to accept values from 0 to 100, in increments of 1. These settings work for the current dataset, but if your dataset includes higher values, choose appropriate start and end points for the scrollbars (see Figure 9.22).

Figure 9.22
Each scrollbar control is formatted to display a certain range of values.

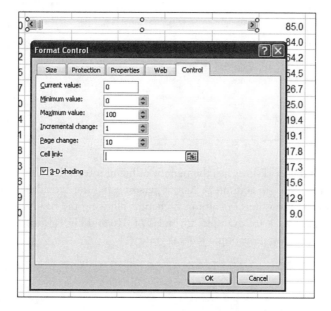

9. Click in the Cell Link text box and then click cell B3 in the worksheet. This tells Excel to get the value for the slider from cell B3. You can optionally type 85 as the initial value for the scrollbar, but in this case, you do not have to because you are copying the original values back in step 15.

10. It is fairly difficult to select cell C3 now, so click in cell C4 and use the up arrow to move to cell C3. Hold down the Shift key and press the right arrow four times to select cells C3:G3.

11. Type Ctrl+C to copy cells C3:G3. If you were careful in step 7 to keep the entire control inside row 3, you have also copied the scrollbar control.

12. Select cells C4:C15 and paste. You now have 12 identical scrollbar controls.

13. Right-click the next scrollbar control and choose Format Control. The control has the same range as the initial control. You will have to reassign the cell link to point to column B of the current row; that will be cell B4 for the second control. You can optionally assign the current value or just wait until step 15 to fix the values in one step.

14. Repeat step 13 for each additional control.

15. If you did not set the initial value for each scrollbar, you will have lost your original data values in column B, as shown in Figure 9.23. Copy the values in H3:H15 and paste them to B3:B15. The sliders on the scrollbar adjust into their proper locations. You can now clear the data from H3:H15.

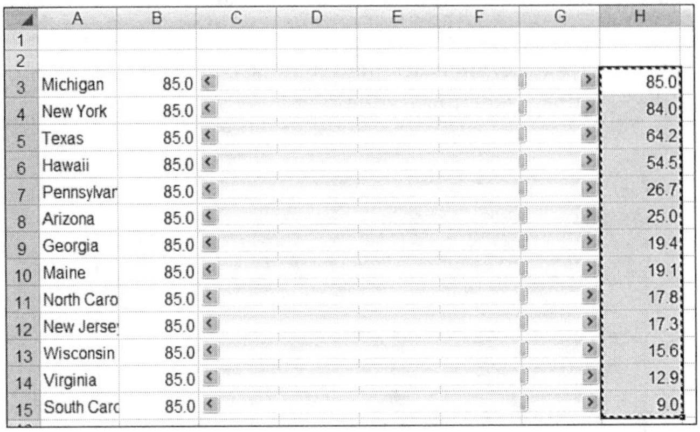

Figure 9.23
Setting up the scroll-bars overwrites the data in column B. You need to copy the temporary values from column H back to column B.

	A	B	C	D	E	F	G	H
1								
2								
3	Michigan	85.0						85.0
4	New York	85.0						84.0
5	Texas	85.0						64.2
6	Hawaii	85.0						54.5
7	Pennsylvar	85.0						26.7
8	Arizona	85.0						25.0
9	Georgia	85.0						19.4
10	Maine	85.0						19.1
11	North Caro	85.0						17.8
12	New Jerse	85.0						17.3
13	Wisconsin	85.0						15.6
14	Virginia	85.0						12.9
15	South Carc	85.0						9.0

This display in the worksheet has the benefit of being interactive. You can build formulas that rely on the values in column B. As the person using the spreadsheet moves the slider on each scrollbar, the values in column B change, allowing the results of the formulas to change. In Figure 9.24, for example, formulas in B16 and H3:H15 use new values in column B as the basis for allocating a federal grant.

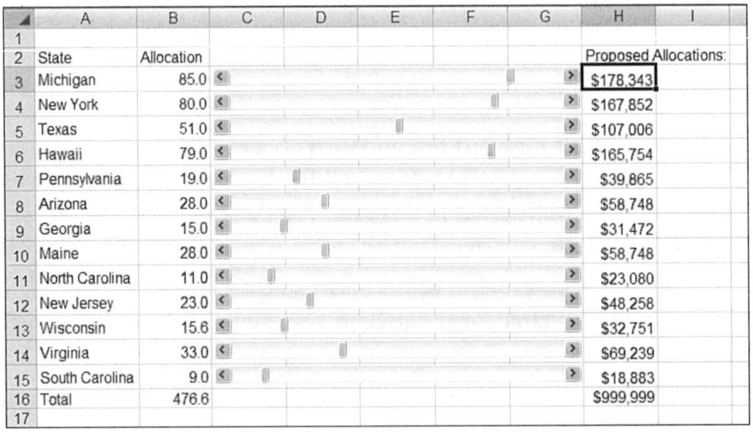

Figure 9.24
As you move the slider, the values in column B and formulas that point to column B automatically adjust.

	A	B	C	D	E	F	G	H	I
1									
2	State	Allocation						Proposed Allocations:	
3	Michigan	85.0						$178,343	
4	New York	80.0						$167,852	
5	Texas	51.0						$107,006	
6	Hawaii	79.0						$165,754	
7	Pennsylvania	19.0						$39,865	
8	Arizona	28.0						$58,748	
9	Georgia	15.0						$31,472	
10	Maine	28.0						$58,748	
11	North Carolina	11.0						$23,080	
12	New Jersey	23.0						$48,258	
13	Wisconsin	15.6						$32,751	
14	Virginia	33.0						$69,239	
15	South Carolina	9.0						$18,883	
16	Total	476.6						$999,999	
17									

Creating Stem-and-Leaf Plots

Stem-and-leaf plots became popular in the 1980s as a means of showing frequency distributions. Figure 9.25 shows two stem-and-leaf plots of the same dataset.

Figure 9.25

A stem-and-leaf plot shows the distribution of numbers in a population.

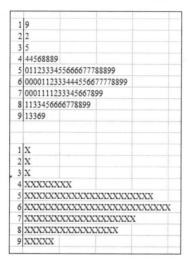

In both of the plots in Figure 9.25, the number to the left of the line indicates groups of 10. The marks to the right of the line indicate how many members of the population occur in that group. In the bottom chart, you can see that one member of the population fell in the 10–19 range, one in the 20–29 range, one in the 30–39 range, and eight in the 40–49 range.

You sometimes see plots such as the bottom plot in Figure 9.25 on the Internet because it is easier to create that plot in Excel than to create the top one. The true stem-and-leaf plot appears at the top of the figure. In this version, the digits to the right of the line indicate the final digit in each member of the population. These numbers are always sorted. The first row in the chart with 1 | 9 indicates that the only member in the population between 10 and 19 is a single member at 19. The next row of 2 | 2 indicates that there is one member of the population in the 20s and that member is 22. The fourth row contains 4 | 44568889. This indicates 8 members of the population fell in the 40s. The members were 44, 44, 45, 46, 48, 48, 48, and 49.

Creating a Stem-and-Leaf Plot with X's as the Leaves

The X-based stem-and-leaf plot requires only a single formula, but it is a rather complex formula. Follow this logic to understand how the formula is built: If you divide 42 by 10, you get 4.2. If you want to know the tens digit of 42, you can take the integer portion of 42/10 to get 4. The Excel function to take the integer portion of a positive number is INT(). Thus, INT(B2) returns a value of 4 for 42 or a value of 6 for 66. This is useful for figuring out in which group a member belongs.

Say you have a heading in A1 and 25 integers in A2:A26, as shown in Figure 9.26. If you want to count how many members of the range A2:A26 fall in the 40s, you can use an IF statement to look at each value. If INT(A2/10)=4, you add 1 to the total. This is a very powerful type of formula in Excel that allows you to check all members of a population at once. This formula returns an array of 25 values, with each value being a 0 or a 1:

```
=IF(INT(A2:A26/10)=4,1,0)
```

You can sum this array to find the number of values that fall in that category. The following formula returns the total:

```
=SUM(IF(INT(A2:A26/10)=4,1,0))
```

After you type this formula, you should not press Enter. Instead, you hold down Ctrl+Shift and then press Enter. This tells Excel to treat the formula as an array formula. Ctrl+Shift+Enter puts Excel in super-formula mode, where Excel figures out the answer to each of the 25 cells in A2:A26 and then adds up the result.

When you have a formula that counts how many members fall in the 40s, you can use the =REPT() function to place the proper number of X's in the stem-and-leaf plot.

Say that you have a population of numbers in A2:A26. You follow these steps to create a stem-and-leaf plot using X's as the markers:

1. Scan the population to find the high and low values. In this case, the values range from the 30s to the 70s. In a new worksheet range, enter the digits 3, 4, 5, 6, and 7 in C2:C6.

2. Select cells C2:C6. From the Border drop-down on the Home ribbon, select Right Border to draw a line to separate the stems in column C from the leaves in column D.

3. In cell D2, type the formula =REPT("X",SUM(IF(INT(A$2:A$26/10)=C2,1,0))), as shown in Figure 9.26. This formula generalizes the array formula discussed previously. Dollar signs in A2:A26 ensure that the formula can be copied. Instead of comparing the integer portion to a specific value, you compare it to the stem value in C2.

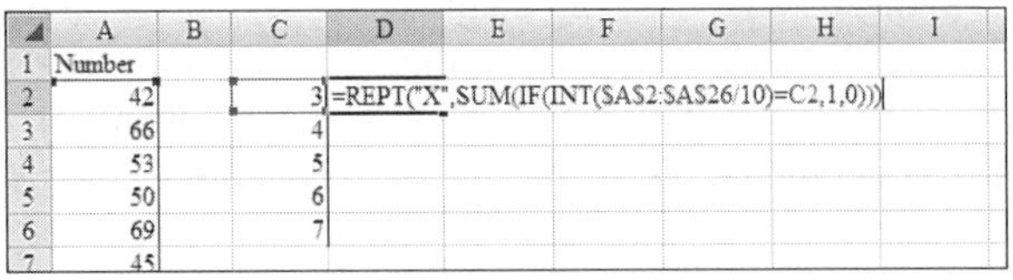

Figure 9.26
You press
Ctrl+Shift+Enter
after typing this
formula.

▲	A	B	C	D	E	F	G	H	I
1	Number								
2	42		3	=REPT("X",SUM(IF(INT($A$2:$A$26/10)=C2,1,0)))					
3	66		4						
4	53		5						
5	50		6						
6	69		7						
7	45								

4. After typing the formula, hold down Ctrl+Shift while pressing Enter. A single X appears.

> **NOTE**
> If you look in the formula bar, you see that Excel has added curly braces around the formula, indicating an array formula. You must take care when copying array formulas. Many people would copy cell D2 and paste to D2:D6, but this will not work. You can copy cell D2 and paste to D3:D6, or you can use the trick in step 5.

5. Select cell D2. Double-click the fill handle in the lower-right corner of the cell to copy the array formula down to D3:D6.

The result is the stem-and-leaf plot shown in Figure 9.27.

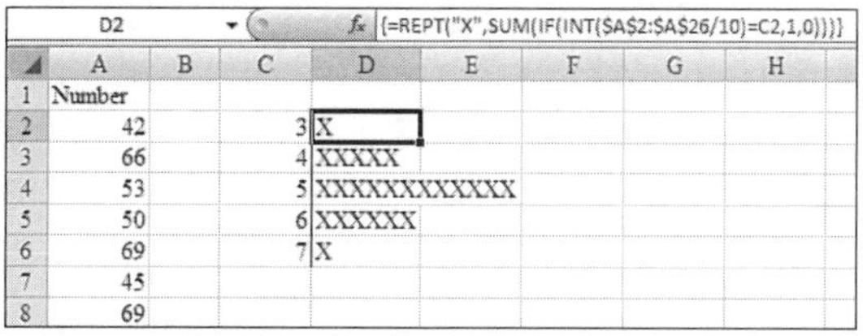

	A	B	C	D	E	F	G	H
1	Number							
2	42		3	X				
3	66		4	XXXXX				
4	53		5	XXXXXXXXXXXX				
5	50		6	XXXXXX				
6	69		7	X				
7	45							
8	69							

Figure 9.27
It is relatively easy to create a stem-and-leaf plot using X's as the leaves.

Creating a Stem-and-Leaf Plot with Digits as the Leaves Using a Long Formula

The stem-and-leaf plot you created in the preceding section requires no sorting of the data and no extra temporary columns, but it does require a horrendous formula that you probably would not want to type.

Assume now that you have the same dataset as in the previous example; the members of the population are in A2:A26. You need to set up the stems by entering the numbers 3 through 7 in cells C2:C6.

The population happens to contain the values 42, 44, 44, 45, and 48. You need to construct a set of leaves for the 40s that show the ones digits from each number: 24458.

The formula in cell D3 could start by repeating the digit 0 once for every occurrence of 40 in the original dataset. Because there is a 4 in cell C3, you use the following formula to show the number of zeros:

```
=REPT("0",COUNTIF(A$2:A$26,C3*10+0)).
```

To find the number of 1s needed in the leaves, you append the following to the above formula:

```
&REPT("1",COUNTIF(A$2:A$26,C3*10+1)).
```

After continuing this concept for all the digits, you end up with the following incredibly long formula:

```
=REPT("0",COUNTIF(A$2:A$26,C2*10+0))&REPT("1",COUNTIF(A$2:A$26,C2*10+1))
&REPT("2",COUNTIF(A$2:A$26,C2*10+2))&REPT("3",COUNTIF(A$2:A$26,C2*10+3))
&REPT("4",COUNTIF(A$2:A$26,C2*10+4))&REPT("5",COUNTIF(A$2:A$26,C2*10+5))
&REPT("6",COUNTIF(A$2:A$26,C2*10+6))&REPT("7",COUNTIF(A$2:A$26,C2*10+7))
&REPT("8",COUNTIF(A$2:A$26,C2*10+8))&REPT("9",COUNTIF(A$2:A$26,C2*10+9)).
```

TIP After entering the formula for the digit 0 in the formula bar and entering the ampersand, you select characters in the formula bar from the R in REPT to the ampersand. Then you press Ctrl+C to copy those characters to the Clipboard. Next, you move the insertion point to the end of the formula. Then you press Ctrl+V nine times to paste nine copies of this text at the end of your formula. You still have to go through and change the "0" and 0 to the appropriate digits in the pasted formula.

Figure 9.28 shows the completed stem-and-leaf plot.

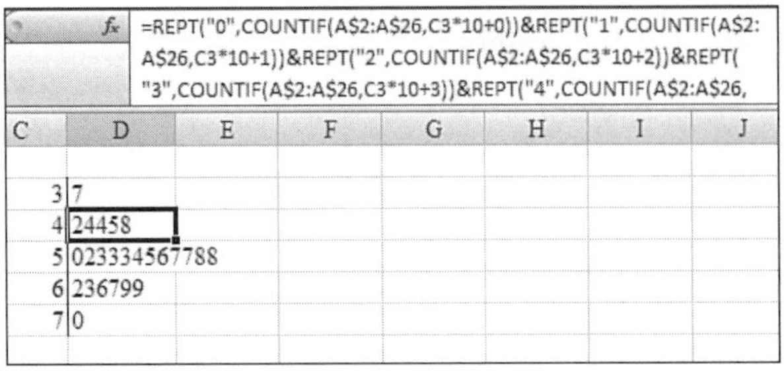

Figure 9.28
A horribly long for-mula creates the leaves for this stem-and-leaf plot.

Creating a Stem-and-Leaf Plot with Digits as the Leaves Using Sorting and Formulas

It is possible, with a bit of sorting, to create a stem-and-leaf plot that does not require a 361-character formula.

Assuming that your data is in A2:A26, you follow these steps to create a stem-and-leaf plot:

1. Sort the data in descending order.

2. Enter the headings Stem, Leaf, and Leaves in cells B1, C1, and D1, respectively.

3. Enter a formula of =INT(A2/10) in cell B2. Copy the formula from cell B2 down to all rows.

4. Enter the formula =A2-B2*10 in cell C2. Copy this formula down to all rows. (You could also use =MOD(A2,10) or =RIGHT(A2,1).)

5. Enter the formula =IF(B2=B3,D3,"")&C2 in cell D2. Copy this formula down to all rows. This formula concatenates all the leaves for the current stem. Because your data is sorted in descending sequence, the best collection of leaves occurs on the first row for each stem. (This is important because the VLOOKUP function used in step 7 returns the first match found.)

6. Enter the numbers 3 through 7 in F2:F6. Add a right border to the edge of this range.

7. Enter the formula =VLOOKUP(F2,B$2:D$26,3,FALSE) in cell G2 to look up the stem number in G2 and find the first Leaves value from column D. Copy this formula down to all rows.

The resulting stem-and-leaf plot is shown in Figure 9.29.

Figure 9.29
This stem-and-leaf plot requires more steps than the one described in the preceding section, but it is a bit more intuitive.

◢	A	B	C	D	E	F	G	H	I	J	K
1	Number	Stem	Leaf	Leaves							
2	75	7	5	5		3	9				
3	69	6	9	023335666789		4	14688				
4	68	6	8	02333566678		5	000457				
5	67	6	7	0233356667		6	023335666789				
6	66	6	6	023335666		7	5				
7	66	6	6	02333566							
8	66	6	6	0233356		Formulas:					
9	65	6	5	023335		B2	=INT(A2/10)				
10	63	6	3	02333		C2	=A2-B2*10				
11	63	6	3	0233		D2	=IF(B2=B3,D3,"")&C2				
12	63	6	3	023		G2	=VLOOKUP(F2,$B$2:$D$26,3,FALSE)				
13	62	6	2	02							
14	60	6	0	0							
15	57	5	7	000457							
16	55	5	5	00045							
17	54	5	4	0004							
18	50	5	0	000							
19	50	5	0	00							
20	50	5	0	0							
21	48	4	8	14688							
22	48	4	8	1468							
23	46	4	6	146							
24	44	4	4	14							
25	41	4	1	1							
26	39	3	9	9							

NOTE
For more formulas you can use to create stem-and-leaf plots, view the January 2007 challenge at MrExcel.com. Readers were invited to submit innovative methods for creating stem-and-leaf plots. More than 20 different approaches were submitted. Review the best entries at www.mrexcel.com.pc16.shtml and the entire thread at www.mrexcel.com/board2/viewtopic.php?p=1202649. Excel MVP Andy Pope created his winning entry by using a stacked bar chart with a custom fill, as shown in Figure 9.30.

Figure 9.30
This stem and leaf plot is an actual stacked bar chart.

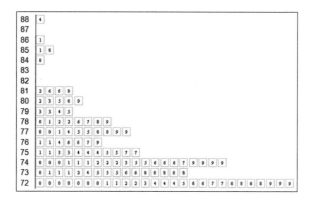

Next Steps

In Chapter 10, "Presenting Your Excel Data on a Map Using Microsoft MapPoint," you will learn how to combine Microsoft Excel with Microsoft MapPoint in order to visually show geographic data. Several of the examples in this chapter show tables of data by state; think of how these examples would take on a whole new meaning if they were plotted on a map. Microsoft MapPoint adds this functionality to Excel.

Presenting Your Excel Data on a Map Using Microsoft MapPoint

10

Plotting Data Geographically

In many cases, the best way to present data is to plot it on a geographic map. Mapping software used to cost thousands of dollars, but Microsoft now offers a product called Microsoft MapPoint 2006. MapPoint debuted in 2001 in both North American and European editions.

Figure 10.1 shows a customer database plotted on a map. Note how many of the customers are around the store, but others travel in from the interstate to shop at the specialty store. Any dataset with a geographic component such as street addresses, zip codes, postal codes, states, or provinces are suitable for mapping.

Figure 10.1
Customers plotted
on a map.

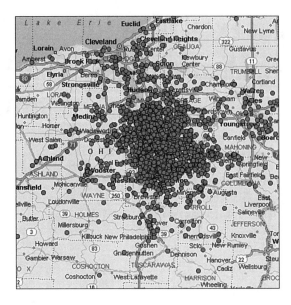

When you install MapPoint, a new add-in is available in Excel 2007 that allows you to plot your data on a map within Excel. For a bit more functionality, you can save your Excel data as an Excel 2003 workbook and import it into MapPoint.

> **TIP**
>
> MapPoint 2006 has a list price of $299 and regularly sells at Amazon.com for $249. However, Microsoft seems to regularly give MapPoint to CIOs as an incentive for attending conferences. Consequently, you can often find brand-new, factory-sealed versions of MapPoint for sale on eBay for less than $100.

Building a Map in Excel

Figure 10.2 shows a database of locations for a chain of stores in the United States. You hope to sell products to those stores and need to analyze their geographic locations.

Figure 10.2
This data lends itself
to geographic
analysis.

	A	B
1	City	State
2	Scottsbor	AL
3	Grand Bay	AL
4	Robertsda	AL
5	Livingstoi	AL
6	Boligee	AL
7	Eutaw	AL
8	Tuscaloos	AL
9	Cottondal	AL
10	Eastaboga	AL
11	Oxford	AL
12	Eutaw	AL

To create a map for this data in Excel 2007, you follow these steps:

1. Make sure that MapPoint is installed on your computer. You should have an extra Add-Ins tab available on the ribbon, with one or more MapPoint Map icons.

2. Select your data in Excel, including headings. MapPoint recognizes headings such as "City," "State," and "Zip Code."

3. Click the MapPoint Map icon on the Add-Ins ribbon. Excel displays the Link Data Wizard dialog. For each column in your selection, Excel shows the column heading and then a drop-down that identifies the data type for that column (see Figure 10.3). Valid data types are Name, Address, City, County, State, Country, Zip Code, Census Tract, Latitude, and Longitude. If you have columns in your data that are not in the list, choose <Other Data> for that column. For example, if you had sales figures for each store, you would select <Other Data>.

Figure 10.3

For each column in your dataset, either identify it as a geographic column or choose <Other Data>.

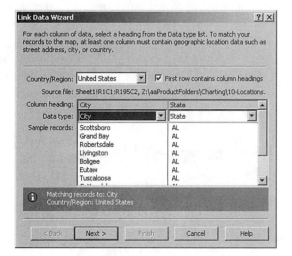

4. Click Next and then click Finish. Excel attempts to find a matching location for each record in your database.

5. After Excel finds all the exact matches, it reports any items that were not matched. In Figure 10.4, for example, there are two possible locations for Centerville, Indiana, so you must choose either the Centerville in Wayne County or the one in Spencer County. For each unmatched record, choose a location and click OK or simply click Skip Record if you don't know the location.

Figure 10.4
You usually have to manually match a few records from a dataset.

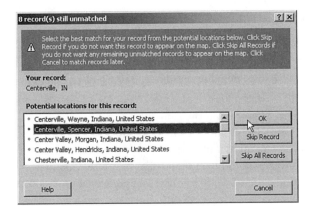

6. Repeat step 5 for each unmatched record. After you match the last record, Excel plots each record as a thumbtack on a map and zooms in to show the complete set of data points.

7. While the map is active, the Excel ribbon is replaced with a MapPoint menu. From the menu, select View, Legend and Overview. Excel adds a sidebar showing the Pushpins set.

8. Right-click the pushpin in the legend and choose Properties, as shown in Figure 10.5.

Figure 10.5
Right-click to access the Properties dialog for the Pushpins set.

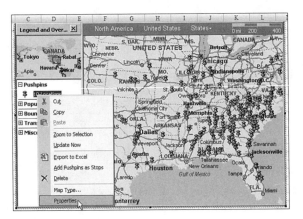

9. In the Properties dialog, change the symbol from a thumbtack to a small circle, as shown in Figure 10.6.

Figure 10.6
The small circle icons work better than thumbtacks on a map with hundreds of mapped points.

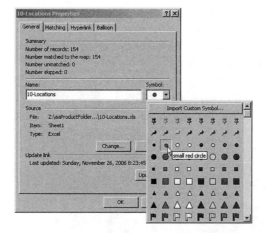

10. Click OK to close the Properties dialog box.

11. Choose View, Legend and Overview to remove the legend.

12. Excel always tightly crops the map to include all the pushpins in the dataset. Use the Zoom Out icon in the toolbar to see a 50,000-foot view of the data. In Figure 10.7, you can see that the stores are concentrated in the southeastern part of the United States.

Figure 10.7
You can zoom out to see the entire country.

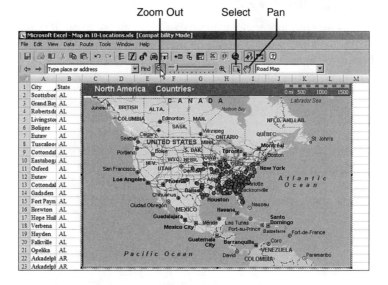

Two icons to the right of the Zoom icon provide you with better control over the zooming process. The Select icon is a rectangle with a mouse arrow in it.

13. Using the Select icon, drag a box around an area and click inside the box. Excel roughly zooms to your selection. For example, you can roughly zoom in on the state of Georgia, as shown in Figure 10.8. To move to a new spot on the map, use the Pan icon. Click anywhere on the map and drag to move the map.

14. Choose View, Map Style. You can select from a road map, a terrain map, data maps, and so on. Figure 10.8 shows a terrain map.

Figure 10.8
A terrain map, zoomed in to show details for the state of Georgia.

Using a Chart on a Map

If your dataset includes some numeric data, you can ask Excel to change the color or size of the circle used for each data point. Figure 10.9 shows a map where the color of the circle indicates the numeric data attached to that city. The white circles are the smaller cities, and the dark gray circles are the larger cities.

Figure 10.9
The color of each circle indicates the size of a numeric column associated with each record.

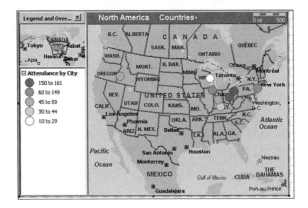

To color the circles on the map, you follow these steps:

1. Create a map as described in the preceding section.

2. Choose View, Legends and Overview.

3. Right-click the appropriate pushpin and choose Map Type. While the properties selection lets you choose a different icon for the pushpin, Map Type allows you to replace the icons with pie charts, column charts, sized circles, or shaded circles.

4. In the dialog that appears next (see Figure 10.10), choose Shaded Circle and click Next.

Figure 10.10
MapPoint offers several different map styles.

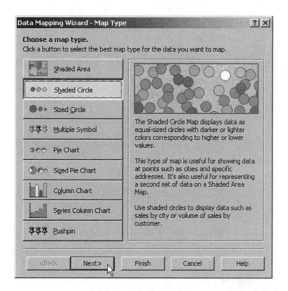

5. Choose to map by city. Click Next.

6. For the range type, choose Equal Data Points. Change the color scheme. If desired, customize the data ranges, as shown in Figure 10.11.

Figure 10.11
You can customize the ranges and colors used for the data points.

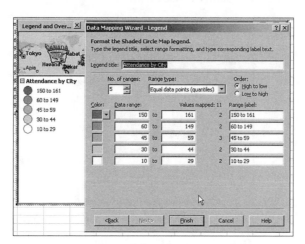

The shaded circle map is better than the sized circle map. With the sized circle map, the largest circle is about five times bigger than the small circle. This makes it nearly impossible to see small dots near the biggest dots. Even with the shaded circles, it is possible for dots to appear too close and for some dots to be obscured. If you zoom in, you can see the detail of the closer dots. Figure 10.12 shows a close-up of the Midwest. At this zoom level, you can see several dots that are hidden at the countrywide level.

Figure 10.12
You can zoom in to see more details.

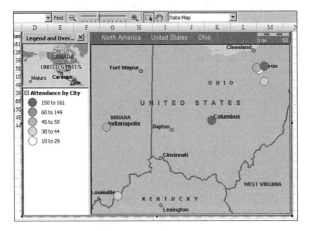

Using Other Map Styles to Illustrate Data

The shaded area map style is great if you have data that can be aggregated by zip code, census tract, county, or state. In Figure 10.13, for example, crime statistics are plotted by zip code. This dataset is a bit too dense to see the entire country at once. You have to zoom in to about a quarter of the country to see the detail.

Figure 10.13
This shaded area map shows crime per capita by zip code.

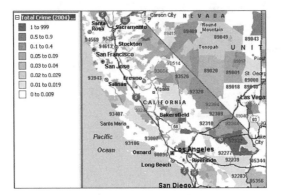

In Figure 10.14, annual rainfall is plotted by county. The county data allows MapPoint to show the entire country. This map illustrates more than 3,000 data points.

Figure 10.14
The map of data by county shows 3,141 data points in a single picture.

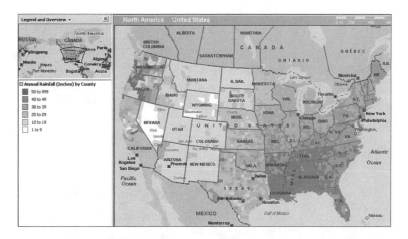

CASE STUDY

Mapping Your Customers

Almost every business has a mailing list of its customers. If you have this data in Excel and you have MapPoint, you can plot up to 10,000 customers on a map.

Seeing your customers on a map helps you to plan advertising and helps you understand how far your customers travel to reach your location. To plot your company's customers on a map, follow these steps:

1. Import your customer list into Excel. Be sure to add headings such as Name, Address, City, State, and Zip Code. Save the data as an Excel 2003 workbook. (At press time, MapPoint 2006 could not import an Excel 2007 file type. It is possible that by the time you are reading this, Microsoft has offered an upgrade to MapPoint.)

2. Start MapPoint. Choose Data, Import Data Wizard.

3. Browse to and select your Excel file.

4. Confirm the field mapping. Click Next and then click Finish. MapPoint matches your fields up with known addresses.

5. If there are unmatched records, MapPoint shows you any close guesses. When you are matching at the address level, you are likely to have a high rate of unmatched addresses. If you are in a hurry, click Skip All Records to map the records that do match.

6. Choose a pushpin map. Click Next.

7. Change the symbol from a thumbtack to a small circle. Click Finish.

Typically, you might have a few stray customers who visited your business while they were traveling. These distant customers cause MapPoint to zoom out to show all the customers. Figure 10.15 shows the customer information with a zoom to show the entire country.

Figure 10.15
A few stray customers from each coast force the map to be zoomed out to show the continental United States.

Use the Select icon (see Figure 10.7) to draw a square around your business location and then click inside the square. You now have a map of the densest concentration of customers, as shown in Figure 10.16. This enables you to determine which newspapers or radio stations might be effective for reaching other customers who live in the same area as your current customers.

Figure 10.16
This is a powerful type of map for a business owner. It helps you see where your customers are from and think about ways to reach other customers in that area.

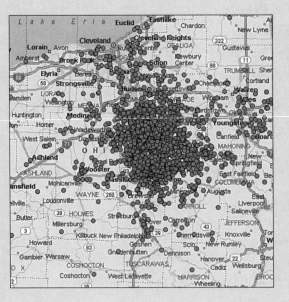

Next Steps

In Chapter 11, "Using SmartArt Graphics and Shapes," you will learn how to use Excel's new business diagramming tools to communicate relationships and organization charts.

Using SmartArt Graphics and Shapes

11

Understanding SmartArt Graphics and Shapes

Images and artwork provide an interesting visual break from tables of numbers. Excel 2007 offers a broad new array of business diagramming tools. The Excel 2003 Insert Diagram menu held six types of business diagrams. The improved gallery of 84 SmartArt graphics in Excel 2007 helps you to communicate messages about your organization and processes.

While SmartArt graphics allow you to create diagrams quickly, they have one annoying limitation in Excel 2007: The text in the shapes is static, so there is no way to link the text in a SmartArt shape to a value calculated in an Excel formula. This is particularly frustrating because Excel has enabled text on shapes to be dynamic since Excel 97.

This one limitation means that to get the most out of SmartArt graphics, you have to understand how to use shapes in your worksheet.

This chapter covers the following:

- **SmartArt**—SmartArt is a collection of similar shapes, arranged to imply a process, groups, or a hierarchy. In former versions of Excel, SmartArt was known as Diagrams. As in the past, with Excel 2007 it is easy to add new shapes, reverse the order of shapes, and change the color of shapes. Office 2007 includes a text editor that allows for Level 1 and Level 2 text for each shape in a diagram. Many styles of SmartArt include the capability to add a small picture or logo to each shape.

- **Shapes**—You can add interesting shapes to a document. A shape can contain words; it is the only art object in which the words can come from a cell on the worksheet. You can add glow, bevel, and 3-D effects to shapes. In previous versions of Excel, shapes were known as AutoShapes. Microsoft has added some new shapes as well as several formatting properties.

- **WordArt**—You use WordArt to present ordinary text in a stylized manner. You can use it to bend, rotate, and twist the characters in text. In Excel 2007, you can add glow, bevel, and material effects. WordArt has been completely redesigned from previous versions of Excel. A limited version of WordArt is available for formatting titles and labels in Excel 2007 charts.

Using SmartArt

You use SmartArt to show a series of similar shapes, where each shape represents a related step, concept, idea, or grouping. SmartArt in Excel 2007 is an enhanced version of business diagrams from previous versions of Excel. In Excel 2007, Microsoft has addressed many of the shortcomings of business diagrams, including the following:

- Each shape has an associated text editor.

- Shapes can contain Level 1 text for headlines and Level 2 text for body copy.

- Some styles now allow shapes to include an image.

- Automatic settings in SmartArt can automatically resize the text in all shapes to allow the longest text to fit.

- SmartArt styles allow you to apply glow and bevels to an entire SmartArt diagram.

The goal of SmartArt is to allow you to create a great-looking graphic with minimal effort. After you define a SmartArt image for your text, you can quickly change to any of the other 84 styles by clicking the desired style in the gallery. Figure 11.1 shows four different SmartArt styles:

- **Basic Process**—In this style, all text is typed as Level 1.

- **Accent Process**—This style puts the Level 1 text in the background and highlights the Level 2 text in the foreground boxes.

- **Picture Accent Process**—This style gives equal weight to the Level 1 and Level 2 text. Pictures are added behind each shape.

- **Picture Accent List**—Unlike the process charts, a list chart does not include arrows to indicate a process.

If you want to fine-tune the text in a particular shape, you can use the Format ribbon to micromanage any element in the SmartArt.

Figure 11.1
Subtle differences in 4 of the 84 possible SmartArt styles give more weight to either Level 1 or Level 2 text. Notice that the Level 1 text is prominent (top), in the background (second), small (third), or vertical (bottom).

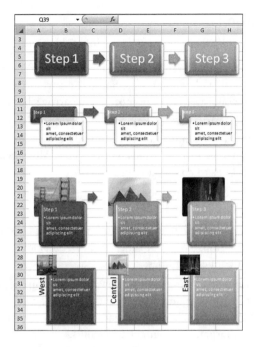

Elements Common Across Most SmartArt

A SmartArt style is a collection of two or more related shapes. In most styles, you can add additional shapes in order to illustrate a longer process. A few styles are limited to only n items. Each shape can contain a headline (Level 1 text), body copy (Level 2 text), and a graphic. Some of the 84 styles show only Level 1 text. If you switch to a style that does not display Level 2 text and then switch back, the shape remembers the Level 2 text it originally had.

Some of the SmartArt styles can include pictures. You should add pictures after you have selected your final style. Changing layout styles always causes pictures to be lost, so you should finalize a layout before adding the images. Some styles include arrows between shapes to illustrate a process.

> **CAUTION**
>
> If you insert pictures in a layout, switch to another layout, and then back to the original layout without closing the document, your pictures do come back. This is somewhat of a privacy concern. After you save and close the document, the hidden pictures are removed.

While you're editing SmartArt, a text pane that is slightly reminiscent of PowerPoint appears. You can type some bullet points in the text pane. If you demote a bullet point, the text changes from Level 1 text to Level 2 text. If you add a new bullet point, Excel adds a new shape to the SmartArt.

11

A Tour of the SmartArt Categories

The SmartArt gallery groups the 84 SmartArt layouts into 7 broad categories:

- **List**—This category is designed to show a nonsequential list of information. Variations include horizontal, vertical, and bending lists. Some lists include chevrons, and some include pictures. In general, these styles do not include arrows between shapes.

- **Process**—This category is designed to show a sequential list of steps. Variations include horizontal, vertical, bending, equations, funnels, gears, and several varieties of arrows. Some process charts allow the inclusion of images. Most styles include arrows or other connectors in order to convey a sequence.

- **Cycle**—This category is designed to show a series of steps that repeat. It includes cycle charts, radial charts, a gear chart, and a pie chart.

- **Hierarchy**—This category is designed to show organization charts, decision trees, and other hierarchical relationships. Variations include horizontal and vertical charts and charts with and without connecting lines.

- **Relationship**—This category is designed to show a relationship between items. Many of the layouts in this category are duplicated from the other six categories. This category includes examples of arrow, chart, cycle, equation, funnel, gear, hierarchy, list, process, pyramid, radial, target, and Venn chart layouts.

- **Matrix**—This category is designed to show four quadrants of a list. Only two options exist: either four quadrants with a central element or four quadrants.

- **Pyramid**—This category is designed to show containment, overlapping, proportional, or interconnected relationships.

Figure 11.2 shows one version of each of the seven categories.

Figure 11.2
SmartArt diagrams exist in seven broad categories.

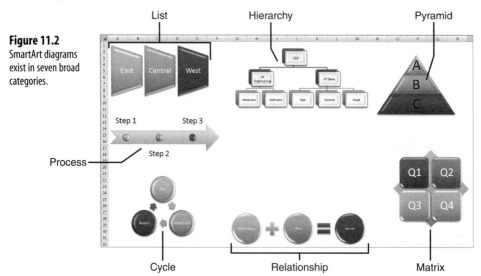

Inserting SmartArt

Although there are 84 different layouts of SmartArt, you follow the same basic steps to insert any SmartArt layout:

1. Select a cell in a blank section of the workbook.

2. From the Insert ribbon, choose SmartArt from the Illustrations group. The Choose a SmartArt Graphic dialog appears.

3. From the left side of the Choose a SmartArt Graphic dialog, select a category.

4. Click a SmartArt type in the center of the Choose a SmartArt Graphic dialog.

5. Read the description on the right side. This description tells you whether the layout is good for Level 1 text, Level 2 text, or both. In Figure 11.3, you can see that the Vertical Chevron List layout is good for large amounts of Level 2 text.

Figure 11.3
The information for each style provides information about whether a particular style is appropriate for more Level 1 or Level 2 text.

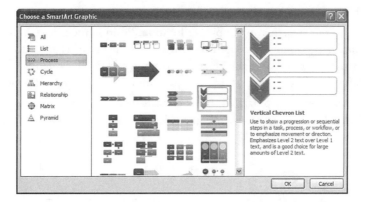

6. Repeat steps 4 and 5 until you find a style suitable for your content. Then click OK. As shown in Figure 11.4, an outline of the SmartArt is drawn on the worksheet. The flashing insertion cursor is in the first item of the text pane. One element of the SmartArt is selected. When you type text at the flashing insertion point, it is added to the selected shape.

Figure 11.4
When you type in the text pane, the text is added to the selected element of the SmartArt.

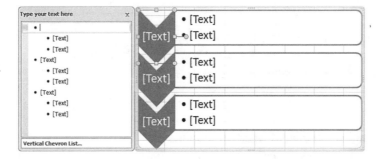

7. Fill in the text pane with text for your SmartArt. You can add, delete, promote, or demote items by using icons in the SmartArt Tools, Design, Create Graphic group. The SmartArt updates as you type more text. In many cases, adding a new Level 1 item adds a new shape element to the SmartArt. If you add longer text to the SmartArt, Excel shrinks all the elements in order to make the text fit.

8. Make the entire SmartArt graphic larger, if needed, by grabbing the resizing handles in the corners of the SmartArt and dragging to a new size. After you resize the graphic, Excel resizes the text to make it fit in the SmartArt at the largest size possible.

9. If you like, change the color scheme of the SmartArt, which initially appears in one color. To do so, from the SmartArt Tools Design ribbon, select Change Colors from the SmartArt Styles group. Excel offers several versions of monochromatic styles and five styles of color variations for each shape.

10. Choose a 2-D or 3-D style from the SmartArt Styles gallery on the Design ribbon. The Inset and Cartoon styles have a suitable mix of effects but are readable.

11. Move the SmartArt to the proper location. Position the mouse over the border of the SmartArt, avoiding the eight resizing areas. The cursor changes to a four-headed arrow. Click and drag the SmartArt to a new location. If you drag the SmartArt to the left side of the worksheet, the text pane moves to the right of the SmartArt.

12. Click outside the SmartArt. Excel embeds the SmartArt graphic in the worksheet and hides the SmartArt ribbons. Figure 11.5 shows some completed SmartArt.

Figure 11.5
You click outside the SmartArt boundary to embed the completed SmartArt.

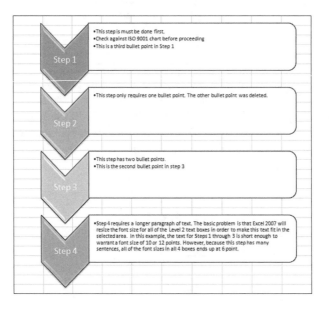

Changing the Color of SmartArt Graphics

The Design ribbon's Change Colors drop-down offers 38 different color schemes for each theme. Five options in the Colorful category offer to mix up the colors used for each shape. Thirty other options offer five varying shades of each of six accent colors.

Changing the Theme colors on the Page Layout ribbon affects the colors offered in the Change Colors drop-down.

Applying a SmartArt Style

The Design ribbon offers a large gallery of 14 different SmartArt styles. There are five 2-D styles in a section labeled Best Fit for Document. There are also nine 3-D styles.

Choosing a style from the gallery applies a different mix of bevel, shadow, transparency, gradient, reflection, and glow to all shapes. The built-in styles range from subtle to outlandish. Some of the later 3-D styles, such as Bird's Eye Scene and Brick Scene, are very hard to read. If you are trying to present bad news that no one can read, you might want to choose the later 3-D styles. Otherwise, the second and third 3-D styles, known as Inset and Cartoon, seem to offer a great mix of effects and readability. Figure 11.6 shows a Continuous Arrow Process graphic with the 14 different styles applied.

Figure 11.6
The SmartArt styles range from simple to over-the-top. The Inset and Cartoon styles offer a mix of style and readability.

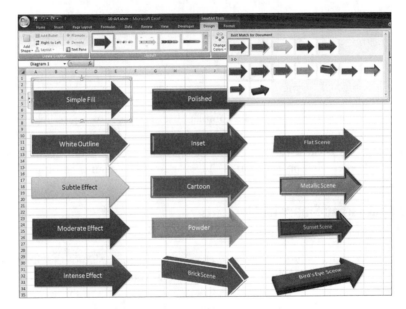

Changing Existing SmartArt to a New Style

There are a couple of ways to change SmartArt to a new style:

- You can left-click the SmartArt and then choose the SmartArt Tools, Layouts from the Design ribbon to choose a new layout. As shown in Figure 11.7, the Layouts drop-down initially shows only the styles that Excel thinks are a close fit to the current style. If you want to access the complete list of styles, you have to select More Layouts. The advantage of this method is that Live Preview shows you the changes before you commit to a style.

Figure 11.7
List Process 2 pro-
vides a new shape
for each bullet point
in Level 2.

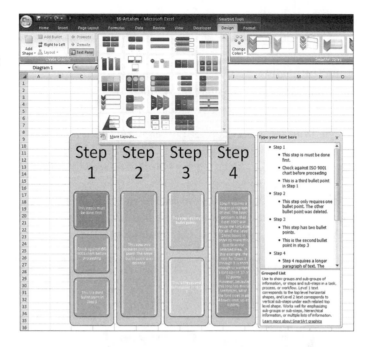

■ A faster way to access the complete list of styles is to right-click between two shapes in the SmartArt and choose Change Layout from the context menu. This step is a little tricky because you cannot click an existing shape; you must click inside the SmartArt border—but on a section of the SmartArt that contains nothing.

Micromanaging SmartArt Elements

The are two ribbons for SmartArt tools: the Design and Format ribbons.

The Design ribbon allows you to change the overall design of the SmartArt. If you stay on the Design ribbon, Microsoft makes sure that your SmartArt looks good. It keeps the font for all Level 2 text consistent for all shapes. It keeps all the shapes proportional. If you have a particular need to override some aspect of one shape, however, you can do so on the Format ribbon.

> **CAUTION**
>
> When you change any setting on the Format ribbon, Microsoft turns off the automatic formatting for the other elements. Changing a setting on the Format ribbon is a great way to make horrible-looking SmartArt. If you absolutely have to use the Format ribbon, you should first get your SmartArt as close as possible to the final version by using the Design ribbon.

Changing Text Formatting in One Element

In Automatic mode, Excel chooses a font size that is small enough to show the longest text completely. This can cause problems if you have one shape with long text and short text everywhere else. In this case, Excel chooses a small font size for the long text and then forces all the other items to have the same tiny text as well. In such a situation, you might want to override the text size for the shape that has the longest text. Excel then automatically resizes the font size in the remaining automatic shapes to be larger.

The mini toolbar is useful for making these types of changes. You select the text either directly in the shape or in the text pane. Immediately after you complete the selection, you should watch for an almost-transparent formatting box to appear. Then you immediately move the mouse to the box to prevent it from disappearing. You can then change the font size by using the drop-down in the mini toolbar. If you allow the mini toolbar to disappear, you can use the formatting tools on the Home ribbon to change the font size.

In Figure 11.8, the long Level 2 text in step 4 was resized. Excel then calculated the proper text size for steps 1 through 3, resulting in the text in the top three shapes automatically growing to a larger font size.

Figure 11.8
When you manually override the font size in the fourth shape, the text in the remaining three shapes automatically becomes larger.

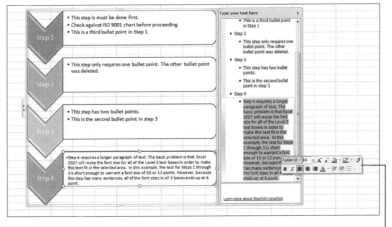

Mini Toolbar

Changing One Shape

There are many items you can edit for a SmartArt shape. To see how this works, you can click any shape in the SmartArt and then try the following:

- Use the green handle to rotate the shape.
- Use the resize handles to resize the shape.
- Use the move handle to nudge the shape.
- Choose Change Shape from the Format ribbon to change the outline to a different shape.

- Choose settings from the Shape Styles group to change fill, outline, and effects for the shape.

- Choose settings from the WordArt Styles group to change the text inside the shape.

- Right-click the shape and choose Format Shape to have complete control over the shape.

In general, SmartArt created on the Design ribbon looks uniform and neat. When you move to the Format ribbon, the possibility for chaos arises. For example, the SmartArt in Figure 11.9 contains mixed effects, font sizes, and rotation; it was created in the Format ribbon.

Figure 11.9
After experimenting with the Format ribbon, you can choose Reset Graphic on the Design ribbon to turn the SmartArt back into something more uniform.

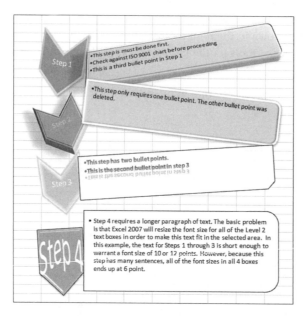

Controlling SmartArt Shapes from the Text Pane

The text pane represents a fantastic improvement over business diagrams in Excel 2003. By using only the keyboard, you can add or delete shapes and promote or demote items. Further, the text pane includes proofing tools, such as spell check. Using the text pane is similar to creating bullet points in a PowerPoint slide.

Figure 11.10 shows a newly inserted pyramid SmartArt in Excel. By default, most new SmartArt diagrams have three shapes, but you can change that number by using the text pane.

Figure 11.10
A default SmartArt includes three shapes. You can edit the number of shapes by using the text pane.

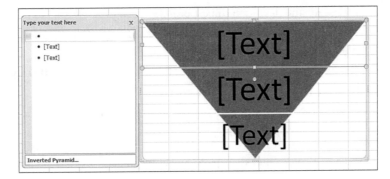

The following rules apply to the text pane for SmartArt:

- You press the Up Arrow and Down Arrow keys to move from one line to another.
- You press the Enter key to insert a new line below the current line. The new line will be at the same level as the current line. Adding a new Level 1 line inserts a new shape in the SmartArt.
- You press the Tab key to demote Level 1 text to Level 2 text.
- You press Shift+Tab to promote Level 2 text to Level 1 text.
- You press the Backspace key on an empty line to delete the line.
- You press Delete at the end of any line to combine text from the next line with this line.
- You press End to move to the end of the current line.
- You press Home to move to the beginning of the current line.

As you add shapes, Excel continues to attempt to squeeze them into the default size. You can resize an entire piece of SmartArt by using the resizing handles around the SmartArt.

As an example of how the text pane works, you can use the following steps to customize the inverted pyramid graphic shown in Figure 11.10 into the one shown in Figure 11.11. This example illustrates how quickly and simply you can change from the default SmartArt with three shapes to any number of shapes:

1. Type **Shape 1** and then press Enter.
2. Type **Subtext** and then press Tab to demote the item. Then press the Down Arrow key to move to text 2.
3. Type **Shape 2** and then press Enter.
4. Type **Point 1** and then press Tab and Enter.
5. Type **Point 2** and then the Down Arrow key.
6. Type **Shape 3** and then press Enter.
7. Type **Point 3** and then press Tab and Enter.

8. Excel wants the next item to be Level 2 text, so press Shift+Tab to promote this item.

9. Type **Shape 4** and then press Enter, type **Shape 5** and then press Enter, type **Shape 6** and then press Enter, and type **Shape 7** and then press Enter.

10. Type **Point 4** and then press Tab, Enter, and Shift+Tab, and then type **8**.

11. Using the mouse, resize the SmartArt so it is larger.

12. From the SmartArt Styles gallery on the Design ribbon, choose a color scheme.

The result is shown in Figure 11.11. As this example shows, by using only the keyboard and the text pane, you can quickly expand SmartArt and add Level 2 subpoints.

Figure 11.11
You can add additional shapes and subpoints simply by using the text pane.

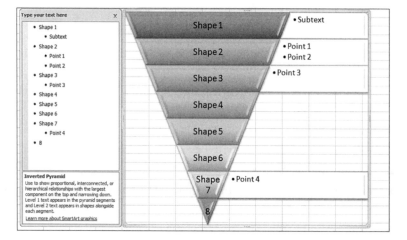

Adding Images to SmartArt

Seven SmartArt layouts in the List category are designed to hold small images in addition to text. In some of these styles, the picture is emphasized; in others, the focus is on the text, and the picture is an accent:

- **Picture Caption List**—This style includes a large picture and is designed to emphasize the picture.

- **Horizontal Picture List**—This style includes a large picture and a large space for text. It is good for a balance of pictures and text.

- **Continuous Picture List**—This style includes a large picture and minimal text.

- **Vertical Picture List**—This style contains a small square picture and text.

- **Vertical Picture Accent List**—This style contains a small round picture on the left and text.

- **Bending Picture Accent List**—This style contains a small circular picture.

- **Picture Accent List**—This style contains a small square picture in the upper right of each block.

When you select one of these styles, you first build the text and then add shapes, as necessary. The SmartArt shows a picture icon in each shape (see Figure 11.12).

Figure 11.12
In the SmartArt styles that include pictures, you should arrange the shapes before trying to add pictures.

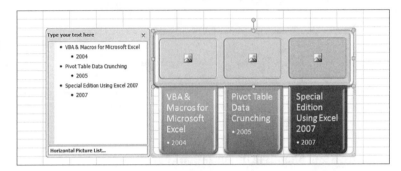

You can click a picture icon to display the Insert Picture dialog. You can then choose a picture and click Insert. You repeat this process to add each additional picture. The pictures are automatically resized to fit the allotted area, as shown in Figure 11.13.

Figure 11.13
Pictures have been added to each shape. Only seven SmartArt styles are prebuilt with placeholders for pictures.

> **CAUTION**
>
> If you change the layout of SmartArt after adding pictures, the picture information is lost. This is particularly frustrating when you switch from one picture style to another picture style.

Special Considerations for Organization Charts

Hierarchical SmartArt can contain more than two text levels. As you add more levels to the SmartArt, Excel continues to intelligently add boxes and resize them to fit.

Figure 11.14 shows a diagram created in the Hierarchy style. In this style, each level is assigned a different color.

Figure 11.14
Hierarchical
SmartArt can contain more than two
levels.

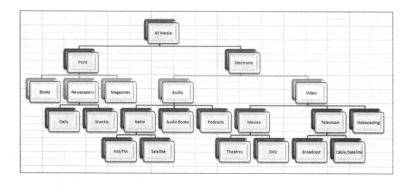

Using Assistant Shapes in Organization Charts

The first style available in the Hierarchy category is the Organization Chart style. You use this style to describe reporting relationships in an organization. There are a few extra options in the ribbon for organization charts. For example, select one manager shape in your organizational chart diagram. The Add Shape drop-down on the Design ribbon includes the option Add Assistant, as shown in Figure 11.15. You can select this option to add an extra shape immediately below the selected level.

Figure 11.15
The Add Assistant
selection adds a box
for an assistant
below the selected
shape.

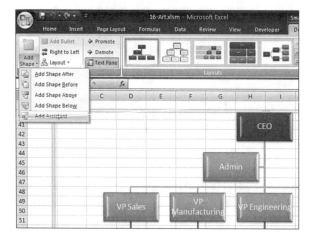

Arranging Subordinates on an Organization Chart

In the Create Graphic group of the Design ribbon, the Layout drop-down offers four options for showing the boxes within a group. First, you select the manager for the group. Then you select the appropriate type from the drop-down to affect all direct reports for the manager. Figure 11.16 illustrates the four options for the Layout drop-down:

- **VP of Sales**—This option shows a standard organization chart. The regions are arranged side-by-side.
- **VP of Manufacturing**—This option has a right hanging group. The departments are arranged vertically to the right of the line.

- **VP of Engineering**—This option has a left hanging group. The departments are arranged vertically to the left of the line.

- **CFO**—This option has a Both group. The direct reports are listed in two columns under the manager, on both sides of the vertical line.

In each group, the assistant box is arranged to the left of the vertical line.

Figure 11.16
Organization charts include options to control the arrangement of direct reports.

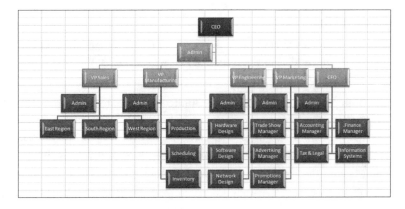

Showing Dotted-Line Reporting Relationships

The SmartArt graphics engine cannot automatically create dotted-line reporting relationships. However, you can manually add a line to a diagram.

> **NOTE**
> You should get your graphic as close to being done as possible before adding manual shapes. Any subsequent changes to the text pane require manual repositioning of the lines.

To add a dotted line, you follow these steps:

1. Prepare the organization chart, using the SmartArt tools.

2. From the Insert ribbon, choose the Shapes drop-down.

3. Click the elbow connector.

4. Draw a line that connects the appropriate two boxes on the organization chart. Grab the yellow diamond handle to lower the horizontal portion of the line to be at the same height as the lower box. Don't worry that the line is the wrong weight and style.

5. Click the line to select it.

6. In the Drawing Tools, Format tab, choose the Shape Outline drop-down. From the Weight fly-out menu, choose a thicker line style, such as 3 pt.

7. Access the Shape Outline drop-down again. From the Dashes fly-out menu, choose one of the dotted-line styles.

11

Figure 11.17
Add the shape, drag
the yellow diamond
into position, then
format the line as
dotted.

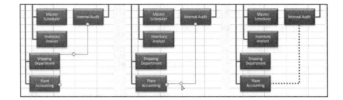

Using Limited SmartArt

Most of the SmartArt examples described so far are expandable: As you add Level 1 text, new shapes are added to the SmartArt. However, some SmartArt styles cannot be expanded (see Figure 11.18):

- Both gear and funnel charts are limited to three items. If you add additional items to the text pane, each appears with a red x. These items do not display in the SmartArt, but they are stored in case you later change to another SmartArt layout. For privacy reasons, the extra text is discarded when you save and close the file.

- Many of the arrow layouts in the Relationship category are limited to two shapes.

- The Matrix layouts are limited to four quadrants. Grid Matrix offers four quadrants plus a title, as shown in the center of Figure 11.18.

- The Segmented Pyramid style can be expanded, but it must contain 1, 4, 9, or 16 shapes. As soon as you add a fifth style to the SmartArt in the upper-left corner of the display, an entire row is added to the bottom of the pyramid, resulting in the SmartArt shown in the lower right of Figure 11.18.

- The Equation style can be expanded, but the answer is always the last Level 1 item in the text pane.

Figure 11.18
Arrows, gears, fun-
nels, and matrix
shapes have certain
limitations on the
number of shapes
they can contain.

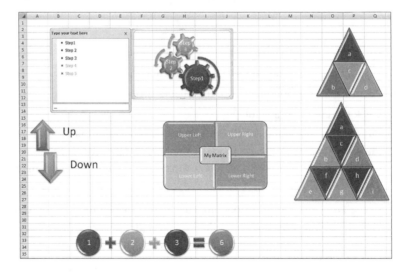

Choosing the Right Layout for Your Message

With 84 built-in layouts of SmartArt graphics, choosing the right layout can be daunting.

The following questions are designed to help you narrow down your choices, assuming that you do not want to further customize the look of a graphic:

- Do you need accent images in the shape? If so, choose Bending Picture Accent List, Picture Caption List, Horizontal Picture List, Picture Accent List, Continuous Picture List, Vertical Picture Accent List, Vertical Picture List, Picture Accent Process, or Radial List.

- Do you have extremely long sentences of Level 2 text? If so, choose Vertical Box List or Vertical Bullet List.

- Do you need to show a continuous process? If so, choose one of the cycle charts: Text Cycle, Basic Cycle, Continuous Cycle, Block Cycle, or Segmented Cycle.

- Do you need to show a circular process that can travel both ways? If so, choose Multidirectional Cycle.

- Do you need to show a process that progresses from left to right? If so, choose Basic Process, Accent Process, Continuous Arrow Process, Alternating Flow, Process Arrows, Detailed Process, Continuous Block Process, Picture Accent Process, Basic Chevron Process, or Closed Chevron Process.

- Do you need to show many processes that progress from left to right? If so, choose Chevron List.

- Do you need to show a process that progresses from top to bottom? If so, choose Vertical Process, Segmented Process, Vertical Chevron List, or Staggered Process.

- Do you need to show a one-way process and need to fit many shapes into a small area? If so, choose Basic Bending Process, Circular Bending Process, Repeating Bending Process, or Vertical Bending Process.

- Do you need to show an organization? If so, choose Organization Chart.

- Do you need to show a hierarchy? If so, choose one of the pyramid, radial, matrix, target, or hierarchy layouts.

- Do you need to make a decision between two choices? If so, choose Balance.

- Do you need to show how parts add together to create an output? If so, choose an Equation or a Funnel layout.

- Do you need to illustrate two opposing forces? If so, choose Diverging Arrows, Counterbalance Arrows, Opposing Arrows, Converging Arrows, or Arrow Ribbon.

- Do you need to illustrate a containment chart? If so, choose Nested Target or Stacked Venn.

11

Exploring Business Charts That Use SmartArt Graphics

The examples in this section show off a few of the 84 different SmartArt graphics that might be suitable for your business presentations.

> **NOTE**   To see examples of all 84 styles in use, take a look at *Leveraging SmartArt Graphics in the 2007 Microsoft Office System*, an e-book published by Que (ISBN 0-7686-6833-6).

In particular, a few of the examples in this section show layouts that are a bit more difficult than average to utilize.

Illustrating a Pro/Con Decision by Using a Balance Chart

The Balance layout is used to illustrate weighing two alternatives, as shown in Figure 11.19.

Figure 11.19
This graphic leans either left or right, depending on which side has more Level 2 text entries.

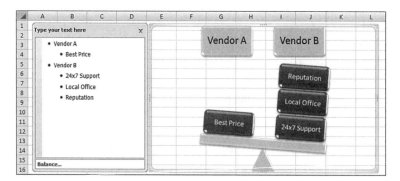

The layout requires two Level 1 text entries to represent the boxes at the top of the graphic. You can then have up to three Level 2 entries for each Level 1 entry. The scale tips in the direction of the side that has more boxes.

Illustrating Growth by Using an Upward Arrow

Microsoft had to create a new shape, called a Swoosh Arrow, in order to add the Upward Arrow layout. This layout holds up to five bullets of Level 1 text. Any Level 2 text is shown below the Level 1 text. This makes it very difficult to fit any Level 2 text beneath the first bullet point of Level 1 text.

In Figure 11.20, a few bullet points of Level 2 text are placed beneath the final Level 1 text entry to provide a caption for the whole chart.

Figure 11.20
The swoosh arrow shows up to five bullets of Level 1 text.

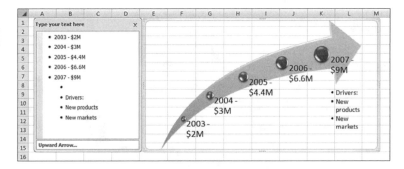

Showing an Iterative Process by Using a Basic Cycle Layout

Several cycle process charts are available in the SmartArt gallery. In some layouts, the arrows are too small to be seen. The Basic Cycle layout offers a good balance between text-holding shapes and arrows (see Figure 11.21).

Figure 11.21
The Basic Cycle layout offers a balance between text and arrows.

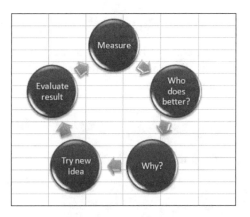

Showing a Company's Relationship to External Entities by Using a Diverging Radial Diagram

The radial layouts show the relationship of one center entity to several entities around the perimeter of the diagram. While many layouts offer a hub-and-spokes arrangement, the Diverging Radial layout adds arrows that point outward from the central diagram to each external shape.

The text for the central circle should be entered as a single bullet of Level 1 text. You build the remaining shapes around the perimeter by adding Level 2 bullets.

11

Figure 11.22
The Diverging Radial layout shows how a central organization supports many other organizations.

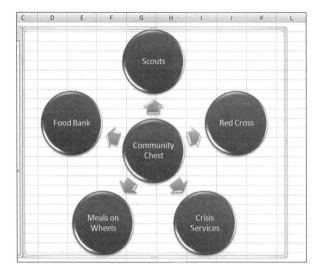

Illustrating Departments Within a Company by Using a Table List Diagram

The Table List layout holds a single entry of Level 1 text as a title across the top of the diagram. Each Level 2 entry causes the diagram to be vertically split. You could show additional bullets in each box by adding Level 3 text (see Figure 11.23).

Figure 11.23
You can illustrate groups within a whole by using the Table List layout.

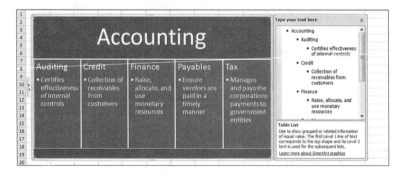

Adjusting Venn Diagrams to Show Relationships

The Basic Venn layout illustrates two to seven overlapping circles. Unfortunately, all the Venn diagrams created by the SmartArt engine show circles that are perfectly overlapping, as shown on the left side of Figure 11.24. This is not how relationships usually happen.

To create Venn diagrams that actually represent relationships, you can usually adjust the size of each circle and the percentage of overlap in the circles. For example, on the right side of Figure 11.24, the diagram indicates that while 80% of the bowling team is made up of people from the accounting department, fewer than one-fifth of the accountants are on the bowling team. To create this chart, you follow these steps:

Figure 11.24
Venn diagrams require adjustment in order to show the real size and proportion of overlap.

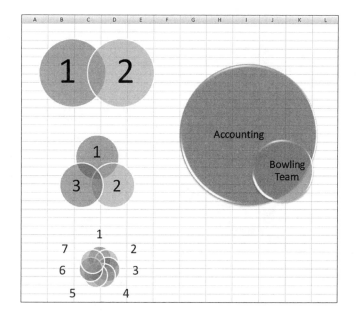

1. Add a SmartArt diagram with a Basic Venn layout.
2. Enter two Level 1 text entries and name them Accounting and Bowling Team.
3. Click the Accounting circle. Excel displays resizing handles. Drag a resizing handle out from the center of the circle to make the circle larger.
4. Click the Bowling circle. Drag a resizing handle inward to make the circle smaller.
5. While the resizing handles are displayed, drag the Bowling circle so that about 80% of that circle is inside the larger circle.

Understanding Labeled Hierarchy Charts

To figure out two of Excel 2007's hierarchy charts—Labeled Hierarchy and Horizontal Labeled Hierarchy—you almost need a Ph.D. However, when you figure out the bizarre layouts required in the text pane, these are really handy hierarchy charts.

The Horizontal Labeled Hierarchy (see Figure 11.25) offers a horizontal hierarchy chart that progresses from left to right. Each level of the chart lies in a colored band with a title. To create this chart, you follow these steps:

Figure 11.25
Getting the titles at the top of each band requires Level 1 shapes at the end of the text pane.

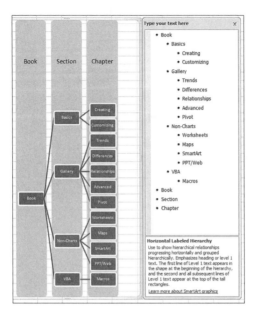

1. Create a single Level 1 item.

2. Beneath the first Level 1 item, build the complete hierarchy of Level 2, Level 3, and so on.

3. Count the number of levels in the hierarchy, including the first level. The chart in Figure 11.25 includes three levels. Remember this number for step 4.

4. At the bottom of the text pane, add new Level 1 entries. The first new Level 1 entry should include the title for the leftmost level of the hierarchy. The second new Level 1 entry should include the title for the second level of the hierarchy. Do not add any Level 2 text to these Level 1 entries.

When the number of bottom Level 1 entries exactly matches the number of levels in the hierarchy, the diagram snaps into place, with the titles lining up in the colored bands.

Using Other SmartArt Layouts

With Excel's 84 built-in layouts, you can use SmartArt graphics in a wide variety of ways. During Power Excel seminars that I conducted during 2006, I often showed a slide with a few of the new graphics, such as the funnel or gear charts. A clever accountant in one of my audiences wryly pointed out that the funnel chart would be perfect for illustrating the ingredients in a martini (see Figure 11.26).

Although Microsoft does not currently allow SmartArt to be created using VBA, it does allow someone with an understanding of XML to create brand-new SmartArt layouts. *Leveraging SmartArt Graphics in the 2007 Microsoft Office System*, an e-book published by Que (ISBN 0-7686-6833-6), includes several examples written by Suat Ozgur. It is easy to create new layouts that use different shapes (for example, pentagons instead of circles) or change the default proportions of the SmartArt layouts. I expect that many third-party vendors will begin offering custom SmartArt types for sale.

Figure 11.26
Your use of SmartArt diagrams for illustrating business concepts is limited only by your imagination.

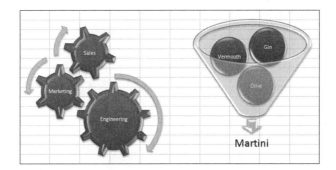

All in all, SmartArt is a great addition to the Office family. The one real drawback related to SmartArt in Excel 2007 is the inability to link cell content to the text in SmartArt. To do that, you have to use shapes, as described in the following section.

Using Shapes to Display Cell Contents

Shapes were known in previous versions of Excel as AutoShapes. Microsoft has added new shapes to the already long list of shapes available in AutoShapes. In addition, Excel 2007 shapes have some new formatting options, such as shadow, glow, and bevel.

Perhaps the best part of shapes is that you can tie the text on a shape to a worksheet cell. In Figure 11.27, for example, the shape is set to display the current value of cell B26. Every time the worksheet is calculated, the text on the shape is updated.

Figure 11.27
Shapes can be set to display the current value of a cell.

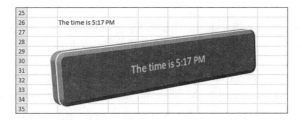

You follow these steps to insert a shape into a worksheet:

1. Select a blank area of the worksheet.

2. From the Insert ribbon, open the Shapes drop-down.

3. Select 1 of the 159 basic shapes, as shown in Figure 11.28.

Figure 11.28
Choose from these
shapes.

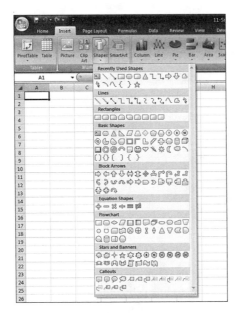

4. When the mouse pointer changes to a small crosshair, click and drag in the worksheet to draw the shape.

5. Choose a color scheme from the Shapes Styles drop-down.

6. Select Shape Effects, Preset and select an effect.

7. Look for a yellow diamond on the shape. Change the inflection point for the shape, if necessary. On the rounded rectangle, for example, sliding the yellow diamond controls how wide the rounded corners are.

8. Look for a green circle on the outside of the shape. Drag this circle to rotate the shape, if necessary.

9. To include static text in the shape, click in the middle of the shape and type the text. You can control the style by using the WordArt Styles drop-down. You can control text size and color by using the formatting buttons on the Home ribbon. The shape can include text from any cell, but it cannot perform a calculation. If you want the shape to include a calculated value, skip this step and follow steps 10 through 12.

10. If desired, add a new cell that will format a message for the WordArt. As shown in Figure 11.29, you can add the formula `="We are at "&TEXT(B13,"0%")&" of our goal!"` to an empty cell to convert the calculation in cell B13 to a suitable message.

11. Click in the middle of the text box as if you were about to type some text.

12. Click in the formula bar and type `=B14` and then press Enter. As shown in Figure 11.29, the shape displays the results from the selected cell.

Figure 11.29
This shape picks up the formula from cell B14 to show a message that changes with the worksheet.

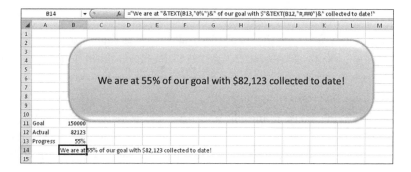

Working with Shapes

The Drawing Tools Format ribbon contains options to change the shape style, fill, outline, effects, and WordArt effects.

In the Insert Shapes group of the Format ribbon, you use the Edit Shape, Change Shape command to choose another shape style.

If you right-click a shape and choose Format Shape, Excel displays the Format Shape dialog, with the fine-tuning settings Fill, Line, Line Style, Shadow, 3-D Format, 3-D Rotation, and Text Placement.

Using the Freeform Shape to Create a Custom Shape

Despite my friendly relationship with Microsoft, I have not convinced them to add the MrExcel logo to the Shapes gallery (yet). However, you can build any shape by using the Freeform line tools in the Shapes gallery.

After you create a shape, you can add 3-D effects, glow, and so on to make a cool-looking version of your company logo, as shown in Figure 11.30.

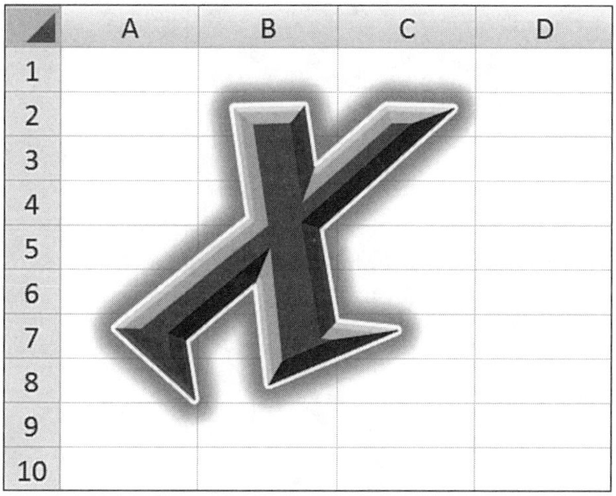

Figure 11.30
This shape was created with the Freeform shape tool and then enhanced using the Drawing Tools section of the Format ribbon.

To create a custom shape, you follow these steps:

1. Insert a picture of the shape that you can use as a guide to trace.
2. From the Insert ribbon, choose the Shapes drop-down. In the Lines section, the last two shapes are Freeform and Scribble. Select the Freeform shape.
3. Click one corner of your logo.
4. Move the mouse to the adjacent corner of the logo and click again.
5. Repeat step 4 for each corner. If your logo has a curve, click several times around the perimeter of the curve. The more often you click, the better the curve will be.
6. When you arrive back at the original corner, click one final time to close the shape and complete the drawing.
7. Use the effect and fill settings to color and stylize the logo.

Using WordArt for Interesting Titles and Headlines

WordArt has been rewritten in Excel 2007. As in previous versions, WordArt is best used sparingly—possibly for a headline or title at the top of a page. It is best used for impressive display fonts to add interest to a report. You would probably not want to create an entire 20-page document in WordArt.

To use WordArt, you follow these steps:

1. Select a blank section of a worksheet.
2. From the Insert ribbon, choose the WordArt drop-down.
3. As shown in Figure 11.31, choose from the 25 WordArt presets in the drop-down. Don't worry that these presets seem less exciting than the WordArt in prior versions of Excel. You will be able to customize the WordArt later.

Figure 11.31
Excel offers 25 WordArt presets.

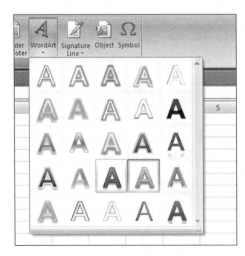

4. Excel adds the generic text *Your Text Here* in the preset WordArt you chose. Select this default text and then type your own text.

5. Select the text. Choose a new font style by using either the mini toolbar that appears or the Home ribbon.

6. Use the WordArt Styles group on the Drawing Tools Format ribbon to color the WordArt. To the right of the Styles drop-down are icons for text color and line color and a drop-down for effects. The Effects drop-down includes the fly-out menus Shadow, Reflection, Glow, Bevel, and 3-D Rotation.

7. To achieve the old-style WordArt effects, from the Format ribbon, select Drawing Tools, WordArt Styles, Text Effects, Transform and then select a shape for the text. Figure 11.32 shows the WordArt with a Wave 1 transformation.

Figure 11.32
WordArt includes the Transform menu to bend and twist type.

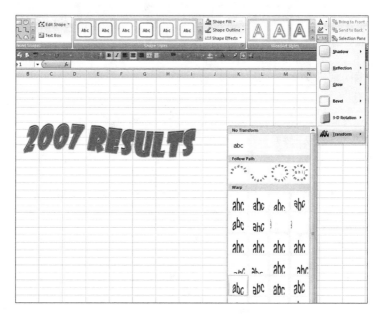

11

CASE STUDY

Converting SmartArt to Shapes to Allow Dynamic Diagrams

Microsoft's official position is that you cannot use formulas to populate the text pane in SmartArt diagrams. However, using the steps in this section, you can simulate this effect.

The diagram in Figure 11.33 looks like a SmartArt Table Hierarchy layout, yet the values in all the shapes are fed from formulas on the Excel worksheet.

Figure 11.33
This looks like a SmartArt diagram, but the values come from formulas on the worksheet. Although using formulas this way sounds simple, the feature is not hooked up in Excel 2007.

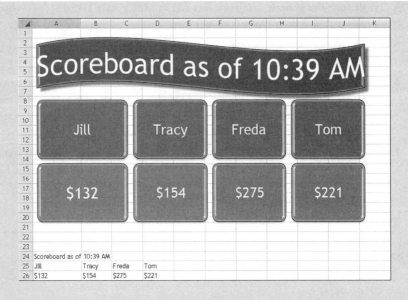

You achieve the live formulas in the SmartArt diagram by cheating slightly. In the steps that follow, you first use the SmartArt diagram engine and then convert the SmartArt diagram to a collection of shapes.

CAUTION

This solution does not work when the number of shapes needs to change in response to the values in the Excel worksheet. The number of shapes has to remain the same. Only the text in the shapes is based on live formulas.

To build the workbook shown in Figure 11.34, you follow these steps:

Figure 11.34
You build the SmartArt diagram with sample text of about the same length as that with which you expect to populate the diagram.

1. Choose Insert, SmartArt and choose a Table Hierarchy from the relationship group.

2. Build a static SmartArt diagram with a single Level 1 item, four Level 2 items, and a Level 3 item for each Level 2 item. Type sample values in the text pane, as shown in Figure 11.34. The sample values should be about the same size as the real values that you expect to have in the final diagram.

3. On the Page Layout tab, change the Theme to Opulent.

4. On the SmartArt Tools Design tab, change the SmartArt Styles to Cartoon.

5. Use the Change Colors tab to select Colorful, Accent Colors.

6. Click on the Level 1 shape. On the Format tab, use the Change Shape drop-down to select a wave shape.

7. Also on the Format tab, choose Shape Styles, Shape Effects, Shadow, Offset Diagonal Bottom Right.

8. Choose Shape Styles, Shape Effects, Shadow, Shadow Options.

9. In the Format Shape dialog box, change the distance from 4 points to 9 points.

10. Select the text within the Level 1 shape. On the Format ribbon, choose WordArt Styles, Text Effects, Transform, Wave1.

11. Click one of the Level 3 shapes. Press Ctrl+A to select the remaining shapes in the diagram.

12. Press Ctrl+C to copy the shapes in the diagram.

13. Choose a blank cell below the SmartArt diagram and press Ctrl+V to paste the nine shapes in formation.

14. Click in the range of the original SmartArt diagram, but not on any shape in the SmartArt diagram. This selects the entire SmartArt diagram. Press the Delete key to delete the static SmartArt diagram.

15. If necessary, delete the rows or columns where the old diagram was.

16. Create an external query in row 30 to retrieve TicketID, Associate, and SaleTotal from a point-of-sale system. Set up the query properties to refresh every minute.

17. In cell A24, enter the formula `="Scoreboard as of "&TEXT(NOW(),"H:MM AM/PM")`.

18. In cells A25:D25, type the names of the four associates working in the store today.

19. In cell A26, enter the formula `=TEXT(SUMIF($B$31:$B$300,A25,$C$31:$C$300),"$#,##0")`.

20. Copy the formula from cell A26 to B26:D26.

21. Select the text in one shape. Click in the formula bar and type a formula such as `=A24`.

22. Use the mini toolbar to center the text and select the same size as used for similar shapes in the diagram.

23. Repeat steps 21 and 22 for the other eight shapes.

Throughout the day, the external query brings new data into the worksheet, and it is presented in the scoreboard diagram (refer to Figure 11.33).

Although this is a tedious process, it is a way to use the SmartArt engine to create a great-looking scoreboard in Excel. It is unfortunate that Microsoft did not have time to hook up the decade-old Shapes formula functionality for SmartArt graphics. Perhaps this will be added in the next version of Office.

Next Steps

In Chapter 12, "Exporting Your Charts for Use Outside of Excel," you will learn how to share your charts and graphics with others through either PowerPoint or by publishing to the web. While the charting functionality between Excel and PowerPoint left much to be desired in Excel 2003, you should be able to flawlessly share charts and SmartArt graphics between Excel 2007 and PowerPoint 2007.

11

Exporting Your Charts for Use Outside of Excel

Presenting Excel Charts in PowerPoint or Word

Although Excel is a great place for you to create charts, you might need to share charts with others, either in PowerPoint, as Word documents, as Web pages, or simply as graphic files.

Word 2007 and PowerPoint 2007 use the new charting engine in Excel 2007, so you now get a better result when you copy a chart from Excel to one of those products. However, there are a number of different ways to copy a chart, and each method has different ramifications. If you are not careful, you might end up sending an entire 20-sheet workbook along with your PowerPoint presentation when you mean to send only a single chart.

There are a number of frustrating gotchas when you copy charts from Excel to PowerPoint. In previous versions of Office, the gotchas were so bad that most tipsters, including me, recommended that you simply copy your charts from Excel to PowerPoint as static pictures.

Office 2007 adds a new wrinkle that makes the issue less cut and dried. In Office 2007, a chart copied from Excel and pasted to PowerPoint is completely editable. All the great tools on the Charting Tools ribbon in Excel are available in PowerPoint. You can also make your charts match the themes in PowerPoint. I am so enamored with the charting tools in Office 2007 that the ability to copy the charts as live charts is worth the hassles.

12

My concerns with copying the charts revolve around several issues:

- **Privacy**—Even though you copy just the chart, Excel brings along all the data in the entire workbook. This means that the recipient of your PowerPoint presentation can right-click the slide and open a complete copy of all 50 worksheets in your workbook.

- **Links**—Depending on how the chart is pasted, the recipient might need to have a copy of the underlying workbook if he or she wants to edit the chart.

- **Live data**—If you want the chart in PowerPoint to reflect the current values from the Excel file, you have to have access to the Excel file.

There are at least eight different ways of getting charts from Excel to PowerPoint or Word. Considering all the positives and negatives, I prefer copying the underlying chart data from Excel to PowerPoint and re-creating the chart in PowerPoint. This method requires a few extra steps, but it allows you to have an editable chart without sending along the entire 50MB workbook.

Table 12.1 shows some of the methods and the advantages and disadvantages of each method.

Table 12.1   Methods for Moving Excel Charts to PowerPoint or Word

Method	Advantages	Disadvantages
Copy the chart in Excel and paste it into PowerPoint	Full access to the Charting Tools ribbon. Data updates when the underlying Excel data updates.	Recipient must have access to the original Excel file to edit data. Recipient can see all worksheets of the underlying Excel file by right-clicking the chart.
After pasting to PowerPoint, use the Format icon to select Excel Chart, Entire Workbook	Full access to the Charting Tools ribbon.	Recipient can see all worksheets of the underlying Excel file by right-clicking the chart. Chart does not update when the original Excel file changes. PowerPoint file size increases by the size of the Excel file.
After pasting to PowerPoint, use the Format icon to select Paste as Picture	No privacy concerns. Small file size. No linking issues.	Cannot update the chart (other than by using the Picture Tools ribbon).
Use Paste Special, Microsoft Office Excel Chart Object	None	No access to the Charting Tools ribbon. Access to copy of entire workbook.
Use Paste Special, Microsoft Office Graph Object	Access to the Charting Tools ribbon.	Can access to a copy of the entire workbook.

Method	Advantages	Disadvantages
Use Paste Special, Paste as Picture	No privacy concerns. Small file size. No linking issues.	Cannot update the chart (other than by using the Picture Tools ribbon).
Use Paste Special, Link, Microsoft Office Excel Chart Object	Works with files saved in Compatibility mode.	Have to right-click and choose Update in order to get new data. Need to have access to the original Excel file in order to update. No access to the Charting Tools ribbon.
Create the chart in PowerPoint and copy and paste the original data from the original Excel file	Full access to the Charting Tools ribbon. Small file size. No linking issues.	Does not reflect changes in the original workbook.

Copying a Chart as a Live Chart Linked to the Original Workbook

Copying a chart as a live chart linked to the original workbook is the easiest method of getting a chart from Excel to PowerPoint. You basically just copy the chart from Excel and paste it to PowerPoint.

With this method, you have full access to all the Charting Tools ribbon tabs in PowerPoint. You can customize the chart to match the theme of the PowerPoint presentation, and you can choose new layouts, styles, and so on.

The data remains linked to the original workbook. If you change the workbook and later open the PowerPoint presentation, the chart reflects the new numbers from the Excel workbook. Obviously, this feature works only if the PowerPoint presentation still has access to the original Excel file. Otherwise, PowerPoint shows a static version of the last-known numbers in the chart.

To copy the chart, you follow these steps:

1. Open both PowerPoint and Excel.
2. In Excel, click the chart.
3. Press Ctrl+C or click the Copy icon on the Home ribbon.
4. Switch to PowerPoint by pressing Alt+Tab.
5. Paste by pressing Ctrl+V or clicking the Paste icon on the Home ribbon.

The chart fills the text area of the slide. The Chart Tools ribbon icons are available, as shown in Figure 12.1.

12

Figure 12.1
Copying and pasting is the simplest method for getting a chart from Excel to PowerPoint.

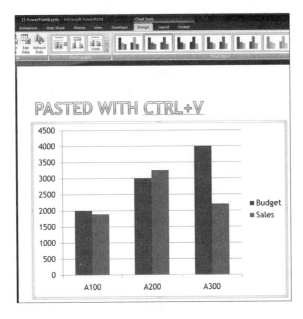

Copying a Chart as a Live Chart Linked to a Copy of the Original Workbook

The problem with a straight copy and paste is that the PowerPoint slide and the original Excel workbook must remain on the same computer in order to maintain the link. If you plan on distributing the PowerPoint file to others, you can copy the chart along with the entire workbook.

To copy the chart, you follow these steps:

1. Open both PowerPoint and Excel.

2. In Excel, click the chart.

3. Press Ctrl+C or click the Copy icon on the Home ribbon.

4. Switch to PowerPoint by pressing Alt+Tab.

5. Paste by pressing Ctrl+V.

6. An icon appears at the lower-right corner of the pasted chart. Hover over the icon, and a drop-down arrow appears. Click the drop-down arrow. Choose Excel Chart (Entire Workbook), as shown in Figure 12.2.

One advantage of this method is that you can send the PowerPoint presentation to any recipient whose computer has Office 2007. The recipient can right-click the chart, choose Edit, and see the entire Excel workbook. If that person makes changes to the assumptions in the workbook, the chart updates. The recipient also has full access to the Charting Tools ribbons in PowerPoint.

Figure 12.2
After pasting, you choose
to embed the entire
workbook.

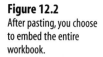
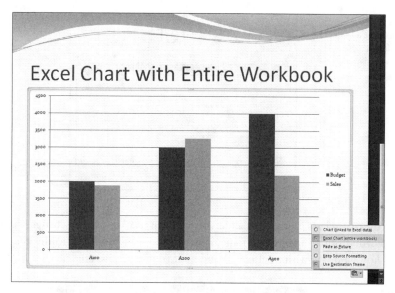

The main advantage of this method is also a disadvantage. Even though you paste a single chart, Office 2007 embeds the entire workbook. This can create privacy concerns if the workbook contains sensitive data on other worksheets or file size concerns if you have millions of cells on other worksheets in the workbook.

Copying a Chart as a Picture

You can paste a picture of a chart in a PowerPoint slide. The picture is initially the same size as the chart in the Excel worksheet. Instead of having access to the Charting Tools ribbon, you only have access to the Picture Tools ribbon. The Picture Tools ribbon might allow you to change the chart to grayscale or a monochrome color, but you do not have access to the rich chart formatting tools.

To paste a chart as a picture, you copy the chart in Excel. On the PowerPoint slide, you can perform either of the following tasks:

- Press Ctrl+V to paste the chart. Then use the drop-down arrow to the lower right of the chart and choose Paste As Picture.

- Select the drop-down arrow on the Paste icon in the PowerPoint Home ribbon. Choose Paste Special and then those to paste the picture as PNG, GIF, JPEG, bitmap, Enhanced Metafile, or Windows Metafile.

The Paste Special dialog is shown in Figure 12.3.

12

Figure 12.3
You can choose a picture format in the Paste Special dialog.

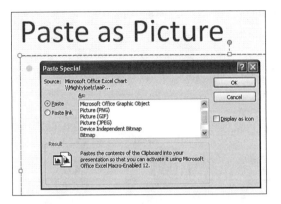

After the chart is pasted as a picture, you can use any of the settings on the Picture Tools Format ribbon to apply a frame, bevel, shadow, or reflection to the chart. Figure 12.4 shows a frame with a reflection and a bit of perspective angle.

Figure 12.4
The picture formatting tools offer interesting possibilities but do not have the flexibility of the charting tools.

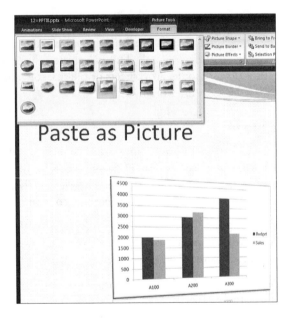

Pasting a Chart as a Linked Object

If you plan to save your chart in Compatibility mode, to be shared with people using PowerPoint 2003, you might consider using the linked object choice in the Paste Special dialog.

First, you copy the chart from Excel. In PowerPoint, you choose Home, Paste, Paste Special, Paste Link, Microsoft Office Excel Chart Object, and then you click OK. This choice is far more limiting than the choices described so far in this chapter. In order to update the chart, you have to right-click the chart and choose Update. To edit the chart, you right-click the chart and choose Linked Worksheet Object, Edit. This means that the person using the PowerPoint file must have access to the original Excel file.

Creating a Chart in PowerPoint and Copying Data from Excel

Creating a chart in PowerPoint and copying data from Excel may seem to be the most tedious method, but it has the advantage of getting a completely editable chart into PowerPoint without the need to copy an entire workbook into the PowerPoint file.

You follow these steps to create the chart:

1. In PowerPoint, choose New Slide from the Home ribbon. A new slide appears, with six icons in the center of the slide (see Figure 12.5).

Figure 12.5
When you insert a new slide in PowerPoint, six icons appear in the center of the slide.

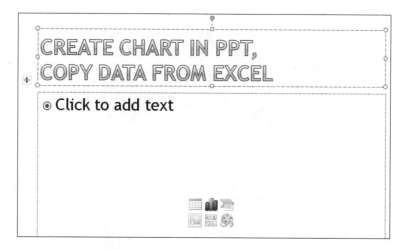

2. Click the Chart icon in the center of the slide.
3. Choose a chart type and click OK. You see your PowerPoint slide on the left and a new Excel worksheet on the right. The worksheet is called Chart in Microsoft Office PowerPoint - Microsoft Excel (see Figure 12.6).
4. Click the original Excel workbook in the taskbar.
5. Highlight your source data and press Ctrl+C to copy it to the Clipboard.
6. Click the new workbook in the taskbar. Click in cell A1 and press Ctrl+V to paste the data. Your data will probably cover a smaller or larger range of data than the default dataset. If your dataset is smaller, remnants of the default dataset will appear outside your paste area, as shown in Figure 12.7.

12

Figure 12.6
PowerPoint creates a
new workbook with
default data.

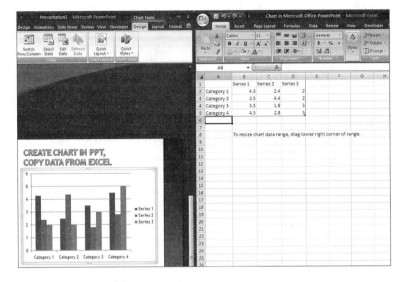

Figure 12.7
You paste your data
over the default
data.

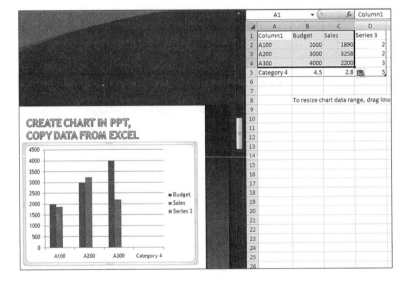

7. A blue outline appears around A1:D5. Grab the blue handle in the corner of cell D5 and drag the handle to match the size of your pasted data.

8. Click the maximize button in the title bar of the PowerPoint application to return to PowerPoint.

You've now created a new chart in PowerPoint. The chart can be edited using the Chart Tools ribbon tabs. You've also minimized the size of the Excel data that must travel with the PowerPoint file.

Presenting Charts on the Web

You can export a chart to appear on a webpage. This technique is also the easiest way to make a GIF version of your chart.

You follow these steps to create an HTML page with a chart:

1. Save your Excel file as an Excel file.
2. If your chart is embedded on a worksheet, click the chart. On the Design ribbon, choose Move Chart. Choose to move the chart to a new sheet.
3. From the Office icon, choose Save As, Other Formats.
4. In the Save As dialog that appears, choose Web Page (*.htm; *.html) from the Save As Type drop-down. Excel warns you that some features of the workbook will be lost. Because you already saved a copy of the workbook in step 1, this is okay.
5. At the bottom of the Save As dialog, change Entire Workbook to Chart.
6. Specify a filename, such as `MyChart.html`.
7. Click either Publish or Save.

If you browse to the selected path, you will find your HTML file and also a new folder. In the preceding example, the folder would be called `MyChart`. This folder contains a GIF version of your chart.

Exporting Charts to Graphics

The steps in the preceding section are a convoluted way of creating a GIF version of a chart. If you don't mind typing a bit of VBA code, you can export the active chart quickly.

Using VBA to Export Charts as Images

VBA is the macro language behind Excel. Although Chapter 13, "Using Excel VBA to Create Charts," takes a more in-depth look at VBA, this section takes a quick peek into using VBA to convert charts to graphics files.

You need to display the Developer tab in the ribbon. If this tab is not on your computer, select the Office icon, Excel Options and then check the Show Developer Tab in the Ribbon check box.

When the Developer tab is available, you follow these steps to export a chart to a graphic file:

1. Select a chart.
2. From the Developer tab, choose Visual Basic.
3. Press Ctrl+G to display the Immediate window.
4. Type the following line of code and then press Enter:
   ```
   ActiveChart.Export "C:MyChart.JPG", "JPG"
   ```

12

You can, of course, specify any path and filename instead of the name shown in the preceding code snippet. The file type can be GIF, JPG, or any other graphics filter installed on your computer's copy of Office.

Using Snag-It or OneNote to Capture Charts

Screen capture tools such as Snag-It from Camtasia and the Insert Screen Clipping feature of Microsoft OneNote allow you to capture a specific region of the screen.

Snag-It allows you to specify an output file type of BMP, GIF, JPG, PCX, PNG, TGA, or TIF. You can also specify a higher resolution, suitable for printing using Snag-It.

Converting to XPS or PDF

PDF is the ubiquitous Portable Document Format from Adobe. XML Paper Specification (XPS) is the new open-source competitor from Microsoft. In October 2005, Microsoft announced that it would add support to Office 2007 to save files as PDF files. Early beta versions of the product included a menu item to save to PDF or XPS. But a European court decided that Microsoft could not include this technology with Office. You thus have to jump through a few hoops in order to install a free utility to convert a document to PDF or XPS.

To install the free utility, you follow these steps:

1. From the Office icon, choose Save As, Find Add-ins for Other File Formats.
2. In the Help topic, follow the link to Microsoft Save as PDF or XPS Add-in for 2007 Microsoft Office Programs.
3. If validation is required, click Continue.
4. If asked to download a Genuine Advantage plug-in, do so.
5. After installing the plug-in, click Continue.
6. Click Download to download the actual code for saving files as PDF. If you are using FireFox as a browser, note the location where the program is downloaded.
7. Run the download by double-clicking on the file downloaded in step 6.
8. Accept the user agreement and click Continue.

Your Save As menu now includes an entry to save as PDF or XPS.

After the add-in is installed, you can select Office icon, Save As, PDF or XPS to print to a PDF file.

Next Steps

In Chapter 13, you will learn how to use VBA macros to automate the creation and formatting of charts. VBA is a macro language that has been in Excel for over a decade; you can use it to automate repetitive tasks.

Using Excel VBA to Create Charts

Introducing VBA

Version 5 of Excel introduced a powerful new macro language called Visual Basic for Applications (VBA). Every copy of Excel shipped since 1993 has had a copy of the powerful VBA language hiding behind the worksheets. VBA allows you to perform steps that you normally perform in Excel, but to perform them very quickly and flawlessly. A VBA program can turn a process that used to take days each month into a single button click and a minute of processing time. If you have a lot of charts to create, you can set up a macro to automatically produce a series of charts. This is appropriate if you regularly have to produce a similar set of charts every day, week, or month.

You shouldn't be intimidated by VBA. The VBA macro recorder tool gets you 80% of the way to a useful macro, and the examples in this chapter get you the rest of the way there.

Every example in this chapter is available for download from www.mrexcel.com/chart2007data.html.

> **NOTE**
> There is usually a nagging subset of features that work in the current version of Excel but do not work in prior versions of Excel. However, all the good features in charting are new to Excel 2007; consequently, hardly any of the code in this chapter is backward compatible with Excel 97–Excel 2003. If you need to write code to create Excel 2003 charts, you can use the examples from Chapter 10 of my book *VBA and Macros for Microsoft Excel* (ISBN 978-0789731296, Que Publishing). The project file from that chapter is available at www.mrexcel.com/chart2007data.html.

13

Enabling VBA in Your Copy of Excel

By default, VBA is disabled in Office 2007. Before you can start using VBA, you need to enable macros in the Trust Center. From the Office icon menu, you choose Excel Options, Trust Center, Trust Center Settings, Macro Settings. Then you choose Enable All Macros.

> **TIP**
>
> If you have previously enabled the Developer tab of the Ribbon, you can use the Macro Security icon to jump quickly to the Trust Center dialog box.

Further, when you save your files, you have to save the files as Excel 2007 macro-enabled workbooks, with the .xlsm extension.

Enabling the Developer Ribbon

Most of the VBA tools are located on the Developer tab of the Excel 2007 Ribbon. By default, this tab is not displayed. To enable it, from the Office icon menu, you select Excel Options, Popular. Then you choose Show Developer Tab in the Ribbon.

As shown in Figure 13.1, the Code group on the Developer tab of the Ribbon offers icons for accessing the Visual Basic Editor, the Macros dialog box, macro recording tools, and the Macro Security setting.

Visual Basic Editor

Macro Recording Tools

Figure 13.1
You need to enable the Developer ribbon to access the VBA tools.

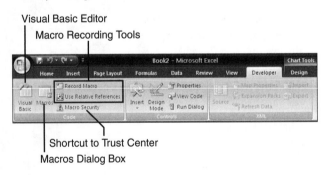

Shortcut to Trust Center

Macros Dialog Box

The Visual Basic Editor

From Excel, you press Alt+F11 or, from the Developer ribbon, you choose Code, Visual Basic to open the Visual Basic Editor. The VBA Editor, shown in Figure 13.2, has three main sections:

Figure 13.2
The Visual Basic Editor window is lurking behind every copy of Excel shipped since 1993.

Project Explorer   Code Window

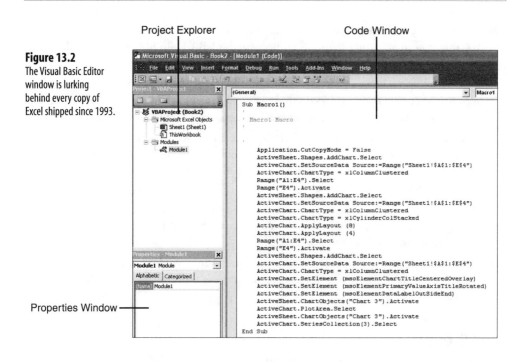

If this is your first time using VBA, some of these items may be disabled. Follow the instructions given in the following list to make sure each is enabled.

- **Project Explorer**—This pane displays a hierarchical tree of all open workbooks. You can expand the tree to see the worksheets and code modules present in the workbook. If the Project Explorer is not visible, you can enable it by pressing Ctrl+R.

- **Properties window**—The Properties window is important when you begin to program user forms. It is also useful when you're writing normal code. You enable it by pressing F4.

- **Code window**—This is the area where you write your code. Code is stored in one or more code modules attached to the workbook. To add a code module to a workbook, you select Insert, Code Module from the application menu.

Visual Basic Tools

Visual Basic is a powerful development environment. Although this chapter cannot offer a complete course on VBA, if you are new to VBA, you should take advantage of the following:

- As you begin to type code, Excel usually offers a drop-down with valid choices. This feature, known as AutoComplete, allows you to type code faster and eliminate typing mistakes.

- For assistance with any keyword, you can put the cursor in the keyword and press F1. You might need your installation CDs because the VBA Help file can be excluded from the installation of Office 2007.

- Excel checks each line of code as you finish it. Lines in error appear in red. Comments appear in green. You can add a comment by typing a single apostrophe. You should use lots of comments so you can remember what each section of code is doing.

- Despite the aforementioned error checking, Excel may still encounter errors at run-time. If this happens, you can click the Debug button. The line that caused the error is highlighted in yellow. You can then hover your mouse cursor over any variable to see the current value of the variable.

- When you are in Debug mode, you can use the Debug menu to step through code line-by-line. You can toggle back and forth between Excel and VBA to see the effect of running a line of code on the worksheet.

- Other great debugging tools are breakpoints, the Watch window, the Object Browser, and the Immediate window. You can read about these tools in the Excel VBA Help menu.

The Macro Recorder

Excel offers a macro recorder that is about 60% perfect for charts. Unfortunately, the last 40% is frustrating. Code that you record to work with one dataset is hard-coded to work only with that dataset. This behavior might work fine if your chart data occupies cells A1:E7 every single day, but if you might have a different number of customers each day, it is unlikely that you will have the same number of rows each day. Given that you might need to work with other data, it would be a lot better if Excel could record your actions of selecting cells when you use the End key. This is one of the shortcomings of the macro recorder.

Excel pros often use the macro recorder to record code and expect to have to then clean up the recorded code. While this approach works perfectly with pivot tables and many other features, it seems that Microsoft ran out of time or was not interested in hooking up the macro recorder for most of the chart formatting tasks. You therefore have to write that code from scratch.

13

> **CAUTION**
>
> The macro recorder is able to record most actions on the Design and Layout ribbons, but it completely ignores actions on the Format ribbon or in the Format dialog boxes. VBA code is available to micro-format chart elements, but you have to write code to perform actions on the Format ribbon from scratch.

Understanding Object-Oriented Code

If you took a class in BASIC a long time ago, the recorded code in VBA is going to appear rather foreign to you. Whereas BASIC is a procedural language, VBA is an object-oriented language. Most lines of VBA code follow the *Noun.Verb*, or *Object.Method*, syntax. Objects can be workbooks, worksheets, cells, or ranges of cells. Methods can be typical Excel actions, such as Copy, Paste, and PasteSpecial.

Many methods allow adverbs—that is, parameters you use to specify how to perform a method. If you see a construction that includes a colon and an equals sign, it is an adverb, and you know that the macro recorder is describing how the method should work.

You might also see adjectives, or *properties*. If you set ActiveCell.Font.ColorIndex = 3, you are setting the font color (the property) of the active cell to red (the value). Note that when you are dealing with properties, there is only an equals sign, not a colon and an equal sign.

Learning Tricks of the VBA Trade

You need to master a few simple techniques to be able to write efficient VBA code. These techniques will help you make the jump to writing effective code.

Writing Code to Handle a Data Range of Any Size

The macro recorder hard-codes the fact that your data is in a range, such as A1:E7. Although this hard-coding works for today's dataset, it may not work as you get new datasets. You need to write code that can deal with different sizes of datasets.

One method is to use the CurrentRegion property. If you specify one nonblank cell and ask for the current region, Excel extends the selection in each direction until it encounters the edge of the worksheet, a blank row, or a blank column. In Figure 13.3, for example, the following line of code selected A1:E4:

```
Range("B1").CurrentRegion.Select
```

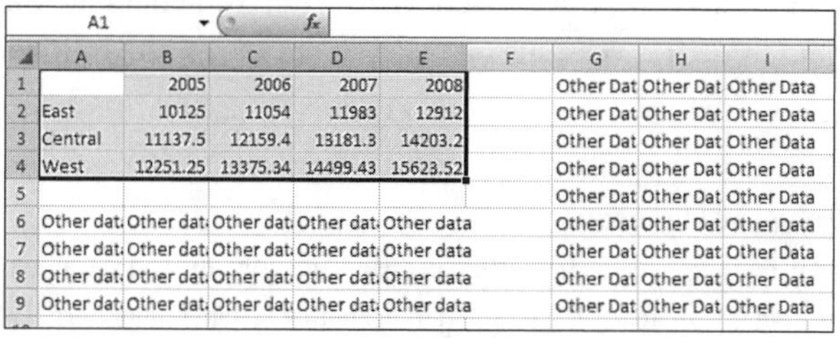

Figure 13.3

Selecting the current region extends the selection out until a blank row/column is encountered.

If you are absolutely sure that cell B1 is nonblank and that no other data touches your chart data, you could use the CurrentRegion approach to specify the data to a chart.

The macro recorder uses syntax such as Range("H12") to refer to a cell. However, it is more flexible to use Cells(12, 8) to refer to the cell in row 12, column 8. Similarly, the macro recorder refers to a rectangular range using syntax such as Range("A1:K415501"). However, it is more flexible to use the `Cells` syntax to refer to the upper-left corner of the range and then use the `Resize()` syntax to refer to the number of rows and columns in the range:

```
Cells(1, 1).Resize(415501,11)
```

This approach is more flexible than using `Range("A1:K415501")` because you can replace any of the numbers with a variable.

In the Excel user interface, you can use the End key on the keyboard to jump to the end of a range of data. If you move the cell pointer to the final row on the worksheet and press the End key and then the Up Arrow key, the cell pointer jumps to the last row that contains data. The equivalent of doing this in VBA is to use the following code:

```
Range("A1048576").End(xlUp).Select
```

You don't need to select this cell; you just need to find the row number that contains the last row. The following code locates this row and saves the row number to a variable named `FinalRow`:

```
FinalRow = Range("A1048576").End(xlUp).Row
```

There is nothing magical about the variable name `FinalRow`. You could call this variable `x` or `y`, or even give it your dog's name. However, because VBA allows you to use meaningful variable names, you should use something such as `FinalRow` to describe the final row.

> **NOTE**
>
> Excel 2007 offers 1,048,576 rows and 16,384 columns. Excel 97 through Excel 2003 offered 65,536 rows and 256 columns. To make your code flexible enough to handle any versions of Excel, you can use `Rows.Count` to learn the total number of rows in the currently running version of Excel. The preceding code could then be generalized like so:
>
> ```
> FinalRow = Cells(Rows.Count, 1).End(xlUp).Row
> ```

You can also find the final column in a dataset. If you are relatively sure that the dataset begins in row 1, you can use the End key in combination with the Left Arrow key to jump from cell XFD1 to the last column that contains data. To generalize for the possibility that the code is running in earlier versions of Excel, you can use the following code:

```
FinalCol = Cells(1, Columns.Count).End(xlToLeft).Column
```

End+Down Arrow Versus End+Up Arrow

You might be tempted to find the final row by starting in cell A1 and using the End key in conjunction with the Down Arrow key. You should avoid this approach. Data coming from another system is imperfect. If your program will import 500,000 rows from a legacy computer system every day for the next five years, a day will come when someone manages to key a null value into the dataset. This value will cause a blank cell or even a blank row to appear in the middle of your dataset. The formula `Range("A1").End(xlDown)` will then stop prematurely at the blank cell instead of including all your data. This blank cell will cause that day's report to miss thousands of rows of data, a potential disaster that will call into question the credibility of your report. You should take the extra step of starting at the last row in the worksheet to greatly reduce the risk of problems.

Using Super-Variables: Object Variables

In typical programming languages, a variable holds a single value. You might use x = 4 to assign a value of 4 to the variable x.

Many properties describe a single cell in Excel. A cell might contain a value such as 4, and the cell also has a font size, a font color, a row, a column, possibly a formula, possibly a comment, a list of precedents, and more. It is possible to use VBA to create a super-variable that contains all the information about a cell or any other object. A statement to create a typical variable such as x = Range("A1") assigns the current value of cell A1 to the variable x.

You can use the Set keyword to create an object variable:

```
Set x = Range("A1")
```

This formula creates a super-variable that contains all the properties of the cell. Instead of having a variable with only one value, you now have a variable in which you can access the value of many properties associated with that variable. You can reference x.Formula to learn the formula in cell A1 or x.Font.ColorIndex to learn the color of the cell.

Using object variables can make it easier to write code. Rather than continuously referring to ThisWorkbook.Worksheets("Income Statement"), you can define an object variable and use that as shorthand. For example, the following code repeatedly refers to the same workbook:

```
ThisWorkbook.Worksheets("Income Statement").ChartObjects("Chart1").Chart _
    .SetSourceData Source:= ThisWorkbook.Worksheets("Income Statement") _
    .Range("A1:E4")
ThisWorkbook.Worksheets("Income Statement").ChartObjects("Chart1").Left = 10
ThisWorkbook.Worksheets("Income Statement").ChartObjects("Chart1").Top = 30
ThisWorkbook.Worksheets("Income Statement").ChartObjects("Chart1").Width = 300
ThisWorkbook.Worksheets("Income Statement").ChartObjects("Chart1").Height = 200
```

If you define an object variable first, the code becomes shorter and easier to write.

```
Dim WS as Worksheet
Set WS = ThisWorkbook.Worksheets("Income Statement")
WS.ChartObjects("Chart1").Chart.SetSourceData Source:= WS.Range("A1:E4")
WS.ChartObjects("Chart1").Left = 10
WS.ChartObjects("Chart1").Top = 30
WS.ChartObjects("Chart1").Width = 300
WS.ChartObjects("Chart1").Height = 200
```

13

> **NOTE** Provided that you do not type Option Explicit in the code window, VBA does not require you to declare your variables with the Dim statement. I tend not to declare regular variables. However, there is a benefit if you use Dim to declare your object variables; Excel will offer AutoComplete dropdowns showing all of the methods and properties available for the object variable. For this reason, I take the extra time to declare the object variables at the top of each macro.

Using `With` and `End With` When Referring to an Object

In the previous code, several lines all refer to the same chart object. Rather than reference this object on every line of code, you could specify the chart object once in a `With` statement. In each subsequent line, you could leave off the name of the chart and begin the line with a period. You would end the block of code with an `End With` statement. This is faster to write than typing the complete object name multiple times, and it executes faster because Excel only has to figure out what `WS.ChartObjects("Chart1")` means once. The following code uses the `With` syntax while setting five properties:

```
Dim WS as Worksheet
Set WS = ThisWorkbook.Worksheets("Income Statement")
With WS.ChartObjects("Chart1")
    .Chart.SetSourceData Source:= WS.Range("A1:E4")
    .Left = 10
    .Top = 30
    .Width = 300
    .Height = 200
End With
```

Continuing a Line

Some lines of code can get very long. To improve readability, you can break a line and continue it. To indicate that the current line is continued on the next line, you can type a space and then an underscore character. Typically, the convention is to then indent the continued line of code. This is not required by VBA, but improves readability. For example, the following two lines of code are really a single line of code:

```
FinalCol = Cells(1, Columns.Count). _
    End(xlToLeft).Column
```

> **NOTE** You are likely to break a line only when you reach the right edge of the code window, but the physical limitations of this book require lines to be broken into much smaller segments. Feel free to rejoin continued lines into a single line of code in your project.

Adding Comments to Code

When you figure out an interesting technique in code, it's a good idea to add comments in the code. This will help you if you return to the code several months later, and it will help others who have to troubleshoot your code.

The comment character in VBA is a single apostrophe ('). You can use a single-line comment, a several-line comment, or a comment that takes up only the end of a line. The Visual Basic Editor changes the color of your comments to green in order to differentiate them from other code. The following macro has comments to document where you can turn to for more information:

```
Sub CommentsImproveReadability()
    Dim WS As Worksheet
```

```
    Set WS = Worksheets("Sheet1")
    ' Create a chart on a new sheet
    Charts.Add
    ' This technique is from chapter 13
    ' of the Excel Charting book
    ActiveChart.ChartType = xlColumnClustered
    ActiveChart.SetSourceData Source:=WS.Range("A1:B4")
    ActiveChart.Interior.ColorIndex = 4 ' Green
End Sub
```

Coding for New Charting Features in Excel 2007

Charts have been completely rewritten in Excel 2007. Most code from Excel 2003 will continue to work in Excel 2007. However, if you write code to take advantage of the new charting features, that code will not be backward compatible with Excel 2003.

The following are some of the new methods and features available in Excel 2007:

- **ApplyLayout**—This method applies one of the chart layouts available on the Design ribbon.

- **SetElement**—This method chooses any of the built-in element choices from the Layout ribbon.

- **ChartFormat**—This object allows you to change the fill, glow, line, reflection, shadow, soft edge, or 3-D format of most individual chart elements. This is similar to settings on the Format ribbon.

- **AddChart**—This method allows you to add a chart to an existing worksheet.

Referencing Charts and Chart Objects in VBA Code

If you go back far enough in Excel history, you find that all charts used to be created as their own chart sheets. Then, in the mid-1990s, Excel added the amazing capability to embed a chart right onto an existing worksheet. This allowed a report to be created with tables of numbers and charts all on the same page, something we take for granted today.

These two different ways of dealing with charts have made it necessary for us to deal with two separate object models for charts. When a chart is on its own standalone chart sheet, you are dealing with a Chart object. When a chart is embedded in a worksheet, you are dealing with a ChartObject object. Excel 2007 introduces a third evolutionary branch because objects on a worksheet are also a member of the Shapes collection.

In Excel 2003, to reference the color of the chart area for an embedded chart, you would have to refer to the chart in this manner:

```
Worksheets("Jan").ChartObjects("Chart 1").Chart.ChartArea.Interior.ColorIndex = 4
```

In Excel 2007, you can instead use the Shapes collection:

```
Worksheets("Jan").Shapes("Chart 1").Chart.ChartArea.Interior.ColorIndex = 4
```

13

In any version of Excel, if a chart is on its own chart sheet, you don't have to specify the container; you can simply refer to the Chart object:

```
Sheets("Chart1").ChartArea.Interior.ColorIndex = 4
```

Creating a Chart

In previous versions of Excel, you used the Charts.Add command to add a new chart. You then specified the source data, the type of chart, and whether the chart should be on a new sheet or embedded on an existing worksheet. The first three lines of the following code create a clustered column chart on a new chart sheet. The fourth line moves the chart back to be an embedded object in Sheet1:

```
Charts.Add
ActiveChart.SetSourceData Source:=Worksheets("Sheet1").Range("A1:E4")
ActiveChart.ChartType = xlColumnClustered
ActiveChart.Location Where:=xlLocationAsObject, Name:="Sheet1"
```

If you plan on sharing your macros with people who still use Excel 2003, you should use the Charts.Add method. However, if your application will only be running in Excel 2007, you can use the new AddChart method. The code for the AddChart method can be as simple as the following:

```
' Create chart on the current sheet
ActiveSheet.Shapes.AddChart.Select
ActiveChart.SetSourceData Source:=Range("A1:E4")
ActiveChart.ChartType = xlColumnClustered
```

Or you can specify the chart type, size, and location as part of the AddChart method, as described in the next section.

Specifying the Size and Location of a Chart

The AddChart method has additional parameters you can use to specify the type of chart, the chart's location on the worksheet, and the size of the chart.

The location and size of a chart are specified in points (72 points = 1 inch). For example, the Top parameter requires the number of points from the top of row 1 to the top edge of the worksheet.

The following code creates a chart that roughly covers the range C11:J30:

```
Sub SpecifyLocation()
    Dim WS As Worksheet
    Set WS = Worksheets("Sheet1")
    WS.Shapes.AddChart(xlColumnClustered, _
        Left:=100, Top:=150, _
        Width:=400, Height:=300).Select
    ActiveChart.SetSourceData Source:=WS.Range("A1:E4")
End Sub
```

It would require a lot of trial and error to randomly figure out the exact distance in points to cause a chart to line up with a certain cell. Luckily, you can ask VBA to tell you the distance in points to a certain cell. If you ask for the Left property of any cell, you find the distance to the top-left corner of that cell. You can also ask for the width of a range or the height of a range. For example, the following code creates a chart in exactly C11:J30:

```
Sub SpecifyExactLocation()
    Dim WS As Worksheet
    Set WS = Worksheets("Sheet1")
    WS.Shapes.AddChart(xlColumnClustered, _
        Left:=WS.Range("C11").Left, _
        Top:=WS.Range("C11").Top, _
        Width:=WS.Range("C11:J11").Width, _
        Height:=WS.Range("C11:C30").Height _
        ).Select
    ActiveChart.SetSourceData Source:=WS.Range("A1:E4")
End Sub
```

In this case, you are not moving the location of the Chart object; rather, you are moving the location of the container that contains the chart. In Excel 2007, it is either the ChartObject or the Shape object. If you try to change the actual location of the chart, you move it within the container. Because you can actually move the chart area a few points in either direction inside the container, the code will run, but you will not get the desired results.

To move a chart that has already been created, you can reference either ChartObject or the Shape and change the Top, Left, Width, and Height properties as shown in the following macro:

```
Sub MoveAfterTheFact()
    Dim WS As Worksheet
    Set WS = Worksheets("Sheet1")
    With WS.ChartObjects("Chart 9")
        .Left = WS.Range("C21").Left
        .Top = WS.Range("C21").Top
        .Width = WS.Range("C1:H1").Width
        .Height = WS.Range("C21:C25").Height
    End With
    End Sub
```

Later Referring to a Specific Chart

When a new chart is created, it is given a sequential name, such as Chart 1. If you select a chart and then look in the name box, you see the name of the chart. In Figure 13.4, the name of the chart is Chart 16. This does not mean that there are 16 charts on the worksheet. In this particular case, many individual charts have been created and deleted.

13

Figure 13.4
You can select a chart and look in the name box to find the name of the chart.

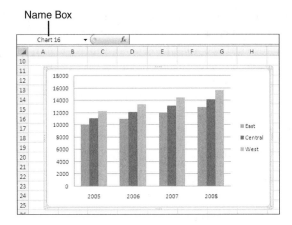

Name Box

This means that on any given day that your macro runs, the `Chart` object might have a different name. If you need to reference the chart later in the macro, perhaps after you have selected other cells and the chart is no longer active, you might ask VBA for the name of the chart and store it in a variable for later use, as shown here:

```
Sub RememberTheName()
    Dim WS As Worksheet
    Set WS = Worksheets("Sheet1")
    WS.Shapes.AddChart(xlColumnClustered, _
        Left:=WS.Range("C11").Left, _
        Top:=WS.Range("C11").Top, _
        Width:=WS.Range("C11:J11").Width, _
        Height:=WS.Range("C11:C30").Height _
        ).Select
    ActiveChart.SetSourceData Source:=WS.Range("A1:E4")
    ' Remember the name in a variable
    ThisChartObjectName = ActiveChart.Parent.Name
    ' more lines of code...
    ' then later in the macro, you need to re-assign the chart
    With WS.Shapes(ThisChartObjectName)
        .Chart.SetSourceData Source:=WS.Range("A20:E24"), PlotBy:=xlColumns
        .Top = WS.Range("C26").Top
    End With
End Sub
```

In the preceding macro, the variable `ThisChartObjectName` contains the name of the chart object. This method works great if your changes will happen later in the same macro. However, after the macro finishes running, the variable will be out of scope, and you won't be able to access the name later.

If you want to be able to remember a chart name, you could store the name in an out-of-the-way cell on the worksheet. The first macro here stores the name in cell Z1, and the second macro then later modifies the chart using the name stored in cell Z1:

```
Sub StoreTheName()
    Dim WS As Worksheet
    Set WS = Worksheets("Sheet1")
    WS.Shapes.AddChart(xlColumnClustered, _
```

```
        Left:=WS.Range("C11").Left, _
        Top:=WS.Range("C11").Top, _
        Width:=WS.Range("C11:J11").Width, _
        Height:=WS.Range("C11:C30").Height _
        ).Select
    ActiveChart.SetSourceData Source:=WS.Range("A1:E4")
    Range("Z1").Value = ActiveChart.Parent.Name
End Sub
```

After the previous macro stored the name in cell Z1, the following macro will use the value in Z1 to figure out which macro to change:

```
Sub ChangeTheChartLater()
    Dim WS As Worksheet
    Set WS = Worksheets("Sheet1")
    MyName = WS.Range("Z1").Value
    With WS.Shapes(MyName)
        .Chart.SetSourceData Source:=WS.Range("A20:E24"), PlotBy:=xlColumns
        .Top = WS.Range("C26").Top
    End With

End Sub
```

If you need to modify a preexisting chart—such as a chart that you did not create—and there is only one chart on the worksheet, you can use this line of code:

```
WS.ChartObjects(1).Chart.Interior.ColorIndex = 4
```

If there are many charts and you need to find the one with the upper-left corner located in cell A4, you could loop through all the chart objects until you find one in the correct location, like this:

```
For each Cht in ActiveSheet.ChartObjects
    If Cht.TopLeftCell.Address = "$A$4" then
        Cht.Interior.ColorIndex = 4
    end if
Next Cht
```

Recording Commands from the Layout or Design Ribbons

With charts in Excel 2007, there are three levels of chart changes. The global chart settings—chart type and style—are on the Design ribbon. Selections from the built-in element settings appear on the Layout ribbon. You make micro-changes by using the Format ribbon.

The macro recorder in Excel 2007 does a great job of recording changes on the Design and Layout ribbon, so if you need to make certain changes, you can quickly record a macro and then copy its code.

Specifying a Built-in Chart Type

There are 73 built-in chart types in Excel 2007. To change a chart to one of the 73 types, you use the ChartType property. This property can either be applied to a chart or to a series within a chart. Here's an example that changes the type for the entire chart:

```
ActiveChart.ChartType = xlBubble
```

To change the second series on a chart to a line chart, you use this:

```
ActiveChart.Series(2).ChartType = xlLine
```

Table 13.1 lists the 73 chart type constants that you can use to create various charts. The sequence of Table 13.1 matches the sequence of the charts in the Chart Type dialog.

Table 13.1   Chart Types for Use in VBA

	Chart Type	Constant		Chart Type	Constant
	Clustered Column	xlColumnClustered		3-D Cone	xlConeCol
	Stacked Column	xlColumnStacked		Clustered Pyramid	xlPyramid ColClustered
	100% Stacked Column	xlColumnStacked100		Stacked Pyramid	xlPyramid ColStacked
	3-D Clustered Column	xl3DColumnClustered		100% Stacked Pyramid	xlPyramidCol Stacked100
	Stacked Column in 3-D	xl3DColumnStacked		3-D Pyramid	xlPyramidCol
	100% Stacked Column in 3-D	xl3DColumn Stacked100		Line	xlLine
	3-D Column	xl3DColumn		Stacked Line	xlLineStacked
	Clustered Cylinder	xlCylinder ColClustered		100% Stacked Line	xlLineStacked100
	Stacked Cylinder	xlCylinder ColStacked		Line with Markers	xlLineMarkers
	100% Stacked Cylinder	xlCylinder ColStacked100		Stacked Line with Markers	xlLineMarkers Stacked
	3-D Cylinder	xlCylinderCol		100% Stacked Line with Markers	xlLineMarkers Stacked100
	Clustered Cone	xlCone ColClustered		3-D Line	xl3DLine
	Stacked Cone	xlConeColStacked		Pie	xlPie
	100% Stacked Cone	xlConeCol Stacked100		Pie in 3-D	xl3DPie

	Chart Type	Constant		Chart Type	Constant
	Pie of Pie	`xlPieOfPie`		100% Stacked Horizontal Cone	`xlConeBarStacked100`
	Exploded Pie	`xlPieExploded`		Clustered Horizontal Pyramid	`xlPyramidBarClustered`
	Exploded Pie in 3-D	`xl3DPieExploded`		Stacked Horizontal Pyramid	`xlPyramidBarStacked`
	Bar of Pie	`xlBarOfPie`		100% Stacked Horizontal Pyramid	`xlPyramidBar Stacked100`
	Clustered Bar	`xlBarClustered`		Area	`xlArea`
	Stacked Bar	`xlBarStacked`		Stacked Area	`xlAreaStacked`
	100% Stacked Bar	`xlBarStacked100`		100% Stacked Area	`xlAreaStacked100`
	Clustered Bar in 3-D	`xl3DBarClustered`		3-D Area	`xl3DArea`
	Stacked Bar in 3-D	`xl3DBarStacked`		Stacked Area in 3-D	`xl3DAreaStacked`
	100% Stacked Bar in 3-D	`xl3DBarStacked100`		100% Stacked Area in 3-D	`xl3DAreaStacked100`
	Clustered Horizontal Cylinder	`xlCylinderBar Clustered`		Scatter with Only Markers	`xlXYScatter`
	Stacked Horizontal Cylinder	`xlCylinderBar Stacked`		Scatter with Smooth Lines and Markers	`xlXYScatterSmooth`
	100% Stacked Horizontal Cylinder	`xlCylinderBar Stacked100`		Scatter with Smooth Lines	`xlXYScatter SmoothNoMarkers`
	Clustered Horizontal Cone	`xlConeBar Clustered`		Scatter with Straight Lines and Markers	`xlXYScatterLines`
	Stacked Horizontal Cone	`xlConeBarStacked`			

continues

Table 13.1 continued

	Chart Type	Constant		Chart Type	Constant
	Scatter with Straight Lines	xlXYScatter LinesNoMarkers		Wireframe Contour	xlSurfaceTopView Wireframe
	High-Low-Close	xlStockHLC		Doughnut	xlDoughnut
	Open-High-Low-Close	xlStockOHLC		Exploded Doughnut	xlDoughnutExploded
	Volume-High-Low-Close	xlStockVHLC		Bubble	xlBubble
	Volume-Open-High-Low-Close	xlStockVOHLC		Bubble with a 3-D Effect	xlBubble3DEffect
	3-D Surface	xlSurface		Radar	xlRadar
	Wireframe 3-D Surface	xlSurfaceWireframe		Radar with Markers	xlRadarMarkers
	Contour	xlSurfaceTopView		Filled Radar	xlRadarFilled

Specifying a Template Chart Type

In "Creating a Chart Template" in Chapter 2, you learned how to create a custom chart template. This is a great technique for saving time when you are creating a chart with a lot of custom formatting.

A VBA macro can make use of a custom chart template, provided that you plan on distributing the custom chart template to each person who will run your macro.

In Excel 2007, you save custom chart types as .crtx files and stored them in the %appdata%\Microsoft\Templates\Charts\ folder.

To apply a custom chart type, you use the following:

```
ActiveChart.ApplyChartTemplate ("MyChart.crtx")
```

If the chart template does not exist, VBA returns an error. If you would like Excel to simply continue without displaying a debug error, you can turn on an error handler before the code and turn it back on when you are done. Here's how you do that:

```
On Error Resume Next
ActiveChart.ApplyChartTemplate ("MyChart.crtx")
On Error GoTo 0 ' that final character is a zero
```

Changing a Chart's Layout or Style

Two galleries—the Chart Layout gallery and the Styles gallery—make up the bulk of the Design ribbon.

The Chart Layout gallery offers from 4 to 12 combinations of chart elements. These combinations are different for various chart types. When you look at the gallery shown in Figure 13.5, the ToolTips for the layouts show that the layouts are imaginatively named Layout 1 through Layout 11.

Figure 13.5
The built-in layouts for column charts are numbered 1 through 11. For other chart types, you might have 4 to 12 layouts

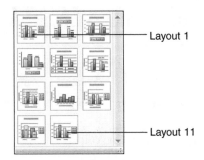

Layout 1

Layout 11

In order to apply one of the built-in layouts in a macro, you have to use the `ApplyLayout` method with a number from 1 through 12 to correspond to the built-in layouts. The following code will apply Layout 1 to the active chart:

```
ActiveChart.ApplyLayout 1
```

> **CAUTION**
>
> While line charts offer 12 built-in layouts, other types such as radar charts offer as few as four built-in layouts. If you attempt to specify apply a layout number that is larger than the layouts available for the current chart type, Excel will return a runtime error 5. Unless you just created the active chart in the same macro, there is always the possibility that the person running the macro changed your line charts to radar charts, so include some error handling before you use the `ApplyLayout` command.

Clearly, in order to effectively use a built-in layout, you must have actually built a chart by hand and found a layout that you actually like.

As shown in Figure 13.6, the Styles gallery contains 48 styles. These layouts are also numbered sequentially, with Styles 1 through 8 in row 1, Styles 9 through 16 in row 2, and so on. These styles actually follow a bit of a pattern:

13

Figure 13.6
The built-in styles are numbered 1 through 48.

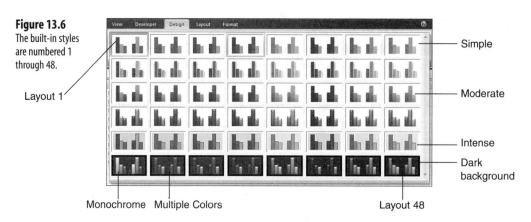

- Styles 1, 9, 17, 25, 33, and 41 (that is, the styles in column 1) are monochrome.
- Styles 2, 10, 18, 26, 34, and 42 (that is, the styles in column 2) use different colors for each point.
- All the other styles use hues of a particular theme color.
- Styles 1 through 8 use simple effects.
- Styles 9 through 17 use moderate effects.
- Styles 33 through 40 use intense effects.
- Styles 41 through 48 appear on a dark background.

If you are going to mix styles in a single workbook, you should consider staying within a single row or a single column of the gallery.

To apply a style to a chart, you use the ChartStyle property, assigning it a value from 1 to 48:

```
ActiveChart.ChartStyle = 1
```

The ChartStyle property changes the colors in the chart. However, a number of formatting changes from the Format ribbon do not get overwritten when you change the ChartStyle property. For example, in Figure 13.7, the second series previously had a glow applied and the third series had a clear glass bevel applied. Running the preceding code did not clear that formatting.

Figure 13.7
Setting the ChartStyle property does not override all settings.

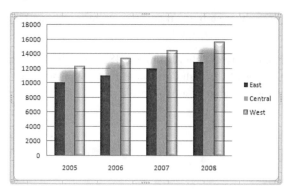

To clear any previous formatting, you use the `ClearToMatchStyle` method:

```
ActiveChart.ChartStyle = 1
ActiveChart.ClearToMatchStyle
```

Using `SetElement` to Emulate Changes on the Layout Ribbon

As discussed in Chapter 2, "Customizing Charts," the Layout ribbon contains a number of built-in settings. Figure 13.8 shows a few of the built-in menu items for the Legend tab. There are similar menus for each of the icons in the figure.

Figure 13.8
There are built-in menus similar to this one for each icon. If your choice is in the menu, the VBA code uses the `SetElement` method.

If you use a built-in menu item to change the titles, legend, labels, axes, gridlines, or background, it is probably handled in code that uses the `SetElement` method, which is new in Excel 2007.

`SetElement` does not work with the More choices at the bottom of each menu. It also does not work with the 3-D Rotation button. Other than that, you can use `SetElement` to change everything in the Labels, Axes, Background, and Analysis groups.

The macro recorder always works for the built-in settings on the Layout ribbon. If you don't feel like looking up the proper constant in this book, you can always quickly record a macro.

The `SetElement` method is followed by a constant that specifies which menu item to select. For example, if you want to choose Show Legend at Left, you can use this code:

```
ActiveChart.SetElement msoElementLegendLeft
```

Table 13.2 shows all the available constants that you can use with the `SetElement` method. These are in roughly the same order as they appear on the Layout ribbon.

13

Table 13.2   Constants Available with SetElement

Layout Ribbon Icon	Chart Element Constant
Chart Title	msoElementChartTitleNone
Chart Title	msoElementChartTitleCenteredOverlay
Chart Title	msoElementChartTitleAboveChart
Axis Titles	msoElementPrimaryCategoryAxisTitleNone
Axis Titles	msoElementPrimaryCategoryAxisTitleBelowAxis
Axis Titles	msoElementPrimaryCategoryAxisTitleAdjacentToAxis
Axis Titles	msoElementPrimaryCategoryAxisTitleHorizontal
Axis Titles	msoElementPrimaryCategoryAxisTitleVertical
Axis Titles	msoElementPrimaryCategoryAxisTitleRotated
Axis Titles	msoElementSecondaryCategoryAxisTitleAdjacentToAxis
Axis Titles	msoElementSecondaryCategoryAxisTitleBelowAxis
Axis Titles	msoElementSecondaryCategoryAxisTitleHorizontal
Axis Titles	msoElementSecondaryCategoryAxisTitleNone
Axis Titles	msoElementSecondaryCategoryAxisTitleRotated
Axis Titles	msoElementSecondaryCategoryAxisTitleVertical
Axis Titles	msoElementPrimaryValueAxisTitleAdjacentToAxis
Axis Titles	msoElementPrimaryValueAxisTitleBelowAxis
Axis Titles	msoElementPrimaryValueAxisTitleHorizontal
Axis Titles	msoElementPrimaryValueAxisTitleNone
Axis Titles	msoElementPrimaryValueAxisTitleRotated
Axis Titles	msoElementPrimaryValueAxisTitleVertical
Axis Titles	msoElementSecondaryValueAxisTitleBelowAxis
Axis Titles	msoElementSecondaryValueAxisTitleHorizontal
Axis Titles	msoElementSecondaryValueAxisTitleNone
Axis Titles	msoElementSecondaryValueAxisTitleRotated
Axis Titles	msoElementSecondaryValueAxisTitleVertical
Axis Titles	msoElementSeriesAxisTitleHorizontaI
Axis Titles	msoElementSeriesAxisTitleNone
Axis Titles	msoElementSeriesAxisTitleRotated
Axis Titles	msoElementSeriesAxisTitleVertical
Axis Titles	msoElementSecondaryValueAxisTitleAdjacentToAxis

13

Layout Ribbon Icon	Chart Element Constant
Legend	msoElementLegendNone
Legend	msoElementLegendRight
Legend	msoElementLegendTop
Legend	msoElementLegendLeft
Legend	msoElementLegendBottom
Legend	msoElementLegendRightOverlay
Legend	msoElementLegendLeftOverlay
Data Labels	msoElementDataLabelCenter
Data Labels	msoElementDataLabelInsideEnd
Data Labels	msoElementDataLabelNone
Data Labels	msoElementDataLabelInsideBase
Data Labels	msoElementDataLabelOutSideEnd
Data Labels	msoElementDataLabelTop
Data Labels	msoElementDataLabelBottom
Data Labels	msoElementDataLabelRight
Data Labels	msoElementDataLabelLeft
Data Labels	msoElementDataLabelShow
Data Labels	msoElementDataLabelBestFit
Data Labels	msoElementDataTableNone
Data Labels	msoElementDataTableShow
Data Labels	msoElementDataTableWithLegendKeys
Axis	msoElementPrimaryCategoryAxisNone
Axis	msoElementPrimaryCategoryAxisShow
Axis	msoElementPrimaryCategoryAxisWithoutLabels
Axis	msoElementPrimaryCategoryAxisReverse
Axis	msoElementPrimaryCategoryAxisThousands
Axis	msoElementPrimaryCategoryAxisMillions
Axis	msoElementPrimaryCategoryAxisBillions
Axis	msoElementPrimaryCategoryAxisLogScale
Axis	msoElementSecondaryCategoryAxisNone
Axis	msoElementSecondaryCategoryAxisShow
Axis	msoElementSecondaryCategoryAxisWithoutLabels

13

continues

Table 13.2   continued

Layout Ribbon Icon	Chart Element Constant
Axis	`msoElementSecondaryCategoryAxisReverse`
Axis	`msoElementSecondaryCategoryAxisThousands`
Axis	`msoElementSecondaryCategoryAxisMillions`
Axis	`msoElementSecondaryCategoryAxisBillions`
Axis	`msoElementSecondaryCategoryAxisLogScale`
Axis	`msoElementPrimaryValueAxisNone`
Axis	`msoElementPrimaryValueAxisShow`
Axis	`msoElementPrimaryValueAxisThousands`
Axis	`msoElementPrimaryValueAxisMillions`
Axis	`msoElementPrimaryValueAxisBillions`
Axis	`msoElementPrimaryValueAxisLogScale`
Axis	`msoElementSecondaryValueAxisNone`
Axis	`msoElementSecondaryValueAxisShow`
Axis	`msoElementSecondaryValueAxisThousands`
Axis	`msoElementSecondaryValueAxisMillions`
Axis	`msoElementSecondaryValueAxisBillions`
Axis	`msoElementSecondaryValueAxisLogScale`
Axis	`msoElementSeriesAxisNone`
Axis	`msoElementSeriesAxisShow`
Axis	`msoElementSeriesAxisReverse`
Axis	`msoElementSeriesAxisWithoutLabeling`
GridLines	`msoElementPrimaryCategoryGridLinesNone`
GridLines	`msoElementPrimaryCategoryGridLinesMajor`
GridLines	`msoElementPrimaryCategoryGridLinesMinor`
GridLines	`msoElementPrimaryCategoryGridLinesMinorMajor`
GridLines	`msoElementSecondaryCategoryGridLinesNone`
GridLines	`msoElementSecondaryCategoryGridLinesMajor`
GridLines	`msoElementSecondaryCategoryGridLinesMinor`
GridLines	`msoElementSecondaryCategoryGridLinesMinorMajor`
GridLines	`msoElementPrimaryValueGridLinesNone`
GridLines	`msoElementPrimaryValueGridLinesMajor`

13

Layout Ribbon Icon	Chart Element Constant
GridLines	msoElementPrimaryValueGridLinesMinor
GridLines	msoElementPrimaryValueGridLinesMinorMajor
GridLines	msoElementSecondaryValueGridLinesNone
GridLines	msoElementSecondaryValueGridLinesMajor
GridLines	msoElementSecondaryValueGridLinesMinor
GridLines	msoElementSecondaryValueGridLinesMinorMajor
GridLines	msoElementSeriesAxisGridLinesNone
GridLines	msoElementSeriesAxisGridLinesMajor
GridLines	msoElementSeriesAxisGridLinesMinor
GridLines	msoElementSeriesAxisGridLinesMinorMajor
Plot Area	msoElementPlotAreaNone
Plot Area	msoElementPlotAreaShow
Chart Wall	msoElementChartWallNone
Chart Wall	msoElementChartWallShow
Chart Floor	msoElementChartFloorNone
Chart Floor	msoElementChartFloorShow
Trendline	msoElementTrendlineNone
Trendline	msoElementTrendlineAddLinear
Trendline	msoElementTrendlineAddExponential
Trendline	msoElementTrendlineAddLinearForecast
Trendline	msoElementTrendlineAddTwoPeriodMovingAverage
Lines	msoElementLineNone
Lines	msoElementLineDropLine
Lines	msoElementLineHiLoLine
Lines	msoElementLineDropHiLoLine
Lines	msoElementLineSeriesLine
Up/Down Bars	msoElementUpDownBarsNone
Up/Down Bars	msoElementUpDownBarsShow
Error Bar	msoElementErrorBarNone
Error Bar	msoElementErrorBarStandardError
Error Bar	msoElementErrorBarPercentage
Error Bar	msoElementErrorBarStandardDeviation

13

> **CAUTION**
>
> If you attempt to format an element that is not present, Excel returns a -2147467259 Method Failed error.

Changing a Chart Title Using VBA

The Layout ribbon's built-in menus let you add a title above a chart, but they don't offer you the ability to change the characters in a chart title or axis title

In the user interface, you can simply double-click the chart title text and type a new title to change the title. Unfortunately, the macro recorder does not record this action.

To specify a chart title, you must type this code:

```
ActiveChart.ChartTitle.Caption = "My Chart"
```

Similarly, you can specify the axis titles by using the `Caption` property. The following code will change the axis title along the category axis:

```
ActiveChart.Axes(xlCategory, xlPrimary).AxisTitle.Caption = "Months"
```

Emulating Changes on the Format Ribbon

In Excel 2007, the macro recorder does not record any actions that happen in the Format ribbon or in the More dialog boxes on the Layout ribbon. This is incredibly frustrating. It is particularly frustrating because Excel 2003 could record these changes with the macro recorder. One solution, if you still have Excel 2003 installed, is to format your chart in Excel 2003 while the macro recorder is on. You can then use that code in Excel 2007, although you then can't make use of all the new formatting features. For information on discovering charting elements without the assistance of the macro recorder, see "Using the Watch Window to Discover Object Settings," later in this chapter.

Using the `Format` Method to Access New Formatting Options

Excel 2007 introduces a new object called the `ChartFormat` object. This object contains the settings for `Fill`, `Glow`, `Line`, `PictureFormat`, `Shadow`, `SoftEdge`, `TextFrame2`, and `ThreeD`. You can access the `ChartFormat` object by using the `Format` method on many chart elements. Table 13.3 lists a sampling of chart elements that can be formatted using the `Format` method.

The `Format` method is the gateway to settings for `Fill`, `Glow`, and so on. Each of those objects has different options. The following sections give examples of how to set up each type of format.

Chart Element	VBA to Refer to This Chart Element

Table 13.3 Chart Elements to Which Formatting Applies

Chart Element	VBA to Refer to This Chart Element
Chart Title	ChartTitle
Axis Title - Category	Axes(xlCategory, xlPrimary).AxisTitle
Axis Title - Value	Axes(xlValue, xlPrimary).AxisTitle
Legend	Legend
Data Labels for Series 1	SeriesCollection(1).DataLabels
Data Labels for Point 2	SeriesCollection(1).DataLabel(2), or SeriesCollection(1).Points(2).DataLabels
Data Table	DataTable
Axes - Horizontal	Axes(xlCategory, xlPrimary)
Axes - Vertical	Axes(xlValue, xlPrimary)
Axis - Series (Surface Charts Only)	Axes(xlSeries, xlPrimary)
Major Gridlines	Axes(xlValue, xlPrimary).MajorGridlines
Minor Gridlines	Axes(xlValue, xlPrimary).MinorGridlines
Plot Area	PlotArea
Chart Area	ChartArea
Chart Wall	Walls
Chart Back Wall	BackWall
Chart Side Wall	SideWall
Chart Floor	Floor
Trendline for Series 1	SeriesCollection(1).TrendLines(1)
Droplines	ChartGroups(1).DropLines
Up/Down Bars	ChartGroups(1).UpBars
Error Bars	SeriesCollection(1).ErrorBars
Series(1)	SeriesCollection(1)
Series(1) DataPoint	SeriesCollection(1).Points(3)

Changing an Object's Fill

As shown in Figure 13.9, the Shape Fill drop-down on the Format ribbon allows you to choose a single color, a gradient, a picture, or a texture for the fill.

13

Figure 13.9

Fill options include a solid color, a gradient, a texture, or a picture.

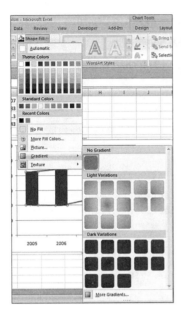

To apply a specific color, you can use the RGB (red, green, blue) setting. To create a color, you specify a value from 0 to 255 for levels of red, green, and blue. The following code applies a simple blue fill:

```
Dim cht As Chart
Dim upb As UpBars
Set cht = ActiveChart
Set upb = cht.ChartGroups(1).UpBars
upb.Format.Fill.ForeColor.RGB = RGB(0, 0, 255)
```

If you would like an object to pick up the color from a specific theme accent color, you use the ObjectThemeColor property. The following code changes the bar color of the first series to accent color 6 (which is an orange color in the Office theme but might be another color if the workbook is using a different theme):

```
Sub ApplyThemeColor()
    Dim cht As Chart
    Dim ser As Series
    Set cht = ActiveChart
    Set ser = cht.SeriesCollection(1)
    ser.Format.Fill.ForeColor.ObjectThemeColor = msoThemeColorAccent6
End Sub
```

To apply a built-in texture, you use the PresetTextured method. The following code applies a green marble texture to the second series, but there are 20 different textures that can be applied:

```
Sub ApplyTexture()
    Dim cht As Chart
    Dim ser As Series
    Set cht = ActiveChart
```

```
    Set ser = cht.SeriesCollection(2)
    ser.Format.Fill.PresetTextured (msoTextureGreenMarble)
End Sub
```

> **TIP** When you type `PresetTextured` followed by an open parenthesis, the VBA editor offers a complete list of possible texture values.

To fill the bars of a data series with a picture, you use the `UserPicture` method and specify the path and filename of an image on the computer, as in the following example:

```
Sub FormatWithPicture()
    Dim cht As Chart
    Dim ser As Series
    Set cht = ActiveChart
    Set ser = cht.SeriesCollection(1)
    MyPic = "C:\PodCastTitle1.jpg"
    ser.Format.Fill.UserPicture (MyPic)
End Sub
```

Gradients are more difficult to specify than fills. Excel 2007 offers three methods that help you set up the common gradients. The `OneColorGradient` and `TwoColorGradient` methods require that you specify a gradient direction such as `msoGradientFromCorner`. You can then specify one of four styles, numbered 1 through 4, depending on whether you want the gradient to start at the top left, top right, bottom left, or bottom right. After using a gradient method, you need to specify the `ForeColor` and the `BackColor` settings for the object. The following macro sets up a two-color gradient using two theme colors:

```
Sub TwoColorGradient()
    Dim cht As Chart
    Dim ser As Series
    Set cht = ActiveChart
    Set ser = cht.SeriesCollection(1)
    MyPic = "C:\PodCastTitle1.jpg"
    ser.Format.Fill.TwoColorGradient msoGradientFromCorner, 3
    ser.Format.Fill.ForeColor.ObjectThemeColor = msoThemeColorAccent6
    ser.Format.Fill.BackColor.ObjectThemeColor = msoThemeColorAccent2
End Sub
```

When using the `OneColorGradient` method, you specify a direction, a style (1 through 4), and a darkness value between 0 and 1 (0 for darker gradients or 1 for lighter gradients).

When using the `PresetGradient` method, you specify a direction, a style (1 through 4), and the type of gradient (for example, `msoGradientBrass`, `msoGradientLateSunset`, or `msoGradientRainbow`). Again, as you are typing this code in the VBA editor, the AutoComplete tool provides a complete list of the available preset gradient types.

Formatting Line Settings

The `LineFormat` object formats either a line or the border around an object. You can change numerous properties for a line, such as the color, arrows, dash style, and so on.

13

The following macro formats the trendline for the first series in a chart:

```
Sub FormatLineOrBorders()
    Dim cht As Chart
    Set cht = ActiveChart
    With cht.SeriesCollection(1).Trendlines(1).Format.Line
        .DashStyle = msoLineLongDashDotDot
        .ForeColor.RGB = RGB(50, 0, 128)
        .BeginArrowheadLength = msoArrowheadShort
        .BeginArrowheadStyle = msoArrowheadOval
        .BeginArrowheadWidth = msoArrowheadNarrow
        .EndArrowheadLength = msoArrowheadLong
        .EndArrowheadStyle = msoArrowheadTriangle
        .EndArrowheadWidth = msoArrowheadWide
    End With
End Sub
```

When you are formatting a border, the arrow settings are not relevant, so the code is shorter than the code for formatting a line. The following macro formats the border around a chart:

```
Sub FormatBorder()
    Dim cht As Chart
    Set cht = ActiveChart
    With cht.ChartArea.Format.Line
        .DashStyle = msoLineLongDashDotDot
        .ForeColor.RGB = RGB(50, 0, 128)
    End With
End Sub
```

Formatting Glow Settings

To create a glow, you have to specify a color and a radius. The radius value can be from 1 to 20. A radius of 1 is barely visible, and a radius of 20 is often way too thick.

> **NOTE** A glow is actually applied to the shape outline. If you try to add a glow to an object where the outline is set to None, you cannot see the glow.

The following macro adds a line around the title and adds a glow around that line:

```
Sub AddGlowToTitle()
    Dim cht As Chart
    Set cht = ActiveChart
    cht.ChartTitle.Format.Line.ForeColor.RGB = RGB(255, 255, 255)
    cht.ChartTitle.Format.Line.DashStyle = msoLineSolid
    cht.ChartTitle.Format.Glow.Color.ObjectThemeColor = msoThemeColorAccent6
    cht.ChartTitle.Format.Glow.Radius = 8
End Sub
```

Formatting Shadow Settings

A shadow is composed of a color, a transparency, and the number of points by which the shadow should be offset from the object. If you increase the number of points, it appears that the object is farther from the surface of the chart. The horizontal offset is known as OffsetX, and the vertical offset is known as OffsetY.

The following macro adds a light blue shadow to the box surrounding a legend:

```
Sub FormatShadow()
    Dim cht As Chart
    Set cht = ActiveChart
    With cht.Legend.Format.Shadow
        .ForeColor.RGB = RGB(0, 0, 128)
        .OffsetX = 5
        .OffsetY = -3
        .Transparency = 0.5
        .Visible = True
    End With
End Sub
```

Formatting Reflection Settings

No chart elements can have reflections applied. The Reflection settings on the Format ribbon are constantly grayed out when a chart is selected. Similarly, the ChartFormat object does not have a reflection object.

Formatting Soft Edges

There are six levels of soft edge settings. The settings feather the edges by 1, 2.5, 5, 10, 25, or 50 points. The first setting is barely visible. The biggest settings are usually larger than most of the chart elements you are likely to format.

Microsoft says that the following is the proper syntax for SoftEdge:

```
Chart.Series(1).Points(i).Format.SoftEdge.Type = msoSoftEdgeType1
```

However, msoSoftEdgeType1 and words like it are really variables defined by Excel. To try a cool trick, go to the VBA editor and open the Immediate pane by pressing Ctrl+G. In the Immediate pane, type **Print msoSoftEdgeType2** and press Enter. The Immediate window tells you that using this word is equivalent to typing 2. So, you could either use msoSoftEdgeType2 or the value 2.

If you use msoSoftEdgeType2, your code will be slightly easier to understand than if you use simply 2. However, if you hope to format each point of a data series with a different format, you might want to use a loop such as this one, in which case it is far easier to use just the numbers 1 through 6 than msoSoftEdgeType1 through msoSoftEdgeType6 as shown in this macro:

```
Sub FormatSoftEdgesWithLoop()
    Dim cht As Chart
    Dim ser As Series
    Set cht = ActiveChart
    Set ser = cht.SeriesCollection(1)
    For i = 1 To 6
        ser.Points(i).Format.SoftEdge.Type = i
    Next i
End Sub
```

13

It is a bit strange that the soft edges are defined as a fixed number of points. In a chart that is sized to fit an entire sheet of paper, a 10-point soft edge might work fine. However, if you resize the chart so that you can fit six charts on a page, a 10-point soft edge applied to all sides of a column might make the column completely disappear.

Formatting 3-D Rotation Settings

The 3-D settings handle three different menus on the Format ribbon. In the Shape Effects drop-down, settings under Preset, Bevel, and 3-D are all actually handled by the ThreeD object in the ChartFormat object. This section discusses settings that affect the 3-D rotation. The next section discusses settings that affect the bevel and 3-D format.

The methods and properties that can be set for the ThreeD object are very broad. In fact, the 3-D settings in VBA include more preset options than do the menus on the Format ribbon.

Figure 13.10 shows the presets available in the 3-D Rotation fly-out menu.

Figure 13.10
Whereas the 3-D Rotation menu offers 25 presets, VBA offers 62 presets.

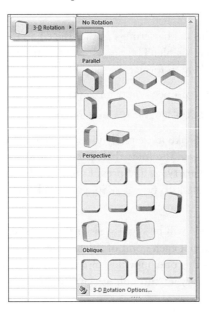

In order to apply one of the 3-D rotation presets to a chart element, you use the SetPresetCamera method, as shown here:

```
Sub Assign3DPreset()
    Dim cht As Chart
    Dim shp As Shape
    Set cht = ActiveChart
```

```
    Set shp = cht.Shapes(1)
    shp.ThreeD.SetPresetCamera msoCameraIsometricLeftDown
End Sub
```

Table 13.4 lists all the possible SetPresetCamera values. If the first column indicates that it is a bonus or an Excel 2003 style, the value is a preset that is available in VBA but was not chosen by Microsoft to be included in the 3-D Rotation fly-out menu.

Table 13.4   3-D Preset Formats and Their VBA Constant Values

Menu Location	Description	VBA Value
Parallel group, row 1, column 1	Isometric Left Down	`msoCameraIsometricLeftDown`
Parallel group, row 1, column 2	Isometric Right Up	`msoCameraIsometricRightUp`
Parallel group, row 1, column 3	Isometric Top Up	`msoCameraIsometricTopUp`
Parallel group, row 1, column 4	Isometric Bottom Down	`msoCameraIsometric BottomDown`
Parallel group, row 2, column 1	Isometric OffAxis1 Left	`msoCameraIsometric OffAxis1Left`
Parallel group, row 2, column 2	Isometric OffAxis1 Right	`msoCameraIsometric OffAxis1Right`
Parallel group, row 2, column 3	Isometric OffAxis1 Top	`msoCameraIsometric OffAxis1Top`
Parallel group, row 2, column 4	Isometric OffAxis2 Left	`msoCameraIsometric OffAxis2Left`
Parallel group, row 3, column 1	Isometric OffAxis2 Right	`msoCameraIsometric OffAxis2Right`
Parallel group, row 3, column 2	Isometric OffAxis2 Top	`msoCameraIsometric OffAxis2Top`
Parallel group, bonus selection	Isometric Bottom Up	`msoCameraIsometricBottomUp`
Parallel group, bonus selection	Isometric Left Up	`msoCameraIsometricLeftUp`
Parallel group, bonus selection	Isometric OffAxis3 Bottom	`msoCameraIsometric OffAxis3Bottom`
Parallel group, bonus selection	Isometric OffAxis3 Left	`msoCameraIsometric OffAxis3Left`
Parallel group, bonus selection	Isometric OffAxis3 Right	`msoCameraIsometric OffAxis3Right`
Parallel group, bonus selection	Isometric OffAxis4 Bottom	`msoCameraIsometric OffAxis4Bottom`
Parallel group, bonus selection	Isometric OffAxis4 Left	`msoCameraIsometric OffAxis4Left`

13

continues

Table 13.4   continued

Menu Location	Description	VBA Value
Parallel group, bonus selection	Isometric OffAxis4 Right	`msoCameraIsometric OffAxis4Right`
Parallel group, bonus selection	Isometric Right Down	`msoCameraIsometricRightDown`
Parallel group, bonus selection	Isometric Top Down	`msoCameraIsometricTopDown`
Perspective group, row 1, column 1	Perspective Front	`msoCameraPerspectiveFront`
Perspective group, row 1, column 2	Perspective Left	`msoCameraPerspectiveLeft`
Perspective group, row 1, column 3	Perspective Right	`msoCameraPerspectiveRight`
Perspective group, row 1, column 4	Perspective Below	`msoCameraPerspectiveBelow`
Perspective group, row 2, column 1	Perspective Above	`msoCameraPerspectiveAbove`
Perspective group, row 2, column 2	Perspective Relaxed Moderately	`msoCameraPerspective RelaxedModerately`
Perspective group, row 2, column 3	Perspective Relaxed	`msoCameraPerspectiveRelaxed`
Perspective group, row 2, column 4	Perspective Contrasting Left Facing	`msoCameraPerspective ContrastingLeftFacing`
Perspective group, row 3, column 1	Perspective Contrasting Right Facing	`msoCameraPerspective ContrastingRightFacing`
Perspective group, row 3, column 2	Perspective Heroic Extreme Left Facing	`msoCameraPerspective HeroicExtremeLeftFacing`
Perspective group, row 3, column 3	Perspective Heroic Extreme Right Facing	`msoCameraPerspective HeroicExtremeRightFacing`
Perspective group, bonus selection	Perspective Above Left Facing	`msoCameraPerspective AboveLeftFacing`
Perspective group, bonus selection	Perspective Above Right Facing	`msoCameraPerspective AboveRightFacing`
Perspective group, bonus selection	Perspective Heroic Left Facing	`msoCameraPerspective HeroicLeftFacing`
Perspective group, bonus selection	Perspective Heroic Right Facing	`msoCameraPerspective HeroicRightFacing`
Perspective group, Excel 2003 styles	Legacy Perspective Bottom	`msoCameraLegacy PerspectiveBottom`
Perspective group, Excel 2003 styles	Legacy Perspective Lower Left	`msoCameraLegacy PerspectiveBottomLeft`
Perspective group, Excel 2003 styles	Legacy Perspective Lower Right	`msoCameraLegacy PerspectiveBottomRight`

Menu Location	Description	VBA Value
Perspective group, Excel 2003 styles	Legacy Perspective Front	`msoCameraLegacy` `PerspectiveFront`
Perspective group, Excel 2003 styles	Legacy Perspective Left	`msoCameraLegacy` `PerspectiveLeft`
Perspective group, Excel 2003 styles	Legacy Perspective Right	`msoCameraLegacy` `PerspectiveRight`
Perspective group, Excel 2003 styles	Legacy Perspective Top	`msoCameraLegacy` `PerspectiveTop`
Perspective group, Excel 2003 styles	Legacy Perspective Upper Left	`msoCameraLegacy` `PerspectiveTopLeft`
Perspective group, Excel 2003 styles	Legacy Perspective Upper Right	`msoCameraLegacy` `PerspectiveTopRight`
Oblique group, row 1, column 1	Oblique Upper Left	`msoCameraObliqueTopLeft`
Oblique group, row 1, column 2	Oblique Upper Right	`msoCameraObliqueTopRight`
Oblique group, row 1, column 3	Oblique Lower Left	`msoCameraObliqueBottomLeft`
Oblique group, row 1, column 4	Oblique Lower Right	`msoCameraObliqueBottomRight`
Oblique group, bonus selection	Oblique Bottom	`msoCameraObliqueBottom`
Oblique group, bonus selection	Oblique Left	`msoCameraObliqueLeft`
Oblique group, bonus selection	Oblique Right	`msoCameraObliqueRight`
Oblique group, bonus selection	Oblique Top	`msoCameraObliqueTop`
Oblique group, bonus selection	Orthographic Front	`msoCameraOrthographicFront`
Oblique group, Excel 2003 styles	Legacy Oblique Bottom	`msoCameraLegacy` `ObliqueBottom`
Oblique group, Excel 2003 styles	Legacy Oblique Lower Left	`msoCameraLegacy` `ObliqueBottomLeft`
Oblique group, Excel 2003 styles	Legacy Oblique Lower Right	`msoCameraLegacy` `ObliqueBottomRight`
Oblique group, Excel 2003 styles	Legacy Oblique Front	`msoCameraLegacyObliqueFront`
Oblique group, Excel 2003 styles	Legacy Oblique Left	`msoCameraLegacyObliqueLeft`
Oblique group, Excel 2003 styles	Legacy Oblique Right	`msoCameraLegacyObliqueRight`
Oblique group, Excel 2003 styles	Legacy Oblique Top	`msoCameraLegacyObliqueTop`
Oblique group, Excel 2003 styles	Legacy Oblique Upper Left	`msoCameraLegacy` `ObliqueTopLeft`
Oblique group, Excel 2003 styles	Legacy Oblique Upper Right	`msoCameraLegacy` `ObliqueTopRight`

13

If you prefer not to use the presets, you can explicitly control the rotation around the x-, y-, or z-axis. You can use the following properties and methods to change the rotation of an object:

- `RotationX`—Returns or sets the rotation of the extruded shape around the x-axis, in degrees. This can be a value from `-90` through `90`. A positive value indicates upward rotation; a negative value indicates downward rotation.

- `RotationY`—Returns or sets the rotation of the extruded shape around the y-axis, in degrees. Can be a value from `-90` through `90`. A positive value indicates rotation to the left; a negative value indicates rotation to the right.

- `RotationZ`—Returns or sets the rotation of the extruded shape around the z-axis, in degrees. Can be a value from `-90` through `90`. A positive value indicates upward rotation; a negative value indicates downward rotation.

- `IncrementRotationX`—Changes the rotation of the specified shape around the x-axis by the specified number of degrees. You specify an increment from `-90` to `90`. Negative degrees tip the object down, and positive degrees tip the object up. (You can use the `RotationX` property to set the absolute rotation of the shape around the x-axis.)

- `IncrementRotationY`—Changes the rotation of the specified shape around the y-axis by the specified number of degrees. A positive value tilts the object left, and a negative value tips the object right. (You can use the `RotationY` property to set the absolute rotation of the shape around the y-axis.)

- `IncrementRotationZ`—Changes the rotation of the specified shape around the z-axis by the specified number of degrees. A positive value tilts the object left, and a negative value tips the object right. (You can use the `RotationZ` property to set the absolute rotation of the shape around the z-axis.)

- `IncrementRotationHorizontal`—Changes the rotation of the specified shape horizontally by the specified number of degrees. You specify an increment from `-90` to `90` to specify how much (in degrees) the rotation of the shape is to be changed horizontally. A positive value moves the shape left; a negative value moves it right.

- `IncrementRotationVertical`—Changes the rotation of the specified shape vertically by the specified number of degrees. You specify an increment from `-90` to `90` to specify how much (in degrees) the rotation of the shape is to be changed horizontally. A positive value moves the shape left; a negative value moves it right.

- `ResetRotation`—Resets the extrusion rotation around the x-axis and the y-axis to `0` so that the front of the extrusion faces forward. This method doesn't reset the rotation around the z-axis.

Changing the Bevel and 3-D Format

There are 12 presets in the Bevel fly-out menu. These presets affect the bevel on the top face of the object. Usually in charts you see the top face; however, there are some bizarre rotations of a 3-D chart where you see the bottom face of charting elements.

The Format Shape dialog contains the same 12 presets as the Bevel fly-out but allows you to apply the preset to the top or bottom face. You can also control the width and height of the bevel. The VBA properties and methods correspond to the settings on the 3-D Format category of the Format Shape dialog. (See Figure 13.11.)

Figure 13.11

You can control the 3-D Format settings, such as bevel, surface, and lighting.

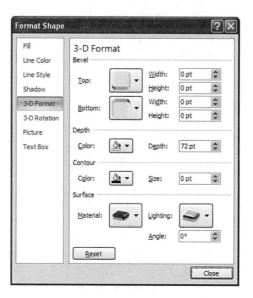

You set the type of bevel by using the `BevelTopType` and `BevelBottomType` properties. You can further modify the bevel type by setting the `BevelTopInset` value to set the width and the `BevelTopDepth` value to set the height. The following macro adds a bevel to the columns of Series 1:

```
Sub AssignBevel()
    Dim cht As Chart
    Dim ser As Series
    Set cht = ActiveChart
    Set ser = cht.SeriesCollection(1)
    ser.Format.ThreeD.Visible = True
    ser.Format.ThreeD.BevelTopType = msoBevelCircle
    ser.Format.ThreeD.BevelTopInset = 16
    ser.Format.ThreeD.BevelTopDepth = 6
End Sub
```

The 12 possible settings for the bevel type are shown in Table 13.5; these settings correspond to the thumbnails shown in Figure 13.12. To turn off the bevel, you use `msoBevelNone`.

Figure 13.12
Samples of the 12 bevel types listed in Table 13.5.

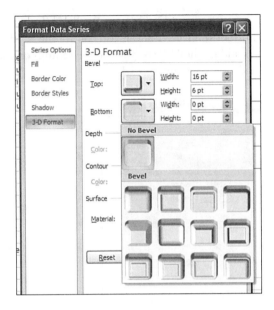

Table 13.5   Bevel Types

	Constant
	msoBevelCircle
	msoBevelRelaxedInset
	msoBevelCross
	msoBevelCoolSlant
	msoBevelAngle
	msoBevelSoftRound
	msoBevelConvex
	msoBevelSlope
	msoBevelDivot
	msoBevelRiblet
	msoBevelHardEdge
	msoBevelArtDeco

Usually, the accent color used in a bevel is based on the color used to fill the object. If you would like control over the extrusion color, however, you first specify that the extrusion color type is custom and then specify either a theme accent color or an RGB color, as in the following example:

```
ser.Format.ThreeD.ExtrusionColorType = msoExtrusionColorCustom
' either use this:
ser.Format.ThreeD.ExtrusionColor.ObjectThemeColor = msoThemeColorAccent1
' or this:
ser.Format.ThreeD.ExtrusionColor.RGB = RGB(255, 0, 0)
```

You use the Depth property to control the amount of extrusion in the bevel, and you specify the depth in points. Here's an example:

```
ser.Format.ThreeD.Depth = 5
```

For the contour, you can specify either a color and a size of the contour or both. You can specify the color as an RGB value or a theme color. You specify the size in points, using the ContourWidth property. Here's an example:

```
ser.Format.ThreeD.ContourColor.RGB = RGB(0, 255, 0)
ser.Format.ThreeD.ContourWidth = 10
```

The Surface drop-downs are controlled by the following properties:

- **PresetMaterial**—This contains choices from the Material drop-down.
- **PresetLighting**—This contains choices from the Lighting drop-down.
- **LightAngle**—This controls the angle from which the light is shining on the object.

Figure 13.13 shows the Material drop-down menu from the 3-D category of the Format dialog box. Although the drop-down offers 11 settings, it appears that Microsoft designed a 12th setting in the object model. It is not clear why Microsoft does not offer the SoftMetal style in the dialog box, but you can use it in VBA. There are also three legacy styles in the object model that are not available in the Format dialog box. In theory, the new Plastic2 material is better than the old Plastic material. The settings for each thumbnail are shown in Table 13.6.

Figure 13.13
Samples of the 11 material types shown in Table 13.6.

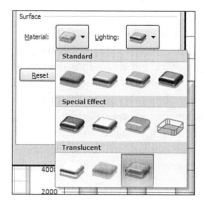

Table 13.6   VBA Constants for Material Types

	Type	VBA Constant	Value
	Matte	msoMaterialMatte2	5
	Warm Matte	msoMaterialWarmMatte	8
	Plastic	msoMaterialPlastic2	6
	Metal	msoMaterialMetal2	7
	Dark Edge	msoMaterialDarkEdge	11
	Soft Edge	msoMaterialSoftEdge	12
	Flat	msoMaterialFlat	14
	Wire Frame	msoMaterialWireFrame	4
	Powder	msoMaterialPowder	10
	Translucent Powder	msoMaterialTranslucentPowder	9
	Clear	msoMaterialClear	13
		msoMaterialMatte	1
		msoMaterialPlastic	2
		msoMaterialMetal	3
	Bonus	msoMaterialSoftMetal	15

In Excel 2003, the material property was limited to matte, metal, plastic, and wire frame. Microsoft apparently was not happy with the old matte, metal, and plastic settings. It left those values in place to support legacy charts but created the new Matte2, Plastic2, and Metal2 settings. These settings are actually available in the dialog box. In VBA, you are free to use either the old or the new settings. The columns in Figure 13.14 compare the new and old settings. The final column is for the SoftMetal setting that Microsoft left out of the Format dialog box. This was probably an aesthetic decision instead of an "oh no; this setting crashes the computer" decision. You can feel free to use msoMaterialSoftMetal to create a look that has a subtle difference from charts others create using the settings in the Format dialog box.

Figure 13.14
Comparison of some new
and old material presets.

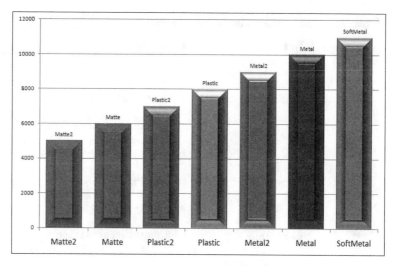

Figure 13.14
Comparison of some new
and old material presets.

Figure 13.15 shows the Lighting drop-down menu from the 3-D category of the Format dialog box. The drop-down offers 15 settings. The Object Model offers these 15 settings, plus 13 legacy settings from the Excel 2003 Lighting toolbar. The settings for each of these thumbnails are shown in Table 13.7.

Figure 13.15
Samples of the 15 light-
ing types shown in Table
13.7.

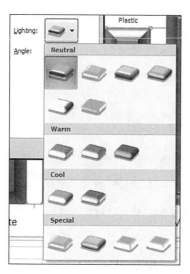

Table 13.7   VBA Constants for Lighting Types

	Type	VBA Constant	Value
	Neutral Category		
	ThreePoint	msoLightRigThreePoint	13
	Balanced	msoLightRigBalanced	14
	Soft	msoLightRigSoft	15
	Harsh	msoLightRigHarsh	16
	Flood	msoLightRigFlood	17
	Contrasting	msoLightRigContrasting	18
	Warm Category		
	Morning	msoLightRigMorning	19
	Sunrise	msoLightRigSunrise	20
	Sunset	msoLightRigSunset	21
	Cool Category		
	Chilly	msoLightRigChilly	22
	Freezing	msoLightRigFreezing	23
	Special Category		
	Flat	msoLightRigFlat	24
	TwoPoint	msoLightRigTwoPoint	25
	Glow	msoLightRigGlow	26
	BrightRoom	msoLightRigBrightRoom	27
	Legacy Category		
	Flat 1	msoLightRigLegacyFlat1	1
	Flat 2	msoLightRigLegacyFlat2	2
	Flat 3	msoLightRigLegacyFlat3	3
	Flat 4	msoLightRigLegacyFlat4	4
	Harsh 1	msoLightRigLegacyHarsh1	9

13

Type	VBA Constant	Value
Harsh 2	`msoLightRigLegacyHarsh2`	10
Harsh 3	`msoLightRigLegacyHarsh3`	11
Harsh 4	`msoLightRigLegacyHarsh4`	12
Normal 1	`msoLightRigLegacyNormal1`	5
Normal 2	`msoLightRigLegacyNormal2`	6
Normal 3	`msoLightRigLegacyNormal3`	7
Normal 4	`msoLightRigLegacyNormal4`	8
Mixed	`msoLightRigMixed`	-2

Automating Changes in the Format Series Dialog

There is a huge gap in the Excel 2007 Ribbon interface. Somewhere between the global changes on the Design ribbon and the set element changes on the Layout ribbon, Microsoft offers no big icons to format the individual data series. Depending on the chart type, the Format Series dialog box holds special settings that can dramatically impact the look of your chart.

There are a few ways to access the Format Series dialog:

- Right-click a series in the chart and choose Format Series from the context menu.
- From the first drop-down in either the Layout or Format ribbon, choose the item that you want to format (for example, choose Series 1 from this drop-down to format Series 1). Then click the Format Selection button immediately below the drop-down.

The special settings appear in the Series Options category of the Format dialog box. The following are some of the settings you can control:

- **Gap Width and Separation**—Control whether the columns in a column chart should be touching each other, as in a histogram, or separated.
- **Plot on Second Axis**—Specifies that a series should be plotted on a secondary axis. This is useful when the magnitude of one series does not match the magnitude of another series.
- **Angle of First Slice**—Rotates pie and doughnut charts. Other settings for the round charts control features such as explosion and hole size.
- **Bar of Pie and Pie of Pie**—Control which categories appear in the secondary chart in these combination charts.
- **Bubble Size**—Controls how the bubbles are sized in a bubble chart.
- **Surface and Radar**—Control certain aspects of these chart types.

13

Understanding How Excel Groups Series into Chart Groups

Although you access many of the series settings in the Format Series dialog box, they actually apply globally to all the series in the chart that have the same chart type.

Say that you have built a chart where Series 1 and Series 2 are column charts and Series 3 is a line chart. If you format the gap width, the setting applies to both of the series that use the column chart type. In VBA, this object is represented by `ChartGroup.Chart.ChartGroups(1)` might apply to the column chart elements, and `Chart.ChartGroups(2)` might apply to the line chart elements. Because the groups can change when you change the chart type for a series, it is safer to use the built-in shortcut methods to select a particular group of series.

The macro recorder uses the relatively risky method of referring to the chart group by index number:

```
ActiveChart.ChartGroups(1).Overlap = 35
```

You could instead use the named shortcut method. Strangely, the shortcut still returns a collection of chart groups, so you still must specify the index number 1:

```
ActiveChart.ColumnGroups(1).Overlap = 35
```

This is inherently safer: Microsoft groups all the series that use column charts into a single chart group.

The shortcut methods available include `AreaGroups`, `BarGroups`, `ColumnGroups`, `DoughnutGroups`, `LineGroups`, and `PieGroups`.

The following sections discuss the various options you can control in the Series Options dialog.

Controlling Gap Width and Series Separation in Column and Bar Charts

Typically, the individual bars in a bar or column chart are separated by gaps. When scientists create histograms, they want to eliminate the gaps between bars.

Excel offers the `GapWidth` property, whose value can range from 0 to 500 to represent 0% to 500%. Figure 13.16 shows a typical chart and a chart where the gap width has been reduced to 25%. Note that reducing the gap size automatically makes the columns thicker. To keep the columns narrow, you should reduce the width of the chart.

The gap width setting applies to chart groups that contain bar or column markers. It can also be used to format the volume markers in volume-high-low-close charts or volume-open-high-low-close charts.

The following macro changes the gap width to 25%:

```
Sub FormatGapWidth()
    Dim cht As Chart
    Set cht = ActiveChart
    cht.ChartGroups(1).GapWidth = 25
    cht.ChartGroups(1).VaryByCategories = True
End Sub
```

Figure 13.16
In the bottom chart, the gap width has been reduced from the default to 25%.

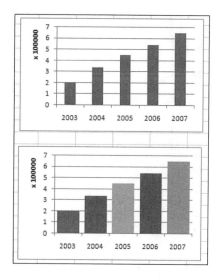

When you create a clustered column chart with two series, the columns for each data point touch, as shown in the top chart in Figure 13.17. You can use the Overlap property to cause the columns to overlap. Values from 1 to 100 cause the columns to overlap anywhere from 1% to 100%. Values from -1 to -100 cause separations between the data points.

The middle chart in Figure 13.17 shows a 50% overlap. The bottom chart shows a –100% overlap.

The following macro creates a 25% overlap between the series:

```
Sub FormatOverLap()
    Dim cht As Chart
    Set cht = ActiveChart
    cht.ChartGroups(1).Overlap = 25
End Sub
```

The Overlap property applies to clustered column and clustered bar charts. It should be set to 100% for the volume series in stock charts.

13

Figure 13.17
The middle chart has an overlap, and the bottom chart has a negative overlap (that is, a separation).

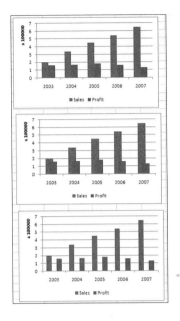

Moving a Series to a Secondary Axis

You might want to communicate data on a chart where the series are different orders of magnitude. In the top chart in Figure 13.18, the first two series represent sales and profit and show numbers in the hundreds of thousands. The third series is a profit percentage where the values are between 20% and 80%. When you plot these three series on a column chart, the columns for the profit percentage series will be so small that they will not be seen.

Figure 13.18
In the top chart, the third series is too small to be seen. In the bottom chart, a secondary axis, a new chart type, and an axis font color solves many problems.

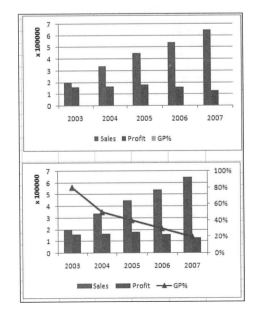

13

The solution is to plot the third series on a secondary axis. The left axis will continue to show hundreds of thousands, but the right axis scales to show percentages from 0% to 100%.

To move a series to the secondary axis, you use the `AxisGroup` property:

```
ActiveChart.SeriesCollection(3).AxisGroup = xlSecondary
```

Using a secondary axis solves one problem but introduces a new problem: How will the reader know that it is the profit percentage series which is plotted against the secondary axis? You can change the chart type of the third series from a column to a line. You can change the `ChartType` property for an individual series as follows:

```
ActiveChart.SeriesCollection(3).ChartType = xlLineMarkers
```

To further help the chart reader, you can change the font color of the tick labels for the secondary axis to match the line color of the third series. In the following macro, the font color for the secondary axis is changed to match the fill color of the third series (see the bottom chart in Figure 13.18):

```
Sub MoveToSecondaryAxis()
    Dim cht As Chart
    Dim ser As Series
    Dim ax As Axis
    Set cht = ActiveChart
    Set ser = cht.SeriesCollection(3)
    ser.AxisGroup = xlSecondary
    ser.ChartType = xlLineMarkers
    Set ax = cht.Axes(xlValue, xlSecondary)
    ax.TickLabels.Font.Color = ser.Format.Fill.ForeColor
End Sub
```

Unfortunately, this is a snapshot type of change. If you later change the theme or the color scheme of the chart, you have to change the tick label color to match the new Series 3 color.

Spinning and Exploding Round Charts

Pie and doughnut charts have rotation and explosion properties. In a typical data series, there might be a few tiny pie slices at the end of the series. These pie slices typically appear in the back of the chart. If you move them around to the front of the chart, they are more visible, and there is more room for the data labels to appear outside the chart.

You control the angle of the first slice of a pie by using the `FirstSliceAngle` property of the `ChartGroup` object. Valid values range from `0` to `360`, representing rotations of 0 to 360 degrees. In the bottom-left chart in Figure 13.19, the original chart was rotated 159 degrees, using the following macro:

```
Sub RotateChart()
    ' Bottom Left Chart in Figure 13.19
    Dim cht As Chart
    Set cht = ActiveChart
    cht.ChartGroups(1).FirstSliceAngle = 159
End Sub
```

13

Figure 13.19
You can rotate or explode pie charts to bring the small slices into view.

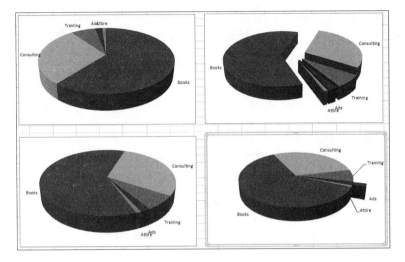

You can also explode pie and doughnut charts. In an exploded view, the individual wedges are separated from each other. You use the Explosion property to change the explosion effect. Valid values range from 0 to 400, representing 0 to 400%. With explosions, tiny values go a long way. The top-right chart in Figure 13.19 represents a 22% explosion and is created with this macro:

```
Sub ExplodeChart()
    ' Top Right Chart in Figure 13.19
    Dim cht As Chart
    Set cht = ActiveChart
    cht.ChartGroups(1).FirstSliceAngle = 159
    cht.ChartGroups(1).Explosion = 22
End Sub
```

Sometimes, a better effect is to explode just a single slice of a pie. You can apply the Explosion property to a single data point. In the bottom-right chart in Figure 13.19, only the Ads slice is exploded. Note that the macro then adjusts the positioning of the adjoining data labels so that they can be seen around the exploded slice:

```
Sub ExplodeOneSlice()
    ' Bottom Right Chart in Figure 13.19
    Dim cht As Chart
    Dim ser As Series
    Dim poi As Point
    Dim dl As DataLabel
    Set cht = ActiveChart
    Set ser = cht.SeriesCollection(1)
    cht.ChartGroups(1).FirstSliceAngle = 114
    ' Explode one slice
    Set poi = ser.Points(4)
    poi.Explosion = 22
    ' fix the labels
    Set dl = ser.Points(3).DataLabel
    dl.Left = dl.Left + 30
    dl.Top = dl.Top - 50
```

```
    Set dl = ser.Points(5).DataLabel
    dl.Left = dl.Left + 10
    dl.Top = dl.Top + 20
End Sub
```

You can also control the hole size in the center of a doughnut chart. A typical doughnut chart starts out with a hole size that is 50% of the doughnut. You use the `DoughnutHoleSize` property to adjust this from 90% to 10%, using values of `90` to `10`. The charts in Figure 13.20 show doughnut hole sizes of 70% on the top and 10% on the bottom. The following macro adjusts the doughnut hole size to 70%:

```
Sub ExplodeChart()
    Dim cht As Chart
    Set cht = ActiveChart
    cht.ChartGroups(1).DoughnutHoleSize = 70
End Sub
```

Figure 13.20
You can change the hole size in doughnut charts.

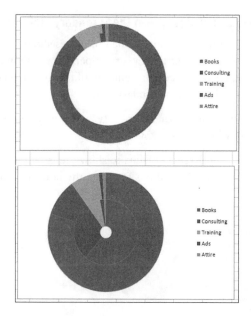

Controlling the Bar of Pie and Pie of Pie Charts

When your data contains many small pie slices and you care about the differences in those small slices, you can ask for the small slices to be plotted in a secondary pie or a secondary bar chart. For complete details on these unique chart types, read "Using a Pie of Pie Chart" in Chapter 4. These chart types are found in the Pie category.

As these charts include two charts inside the chart area, Excel offers many additional settings for controlling the size and placement of each chart in relation to the other. There are also a myriad of ways to determine which pie wedges are represented in the secondary chart. You have complete control of these settings in VBA. You might consider the following:

- How do you decide which wedges are reported in the smaller pie? Excel offers choices to move the last *n* slices, move all slices smaller than *n*%, or to move all slices smaller than a particular value. Excel also offers the custom method for moving the pie slices.

- Do you want leader lines from the "other" slice to the secondary plot? These are generally a good idea, but you can turn them off or even format them, if desired.

- How large should the secondary plot be compared to the first plot? Say that you are preparing charts for a meeting to discuss which product lines should be discontinued. In this case, the focus really is on the tiny wedges, and you might want to have the secondary plot be as large as or larger than the original pie.

- How wide should the gap be between the plots?

The following sections discuss how to adjust each of these settings with VBA.

Using a Rule to Determine Which Wedges Are in the Secondary Plot

Excel offers three built-in rules for determining which pie slices should be in the secondary plot. You can specify that all slices smaller than a certain percentage should be in the secondary plot, that all slices smaller than a certain value should be in the secondary plot, or even that the last *n* slices should be in the secondary plot.

You specify which of these rules to use with the `SplitType` property and then you specify a `SplitValue` setting to indicate where the split should occur.

In Figure 13.21, the top chart used Excel's defaults to show the last four points in the secondary plot. You could use any of these methods to create the bottom chart:

Figure 13.21
In the bottom chart, 80% of the slices appear in the secondary chart.

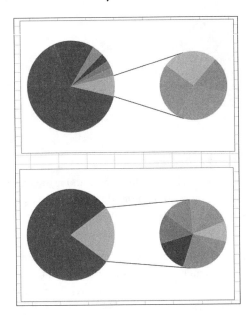

- You could specify a split type of xlSplitByValue and then indicate that any values less than 10 should be in the secondary plot.

- You could specify a split type of xlSplitByPercentValue and then indicate that any values less than 5% should be in the secondary plot.

- You could specify a split type of xlSplitByPosition and then indicate that the last eight values should be in the secondary plot.

Any one of these three macros could be used to create the second chart in Figure 13.21:

```
Sub SmallerThan10ToPlot2()
    Dim cht As Chart
    Dim chtg As ChartGroup
    Set cht = ActiveChart
    Set chtg = cht.ChartGroups(1)
    ' Anything less than 10 to second group
    cht.ChartGroups(1).SplitType = xlSplitByValue
    ActiveChart.ChartGroups(1).SplitValue = 10
End Sub

Sub SmallerThan10PctToPlot2()
    Dim cht As Chart
    Dim chtg As ChartGroup
    Set cht = ActiveChart
    Set chtg = cht.ChartGroups(1)
    ' Anything less than 10% to 2nd plot
    chtg.SplitType = xlSplitByPercentValue
    chtg.SplitValue = 10
End Sub

Sub Last8ToPlot2()
    Dim cht As Chart
    Dim chtg As ChartGroup
    Set cht = ActiveChart
    Set chtg = cht.ChartGroups(1)
    ' Send last 8 slices to secondary plot
    chtg.SplitType = xlSplitByPosition
    chtg.SplitValue = 8
End Sub
```

Defining Specific Categories to Be in the Secondary Plot

You can choose to have complete control over which slices of a pie appear in a secondary chart. If you are trying to decide among three specific products to discontinue, for example, you can move all three of those products to the secondary pie.

To do this with a macro, you first set SplitType to xlSplitByCustomSplit. You can then use the SecondaryPlot property on individual data points. A value of 0 shows the data point in the left pie. A value of 1 sends the data point to the secondary pie.

Because you aren't sure how many items Excel will send to the secondary pie by default, you can write a macro such as the following to first loop through all data points and reset them to the primary pie, and then move three specific slices to the secondary pie:

13

```
Sub CustomPieofPie()
    Dim cht As Chart
    Dim chtg As ChartGroup
    Dim ser As Series
    Dim poi As Point
    Set cht = ActiveChart
    Set chtg = cht.ChartGroups(1)
    Set ser = cht.SeriesCollection(1)
    chtg.SplitType = xlSplitByCustomSplit
    ' Move all slices to first plot
    For Each poi In ser.Points
        poi.SecondaryPlot = 0
    Next poi
    ' Move points 1, 6, 10 to secondary plot
    ser.Points(2).SecondaryPlot = 1
    ser.Points(6).SecondaryPlot = 1
    ser.Points(10).SecondaryPlot = 1
End Sub
```

The results are shown in Figure 13.22. This figure shows a bar of pie chart with three specific wedges moved to the secondary plot.

Figure 13.22
Instead of focusing on the smallest slices, this bar of pie chart focuses on three particular products.

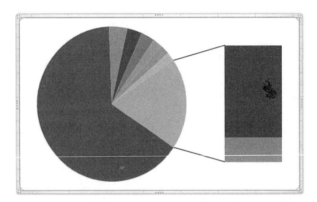

Controlling the Gap, Size, and Lines of a Secondary Plot

You adjust the gap between an original pie and a secondary plot by using the GapWidth property, whose values range from 0 to 500. In Figure 13.23, the bottom chart has a gap of 500, and the middle chart has a gap of 0.

You can turn on or off the two leader lines extending from the main pie to the secondary plot by setting the HasSeriesLines property to True or False. To format those lines, you use the Format property of the SeriesLines object. The following macro moves the secondary plot to the maximum distance and changes the series lines to a dash/dot style:

```
Sub MindTheGap()
    Dim chtg As ChartGroup
    Set chtg = ActiveChart.ChartGroups(1)
    chtg.GapWidth = 500
    chtg.HasSeriesLines = True
    chtg.SeriesLines.Format.Line.DashStyle = msoLineDashDot
End Sub
```

Figure 13.23
You use the *GapWidth* property to move the secondary plot closer to or farther from the main pie.

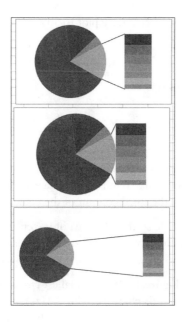

The size of the secondary plot usually starts off at 75% of the original pie. You can use the SecondPlotSize property to change the plot size from 5 to 200, representing 5% to 200% of the original pie chart. Figure 13.24 shows charts with secondary plot sizes of 75%, 5%, and 200%.

Figure 13.24
You can shift the focus toward or away from the secondary plot by adjusting its size.

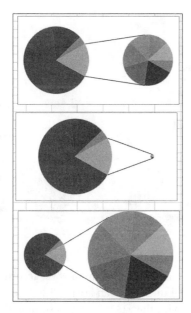

The following macro adjusts the size of the secondary plot to 50% of the size of the main pie:

```
Sub ChangeSize()
    Dim chtg As ChartGroup
    Set chtg = ActiveChart.ChartGroups(1)
    chtg.SecondPlotSize = 50
End Sub
```

Setting the Bubble Size

The bubble chart type includes an incredibly misleading setting that you should always avoid. A bubble chart places circles at particular x and y coordinates. The sizes of the circles are determined by the values specified in the third column of the data series.

By default, Excel scales the size of the circle so that the area of the circle is proportionate to the data. This is an appropriate choice. However, you can override this setting to say that the size represents the width of the circle. This always results in a misleading chart.

For example, in the upper-left chart in Figure 13.25, the smallest circle has a value of 1, and the largest circle has a value of 4. Because this chart uses the xlSizeIsArea setting, the bottom-left circle is four times larger than the top-right circle. The bottom-left chart plots the same data but uses the xlSizeIsWidth setting. With this setting, your circles will be completely out of scale.

Figure 13.25
The bottom-left chart uses *xlSizeIsWidth* and is misleading. The bottom-right chart shows a negative-sized circle, represented by a circle with no fill.

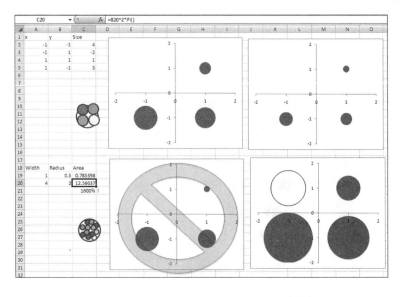

A circle with a width of 1 inch has an area of 0.785 square inches, according to =PI()*(1/2)^2. A circle with a width of 4 inches has an area of 12.56 square inches, according to =PI()*(4/2)^2. This means that with the xlSizeIsWidth setting, the bottom-left circle is 16 times larger than the top-right circle.

It is strange that Excel even offers the `xlSizeIsWidth` setting. Microsoft makes sure to avoid the mistake of resizing markers in two dimensions when dealing with bar or column charts.

You can also choose to scale the circles from 0 to 300% by changing the `BubbleScale` property from `0` to `300`. The top-left chart in Figure 13.25 has a 100% scale. The top-right chart uses a 50% scale. The bottom-right chart uses a 300% scale.

Finally, you can specify whether Excel should show negative-sized circles on a chart. In the lower-right chart in Figure 13.25, the –2 in the upper quadrant is represented by a circle with a white fill instead of a circle with a blue fill.

The following macro demonstrates some of the settings available for bubble charts:

```
Sub BubbleSettings()
    Dim chtg As ChartGroup
    Set chtg = ActiveChart.ChartGroups(1)
    ' Never use the following setting
    ' chtg.SizeRepresents = xlSizeIsWidth
    chtg.SizeRepresents = xlSizeIsArea
    chtg.BubbleScale = 50
    chtg.ShowNegativeBubbles = True
End Sub
```

Controlling Radar and Surface Charts

A couple minor settings affect surface charts and radar charts. A default surface chart uses contour shading within each color band in order to give a 3-D feeling. You can turn this off in a surface chart by using the `Has3DShading` property. In Figure 13.26, the bottom-left chart has the shading turned off. (You may not be able to see it in this monochrome book, but you can download the project files from www.mrexcel.com/chart2007data.html to see the effect in color.)

Radar charts typically have the name of each category at the end of the axis. You can turn this off by setting the `HasRadarAxisLabels` property to `False`. The bottom-right chart in Figure 13.26 shows this setting.

The code for turning off the `Has3DShading` and `HasRadarAxisLabels` properties follows:

```
Sub FormatSurface()
    Dim chtg As ChartGroup
    Set chtg = ActiveChart.ChartGroups(1)
    chtg.Has3DShading = False
End Sub
Sub FormatRadar()
    Dim chtg As ChartGroup
    Set chtg = ActiveChart.ChartGroups(1)
    chtg.HasRadarAxisLabels = False
End Sub
```

13

Figure 13.26
The bottom charts reflect removing the 3-D contour (left) and radar axis labels (right).

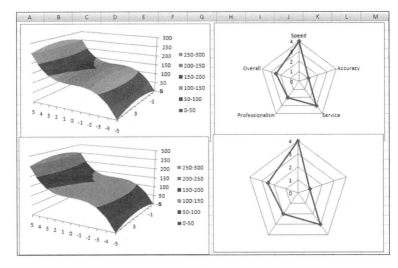

Using the Watch Window to Discover Object Settings

It is frustrating that the macro recorder does not record certain actions when you're working with charts. Actually, there are two levels of frustration. First, the macro recorder does not record the action of creating SmartArt graphics because Microsoft made a conscious decision not to allow you to create SmartArt using VBA. I don't agree with that decision, but I can understand why the macro recorder doesn't record these steps. Second, when you are using the Format ribbon, the macro recorder does nothing; however, you can control all the actions with the Format ribbon by using VBA.

With previous versions of Excel, I relied on the macro recorder to teach me which objects, properties, and methods responded to various actions in the Excel interface. Without the macro recorder, it becomes very difficult to learn these aspects.

In case you need to use a property that is not covered in this book, there is a way to be able to explore the properties for certain chart elements. The following is an example in which the macro defines a Chart object variable and a ChartGroup object variable and then stops:

```
Sub ExploreChartElements()
    Dim cht As Chart
    Dim chtg As ChartGroup
    Dim ser As Series
    Set cht = ActiveChart
    Set chtg = cht.ChartGroups(1)
    Set ser = cht.SeriesCollection(1)
    Stop
End Sub
```

13

The Stop command in the macro is key to the success of this technique. Excel enters Break mode when it encounters the Stop code. This allows you to examine the object variables while they are still in scope.

You follow these steps to discover new chart properties:

1. Enter the preceding macro in your workbook.

2. Create a chart.

3. Select the chart.

4. Run the macro. VBA stops and highlights the Stop line in yellow. You are now in Break mode.

5. Right-click the ser object variable and choose Add Watch. Click OK in the Add Watch dialog box. Excel displays a new Watch window at the bottom of the VBA editor. This window displays a single line with a pair of eyeglasses, a plus sign, and the name of the variable, as shown in Figure 13.27.

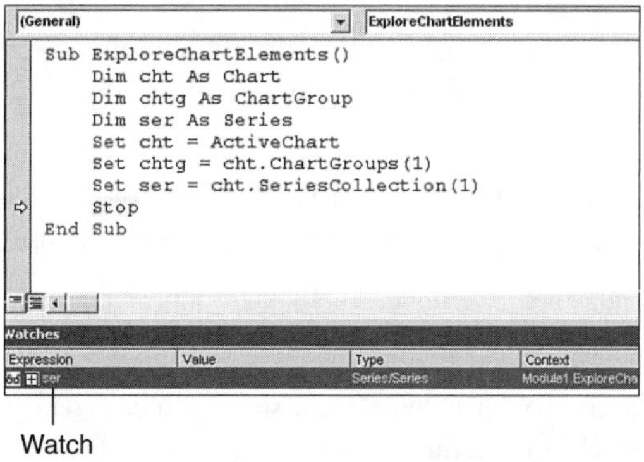

Figure 13.27
Initially, the watched variable shows a single, useless line.

Watch

6. Click the plus sign next to the watch. A list of many properties for the series opens. One property is the Format property. This is where all of the Format ribbon settings are stored.

7. Click the plus sign next to the Format entry. It expands to show the settings for Fill, Glow, Line, and so on.

8. Click the plus sign next to the Fill entry. You see many settings that define the fill used in Series 1. The GradientDegree setting is highlighted in Figure 13.28. You can see that Gradient Degree is a property of the Fill property, and Fill is a property of the Format property. From this, you can ascertain that the proper code would be this:
```
ser.Format.Fill.GradientDegree = 0.8825
```

13

Figure 13.28
After browsing through the Watch window, you can locate a property without the macro recorder.

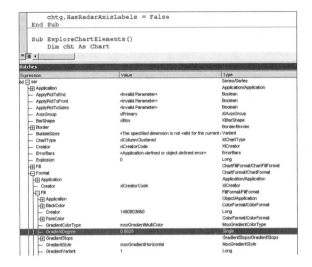

This isn't exactly as easy as using the macro recorder to examine objects, properties, and methods, but it makes it possible to figure out how to write code.

> **NOTE**
> In the ExploreChartElements macro, there are variables for the chart, the series, and the chart group. You might have to add watches for each of these variables and begin exploring to find the actual setting.

The Watch window is "somewhat" live. With a few steps, you can change the chart formatting in the Excel user interface and then return to the VBA Editor to discover the new settings:

1. While in Break mode, switch back to Excel using Alt+Tab or by clicking on Excel in the taskbar.

2. Make some changes to the active chart in Excel. Make sure not to deactivate the chart.

3. Switch back to the VBA Editor.

4. There is a yellow arrow to the left of the Stop line in your code window. Grab this arrow and drag upward to point to the line that set up your watched variable. In the current example, you are watching the ser variable, so you just have to move up one line, to the Set ser line.

5. Press the F8 key to rerun the line highlighted in yellow. The Watch window updates to show the settings you made in step 2.

When you are done exploring, click the Reset button in the VBA toolbar (the square dot located near the Run menu).

CASE STUDY

Using the Watch Window to Learn Rotation Settings

There is one icon on the Layout ribbon that is not recorded by the macro recorder. If you change the rotation of a 3-D chart, the macro recorder records nothing. To see an example of this, you can follow these steps:

1. Turn on the macro recorder.

2. Select a surface chart.

3. Change the rotation settings.

4. Stop the macro recorder.

5. Switch back to Excel and change the formatting of the columns in the first series. Excel records this macro, which is of little use:

   ```
   Sub RotateChartRecordedMacro()
   '
   ' RotateChartRecordedMacro Macro
   '
   '
       ActiveSheet.ChartObjects("Chart 1").Activate
   End Sub
   ```

To solve this problem and learn how to programmatically rotate a chart, you can follow these steps:

1. Type this macro in the VBA Editor:

   ```
   Sub ExploreChartElements()
       Dim cht As Chart
       Set cht = ActiveChart
       Stop
   End Sub
   ```

2. In Excel, select the chart. On the Layout ribbon, choose the 3-D Rotation icon. Note the X, Y, and Perspective settings (for example, 200, 10, and 15).

3. Click Close to close the Format Chart Area dialog.

4. Switch to VBA.

5. Run the ExploreChartElements macro. VBA enters Break mode.

6. Right-click the cht variable and choose Add Watch. Click OK in the Add Watch dialog.

7. In the Watch window, click the plus sign to expand the chart.

8. Scan through the properties. You are looking for properties that might have values of 200, 10, and 15. There is an Elevation property with a value of 10. There is a Rotation property with the value of 200. There is a Perspective setting with a value of 30. This one is maddening because the name is exactly right, but the value is incorrect.

9. Switch back to Excel. Choose 3-D Rotation and change the Perspective setting from 15 to 20 in the Format dialog box.

13

10. Switch back to VBA and rerun the macro. Look in the Watch window. The `Perspective` setting has changed to 40. You can theorize that this is the right property but that the Perspective value shown in the Format dialog box needs to be doubled when entered in VBA.

You now have enough information to write the following macro to change the rotation of the chart using VBA:

```
Sub RotateChart()
    Dim cht As Chart
    Set cht = ActiveChart
    cht.Rotation = 100
    cht.Elevation = 30
    cht.Perspective = 60 ' Really means 30%
End Sub
```

Exporting a Chart as a Graphic

You can export any chart to an image file on your hard drive. The `ExportChart` method requires you to specify a filename and a graphic type. The available graphic types depend on graphic file filters installed in your Registry. It is a safe bet that JPG, BMP, PNG, and GIF will work on most computers.

For example, the following code exports the active chart as a GIF file:

```
Sub ExportChart()
    Dim cht As Chart
    Set cht = ActiveChart
    cht.Export Filename:="C:\Chart.gif", Filtername:="GIF"
End Sub
```

> **CAUTION**
>
> Since Excel 2003, Microsoft has supported an `Interactive` argument in the `Export` method. Excel help indicates that if you set `Interactive` to `TRUE`, then Excel asks for additional settings depending on the file type. However, the dialog to ask for additional settings never appears, at least not for the four standard types of JPG, GIF, BMP, or PNG.

Creating a Dynamic Chart in a UserForm

With the ability to export a chart to a graphic file, you also have the ability to load a graphic file into an `Image` control in a UserForm. This means you can create a dialog box in which someone can dynamically control values used to plot a chart.

To create the dialog shown in Figure 13.29, you follow these steps:

Figure 13.29
This dialog box is a VBA UserForm displaying a chart. The chart redraws based on changes to the dialog controls.

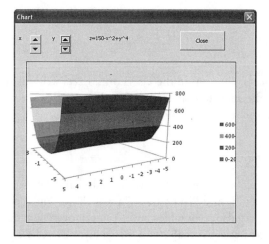

1. In the VBA window, choose Insert, UserForm. In the Properties pane, rename the form frmChart.

2. Resize the UserForm.

3. Add a large Image control to the UserForm.

4. Add two spin buttons named sbX and sbY. Set them to have a minimum of 1 and a maximum of 5.

5. Add a Label3 control to display the formula.

6. Add a command button labeled Close.

7. Enter this code in the code window behind the form:

```
Private Sub CommandButton1_Click()
    Unload Me
End Sub
Private Sub sbX_Change()
    Worksheets("Surface").Range("O2").Value = Me.sbX.Value
    Worksheets("Surface").Shapes(1).Chart.Export "C:\Chart.gif"
    Me.Label3.Caption = Worksheets("Surface").Range("O4").Value
    Me.Image1.Picture = LoadPicture("C:\Chart.gif")
End Sub
Private Sub sbY_Change()
    Worksheets("Surface").Range("O3").Value = Me.sbY.Value
    Worksheets("Surface").Shapes(1).Chart.Export "C:\Chart.gif"
    Me.Label3.Caption = Worksheets("Surface").Range("O4").Value
    Me.Image1.Picture = LoadPicture("C:\Chart.gif")
End Sub

Private Sub UserForm_Initialize()
    Me.sbX = Worksheets("Surface").Range("O2").Value
    Me.sbY = Worksheets("Surface").Range("O3").Value
    Me.Label3.Caption = Worksheets("Surface").Range("O4").Value
    Worksheets("Surface").Shapes(1).Chart.Export "C:\Chart.gif"
    Me.Image1.Picture = LoadPicture("C:\Chart.gif")
End Sub
```

13

8. Use Insert, Module to add a `Module1` component with this code:

```
Sub ShowForm()
    frmChart.Show
End Sub
```

As someone changes the spin buttons in the UserForm, Excel writes new values to the worksheet. This causes the chart to update. The UserForm code then exports the chart and displays it in the UserForm (refer to Figure 13.29).

Creating Pivot Charts

A pivot chart is a chart that uses a pivot table as the underlying data source. As I lamented in Chapter 8, "Creating and Using Pivot Charts," pivot charts don't have the cool "show pages" functionality that regular pivot tables have. You can overcome this problem with a quick VBA macro that creates a pivot table and then a pivot chart based on the pivot table. The macro then adds the customer field to the page field of the pivot table. It then loops through each customer and exports the chart for each customer.

In Excel 2007, you first create a pivot cache by using the `PivotCache.Create` method. You can then define a pivot table based on the pivot cache. The usual procedure is to turn off pivot table updating while you add fields to the pivot table. Then you update the pivot table in order to have Excel perform the calculations.

It takes a bit of finesse to figure out the final range of the pivot table. If you have turned off the column and row totals, the chartable area of the pivot table starts one row below the `PivotTableRange1` area. You have to resize the area to include one fewer row in order to make your chart appear correctly.

After the pivot table is created, you can switch back to the `Charts.Add` code discussed earlier in this chapter. You can use any formatting code to get the chart formatted as you desire.

The following code creates a pivot table and a single pivot chart that summarize revenue by region and product:

```
Sub CreateSummaryReportUsingPivot()
    Dim WSD As Worksheet
    Dim PTCache As PivotCache
    Dim PT As PivotTable
    Dim PRange As Range
    Dim FinalRow As Long
    Dim ChartDataRange As Range
    Dim Cht As Chart
    Set WSD = Worksheets("Data")

    ' Delete any prior pivot tables
    For Each PT In WSD.PivotTables
        PT.TableRange2.Clear
    Next PT
```

13

```
WSD.Range("I1:Z1").EntireColumn.Clear

' Define input area and set up a Pivot Cache
FinalRow = WSD.Cells(Application.Rows.Count, 1).End(xlUp).Row
FinalCol = WSD.Cells(1, Application.Columns.Count). _
    End(xlToLeft).Column
Set PRange = WSD.Cells(1, 1).Resize(FinalRow, FinalCol)

Set PTCache = ActiveWorkbook.PivotCaches.Create(SourceType:= _
    xlDatabase, SourceData:=PRange.Address)

' Create the Pivot Table from the Pivot Cache
Set PT = PTCache.CreatePivotTable(TableDestination:=WSD. _
    Cells(2, FinalCol + 2), TableName:="PivotTable1")

' Turn off updating while building the table
PT.ManualUpdate = True

' Set up the row fields
PT.AddFields RowFields:="Region", ColumnFields:="Product", _
    PageFields:="Customer"

' Set up the data fields
With PT.PivotFields("Revenue")
    .Orientation = xlDataField
    .Function = xlSum
    .Position = 1
End With

With PT
    .ColumnGrand = False
    .RowGrand = False
    .NullString = "0"
End With

' Calc the pivot table
PT.ManualUpdate = False
PT.ManualUpdate = True

' Define the Chart Data Range
Set ChartDataRange = _
    PT.TableRange1.Offset(1, 0).Resize(PT.TableRange1.Rows.Count - 1)

' Add the Chart
WSD.Shapes.AddChart.Select
Set Cht = ActiveChart
Cht.SetSourceData Source:=ChartDataRange
' Format the Chart
Cht.ChartType = xlColumnClustered
Cht.SetElement (msoElementChartTitleAboveChart)
Cht.ChartTitle.Caption = "All Customers"
Cht.SetElement msoElementPrimaryValueAxisThousands
End Sub
```

Figure 13.30 shows the resulting chart and pivot table.

Figure 13.30
VBA creates a pivot table and then a chart from the pivot table. Excel automatically displays the PivotChart Filter pane in response.

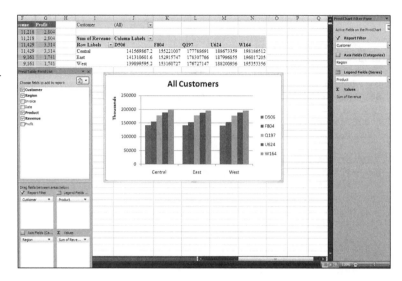

CASE STUDY

Printing a Chart for Each Customer

In this case study, you'll use a pivot table and a pivot chart to summarize data from a pivot table. The goal is to create a pivot table with customers in the filter field area. The pivot table should summarize revenue by year and by product.

After this pivot table is created, you will add a chart with a chart title. You can then loop through each pivot item in the customer field. For each chart, you'll update the pivot table, change the chart title, and then export a chart with the name of the customer.

There is a bit more complexity in this macro than in the others shown so far in this chapter. The process of grouping daily dates up to yearly dates requires you to calculate the pivot table and then select one of the date fields. From `TableRange1`, you have to select a cell that is one row and one column from the top-left corner before you can group up to years.

After the first chart is created, you can loop through each pivot item in the customer pivot field. For each customer, you change the page field, recalculate the pivot table, change the title in the chart, and then export. To do all this, you use the following macro:

```
Sub CreateChartPerCustomer()
    Dim WSD As Worksheet
    Dim PTCache As PivotCache
    Dim PT As PivotTable
    Dim PRange As Range
    Dim FinalRow As Long
    Dim ChartDataRange As Range
    Dim Cht As Chart
    Dim PI As PivotItem
    Set WSD = Worksheets("Data")
```

```vba
' Delete any prior pivot tables
For Each PT In WSD.PivotTables
    PT.TableRange2.Clear
Next PT
WSD.Range("M1:Z1").EntireColumn.Clear

' Define input area and set up a Pivot Cache
FinalRow = WSD.Cells(Application.Rows.Count, 1).End(xlUp).Row
FinalCol = WSD.Cells(1, Application.Columns.Count). _
    End(xlToLeft).Column
Set PRange = WSD.Cells(1, 1).Resize(FinalRow, FinalCol)

Set PTCache = ActiveWorkbook.PivotCaches.Create(SourceType:= _
    xlDatabase, SourceData:=PRange.Address)

' Create the Pivot Table from the Pivot Cache
Set PT = PTCache.CreatePivotTable(TableDestination:=WSD. _
    Cells(2, FinalCol + 2), TableName:="PivotTable1")

' Turn off updating while building the table
PT.ManualUpdate = True

' Set up the row fields
PT.AddFields RowFields:="Product", ColumnFields:="Date", _
    PageFields:="Customer"

' Set up the data fields
With PT.PivotFields("Revenue")
    .Orientation = xlDataField
    .Function = xlSum
    .Position = 1
End With

With PT
    .ColumnGrand = False
    .RowGrand = False
    .NullString = "0"
End With

' Calc the pivot table
PT.ManualUpdate = False
PT.ManualUpdate = True

' Find a date field & group by year

PT.TableRange1.Offset(1, 1).Resize(1, 1).Group Start:=True, End:=True, _
    Periods:=Array(False, False, False, False, False, False, True)

' Calc the pivot table
PT.ManualUpdate = False
PT.ManualUpdate = True

' CreateChart
Set ChartDataRange = _
    PT.TableRange1.Offset(1, 0).Resize(PT.TableRange1.Rows.Count - 1)
```

13

```
' Add the Chart
WSD.Shapes.AddChart.Select
Set Cht = ActiveChart
Cht.SetSourceData Source:=ChartDataRange
' Format the Chart
Cht.ChartType = xlColumnClustered
Cht.SetElement (msoElementChartTitleAboveChart)
Cht.ChartTitle.Caption = "All Customers"
Cht.SetElement msoElementPrimaryValueAxisThousands
' Loop through each customer
For Each PI In PT.PivotFields("Customer").PivotItems

    PT.PivotFields("Customer").ClearAllFilters
    PT.PivotFields("Customer").CurrentPage = PI.Name

    ' Calc the pivot table
    PT.ManualUpdate = False
    PT.ManualUpdate = True

    Cht.ChartTitle.Caption = PI.Name

    Cht.Export Filename:="C:\" & PI.Name & ".jpg", Filtername:="JPG"

Next PI
End Sub
```

Figure 13.31 shows one of the three dozen charts created by this macro in less than a minute.

Figure 13.31
The macro creates dozens of summary charts in under a minute.

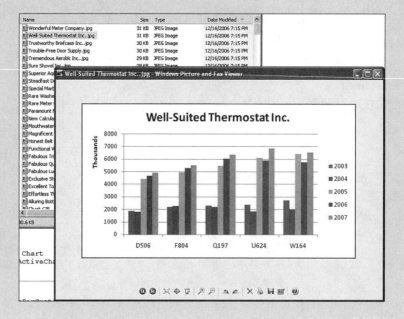

Next Steps

While I hope this book has taught you how to create meaningful charts, the next chapter shows many examples of bad charts. People might try to use bad charts to intentionally mislead the reader or might just create a misleading chart because they think it looks cool. By knowing how to spot bad charts, you can prevent people from misleading you the next time you are sitting through a presentation.

13

Knowing When Someone Is Lying to You with a Chart

14

Lying with Perspective

Excel's 3-D charts all attempts to show a two-dimensional object on a two-dimensional computer screen and give the perception that the objects are rendered in 3-D. Excel provides a lot of support for the 3-D charts, but I do not cover them in great detail in this book because they often misrepresent your data. Hopefully, you will resist the urge to use them.

I took a photography class once. During the lesson on wide-angle lenses, the instructor pointed out that a wide-angle lens makes everything in the foreground look proportionally larger than it is. If you are shooting a portrait of someone who has a big nose, you don't want to use a wide-angle lens for that portrait.

Similarly, with 3-D pie charts, any wedges at the front of the pie look much larger than wedges at the back of the pie. In Figure 14.1, for example, both charts show a labor component of 30%. If you want to impress the union during contract negotiations, you should use the chart where labor is in the front because the labor wedge in that chart is 2.8 times the size of the one in the top chart.

Figure 14.1
Wedges in the front of a 3-D pie appear much larger than those in the back.

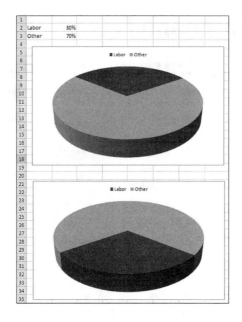

NOTE

If want to lie with a 3-D pie chart, you can accomplish that by changing the rotation of the pie. You right-click the pie, choose Format Series, and then change the rotation angle.

Perspective causes problems with 3-D column charts as well. Is the reader supposed to look at the front or the back of the column?

Look in the top chart in Figure 14.2. Are any of the quarters over 3,000? Count the number of gridlines. The first line is 1,000, then 2,000, then 3,000. None of the bars ever touch the 3,000 line. Yet, in the bottom chart, both the Q3 and Q4 columns are over 3,000.

Figure 14.2
Are you supposed to look at the back or front edge of the 3-D columns? It doesn't really matter because neither appears to reach the 3,000 gridline.

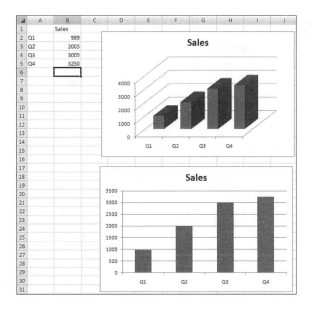

Lying with Shrinking Charts

The pyramid and cone charts should be banned from Excel. You could do without these 14 different charts, which are completely misrepresentative.

Consider a standard stacked bar chart like the top one in Figure 14.3. In this chart, a charity's administrative expenses are fairly high, at 35%. If the charity wants to minimize this in a chart for its donors, it could change the chart to a cone or pyramid chart. Because the chart naturally gets smaller at the top, the 35% in black looks like nothing!

Figure 14.3
To misrepresent the 35% category in black at the top, you can put it in a cone chart.

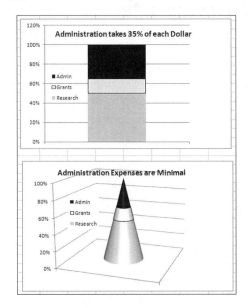

Lying with Scale

To try to prove that values are jumping all over, someone can change the minimum and maximum values along the vertical axis and zoom in to a tight view of the chart series, as shown in the top-left chart in Figure 14.4. If they want to make the sales look smooth, they can change the maximum value on the axis to something several times larger than the usual maximum. In this case, the line looks very smooth, as shown in the bottom of Figure 14.4.

Figure 14.4
Watch out for someone changing the scale in order to push a message.

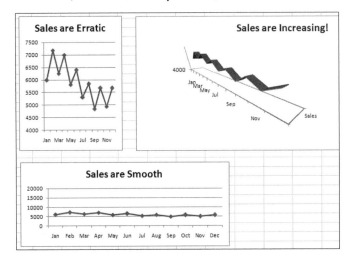

3-D perspective can also be used to distort a message. In the top-right chart in Figure 14.4, sales might even seem to be increasing.

Lying Because Excel Won't Cooperate

I received the chart in Figure 14.5 in a meeting. The person who made the chart was trying to show how cash balances had been consistently increasing year over year. However, because there was no data for the last half of 2007, a thick solid line made the cash balance appear to plummet to 0 in the current month. (The original chart didn't actually have a title, but I penciled one in.)

Figure 14.5
The person making this chart really wanted to show something positive. However, I penciled in my own title, based on the disappearance of all the money.

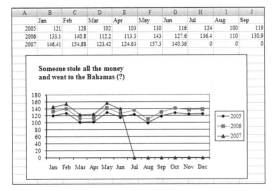

14

This problem actually results from following rules. I always complain when people leave cells blank instead of putting in zeros. I hammer this home in my Power Excel seminars, and I mock Microsoft for all the blank cells in a pivot table. However, this accountant's desire to have zero in the future cells caused the chart line to plummet to zero.

The solution is to replace the future cells with empty cells, using Alt+E+A+A (or selecting Edit, Clear All), or explicitly put =NA() in the future cells. If you use either of these methods, Excel changes the 2007 line to end with a nice 140,000 cash balance, as shown in Figure 14.6.

Figure 14.6

Use a few empty cells instead of zero for future months, and the cash drain disappears.

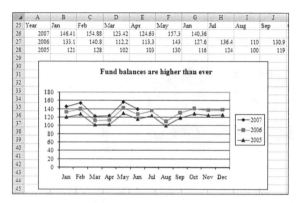

Lying by Obscuring the Data

The message of the chart at the top of Figure 14.7 is that marketing costs more than tripled in three years. If the vice president of marketing wants to defend the marketing spend, he might just mix it in with a bunch of other numbers and show the marketing budget as a middle series in a stacked area chart.

In the chart at the bottom of Figure 14.7, the marketing numbers look flat, possibly even trending down.

In the top chart in Figure 14.8, sales appear to be trending up. The automatic Excel trendline even says so.

Beware of charts that figure a multiyear trend from only two data points. You need to add more data to get the big picture. The bottom chart in Figure 14.8 shows that the last two years might be the bottoming out of a six-year skid.

14

Figure 14.7
Adding data obscures the marketing excesses.

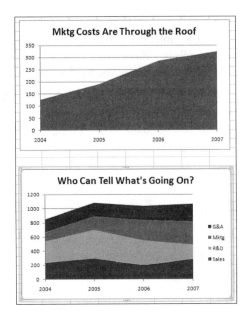

Figure 14.8
Inferring a trend based on a two-point line is dangerous. You need to add more data points to tell the real story.

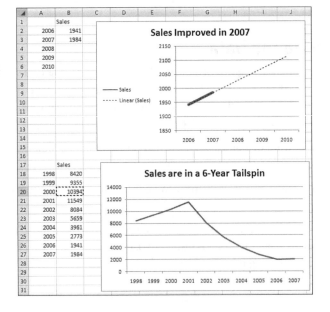

Deliberately Using Charts to Lie

Some people are just good at lying. In Figure 14.9, for example, sales are increasing. Or are they? The chart author reversed the categories along the x-axis. The most recent year is at the left. I bet no one will notice.

Figure 14.9
All is going well.

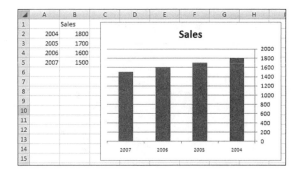

As another example, in Figure 14.10, a city is drastically losing population. Jobs are scarce, education is bad, and people are moving out. The top chart paints a pretty bleak picture. The mayor who has been around for 20 years wants to put a happy spin on the message. His staff prepares the bottom chart, showing how population growth has slowed.

Figure 14.10
When the absolute numbers are bleak, you plot the percentage rate of change.

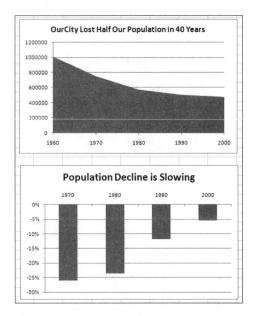

The next example is definitely a non-Excel lie. Even Excel is smart enough not to allow picture markers to extend in both directions. Someone had to make the markers invisible and use clip art to pull off the lie shown in Figure 14.11.

The image on the left is 100 pixels tall and 100 pixels wide. This seems like a reasonable way to represent $100 million in exports. When the chart designer scaled the picture up to 300 pixels for the March data, he allowed both the height and the width to change. The size of the final image contains nine times the area of the first image, even though the exports increased by a factor of three.

14

Figure 14.11
The size of the images increased in both height and width. This causes a 200% increase to look like an 800% increase.

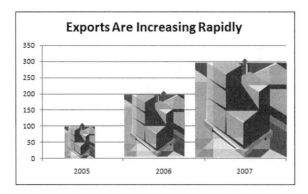

These are just a few of the many ways that people might try to lie to you with charts. Now that you've read this book, you should be able to spot a deception and call it out. You should also be able to use charts to accurately represent data.

Next Steps

Appendix A, "Charting References," lists several additional resources for more information on charting.

Charting References

A
APPENDIX

Other Charting Resources

If you enjoyed this book, there are many more resources for you to investigate. These are people, books, and websites that have had an influence on my charting life.

Websites come and go. I will maintain a list of links to these references and any more that I find at www.MrExcel.com/chartbookdata.html.

Gene Zelazny: The Guru of Business Charting

During a 40-year career at McKinsey & Company, Gene Zelazny has taught two generations of people how to effectively communicate with charts. I learned a lot about charting during a six-month stint on a McKinsey project team. The McKinsey consultants, such as Gino Picasso and Firoz Dosani, who taught me about charting, learned the craft from Gene Zelazny.

I enjoy Gene's work because he focuses on positive ways to effectively communicate by using charts and visuals. While Tufte spends a lot of ink showing why popular charts are bad, Gene cuts right to the chase and shows examples of effective charts.

Pick up anything that you find written by Gene. He first wrote *Say It with Presentation*. His best kit is *The Say It with Charts Complete Toolkit* (see Figure A.1). If you wonder where Microsoft got the idea for SmartArt graphics, you will see that Gene began advocating what Microsoft calls SmartArt long before Microsoft coined the name. The kit includes a book, images on CD-ROM, and more (see www.zelazny.com/charts.html).

A

Figure A.1
Gene Zelazny's toolkit is a great reference to consult before you even think about using Excel. It can help you learn which charts are the best to use in many cases.

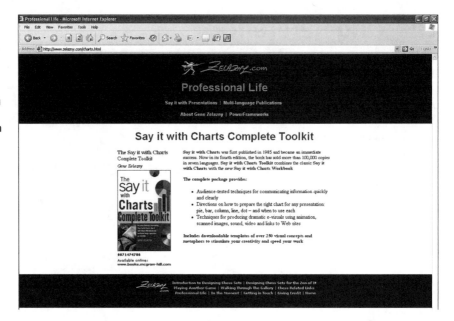

PowerFrameworks.com

If you are the go-to person for charts in your company, then you need to subscribe to PowerFrameworks.com. The $249 annual subscription gives you access to hundreds of charting and presentation templates. Kathy Villella and Lisa Baker are constantly adding new, leading-edge elements to the site. For example, Kathy recently posted an umbrella chart element that you can import into PowerPoint. In addition to the element, Kathy provides several professionally designed ideas about how you could use the chart.

PowerFrameworks hires professional artists to bring its ideas to life. It makes sure that in a lock-and-key chart, the key actually fits in the lock. You can build brilliant-looking animated or still charts using these elements.

The company's ideas alone are worth the price of a PowerFrameworks subscription. Download the templates, label the charts, color with the Formatting ribbon, and you are ready to go. Figure A.2 shows an umbrella chart that I created in a few minutes after downloading from the site.

Figure A.2
An umbrella chart created using a template from PowerFrameworks.com. The downloaded template starts as the black-and-white drawing, but it is designed to be formatted using the Format ribbon.

A subscription to PowerFrameworks can help supercharge your career.

Books by Edward Tufte

I own everything that Professor Edward Tufte writes. He self-publishes his books and really spares no expense in creating fantastic, full-color, beautiful books.

His books are informative and filled with eye candy. I can spend an hour studying the beautiful Napoleon's March chart that manages to communicate seven different series with a single line. Tufte has found examples of good and bad charts throughout history. He coined the term *chartjunk*.

My only complaint is that Tufte comes off as a bit of a curmudgeon. He shows bad charts and explains why they are bad. I am sure that Tufte would skewer some of my charts in this book. After reading Tufte, I am filled with doubt and knowledge about what *not* to do. Zelazny counters this by only telling you what is effective.

Tufte has written the following books:

- *The Visual Display of Quantitative Information*, now in its second edition, contains 250 illustrations of the best and sometimes the worst ways of displaying information.

- *Envisioning Information* covers maps, charts, tables, timetables, and more. This book is aimed at those in the design profession.

- *Visual Explanations: Images and Quantities, Evidence and Narrative* is about the representation of verbs. This book talks about how to pack the most information into a small space and how to use visual information for making decisions.
- *Beautiful Evidence* is a book in which Tufte introduces the concept of sparklines.

Tufte also maintains a website and forum at www.EdwardTufte.com.

Websites with Charting Tutorials

Excel gurus maintain numerous websites. A very few offer a better-than-usual concentration on charting and the process of creating unique charts:

- **Jon Peltier**—Jon, a Microsoft MVP, has several excellent charting examples on his website. If I am Googling a particularly difficult chart problem, I end up at Jon's site more often than not. Visit his site at www.PeltierTech.com.
- **Mike Alexander**—Mike runs a site with a funny name (DataPig Technologies) but great content. Many of his charting ideas made it into Chapter 7, "Using Advanced Chart Techniques." The benefit of Mike's site is that all the tutorials are five-minute videos that allow you to actually watch the charts being built. Visit www.DataPigTechnologies.com.
- **Andy Pope**—Andy maintains a website with amazing chart examples. These examples run circles around even the advanced charts shown in Chapter 7 of this book. Andy is a Microsoft MVP. Visit his website, www.andypope.info/charts.htm.
- **Tushar Mehta**—Tushar, a Microsoft MVP, has some nontraditional charting examples on his website, at www.tushar-mehta.com/excel/charts/.
- **Tom Bunzel**—If you need to present your data with PowerPoint, check out Tom Bunzel's site, www.professorppt.com. Tom writes books about PowerPoint and numerous articles for *InformIT*.

Interactive Training

As I was working on the manuscript for this book, I created an interactive training DVD program for Total Training. This excellent company has been producing top-notch DVD training packages since 1996. Find any designer who uses a Mac and Photoshop and they will tell you that Total Training produces the best training for Adobe products. Total Training is now producing products for Microsoft technologies, including a six-hour Advanced Excel DVD based on my Excel Power Seminar.

The Advanced Excel training contains more than an hour of content on charting in Excel. The DVD publishes in April 2007. I highly recommend any of the training programs Total Training offers. Search www.TotalTraining.com or www.MrExcel.com/chartbookdata.html for more information.

Live Training

If you are an MBA student at a business school, you might be lucky enough to catch Gene Zelazny as a guest speaker at your college. I highly recommend attending his seminar if he visits your town.

Edward Tufte provides a one-day course on charting at various sites around the country. Check out www.edwardtufte.com/tufte/courses for a schedule.

I also cover charting as part of a half-day Power Excel Seminar. For a list of upcoming dates and locations, see www.mrexcel.com/pressappearances.shtml. For information about booking a seminar for your company or organization, see www.mrexcel.com/speaking.html.

Blogs About Charting

A few people are gracing the blogosphere with posts that often touch on charting:

- **Juice Analytics**—Zach and Chris Gemignani seem to be proponents of Edward Tufte. They often critique charts at their Juice Analytics blog, www.juiceanalytics.com/weblog/.

- **Daily Dose of Excel**—Many Excel MVPs contribute topics on various Excel topics to Dick Kusleika's Daily Dose of Excel blog. You can find an archive of the charting posts at www.dailydoseofexcel.com/archives/category/charting/.

- **Visual Business Intelligence**—Steven Few shows off new and innovative visual designs at his blog, http://www.perceptualedge.com/blog/.

- **Instant Cognition**—This wide-ranging blog has several excellent posts on visual report design. See http://blog.instantcognition.com/category/visualization/charts/.

- **Politikal Arithmetik**—Professor Charles Franklin's blog always has the latest political charts and analysis. Visit for inspiration on cool charting ideas: http://politicalarithmetik.blogspot.com/.

In addition, I produce a daily two-minute video podcast about Excel that occasionally dips into the charting realm. You can find a link to charting episodes at www.MrExcel.com/chartbookdata.html.

Visual Design Stores

If you are a fan of visual information and graphic design, then a must-see store on your next trip through Toronto is SWIPE. This store is dedicated to books on advertising and design.

David Michaelides has been running SWIPE for almost 20 years. If there is a book on advertising or design, he either has it or knows where to get it. The store is located at 477 Richmond Street West, Toronto. You can find more information at www.swipe.com.

Plan on spending at least an hour browsing the store.

Professional Chart Designers

Well, I realize that if you are creating charts and getting paid for it, then you, the reader, are a professional chart designer. However, if you are in a pinch and need to find some outside help, check out the services of these three designers:

- **Kyle Fletcher**—Kyle Fletcher designs some innovative charts. Just don't ask him to deliver them as Sharpie charts drawn on his bare chest. Visit http://kylefletcher.com/index.htm.

- **Bob D'Amico**—Bob D'Amico is an illustrator and a designer. Although he drew the humorous charts in Chapters 4 and 6, he has a complete portfolio of serious charting designs he has completed for clients. Whether you need something serious or irreverent, contact Bob via e-mail at CartoonBob@mac.com.

- **Andy Attiliis**—Andy Attiliis operates a professional charting design service at www.ideasiteforbusiness.com/andy/dc.htm.

Charting Utilities and Products

Some charts just aren't easy to create in Excel. The following are some of my favorite utilities for creating different charts:

- **Speedometer Chart Creator**—Mala Singh provides an add-in that can generate speedometer charts in seconds instead of the hour it can take to draw a speedometer with AutoShapes. His charts show a current value plus yesterday's value, so you can get an idea of whether the value is trending up or down (see Figure A.3). Mala also offers the MacroEconomic Supply Curve Chart add-in, in which the width of the column indicates units sold and the height of the column indicates price. You can see these charts and more at www.mrexcel.com/graphics.shtml.

Figure A.3
Mala Singh's
Speedometer Chart
Creator can create a
dashboard full of
speedometer charts.

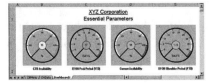

- **SparkMaker**—The SparkMaker add-in comes in a free version that creates only sparklines and a professional version that creates a plethora of tiny charts, including SparkLines, SparkBars, and SparkPies charts (see Figure A.4). You can create the charts either using a special font or as an image (which is easier for distribution). Check out www.bissantz.de/en/.

Figure A.4
Fans of Tufte can create their own sparklines and more using this utility from Bissantz.

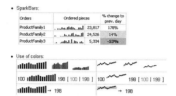

- **Dashboard Reporting with Excel**—This is Charley Kyd's excellent kit about how to create dashboards in Excel. It features an e-book plus a dozen sample Excel files to get you started. Charley is the king of getting small charts readable in Excel; my favorite examples puts 112 readable postage stamp–size charts on a single letter-size sheet of paper. Visit www.ExcelUser.com.

- **Crystal Xcelsius**—This product can use your Excel data to make interactive charts and output them to the web or PowerPoint. Check it out at www.xcelsius.com.

> **NOTE** If you have resources that should be listed here, send them to the email address listed at www.MrExcel.com/chartbookdata.html.

INDEX

Symbols

%AppData% shortcut, 35

' (apostrophe), VBA comments, 364-365

_ (underscore), VBA line continuation, 364

3-D 100% stacked column charts, 12

3-D charts
elements of, 40
lying with perspective, 423-425
rotation, formatting, 66-68
types of, 11-12
walls/floor, formatting, 65-66

3-D clustered column charts, 11

3-D column charts, 12

3-D Format settings, changing with VBA, 390-397

3-D rotation settings
changing with VBA, 386-390
of surface charts, 185

3-D stacked column charts, 11

80/20 rule in pie charts, 137-138

100% stacked bar charts, when to use, 83

100% stacked column charts, 12, 134-135
when to use, 82, 127

1900
dates prior to, 93-97
as leap year problem, 88

A

accuracy of date-based axes, 84

AddChart method, 365-367

adding. *See* inserting

Adjusted Close column (stock charts) for stock splits, 191-193

Alexander, Mike, 434

aligning icon sets with numbers, 292

Alt+F1 shortcut, 17

analysis elements, list of, 40-41

apostrophe ('), VBA comments, 364-365

ApplyLayout method, 365, 373

area charts
drop lines, inserting, 71
when to use, 82

array formulas, 302-303

array functions, 172

arrows, converting columns to, 109-110

assistants in organization charts, adding, 330

Attiliis, Andy, 436

AutoComplete, 359

AutoShapes. *See* shapes

axes
built-in options
depth axis, 53
horizontal axis, 52-53
vertical axis, 53-54
date-based versus text-based, 55-56
logarithmic axis, 54-55
scale, changing, 56-59
secondary axis, inserting, 74
time-based, creating, 56
types of, 51-52

Axis fields, filtering pivot tables, 276-278

U

underscore (_), VBA line
continuation, 364

up/down bars
defined, 41
inserting, 72

Upward Arrow layout
(SmartArt), 334-335

UserForms, creating
dynamic charts with VBA,
414-416

UserPicture method, 383

utilities, list of, 436-437

V

validation drop-downs,
creating dynamic charts
with, 250-253

value filters for pivot
tables, 277

variables
variables, comparing. See
relationships with charts
declaring, 363
object variables, 363

VaryByCategories
property, 399

VBA (Visual Basic for
Applications), 357
axis titles, changing, 380
backward compatibility,
357
built-in layouts,
applying, 373
built-in styles, applying,
373-375

chart titles, changing, 380
chart types, specifying,
369-370, 372
charts
creating, 366-367
moving, 367
referencing, 365-369
comments, 364-365
Developer ribbon,
enabling, 358
dynamic charts, creating,
414-416
enabling, 358
exporting charts as
graphics, 414
Format method, 380-381
3-D rotation settings,
386-390
bevel settings, 390-393
fill options, 381-383
glow settings, 384
lighting settings,
395-397
line settings, 383-384
material settings,
393-395
reflection settings, 385
shadow settings, 384
soft edge settings,
385-386
Format Series dialog,
changes in, 397-398
bar of pie and pie
of pie chart settings,
403-408
bubble size settings,
408-409
gap width settings,
398-400
radar and surface chart
settings, 409-410

rotating and exploding
charts, 401-403
secondary axis settings,
400-401
Layout ribbon changes
with SetElement
method, 375-379
line continuation, 364
macro recorder and, 360
multiple charts, printing,
418-420
new features, 365
object variables, 363
object-oriented code, 361
objects, referencing with
With and End With
statements, 364
pivot charts, creating,
416-420
ranges of data, specifying,
361-362
template chart types,
specifying, 372
tips for, 359-360
variables, declaring, 363
Visual Basic Editor,
358-359
Watch window
object settings, finding,
410-414
rotation settings,
finding, 413-414

Venn diagrams (SmartArt),
336-337

vertical axis, 52
built-in options, 53-54
defined, 39
gridlines/labels, rogue XY
series as, 230-236
scale, changing, 56-59
secondary axis,
inserting, 74

BOOKS ONLINE
ENABLED

THIS BOOK IS SAFARI ENABLED

INCLUDES FREE 45-DAY ACCESS TO THE ONLINE EDITION

The Safari® Enabled icon on the cover of your favorite technology book means the book is available through Safari Bookshelf. When you buy this book, you get free access to the online edition for 45 days.

Safari Bookshelf is an electronic reference library that lets you easily search thousands of technical books, find code samples, download chapters, and access technical information whenever and wherever you need it.

TO GAIN 45-DAY SAFARI ENABLED ACCESS TO THIS BOOK:

- Go to **http://www.quepublishing.com/safarienabled**
- Complete the brief registration form
- Enter the coupon code found in the front of this book on the "Copyright" page

If you have difficulty registering on Safari Bookshelf or accessing the online edition, please e-mail customer-service@safaribooksonline.com.

GET TO WORK WITH BUSINESS SOLUTIONS

Let's face it, when it comes to working with software in your job, you only have time to learn enough to get things going. The time may come, however, when you have to push the limits of Microsoft Excel, Access, and other Office applications to complete more sophisticated tasks. You probably have even less time to learn new software skills now than you did before, and you certainly don't want to read multiple books just to learn how to complete a specific task. Sound familiar? We have a solution.

The **Business Solutions** series was created to provide professionals like you books focused on a specific use or application of a software program. You won't find general software information here, only details on specific software features and functions that help you perform complex tasks related to your particular productivity use. You don't need to be a programmer or a power user to become more proficient with your software. You just need some motivation and a **Business Solutions** book, written by authors who are experienced practitioners of the specific solution presented.

LOOK FOR THESE BOOKS AT YOUR FAVORITE BOOKSTORE
OR VISIT www.quepublishing.com

0789736675

VBA for the 2007 Microsoft® Office System

0789736012

Pivot Table Data Crunching for Microsoft® Office Excel® 2007

0789736829

VBA and Macros for Microsoft® Office Excel® 2007

0789736683

Formulas and Functions with Microsoft® Office Excel® 2007

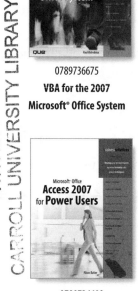

0789736608

Microsoft® Office Access 2007 for Power Users

0789736101

Charts and Graphs for Microsoft® Office Excel® 2007

0789736667

Tricks of the Microsoft® Office 2007 Gurus

0789736691

Microsoft® Office Access 2007 Forms, Reports, and Queries

Don't wait any longer. Stop solving software problems and start focusing on business.
Get a book in the **Business Solutions** series today!